PREDICTIVE ASTROLOGY OF THE HINDUS

PREDICTIVE ASTROLOGY OF THE HINDUS

Jyotish Kalanidhi, Daivagya Shiromani
PANDIT GOPESH KUMAR OJHA

MOTILAL BANARSIDASS PUBLISHERS
PRIVATE LIMITED • DELHI

2nd Reprint: Delhi, ***2018***
First MLBD Edition: Delhi, 2009
By arrangements with Shri Gopesh Kumar Pratishthan
Gurgaon, Haryana-122001
First Published: Gurgaon (Haryana) 1972

ISBN: 978-81-208-3415-6 (Cloth)
ISBN: 978-81-208-3416-3 (Paper)

MOTILAL BANARSIDASS
41 U.A. Bungalow Road, Jawahar Nagar, Delhi 110 007
1 B, Jyoti Studio Compound, Kennedy Bridge, Nana Chowk, Mumbai 400 007
203 Royapettah High Road, Mylapore, Chennai 600 004
236, 9th Main III Block, Jayanagar, Bengaluru 560 011
8 Camac Street, Kolkata 700 017
Ashok Rajpath, Patna 800 004
Chowk, Varanasi 221 001

Printed in India

by RP Jain at NAB Printing Unit,
A-44, Naraina Industrial Area, Phase I, New Delhi–110028
and published by JP Jain for Motilal Banarsidass Publishers (P) Ltd,
41 U.A. Bungalow Road, Jawahar Nagar, Delhi-110007

PREFACE

There are in the market many books on Hindu astrology. I have seen some of them. Still I have been prompted to place a new one before the readers. That is because I feel I have been able to present some new points of view which the readers would not find in other works.

I do not claim to be original in the sense that I have evolved any new theories. It is difficult to do so in a subject which has been successfully dealt with by a host of savants and scholars through the ages. I have been perusing Sanskrit works on astrology since 1927 and have been practising astrology. I have had occasion to go through ten Sanskrit commentaries on the same work by eminent scholars who lived in the preceding centuries. I have been charmed by their subtleties in exposition. Besides, standard works on Hindu astrology deal with the same topics and the number of such works is too large and their perusal is a problem, particularly for the lay readers who do not know Sanskrit. Even many who know Sanskrit will find it a thorny path to follow fully the logic encompassed in difficult diction, for erudition does not always go with straight and simple expression. I have therefore picked and chosen what I have considered best and only presented in cumulative form a few drops of old wine in a new bottle. As such I do not claim that I have evolved any new theories for I am only presenting the quintessence from the works of old masters.

While doing so, I have been conscious that I am writing a book which is to initiate new readers into this sacred science and if I pour into it all the wisdom of ancient seers it would add to the learning but become so formidable that new entrants will find it too difficult to follow, and it would defeat the very purpose of making it a popular text-book for the masses. I am fully conscious that I have not dealt with many intricate calculations and the readings based on them which can be useful for advanced students and scholars, but that would have made the book too voluminous and complex. All these matters I reserve for subsequent volumes.

I have observed that a large number of people are fond of astrology, but their interest in the subject becomes lukewarm as soon as they have to cross the wall of calculations. Only a small percentage has the patience and the perseverance to scale the wall and enjoy the fruit beyond. So I have kept the calculations at the minimum and diffused them in chapters 4, 7 and 12 so that they do not prove an obstacle at any place and present an easy go over. Another feature of calculations is that in ancient India time was reckoned in *Ghatis* and *Palas*. One day, twenty-four hours, was divided into sixty *Ghatis* and each *Ghati* was sub-divided into sixty *Palas*. All calculations in Hindu astrology are on this basis. But now-a-days time is recorded including the birth time, in hours and minutes. Many up-to-date ephemerides also furnish time in hours and minutes. So instead of following the complicated process of finding the sunrise time, calculating the time elapsed since sunrise till birth and calculating the rising sign and the ascending degree, I have introduced the modern method of ascertaining the ascending degree by the trigonometrical method as given in *Raphael's Table of Houses* for the tropical zodiac or *Lahiri's Table of Houses* for the sidereal zodiac.

The duration of each ascendant varies with the latitude and since the tables referred to above cover most of them, that not only makes the calculation simple but more precise also.

Hindu astrology is sidereal. But in the West most of the astrologers base their calculations and inferences on the tropical zodiac. An increasing number of people in the West is, however, taking interest in the predictions on the sidereal basis and they want a text-book on Hindu astrology. To cater to their needs and to enable them to convert a tropical chart into a sidereal one, I have all through provided instructions so that the students and scholars of the West may take full advantage of this text-book. And with this view I have used the nomenclature Sun, Moon, Mars etc. instead of Surya, Chandra, Mangal etc. and Aries, Taurus, Gemini etc. instead of Mesha, Vrishabha, Mithuna and so on. I must add here that Western astrologers use she for Moon and Venus but in the Hindu texts the Moon and Venus are referred to as he. There is a mythology that the Moon had a liaison with Jupiter's wife Tara and thus Tara gave birth to Mercury. Whatever be the import of the mythology, in view of the above and similar statements I find it difficult to refer to the Moon as she. According to Hindu texts Venus has a wife and I have in view of all this stuck to the Hindu code of referring to the Moon and Venus as he. While sticking mainly to the Western terminology I have utilised essential Hindu terminology where no single word in English could have conveyed the full import of the technical term in Sanskrit. Instead of referring to the term by circumlocution of English phraseology which would have been ambiguous and created confusion rather than clarification, I have preferred to use the technical Sanskrit terms which have been fully explained in the appropriate contexts.

Those who are beginners will find that in perusing this book they can start from the scratch and ascend gradually to the high pinnacles of delineations and judgment. Those who are already acquainted with the subject will find many new rules and the discussions enlightening and throwing back the horizon of astrological knowledge. While bearing in mind that a large number of readers might be new to the subject, I have at places explained the various steps at length or clarified the obscure points which may appear unnecessary to those who are already aware of the technicalities or the import of particular configurations in the birth chart. To them my only apology is that though it would have been more convenient for me to skip over the familiar steps it would have landed in difficulty those new readers who have not the grasp of the subject. Their need has also to be kept in mind.

In regard to the calculations and predictions, fairly good matter has been provided. But as in medical sciences, so in astrology, one cannot become proficient by the study of theory alone.

A certain amount of practice is essential.

I look forward to the prospect of this text-book being received with interest and approbation by the reading public. If my hopes are fulfilled I shall feel amply rewarded.

93-Daryaganj,
Delhi-6

GOPESH KUMAR OJHA

CONTENTS

PREFACE v

CHAPTER 1 *The Zodiac*

A general idea of the heavens—the earth's path round the Sun—the zodiac defined and explained—latitude of planets—Sun has no latitude—intersections of the orbits of Moon and earth—nodes of Moon—Rahu and Ketu—the tropical and sidereal zodiacs distinguished—constellations—longitudes of constellations—their geometrical patterns—constellations in each sidereal sign—declination of Sun—equinoxes—precession of equinoxes and nutation—conversion of tropical longitudes into sidereal. 1 — 12

CHAPTER 2 *The Birth Chart*

Birth chart a sketch of heavens—the rising degree at the horizon—the ecliptic—obliquity of the ecliptic—time taken by each sign to rise—difference in durations of rise due to geographical latitude—what is a house—domain of houses—their order—opposite signs. 13 — 18

CHAPTER 3 *Time*

Cycles of time according to ancient Hindu texts—different calendars—the 60 years cycle—name for each year—the twelve Hindu months—tithi (the lunar date) determined on the basis of soli-lunar distance—names of lunar dates—half tithi called a karana—the names of karanas—their order—the Hindu panchanga (ephemeris)—the yogas or time durations based on longitudes of the Sun and Moon—their names and order—Hindu unit of time—ghatis and palas—the modern units of time, hours, minutes and seconds—modern ephemerides—some inauspicious tithis, Karanas and yogas at birth time—some unfavourable constellations for Moon to be in, at birth—their effects. 19 — 32

CHAPTER 4 *Sign Rising (Ascendant)*

Duration taken by each sign to rise at a particular geographical latitude—table of houses—common errors in calculating the rising degree—calculations based on sunrise—how to calculate the rising sign—standard time and local mean time—conversion of standard time into local mean time—sidereal time—example worked out for calculating the ascending degree on a particular date, at a particular time and place—how to find exact longitudes of planets and make the birth chart—different patterns of birth chart, in northern, north-western, southern and eastern India—the occidental pattern—effects for each of the twelve ascending signs—some special effects for particular degrees rising. 33 — 50

CHAPTER 5 *The Signs*

Difference between the tropical and sidereal signs—correlation between signs and parts of human body—correspondence of signs with houses—effects thereof—the physi al appearance of signs—their places, countries, castes, male and female—odd and even—watery and waterless—movable, fixed and common signs—their directions—blind and lame signs—diurnal and nocturnal—biped, quadruped and snails—mineral, vegetable and animal signs—short and long—sign rising with head or back—auspicious and inauspicious degrees occupied by the Moon in signs—the three sectors, 51 — 66

CHAPTER 6 *The Planets*

Only nine planets—Sun, Moon, Mars, Mercury, Jupiter, Venus, Saturn and nodes of the Moon—Rahu and Ketu dealt with in

Hindu astrology—their signs—exaltation and debilitation signs—highest degrees of exaltation and deepest degrees of debilitation—the Sanskrit terms avaroha, aroha, uchchabhilashi, neechabhilashi explained—friendship, neutrality and enmity among planets—natural, temporal and resultant relationship—planetary aspects—the characteristics and portfolio of planets—ingredients of the human body—complexion, some physical characteristics—temperament—glance—flavour—humours of the body—aptitudes—colours—age—jewels—seasons—places—sex—deities—the elements—direction—caste—the type of cloth—biped, quadruped etc. rising with front part, back portion or both ways—qualities pertaining to metal, herb or animal—directional strength—auspicious and inauspicious planets—manner of winning over—geographical regions in India—significance of each planet—planets as significators for particular houses—the Sanskrit terms *papa* and *papi* explained. 67 — 90

CHAPTER 7 *Houses*

What are houses—various systems of house division—older Hindu system—equal house division—example worked out—cusp of each house—domain of each house—house lords—placing a planet in house—what to judge from each house—house lords signifying matters pertaining to houses they are lords of—one and the same matter judged from different houses—subtle distinctions therein—some difference in southern and northern Indian schools of Hindu astrology—parts of human body assigned to each house—matters and affairs judged from first, second, third, fourth, fifth, sixth, seventh, eighth, ninth, tenth, eleventh and twelfth houses—details based on old Sanskrit texts—reference to these—a summary of matters governed by each house. 91 — 115

CHAPTER 8 *Planets in Signs*

Correspondence between signs and houses—Sun in twelve signs Aries to Pisces—the influence exerted by Moon according to his location in a sign—effects of Mars in the various signs of the zodiac—location of Mercury in the twelve signs—position of Jupiter in each sign—effects of Venus occupying any sign Aries to Pisces—an analysis of Saturn's influence on the native according to his position in various signs—effects of Rahu and Ketu analysed signwise—detailed delineation of each planet's effects by location in a sign of exaltation, debilitation or own sign—particularly favourable or unfavourable degrees for each planet occupying a particular sign. 116 — 148

CHAPTER 9 *Planets in Houses*

Sun in twelve houses—first to twelfith—delineation of Moon's influence according to his location in one house or the other—how Mars affects the birth chart and matters connected with the house he occupies—Mercury's location in any of the twelve houses and the results thereof—Jupiter in twelve houses first to twelfth and the effects produced by him due to occupying a particular house—influence of Venus in each of the twelve houses of the birth chart—Saturns location in a house and the effects arising therefrom —Rahu and Ketu's position in any of the twelve houses analysed housewise. 149 — 176

CHAPTER 10 *General Principles of Judgement*

Malefic tenanting his own house—aspect of a benefic or malefic planet in own house conjoined with or aspected by a benefic—a retrograde planet—planet in angle—natural and temporal friendships compared—evil places—occupation of a house by lord of an evil house—consideration of karaka (significator) along with house lord—effect of good or evil combinations—house hemmed in between benefics or malefics—lord of the house similarly placed —a combust house lord—placement of karaka and various considerations to determine his effects—evaluation of aspect of a planet according to his strength—owner of two houses one good and the other evil—lord of two houses occupying one of his houses—lord of ascendant—some astrological terms in Sanskrit explained—apachaya-asta (combust)—dosha—dusthana—karaka—maraka-rajayoga sambandha, upachaya, yoga, yogakaraka. 177 — 192

CHAPTER 11 *Yogas—Combinations of Planets*

Importance of yogas—18 yogas based on ascendant as a factor—9 yogas connected with the lord of the ascendants—6 yogas pertaining to the Sun—20 yogas with Moon as one of the factors—6 yogas connected with births during day or night and concomitant factors—8 yogas based on sign positions of planets—24 yogas based on placement of planets in their own signs or their signs of exaltation—26 yogas formed in birth charts according to positions of planets in houses—66 yogas according to mutual exchange of house lords—24 yogas according to the houses being tenanted by benefics or malefics and their lords occupying good or evil houses —9 yogas connected with lords of houses—2 yogas based on directional strength—5 yogas connected with placement of planets in their signs of debilitation—1 yoga based on retrogression—kendra—trikona yogas fully discussed and guide lines for evaluation of their effects. 193—219

CHAPTER 12 *Judgement of the Twelve Houses*

General principles—comparative assessment of one matter from several connected houses—instructions for judging yogas—conjunctions—counting of houses—first house—second-third-fourth-fifth-sixth-seventh-eighth-ninth-tenth-eleventh and the twelfth house—detailed guide lines for judging each house and some special factors for each house augmenting the good effects or enhancing the evil effects pertaining to health, wealth, eyes, brothers and sisters, valour, mother, land, immovable property, conveyance—intelligence, education, stomach, sons, enemies, illness, wife or husband —partnership legacy duration of life, longevity, death, legacy, religion, general prosperity and good fortune—power—position—income—expenditure, losses etc. 220—249

CHAPTER 13 *Calculation of Mahadashas and Antardashas*

Their importance in a birth chart, the major periods of each planet—their order—Moon's position in the constellation the basis for mahadasha—ready reckoner table to find the balance of mahadasha at birth—proportionate parts for mahadasha according to one or more minutes of arc of Moon—example how to erect table of mahadasha—the duration of each antardasha in each mahadasha—their order—to find the balance of antardasha in a mahadasha at birth—example—how to erect tables of antardashas in mahadashas. 250—259

CHAPTER 14 *Mahadashas—Major Periods of Planets and Judgement*

How to evaluate their effects—good or evil—four schools of Hindu astrology—what effects is the mahadasha likely to show—theory of karakatwa or natural significance of the planet—illustration—effects of Sun, Moon, Mars, Mercury, Jupiter, Venus, Saturn, Rahu and Ketu in respect of matters and affairs they are significators for, according as they are strong and well placed or weak and afflicted—effects of lords of houses—first, second, third, fourth, fifth, sixth, seventh, eighth, ninth, tenth, eleventh and twelfth according as they are beneficially placed and powerful or in evil places and weak—Parashari system—favourable and unfavourable mahadashas of various planets for each ascendant—mahadashas of lords of trines, angles, third, sixth and eleventh—of the eighth lord—of lords of second and twelfth—mahadashas causing serious illness or causing death—favourable mahadashas for wealth and prosperity, for power and prestige. Mahadashas of Rahu and Ketu—favourable and unfavourable mahadashas for each ascendant Aries, Taurus, Gemini, Cancer, Leo, Virgo, Libra, Scorpio, Sagittarius, Capricorn, Aquarius and Pisces—other factors for evaluating the effects of each mahadasha. Planets in signs of exaltation, own sign, signs of great friend, friend, neutral, enemy, great enemy or in debilitated sign—planets which have crossed highest, exaltation or deepest debilitation points—combust or retrograde planet—conjunction with a benefic or malefic planet—planets in signs rising with their hind or front parts, first-timing of mahadasha effects according to the degree occupied by a planet in the radix—other considerations—transit of the planet during his mahadasha—why a mahadasha is at times favourable for certain matters and unfavourable for others—a general discussion. 260—293

CHAPTER 15 *Antardashas—Minor Periods*

General features—balancing of mahadasha and antardasha—if both are good or both evil or one good and the other evil—the mutual position of the two lords and their mutual relationship—antardasha in evil mahadashas—periods of serious illness and likely death—auspicious and inauspicious antardashas according to Parashari system—likely effects of evil antardashas—antardashas of lords of trine and angle—likely periods when the full effect of antardasha may be felt—antardasha in own mahadasha—Saturn in Venus and Venus in Saturn—antardashas in yogakaraka's mahadasha—antardashas of yogakaraka—inferences based on antardasha lord owning houses as counted from the mahadasha lord and an antardasha lord occupying a house as counted from the mahadasha lord—illustrations—sub-periods in antardashas—how to calculate prayantars (sub-periods) importance and necessity of calculating sub-periods in some cases—particular timings for each planet when he may evince marked effect. 294 — 305

CHAPTER 16 *Transits*

Transit defined—importance of Moon—transits computed from the Moon sign—appraising transits for persons whose birth data not known—rule to allot Moon sign according to the first syllable of name—table of syllables and corresponding Moon signs—transits of the Sun in several houses counted from the Moon—sign-transits of Moon from his radical position—transits of Mars, Mercury, Jupiter—some special features—transits of Venus and Saturn —some special features—transits of Rahu and Ketu—effects of transits of all the nine planets housewise—planetary positions which obstruct the effects of good or evil transits—twenty factors which modify transit influences. 306 — 320

APPENDIX Precession of Equinox and Nutation from 1880 to 1972 on the 1st January of each year 321 — 323

GLOSSARY OF ASTROLOGICAL TERMS 324 — 327

INDEX TO SANSKRIT TERMS 329 — 334

INDEX 335 — 347

CHAPTER 1

THE ZODIAC

HINDU Astrology is sidereal. The zodiac is divided into twelve sectors on the basis of certain fixed stars. It is true that even the fixed stars show some motion, but this being very, very slow, infinitesimal, they are for all practical purposes treated as fixed stars.

There are millions, rather trillions of stars in the sky. It is not possible to count or catalogue all of them. In astrology we are however concerned only with the stars which lie in the zodiacal belt. What is the zodiac? It is the belt comprising the apparent path of the Sun. The Sun completes one full revolution in one year. The path through which he* appears to travel is called the ecliptic. Why did we say 'through which the Sun appears to travel'? Why did we not say 'through which the Sun travels'? Because, the Sun does not travel, he only appears to travel. In fact, it is the Earth which travels round the Sun and pursues a particular path — the same path, year after year, century after century. This path of the Earth is called the ecliptic. We, the inhabitants of the Earth move with it round the Sun and although it is the Earth which moves, it appears to us that the Sun is moving.

The ecliptic (the Earth's path) is not circular in shape. It is elliptical or egg-shaped.

* In Hindu astrology all planets, the two luminaries, the five planets and the nodes of the Moon, are referred to as 'he'.

What is the zodiac? This is a belt of the heavens limited by lines of about 8 degrees from the ecliptic on each side. While the Sun's path is along the ecliptic, why should we then have another belt extending to about 8° on either side of the ecliptic and call it the zodiac? This is because the Sun moves along the ecliptic, but the planets do not follow the exact path of the Sun; their paths are sometimes along the ecliptic, sometimes north of the ecliptic and at others south of it. However, they do not swerve to the north or the south of the ecliptic beyond 8°. The distance north of the ecliptic line is called the northern latitude, while the distance south of it is known as the southern latitude. When a planet has neither a northern latitude nor a southern latitude, but is exactly on the ecliptic, it is said to have zero latitude or no latitude at all.

In the Ephemeris, readers will see a column where latitudes of planets have been given for each day. But no latitude is ever given for the Sun. This is so because it is the real motion of the Earth which is given as the motion of the Sun. As explained earlier, it is the Earth which moves. But as the Earth moves, according to the variation in the angle of the Earth or the observers' place, the Sun appears to be in a different direction. So, since the Earth confines itself to the ecliptic, the Sun also appears on the ecliptic. As the Earth does not move north or south of the ecliptic, the Sun also does not appear to move north or south of the ecliptic. The Sun, therefore, does not ever have any latitude, northern or southern. In other words the Sun always has zero latitude.

In astronomy distances are measured in degrees. A circle has 360 degrees. One degree is divided into parts, and each part is called a minute. A minute is further sub-divided into 60 parts, and each sub-division is called a second. This is the division in space. The directions are as usual east, west, north and south.

The Sun has no latitude as said above. But what about the other planets—the Moon, Mars, Mercury, Jupiter, Venus, and Saturn? We have not included Herschel, Neptune or Pluto in the above list of planets because they were discovered only lately and there is no mention of them in ancient Hindu astrology. But Hindu astrology is a complete system in itself and provides detailed guide lines for future predictions. The rules of Hindu predictive astrology are easier to learn and have been found to be more precise in application and capable of yielding more accurate results than other methods of prediction.

The latitude of a planet is important in Hindu astronomy. But in Hindu astrology it has little significance. The point, however, is important in as much as no planet has more than 8° of northern or southern latitude. So the path of the planets is confined along the ecliptic within a belt of 8° on either side. All planets traverse the path within the zodiac.

While explaining the zodiac and the northern or the southern latitudes of planets, it would be appropriate to add that when the Moon in his orbit round the Earth travels to the northern latitude, the point where it cuts the ecliptic is deemed a sensitive point. This is called the northern node of the Moon. The point where the Moon in his orbit round the earth cuts the ecliptic in his passage to the south of the ecliptic is also a very sensitive point and is called the southern node of the Moon. These two points, the northern and the southern nodes of the Moon, are always 180° apart.

These two points are, however, not fixed or stationary in the sense that if the Moon crossed over to the north of the ecliptic at a particular point today, he would cross over the same place the next month or in any subsequent month. Actually, this point recedes, and in about one year it recedes by about 18.84°, with the result that by its backward motion in the zodiac, it comes to the same point in about nineteen years.

In Hindu astrology, great importance is attached to these two points and they are called Rahu and Ketu. The northern node of the Moon is called Rahu, and the southern, Ketu.

In Western astrology the northern node is referred to as Caput Draconis and the southern one as Cauda Draconis. In predictive astrology, some Western astrologers do take these into consideration, but most ignore them. The position of Rahu or the northern node is given in the Ephemeris. The southern node's longitude is not given for the simple reason that Rahu and Ketu are always 180° apart. If the longitude of one is known, that of the other can always be calculated.

These two, Rahu and Ketu, are not planets in the sense of Mars, Mercury, Jupiter, etc. Rahu and Ketu have no mass, no weight, no light, no body. They are simply two sensitive points. In Hindu astrology, the Sun, Moon, Mars, Mercury, Jupiter, Venus, Saturn, Rahu and Ketu are called *Grahas*. The literal meaning of *Graha* is seizing, grasping, laying hold on, gripping, etc. A *Graha* according to Hindu conception is an entity having the power to seize, grasp, grip, lay hold of etc. And since the planets have that power they are called *Grahas*. In English the Sun and Moon are called the luminaries, while Mars, Mercury, Jupiter, etc., are called planets. But for the sake of convenience all these, including the Sun and Moon, are commonly referred to as planets. So in the context of Hindu astrology we may describe all the nine *Grahas* as planets, though Rahu and Ketu have, as already explained, no body.

The Zodiac

While explaining the term ecliptic we passed on to latitude and in that connection explained what the nodes of the Moon were. Our principle subject of discussion was, however, the zodiac. What the zodiac is has been described, but in order to fully understand this we have to know the difference between the Tropical zodiac and the Sidereal zodiac. The same belt of the heaven is referred to by some as the Tropical zodiac and by others as the Sidereal zodiac.

The Tropical and the Sidereal Zodiac

If there be a straight line, every one would begin at one end and terminate at the other, but if a figure were circular or elliptical a question would naturally arise as to the commencing point—where the figure begins. There are no pillars or poles in the zodiac. How is one to locate or identify a particular point? From times immemorial Hindu astronomers have identified the particular regions in the zodiac by means of fixed constellations. The names of the constellations are given below:

1. Ashwini	Arietis			9. Ashlesha	e-Hydrae	
2. Bharani	41 Arietis			10. Magha	Regulus	14
3. Krittika	Alcyone	2		11. Poorva-phalguni	Leonis	
4. Rohini	Aldebaran	3				
5. Mrigashira	Orionis			12. Uttara-phalguni	Denebola	15
6. Ardra	Betelguese	7				
7. Punarvasu	Pollux	11		13. Hasta	Spica	16
8. Pushya	Cancri			14. Chitra	Corvi	

15. Swati	Arcturus	17	22. Shravana	Altair	20
16. Vishakha	a Libra		23. Dhanishtha	Delphini	
17. Anuradha	Scorpii		24. Shatabh-isha	Aquarii	
18. Jyeshtha	Antares	18	25. Poorva-bhadra	Markeb	24
19. Moola	Scorpii		26. Uttara-bhadra	Pegasi	
20. Poorva-shadha	Sagittari		27. Revati	Piscium	
21. Uttara-shadha	Sagittari				

In older Hindu astrology there are references to one more constellation, Abhijit in between Uttarashadha and Shravana, but in later Hindu works it was dropped and now only these twenty-seven constellations are taken as identifying marks round the zodiac. These constellations were also catalogued by Ptolemy and other Western astronomers and the Greek names for these have been given in the above list. During the course of this book, we shall however refer to them by their Sanskrit names. Very detailed descriptions of these constellations have been given in works on Hindu astrology. Some are deemed auspicious for election purposes, i.e., for choosing or selecting a suitable time for commencing an important undertaking, while others are not. Some constellations are specially marked as good for commencing a journey, others for performance of a wedding, and so on. These constellations have also been labelled as benefic and malefic. When the Moon is in benefic constellations, benefic undertakings should be commenced; while for evil deeds, for example, if the object is to set fire, to give poison, to wage a war or to kill or damage an enemy, the Moon in a malefic constellation is more conducive to success! Some have been described as face downwards, others as facing upwards, yet others as having a gaze in a slanting direction. All work such as digging a well is good when the Moon is in a constellation facing downwards, while in all undertakings such as building a house in which we proceed upwards, the Moon in a constellation facing upwards would be more helpful. All this is the field of electional astrology, but we have mentioned this in the present context to show that in Hindu astrology these constellations form the bases.

We give below the identifying marks or characteristics of the constellations to locate them in the sky. We have also given their longitudes in the Sidereal zodiac as on 1st January 1969.

Constellation	*Longitude*	*Shape*	*Number of Stars*
1. Ashwini	0-10- 6-47	Face of a horse	3
2. Bharani	0-24-20-48	Yoni	3
3. Krittika	1- 6- 8- 8	Curved knife	6
4. Rohini	1-15-55-54	Cart	5
5. Mrigashira	1-29-50-59	Face of a deer	3
6. Ardra	2- 4-53-51	Jewel	1
7. Punarvasu	2-29-21-49	House	4
8. Pushya	3-14-51-53	Arrow	3
9. Ashlesha	3-18-29-24	Circular	5
10. Magha	4- 5-58-27	House	5
11. Poorvaphalguni	4-17-27-25	Manchaka	2
12. Uttaraphalguni	4-27-45-48	Small cot	2
13. Hasta	5-19-35-48	Hand	5
14. Chitra	5-29-59- 5	Pearl	1
15. Swati	6- 0-22-37	Coral	1
16. Vishakha	6-21-13-34	Torana	4
17. Anuradha	7- 8-42-52	Vali	4
18. Jyeshtha	7-15-54-19	Like a circular earring	4
19. Moola	8- 0-43-43	Tail of a lion	3
20. Poorvashadha	8-10-43-24	Tusk of an elephant	11
21. Uttarashadha	8-18-31-41	Manchaka	2
22. Shravana	9- 7-54-52	Aeroplane	3
23. Dhanishtha	9-22-29- 7	Mridanga	4
24. Shatabhisha	10-17-43- 7	Elliptic	100
25. Poorvabhadra	10-29-37-47	Manchaka	2
26. Uttarabhadra	11-15-18- 0	Twins	2
27. Revati	11-26- 1-10	Mardala	32

Certain Sanskrit words used under the column 'shape' need explanation. *Yoni* means the shape of the sexual organ of a woman; *Manchaka* is a raised seat dais resting on columns; *Torana* means an arched doorway; *Vali* means a fold or wrinkle, i.e. having curls; *Mridanga* is an oblong leather bag which is filled with air and played upon like a musical instrument; *Mardala* is a kind of drum.

The information provided in reference to the shape or figure, i.e., the various stars constituting the constellation or the number of stars therein are not important for predictive purposes. But the particulars have been furnished to indicate how these constellations are identified in the sky. The longitudes of the constellations relate to the principal star where there are more than one star in the constellation, for naturally the various stars in the constellation will have different longitudes. But for purposes of predictive astrology each constellation is treated as having a jurisdiction of 13° 20′ of longitude. This point is important, as we shall have to refer to this matter in subsequent chapters. How do we arrive at the figure of 13° 20′? This is done by the simple process of dividing 360° by 27. A circle, whether it be an exact circle or an elliptic, has 360° as computed from the centre of it. And the number of constellations is twenty-seven. So by the simple rule of division we get 13° 20′ as the share of each constellation.

Hindu astrology is primarily an astrology based on constellations. The zodiac is covered by twenty-seven constellations named above. Not that there are only these twenty-seven constellations alone in the zodiac, there are many more. But to make a particular position or location in the zodiac these twenty-seven have been treated as permanent pillars or posts. Without any such aid it would become impossible to describe the zodiac in regard to a particular point.

The jurisdiction of each constellation is as described below:

	In signs, degrees & minutes			*In signs, degrees & minutes*		
	D. M.		D. M.	S.D.M.		S.D.M.
1. Ashwini	0- 0	to	13-20	0- 0- 0	to	0-13-20
2. Bharani	13-20	to	26-40	0-13-20	to	0-26-40
3. Krittika	26-40	to	40- 0	0-26-40	to	1-10- 0
4. Rohini	40- 0	to	53-20	1-10- 0	to	1-23-20
5. Mrigashira	53-20	to	66-40	1-23-20	to	2- 6-40
6. Ardra	66-40	to	80- 0	2- 6-40	to	2-20- 0
7. Punarvasu	80- 0	to	93-20	2-20- 0	to	3- 3-20
8. Pushya	93-20	to	106-40	3- 3-20	to	3-16-40
9. Ashlesha	106-40	to	120- 0	3-16-40	to	4- 0- 0
10. Magha	120- 0	to	133-20	4- 0- 0	to	4-13-20
11. Poorvaphalguni	133-20	to	146-40	4-13-20	to	4-26-40
12. Uttaraphalguni	146-40	to	160- 0	4-26-40	to	5-10- 0

13. Hasta	160- 0	to	173-20	5-10- 0	to	5-23-20
14. Chitra	173-20	to	186-40	5-23-20	to	6- 6-40
15. Swati	186-40	to	200- 0	6- 6-40	to	6-20- 0
16. Vishakha	200- 0	to	213-20	6-20- 0	to	7- 3-20
17. Anuradha	213-20	to	226-40	7- 3-20	to	7-16-40
18. Jyestha	226-40	to	240- 0	7-16-40	to	8- 0- 0
19. Moola	240- 0	to	253-20	8- 0- 0	to	8-13-20
20. Poorvashadha	253-20	to	266-40	8-13-20	to	8-26-40
21. Uttarashadha	266-40	to	280- 0	8-26-40	to	9-10- 0
22. Shravana	280- 0	to	293-20	9-10- 0	to	9-23-20
23. Dhanishtha	293-20	to	306-40	9-23-20	to	10- 6-40
24. Shatabhisha	306-40	to	320- 0	10- 6-40	to	10-20- 0
25. Poorvabhadra	320- 0	to	333-20	10-20- 0	to	11- 3-20
26. Uttarabhadra	333-20	to	346-40	11- 3-20	to	11-16-40
27. Revati	346-40	to	360-00	11-16-40	to	12- 0- 0

If we divide the number 27 by 12, the quotient is two and a quarter. Twenty-seven is the number of constellations and twelve is the number of the signs. Thus the jurisdiction of a sign is constituted by two and a quarter constellations. The names of the twelve signs are as follows:

1. Mesha	Aries	7. Tula	Libra
2. Vrishabha	Taurus	8. Vrischika	Scorpio
3. Mithuna	Gemini	9. Dhanu	Sagittarius
4. Karka	Cancer	10. Makara	Capricorn
5. Sinha	Leo	11. Kumbha	Aquarius
6. Kanya	Virgo	12. Meena	Pisces

Along with the Sanskrit names we have also given their English names. There are twelve signs covering 30° each and thus covering 12×30 degrees of the zodiac.

We have already stated that each sign covers two and a quarter constellations. Thus each sign covers the constellations or part thereof as shown below:

1. Mesha	Aries	Ashwini, Bharani and one quarter of Krittika.
2. Vrishabha	Taurus	The remaining three quarters of Krittika, Rohini and the first half of Mrigashira.

3. Mithuna	Gemini	The remaining two quarters of Mrigashira, Ardra and three quarters of Punarvasu.
4. Karka	Cancer	The last quarter of Punarvasu, Pushya and Ashlesha.
5. Sinha	Leo	Magha, Poorvaphalguni and one quarter of Uttaraphalguni.
6. Kanya	Virgo	Three quarters of Uttaraphalguni, Hasta and the first half of Chitra.
7. Tula	Libra	The remaining two quarters of Chitra, Swati and three quarters of Vishakha.
8. Vrischika	Scorpio	The last quarter of Vishakha, Anuradha and Jyeshtha.
9. Dhanu	Sagittarius	Moola, Poorvashadha and one quarter of Uttarashadha.
10. Makara	Capricorn	The remaining three quarters of Uttarashadha, Shravana and first half of Dhanishtha.
11. Kumbha	Aquarius	Last two quarters of Dhanishtha Shatabhisha and three quarters of Poorvabhadra.
12. Meena	Pisces	The last quarter of Poorvabhadra, Uttarabhadra and Revati.

The jurisdiction of each constellation in terms of degrees and minutes and also in terms of signs, degrees and minutes has already been given in tabular form. Below is a Table showing the jurisdiction of each sign in terms of degrees. Hereafter the English names for signs—Aries, Taurus, etc., will be used as that will be more convenient for the readers. The Sanskrit equivalents have already been given above to familiarise the readers with the Hindu nomenclature.

Signs	*Degrees*	*Signs*	*Degrees*
1. Aries	0° to 30°	5. Leo	121° to 150°
2. Taurus	31° to 60°	6. Virgo	151° to 180°
3. Gemini	61° to 90°	7. Libra	181° to 210°
4. Cancer	91° to 120°	8. Scorpio	211° to 240°

9.	Sagittarius	241° to 270°	11.	Aquarius	301° to 330°
10.	Capricorn	271° to 300°	12.	Pisces	331° to 360°

We have already seen how the zodiac is divided into constellations and signs, but the crucial question remains: where to start the zero degree from. The simple answer is that the zero degree commences from Ashwini the fixed star. From this point to 30° is allotted to Aries, the next 30° to Taurus, and so on.

The word 'sidereal' means pertaining to stars, and the Hindu zodiac is the sidereal one, that is, of the constellations of the fixed stars. It is also called the stellar zodiac or pertaining to stars. Since the stars are fixed this is called the fixed zodiac also.

The word 'tropic' may be defined as parallel to latitude 23° 27′ in the north the Tropic of Cancer or in the south the Tropic of Capricorn; these are the two corresponding circles on the celestial sphere where the Sun appears to turn after reaching greatest declination. This requires some explanation.

On or about the 21st March, the Sun rises due east, ascends the heavens and sets in the west—the apparent path of the Sun is thus above the geographical equator. The next day the Sun rises in the east and ascends the heavens to set in the west; but its apparent path is not exactly over the equator but slightly to the north of the equator. This distance between the equator and the path, as measured in degrees, is called the declination. It is called the northern declination if the apparent path of the heavenly body is to the north of the equator and southern declination if the apparent path is to the south of the equator. It is measured in degrees and minutes of arc.

Now from the 21st March onwards, every day the Sun's path becomes increasingly northern till on or about the 21st June, its northern declination becomes maximum. It is about 23° 27′ northern declination on that day. Then the northern declination begins to decrease day by day and on or about the 22nd September, it again rises due east, passes over the equator and sets in the west. The next day he rises in the east, ascends the heavens and sets in the west; but this passage is not exactly over the equator but slightly southwards. This southern declination goes on increasing till about the 22nd December when the declination is 23° 27′ south. Having reached the maximum southern declination the Sun begins to rise and set with less and less southern declination till on or about the 21st March the declination becomes zero; it is neither to the south nor to the north, but exactly above the equator. And the same phenomenon—increasing northern declination reaching the northernmost point, then reverting to a passage over the equator, proceeding with increasing southern declination, reaching the maximum southern declination and reverting to passage over the equator—goes on year after year.

Now the degree of the ecliptic where the Sun in its passage has no declination, i.e., where the Sun is on 21st March and 22nd September, are called equinoxes and such degrees are called the equinoctial degrees.

The word equinoxes may be defined as two points at which the Sun crosses the equator and the day and night are equal.

The equinoctial line might be described as that circle of celestial sphere whose plane is perpendicular to the Earth's axis.

Had these equinoxes been fixed points, there would have been no complication. But these equinoctial points shift backwards. They precede at the rate of 50.25 seconds of arc per annum or roughly one degree in seventy-two years. The equinoctial points seventy-two years ago are not the equinoctial points today. It is one degree backwards or we might say that it has preceded by one degree. After seventy-two years from now it will further precede by one degree.

There is one more peculiarity of the Earth's motion—it resembles the oscillation of a spinning top. The oscillation of the Earth's axis makes a wavy motion at the pole of the equator round the pole of the ecliptic which is called Nutation.

Due to the twin phenomena of precession of equinoxes and nutation the two equinoctial points are ever preceding. The degree in which the Sun is on or about 21st March, when he has no declination, is called the spring equinox and the degree occupied by him on or about the 22nd September when again he has no declination is called the autumnal equinox. Most western astronomers commence the zero degree of the zodiac from the spring equinox and complete 360° by counting 30° for each sign ($12\times30=360°$) from the point. Due to the precession of the equinox, the point also precedes year after year. This commencement from the equinoctial point describes the tropical zodiac. When the Sun's passage reaches the sign of Cancer, the corresponding line below the Sun's passage on Earth is called the Tropic of

Cancer. Similarly, when the Sun reaches the sign of Capricorn, the corresponding line below the passage of the Sun on Earth is known as the Tropic of Capricon. This is called the moving zodiac because the commencing degree or the equinoctial points constantly move by shifting backwards.

Once the two zodiacs, the sidereal and the tropical, were identical when the spring equinoctial point was at zero degree Ashwini, i.e., the beginning of the sidereal zodiac. But through the ages, by constant shifting back of the spring equinoctial point, there is now a distance of about 23° between the commencing points of the two zodiacs. This distance is called the precession of the equinox and nutation.

Since the constellation Ashwini has more than one star, Hindu astrologers also are not all unanimous in regard to the present value of the precession of the equinox and nutation, say, on 1st January 1969. But the majority of eminent astrologers in India approve of the value as given in *Lahiri's Ephemeris*. According to this Indian ephemeris the precession of equinox and nutation on 1st January 1969 was 23° 25′ 25″. The precession of equinox and nutation for the first of January of each year has been given in an appendix at the end of the book.

The attention of readers is again invited to the very important fact that Hindu Astrology is based upon the sidereal or the fixed zodiac. All signs are as in the fixed zodiac and the longitudes of planets also refer to their location in the fixed zodiac.

Readers should therefore verify that the birth chart before them is in the sidereal zodiac. If the cusp of the first and the tenth houses and the longitudes of planets refer to the tropical zodiac and have been taken from Raphael's or any other Western Ephemeris, the value of the precession of the equinox and nutation on the date of birth must be ascertained from the Appendix and deducted from the tropical longitudes, to convert them into sidereal ones. In a subsequent chapter we shall indicate how to calculate the rising degree, minute and second at a particular hour at any place on the earth.

CHAPTER 2

THE BIRTH CHART

THE BIRTH chart is a sketch of the heavens at the time of birth as viewed from the place of birth. Thus three elements are required to make the birth chart: (i) the date of birth, (ii) the time of birth, and (iii) the longitude and latitude of the place of birth. The birth place is important because the positions of the rising sign and mid-heaven are taken as viewed from the place of birth. The longitudes of the planets entered in the chart are geocentric, i.e., as if viewed from the centre of the earth. Thus the geocentric degree, minute and second in a particular sign will be the same at a particular time whether the birth is in India or America or Australia or any other place. But at a time when it is noon in India it will be mid-night in America, and when the Sun is in the mid-heaven in India it will be at the nadir in America. Thus the house position of the Sun will differ.

The point of the ecliptic touching or cutting the eastern horizon is called the ascendant. It is called the ascendant because it ascends or goes up. This needs explaining. Suppose the birth is at sunrise when the Sun is rising on the Eastern horizon; the degree of the ecliptic rising will be the same as the longitude occupied by the Sun. After a couple of hours the Sun will be higher up in the east and the degree which was rising in the east at the time will also go up. After another two hours the Sun and degree rising, both being identical, will further go up. After another hour it will go up further still. We cannot see or identify the degree rising at the time of birth with the naked eye. But we can see the Sun, and since the degree rising and the Sun at sunrise have identical locality, when we see the Sun rising we infer that the degree which was at birth touching the eastern horizon is also rising. Now this phenomenon of rising is called ascending and the degree rising on the eastern horizon at the time of birth is called the ascendant. Correctly speaking, the ascending degree, minute, and second is the point of the ascendant; but in common parlance if the degree falls in the sign Aries, we call Aries as the ascendant; if it falls in Taurus, we deem Taurus as the ascendant, and so on.

In Sanskrit the ascendant is called the *Lagnam*. The word *Lagnam* means 'attached to.' Attached to what? To the eastern horizon.

Since the Earth by its revolving motion round its axis completes one revolution in twenty-four hours, all the signs rise in succession, and the rising of the twelve signs is completed in twenty-four hours.

Because the Earth is inclined in relation to the plane of the ecliptic and since the path of the Earth is also elliptic, the durations of the signs rising, i.e., the durations of the signs, at the eastern horizon, differ. This difference is also caused by the latitude of the place of birth. To explain this further: If we draw an ellipse on paper and draw twelve lines from the centre to the circumference, each making an angle of 30° with the centre, although the degrees of each sector at the centre will be 30° the arcs on the elliptical circumference made by these radial lines will be of unequal lengths.

At a particular given place the following pairs of signs take equal time to rise:

Aries and Pisces,
Taurus and Aquarius,
Gemini and Capricorn,
Cancer and Sagittarius,
Leo and Scorpio,
Virgo and Libra.

From the equator as we proceed to the north, the ascending time of Aries, Taurus and Gemini as also of Pisces, Aquarius and Capricorn goes on decreasing, and the ascending time of Cancer,

Leo and Virgo, as also of Sagittarius, Scorpio and Libra goes on increasing. In southern latitudes it is the reverse.

We shall explain subsequently to calculate the ascending degree. But before we do so, it is necessary to explain what is meant by house division. The eastern horizon is denoted in the birth chart as we draw it on paper, representing a rough sketch of the heavens, by the ascendant; the western horizon by the descendant; the mid-heaven by the tenth house, and the nadir by the fourth house. If a person is born at sunrise, the Sun is in the east. So the Sun will be in the ascendant. If a person is born at sunset, the Sun will be in the west. So the Sun will be in the descendant or the seventh house. Similarly, if a person is born at noon his Sun will be in mid-heaven and therefore in the tenth house. Correspondingly, if the birth is at midnight the Sun will be exactly below, i.e., in the fourth house.

The eastern horizon is to the east, the western is to the west. The mid-heaven in the south and the nadir in the north. The sign rising in the east is the first house; just below the eastern horizon is the second house; then further below it in the sky below the Earth is the third house; then further below is the fourth, then the fifth, then the sixth and at the western horizon the seventh. From the western horizon we go up and that is the eighth house; then still further up will be the ninth, and in mid-heaven will be the tenth house. As we proceed from the mid-heaven towards the east there will be the eleventh house and then just above the horizon will be the twelfth house. In other words, we count the signs or the houses from the eastern horizon; we have to proceed from the eastern horizon via below the earth come to the western horizon, then go up to mid-heaven and complete the circle by coming to the eastern horizon. Let us further clarify this.

Suppose the sign rising on the eastern horizon is Aries. We are for the time being not paying attention to the degree in Aries which like all others, has 30°, but taking the sign Aries as a whole. Then Taurus will be below the Earth, with Gemini under it, then Cancer in the sky below the Earth, with Leo also under the Earth and with Virgo also under the Earth. At the western horizon there will be Libra. We go higher up and there will be Scorpio. Further higher up will be Sagittarius and at the mid-heaven point will be Capricorn. As we proceed from mid-heaven towards the eastern horizon, there will be found Aquarius and then Pisces. This is generally the case near the equator. But in very high latitudes, due to the arc from the mid-heaven to the eastern horizon being very unequal to the arc from the eastern horizon to the nadir, there is slight variation in the sign at mid-heaven. But the order of the signs Aries, Taurus, Gemini, etc., or of the first house, second house, and so on, never varies.

What is intended to convey is that when we commence from the point rising at the eastern horizon or the ascending degree, we travel east, north, west, south and east again, i.e., via the heavens below the Earth and not the other way round.

What Is a House?

In the above discussion we have used the word 'house.' Readers well acquainted with astrology will know what the word 'house' actually means in the astrological context. In fact to such readers as are well acquainted with astrological terminology, the entire first chapter and much of this and subsequent chapters will appear to be covering the ground they are well familiar with. But since interest in Hindu astrology is increasing and a large number of readers will be treading untrodden ground, it is necessary to explain each link and each technical word, for if a new reader is not acquainted with the basic terminology or misses a link, he will not be able to follow the subsequent steps. Those who are already familiar with the technical words of astrology or know how to cast a birth chart can conveniently skip over the following pages.

According to older Hindu texts, the words signs and houses fall on each other, but the count of the signs is always made from Aries which is the first sign. If we say a planet is in the first sign, it means that he is in Aries. If we say, it is in the fifth sign, it will be in Leo. If we say, it is in the twelfth sign, it will be in Pisces because Pisces is the last and the twelfth sign. We must remember that when referring to a sign we always count Aries as the first and then proceed in the regular order of the signs.

But a house begins from the ascendant. We must first know which is the sign ascending at the particular moment at a particular place. The mathematical procedure for finding this will be described in subsequent pages. The Earth is globular. It is like a globe with the sky all around. There is no part of the sky which is not to the east of any locality of the Earth. We can explain this further by giving a practical example. The Sun always appears to be somewhere on the ecliptic. In fact, he is not on the ecliptic; it is the Earth which is on the ecliptic and as viewed from the Earth, the Sun appears to be in line with some place on the ecliptic. But for practical purpose, we may say that the Sun is somewhere in the zodiac. Now this Sun at any time appears in the east, in some part or the other of the Earth. So we may state that as the zodiac is a circular ring in the skies, though in fact it is elliptic, going all round, some part of the ring, i.e., the zodiac is on the eastern horizon somewhere.

Now suppose that at a particular time the sign Leo is rising at the eastern horizon. Then Leo will constitute the first house, Virgo the second house, Libra the third house, Scorpio the fourth house, Sagittarius the fifth house, Capricorn the sixth house, Aquarius the seventh house, Pisces the eighth house, Aries the ninth house, Taurus the tenth house, Gemini the eleventh house and Cancer the twelfth house. Now suppose that the Sun is in Aquarius. So we say the Sun is in the seventh house or setting in the western horizon.

If suppose Scorpio was rising at New Delhi. Then Scorpio will be the first house, Sagittarius the second house. Capricorn the third house and so on; and the Sun being in Aquarius he will be in the fourth house.

Delhi's longitude is 77° 13′ East and 28° 39′ North. Now it is elementary geography that when the Sun is setting at Delhi, it is rising at a place having the longitude 77° 13′ West and 28° 39′ North. The Sun is in Aquarius. So the sign Aquarius is rising there and constitutes the first house, Pisces the second house, Aries the third house, Taurus the fourth house, Gemini the fifth house, Cancer the sixth house, Leo the seventh house, Virgo the eighth house, Libra the ninth house, Scorpio the tenth house, Sagittarius the eleventh house, and Capricorn the twelfth house. Now since the Sun is in Aquarius we say the Sun is in the first house.

And what happens when Scorpio rises at Delhi having 77° 13′ East longitude. At the corresponding place having 77° 13′ West longitude and having the same latitude as Delhi, i.e., 28° 39′ North, the opposite sign Taurus rises; so Taurus will be the first house, Gemini the second house, and so on, Aquarius being the tenth house. Since the Sun is in Aquarius, the Sun will be in the tenth house.

The following signs being in opposition at 180°, to each other are called opposition signs:

Aries is in opposition to Libra and Libra to Aries
Taurus is in opposition to Scorpio and Scorpio to Taurus
Gemini is in opposition to Sagittarius and Sagittarius to Gemini
Cancer is in opposition to Capricorn and Capricorn to Cancer
Leo is in opposition to Aquarius and Aquarius to Leo
Virgo is in opposition to Pisces and Pisces to Virgo

We may further clarify this point by citing the example of a cycle wheel. Suppose the wheel has twelve spokes at 30° each. The circumference of the wheel is thus divided into twelve sectors. We shall call them Aries, Taurus, etc. Now rotate the wheel. Different sections of the circumference will appear to the east of the centre of the wheel. Sometimes Aries will be to the east, at others Taurus or Gemini, and so on. This is exactly what happens in the case of the Earth, with the difference that here the zodiac is constant; it does not move: But the Earth turns round, completes a full revolution in about twenty-four hours, and as the Earth turns round on its axis an inhabitant on Earth at a fixed place, say Delhi facing the east will find certain parts of the zodiac on the east, and after about twenty-four hours the same sign will come to the east, and thus the cycle continues.

So we must remember that the sign rising to the east at a particular time depends upon the time, date, month, year and the longitude and latitude of the place.

The latitude is very important because the duration of a sign rising differs from latitude to latitude.

CHAPTER 3

TIME

TIME IS eternal. Its beginning or end cannot be conceived. But still to identify a particular moment we have to take recourse to some kind of marking. According to Hindu astrology the Earth comes into being and is then destroyed, again it comes into being and is again destroyed, and thus the cycle goes on. According to the conception of the Hindus, one cycle continues for 43,20,000, years. This epoch has been divided into four sub-epochs as follows:

Satayuga	4,32,000 × 4	17,28,000 years
Tretayuga	4,32,000 × 3	12,96,000 ,,
Dwaparayuga	4,32,000 × 2	8,64,000 ,,
Kaliyuga	4,32,000 × 1	4,32,000 ,,
	TOTAL	43,20,000 years

We are at present in *Kaliyuga*. On 15th April 1969, *Kaliyuga* year 5070 commenced.

Other calendar years like the *Yudhishthira* year, *Buddha* year, also came into use from time to time, but with the passage of time they passed on into oblivion. But there are still current various calendars for reckoning different kinds of years in different parts of India, for example the Bengali san whose 1376th year commenced on 14th April 1969, *Kollam* era in Kerala whose 1145th year began on 17th August 1969; but the most widely current eras at present are the Vikrama Samvata whose 2026th year commenced on 19th March 1969 and the *Shaka* era whose 1891st year began on 14th April 1969. The Vikrama year is a lunar year, while the Shaka year is a solar year.

There is a sixty year cycle known as Jupiter's cycle. The names assigned to the various years in the sixty year cycle are as follows:

1. Prabhava	21. Sarvajit	41. Plavanga
2. Vibhava	22. Sarvadhari	42. Keelaka
3. Shukla	23. Virodhi	43. Saumya
4. Pramoda	24. Vikrita	44. Sadharana
5. Prajapati	25. Khara	45. Virodhakrit
6. Angira	26. Nandana	46. Paridhavi
7. Shrimukha	27. Vijaya	47. Pramathi
8. Bhava	28. Jaya	48. Ananda
9. Yuva	29. Manmatha	49. Rakshasa
10. Dhata	30. Durmukha	50. Anala
11. Ishwara	31. Hemalamba	51. Pingala
12. Bahudhanya	32. Vilamba	52. Kalayukta
13. Pramathi	33. Vikari	53. Siddhartha
14. Vikrama	34. Sharvari	54. Raudra
15. Vrisha	35. Plava	55. Durmati
16. Chitra bhanu	36. Shubhakrit	56. Dundubhi
17. Subhanu	37. Shobhana	57. Rudhirodgari
18. Tarana	38. Krodhi	58. Raktaksha
19. Parthiva	39. Vishwavasu	59. Krodhana
20. Vyaya	40. Parabhava	60. Kshaya.

Certain effects on nativities and on mundane affairs have been attributed to each of the years, but it would be too academic to discuss them here. A broad outline of the conception of time and the various eras and epochs have been provided to convey an idea of the background of Hindu astrology. The subject we are dealing with in this volume is primarily the reading of the birth chart on the basis of the planetary positions and we shall revert to this.

In Hindu nativities worked out in Sanskrit the date is expressed in terms of Samvata, the Hindu name of the month, the lunar date of the month, and the time of birth as *Ghatis* and *Palas* after sunrise is given. Some astrologers put the shaka year also in addition to the Samvata year. In northern India the Vikram Samvata commences from Chaitra Shukla, but in Gujarat and some western and southern parts of India the Vikram Samvata commences after seven months on Kartika Shukla.

The names of the twelve months are:

1.	Chaitra	7.	Ashwina
2.	Vaishakha	8.	Kartika
3.	Jyeshtha	9.	Margashirsha
4.	Ashadha	10.	Pausha
5.	Shravana	11.	Magha
6.	Bhadra	12.	Phalguna.

These are lunar months. When after the conjunction of the Sun and the Moon, the Moon having much faster motion than the Sun goes ahead of the Sun, it is called *Shukla*. The word *Shukla* means white or bright in Sanskrit. The period from now onwards for about fifteen days is called *Shukla* because the Moon having crossed the conjunction of the Sun is now proceeding towards the opposition of the Sun. If the Moon has one bright digit, today, he will have two bright digits tomorrow, and so on until on or about the fifteenth day there will be full Moon. This is called the bright half of the month or the *Shukla Paksha.* When the Moon has reached the opposition of the Sun, i.e., is exactly at 180° from the Sun, the dark half of the month commences. The bright part of the Moon's disc starts shedding one digit each day until on or about the fifteenth day the Moon having no bright digit at all is invisible.

The angular distance of 12° from the Sun constitutes one lunar day, which is called *Tithi* in Sanskrit. We may in terms of soli-lunar distance express the Hindu lunar day or *Tithi* as follows:

When the distance between the Sun and the Moon is	*Increasing distance between the Sun and the Moon or bright fortnight*
From 0 to 12 degrees	*Tithi* 1
„ 12 „ 24 „	„ 2
„ 24 „ 36 „	„ 3
„ 36 „ 48 „	„ 4

,,	48	,,	60	,,	,,	5
,,	60	,,	72	,,	,,	6
,,	72	,,	84	,,	,,	7
,,	84	,,	96	,,	,,	8
,,	96	,,	108	,,	,,	9
,,	108	,,	120	,,	,,	10
,,	120	,,	132	,,	,,	11
,,	132	,,	144	,,	,,	12
,,	144	,,	156	,,	,,	13
,,	156	,,	168	,,	,,	14
,,	168	,,	180	,,	,,	15

Decreasing distance from the Sun

Now the Moon having reached 180° from the Sun, the distance between the two goes on decreasing gradually.

When the distance between the Sun and the Moon is				*Decreasing distance between the Sun and the Moon or dark fortnight*	
From	180	degrees to	168	*Tithi*	1
,,	168	,,	156	,,	2
,,	156	,,	144	,,	3
,,	144	,,	132	,,	4
,,	132	,,	120	,,	5
,,	120	,,	108	,,	6
,,	108	,,	96	,,	7
,,	96	,,	84	,,	8
,,	84	,,	72	,,	9
,,	72	,,	60	,,	10
,,	60	,,	48	,,	11
,,	48	,,	36	,,	12
,,	36	,,	24	,,	13
,,	24	,,	12	,,	14
,,	12	,,	0	,,	30

Readers will note that we have put 30 after 14 because 30 symbolically represents the end of the lunar month of 30 days. The

Hindu names of *Tithis* are given below:

1.	Pratipat	8.	Ashtami
2.	Dwiteeya	9.	Navami
3.	Triteeya	10.	Dashami
4.	Chaturthi	11.	Ekadashi
5.	Panchami	12.	Dwadashi
6.	Shashthi	13.	Trayodashi
7.	Saptami	14.	Chaturdashi.

The *Tithi* given as 15 is called *Poornima* or full Moon. The *Tithi* given as 30 is called *Amavasya*. The end of *Amavasya* is called new Moon. Since the names of the fourteen *tithis* are the same a prefix *Shukla Paksha*, meaning bright half of the month, or *Krishna Paksha*, meaning dark half of the month, is added to indicate whether the Moon is waxing or waning. Some Hindu Ephemerides begin with the bright half of the month and take it in regular order upto 30, which is the end of the lunar month or *Amavasya*.

Now if the relative motion of the Sun and the Moon be unchanged all *Tithis* and lunar months would be of equal duration. But since the motion of the Sun and the Moon is varying, sometimes the Moon is faster, at others he is slower; thus the time taken by him to cover a particular distance from the Sun is different and so the durations of the *Tithis* differ and that of the lunar months also. A lunar month's average duration is 29 days, 12 hours and 44 minutes.

As the lunar year covers about 354 days and the sidereal year is of about 365 days and 6 hours, Hindu astrologers have from times immemorial adopted the practice of adding an intercalary month once in about three years. When a lunar month falls between two ingresses of the Sun—when the Sun enters a sign it is called an ingress—an intercalary lunar month is added. This is known in Hindu astrology as *Adhikamasa*, and bears the same name as the just preceding lunar month; but the word *Adhika* or additional is added to indicate that it is an intercalary month.

All this information is provided so that the reader may become conversant with the terminology signifying various particulars as stated in a Hindu horoscope.

PANCHANGA

The Hindu ephemeris is called a *Panchanga.* The word *Panchanga* means five constituents:

(i) The day of the week. It is the same as in English — Sunday, Monday Moon's day, Tuesday Mars, Wednesday Mercury, Thursday Jupiter, Friday Venus, Saturday Saturn.

(ii) The *Tithi* or the lunar day. This has already been explained.

(iii) The *Karana.*

Half of a *Tithi* is called a *Karana.* The following table gives an idea of the two *Karanas* into which a *Tithi* is divided.

Bright Half of the Month (Shukla Paksha)		*Dark Half of the Month (Krishna Paksha)*	
Tithi First Karana	*Second Karana*	*Tithi First Karana*	*Second Karana*
1. Kinstughna	Bava	1. Balava	Kaulava
2. Balava	Kaulava	2. Taitila	Gara
3. Taitila	Gara	3. Vanija	Vishti
4. Vanija	Vishti	4. Bava	Balava
5. Bava	Balava	5. Kaulava	Taitila
6. Kaulava	Taitila	6. Gara	Vanija
7. Gara	Vanija	7. Vishti	Bava
8. Vishti	Bava	8. Balava	Kaulava
9. Balava	Kaulava	9. Taitil	Gara
10. Taitila	Gara	10. Vanija	Vishti
11. Vanija	Vishti	11. Bava	Balava
12. Bava	Balava	12. Kaulava	Taitila
13. Kaulava	Taitila	13. Gara	Vanija
14. Gara	Vanija	14. Vishti	Shakuna
15. Vishti	Bava	30. Chatushpada	Naga

Thus, if you divide the duration of the first lunar *tithi* of the bright half of the month into two parts, during the first half there will be *Kinstughna Karana,* in the second half *Bava Karana.*

These seven *Karanas, Bava, Balava, Kaulava, Taitila, Gara, Vanija* and *Vishti,* come in regular order, as will be evident from the above Table.

They are repeated eight times in a month. But the *Shakuna*

Karana during the latter half of *Chaturdashi* in the dark half of the month, *Chatushpade Karana* during the first half of *Amavasya, Naga Karana* during the second or last half of *Amavasya,* and *Kinstughna Karana* during the first half of the first *Tithi* in the bright half of the month occur only once.

Certain predictions for natives born during particular *Karana* have been given in Hindu text-books, but as they are too general we shall not deal with them here.

(iv) *Nakshatra.* This we have already explained.

(v) *Yoga.* This is a Sanskrit word which literally means 'addition.' To find a *Yoga* at a particular time the longitudes of the Sun and the Moon are added. Whenever the word longitude is used, unless otherwise stated they refer to the sidereal longitudes and not to the tropical longitudes. If a reader has an Ephemeris giving tropical longitudes of planets, such as *Raphael's Ephemeris,* the first step should be to convert them into sidereal ones, by deducting the precession of equinoxes and nutation for the particular day. The necessary Table is given in Appendix I at the end of the book.

There are 27 *Yogas* as given below.

Now to find the Yoga, add the longitudes of the Sun and the Moon on a particular date at a particular time. Suppose you have to find the *Yoga* at 5.30 a.m. Indian Standard Time on 1st January 1969.

	S.	D.	M.	S.*
The longitude of the Sun	8-	16-	58-	44
The longitude of the Moon	1-	16-	51-	18
Total:	10-	3-	50-	2

If the Sum exceeds 12 signs, deduct 12 from the figure for signs. The degrees, minutes and seconds should be allowed to stand unaltered. In the present example, since the number of signs is 10 only, i.e., less than 12, no question of deducting 12 arises.

Now the *Yoga* at the time is determined according to the figure arrived at by adding the longitudes of the Sun and the Moon.

* S.D.M.S. Means signs, degrees, minutes and seconds.

		S. D. M.		S. D. M.	*Yoga*
1.	From	0- 0- 0	to	0-13-20	*Vishkumbha*
2.	,,	0-13-20	to	0-26-40	*Priti*
3.	,,	0-26-40	to	1-10- 0	*Ayushmana*
4.	,,	1-10- 0	to	1-23-20	*Saubhagya*
5.	,,	1-23-20	to	2- 6-40	*Shobhana*
6.	,,	2- 6-40	to	2-20- 0	*Atiganda*
7.	,,	2-20- 0	to	3- 3-20	*Sukarma*
8.	,,	3- 3-20	to	3-16-40	*Dhriti*
9.	,,	3-16-40	to	4- 0- 0	*Shoola*
10.	,,	4- 0- 0	to	4-13-20	*Ganda*
11.	,,	4-13-20	to	4-26-40	*Vriddhi*
12.	,,	4-26-40	to	5-10- 0	*Dhruva*
13.	,,	5-10- 0	to	5-23-20	*Vyaghata*
14.	,,	5-23-20	to	6- 6-40	*Harshana*
15.	,,	6- 6-40	to	6-20- 0	*Vajra*
16.	,,	6-20- 0	to	7- 3-20	*Siddhi*
17.	,,	7- 3-20	to	7-16-40	*Vyatipata*
18.	,,	7-16-40	to	8- 0- 0	*Variyana*
19.	,,	8- 0- 0	to	8-13-20	*Parigha*
20.	,,	8-13-20	to	8-26-40	*Shiva*
21.	,,	8-26-40	to	9-10- 0	*Siddha*
22.	,,	9-10- 0	to	9-23-20	*Sadhya*
23.	,,	9-23-20	to	10- 6-40	*Shubha*
24.	,,	10- 6-40	to	10-20- 0	*Shukla*
25.	,,	10-20- 0	to	11- 3-20	*Brahma*
26.	,,	11- 3-20	to	11-16-40	*Indra*
27.	,,	11-16-40	to	12- 0- 0	*Vaidhriti*

Now let us find in which sector 10-3-50, the sum of the longitudes of the Sun and the Moon in the example taken by us falls. On going through the above table we find that 23 is from 9-23-20 to 10-6-40. Against this we find *Shubha*. So on 1st January 1969 at 5-30 a.m. there was *Shubha Yoga.*

Certain general effects have been described for birth according to the month, day of the week, or the *Yoga* and *Nakshatra*. They are too general and if given would unnecessarily add complications. So we have given only the effects of important *Nakshatras* at the end of this Chapter. These—the day of the week, *Tithi*,

Nakshtra and *Yoga*—are also taken into account for selection of auspicious time for commencing or performing important acts and ceremonies. But here we are concerned only with a discussion of birth charts.

Time in Hindu astrology is expressed in *Ghatis* and *Palas*.

One day and night	= 60 Ghatis
1 *Ghati*	= 60 Palas
1 *Pala*	= 60 Vipals

Commonly a day and night is taken to cover 24 hours.*

So 1 *Ghati*	= 24 minutes
1 *Pala*	= 24 seconds

In olden times when there were no watches, time used to be computed by sundials or water meters, which were cup shaped vessels with a small hole at the bottom. These were placed in a big can full of water. Water through the hole would gradually enter the cup and when filled with water coming into it through the fine orifice at the bottom, it would sink to the bottom of the can full of water. The markings on the cup indicated the water level and with the help of this contrivance time was computed. There was another method of measuring time. A small straight stick was fixed on level ground, and by measuring the length of the shadow cast by this stick, time was computed. All these measures have become obsolete and do not have the precision which a good watch has. Nor is time now spoken of in *Ghatis* and *Palas*. It is referred to in hours and minutes. So we shall throughout this book refer to hours and minutes which are in current usage.

The *Panchangas* or Indian Ephemerides continue to give the duration of *Tithi, Nakshatra, Yoga,* etc., in *Ghatis* and *Palas*. Some have introduced the system of giving the duration in hours and minutes also; while other modern Ephemerides give the duration in hours and minutes only and not in *Ghatis* and *Palas*. There are hundreds of *Panchangas* in current usage in India. Local astrologers consider it a mark of respect and prestige to be the authors of a *Panchanga* and so they make one and sell it directly or through some publisher. But most of them are incorrect. This is due to two reasons. The old formulae given in the *Surya*

* Sidereal day in civil hours = 23 hours, 56 minutes, 4 secs. Civil day in sidereal hours = 24 hours, 3 minutes, 56 secs. = 24 hours.

Siddhanta and other astronomical works do not hold good today. There has been some variation in the regular motions of the astral bodies as given in the older texts. Formerly Hindu astronomers used to rectify these formulae by prescribing certain additions or subtractions to arrive at correct results. These additions or subtractions used to be called *Beeja Sanskara.* The practice and the tradition of providing *Beeja Sanskara* was discontinued in later times.

The other reason for the inaccuracy of many of the *Panchangas* is that the calculation of daily longitudes of planets for 360 days involves much time and labour and a certain amount of mathematical accuracy and for precision, checking and rechecking is necessary and this is lacking in a majority of the *Panchangas* and their authors.

Most of the up-to-date *Panchangas* or Ephemerides published in India take the longitudes of planets from western Ephemerides and convert the tropical longitudes into sidereal.

We would, therefore, suggest that unless correct Hindu *Panchangas* giving the exact longitudes of planets for each day are available readers would do well to use *Raphael's Ephemeris,* convert the Standard Time of birth into Greenwich Mean Time and calculate the longitudes. These will, however, be longitudes in the tropical zodiac. Deduct the precession of equinoxes and nutation on the birth date from the tropical longitudes, and you will have the correct longitudes in the sidereal zodiac.

An objection might be raised that the longitudes given in Raphael's or other western Ephemerides are geocentric, i.e., as the planets would appear if viewed from the centre of the earth, whereas the correct longitudes should be as would appear from the place of observation or place of birth on the surface of the earth. The distances of the Sun, Mars, Mercury, Jupiter, Venus, and Saturn are so great that the angles between the geographical positions and the geocentric positions of the Sun and other planets would be very small and therefore negligible. In the case of the Moon, due to the distance of the Moon being not so far away from the earth, there would be a difference between the two longitudes as viewed from the place of birth and the centre of the earth, i.e., the geographical position and the geocentric one. This is called parallax. But the calculation of parallax involves much time and energy and also mathematical ability and it would be beyond the scope of this volume to give complete instructions for the calculation of parallax. Those who are interested in the study and calculations of parallax are advised to refer to more advanced books on the subject.

Even among the current sidereal Ephemerides, such as *Lahiri's*, only geocentric longitudes of the Moon are given and the readers are advised to use the geocentric longitudes of the Moon after deducting the precession of the equinoxes and nutation from the tropical longitudes.

Once we have calculated the longitudes of the Sun and the Moon, we can easily calculate the *Nakshatra, Tithi* and *Yoga*. We repeat that the *Nakshatra* is determined by the sidereal longitude of the Moon. The *Tithi* is determined by the relative distance between the Sun and the Moon; and *Yoga* is calculated by adding the sidereal longitudes of the Sun and the Moon. So readers can calculate these even if they have no Hindu *Panchanga*. We shall work out an example to show how this is done.

Suppose a person was born at 5-30 a.m. on 1st January 1969, Indian Standard Time. First calculate the sidereal longitudes of the Sun and the Moon at 5-30 a.m. Indian Standard Time as 5-30 a.m. will be 12 midnight between 31st December 1968 and 1st January 1969 Greenwich Mean Time. Now calculate the longitudes at 12 midnight Greenwich Mean Time and deduct the precession of the equinoxes and nutation from the tropical longitudes, and you will have the sidereal longitudes of the Sun and the Moon. Or take these sidereal longitudes from an ephemeris giving sidereal longitudes.

For example, the sidereal longitudes of the Sun and the Moon on 1st January 1969 at 5-30 a.m. Indian Standard Time as given in *Lahiri's Ephemeris* are as follows:

	S. D. M. S.
Longitude of the Sun	8-16-58-44
Longitude of the Moon	1-16-51-18

We have already given an example earlier as to how a *Yoga* is calculated.

Now let us give an example of how the *Nakshatra, Tithi* and *Karana* are worked out. To take *Nakshatra* first, for which we require only the Moon's longitude, on referring to an earlier page we find that from 1-10-0-0 to 1-23-20-0 is *Rohini*. So we say that the Moon is in *Rohiṇi Nakshtra* or in the astrological parlance there is *Rohini Nakshatra.*

When we say today is *Rohini Nakshtra,* what do we mean? The *Rohini Nakshatra* was in the heavens before today for innumerable centuries and will be even after centuries from today. But when we say today is *Rohini,* it is an abbreviated form of the statement, 'the Moon is in *Rohini Nakshatra* today.'

Now let us come to *Tithi.* Convert the signs into degrees and the Moon's longitude will be 46° 51′ 18″. The Sun's longitude will be 256° 58′ 44″. Now subtract the Sun's longitude from the Moon's.

Moon	46° 51′ 18″
Sun	256° 58′ 44″

When the Moon's longitude, as in the present case, is less than the Sun's, add 360 degrees to the Moon's longitude and then subtract.

Moon	406° 51′ 18″
Sun	256° 58′ 44″
	149° 52′ 34″

Now referring to an earlier page we find that this is *Shukla Paksha Trayodashi.* Why *Shukla Paksha* or the bright half? Because the Moon is proceeding towards the opposition of the Sun.

Now *Trayodashi Tithi* is when the distance of the Moon from the Sun is 144° to 156°.

The distance between 144° and 156° is 12 degrees. Divide this into sectors of 6 degrees each: (i) 144 to 150 and (ii) 150 to 156 degrees. These two sectors represent the two sectors or *Karanas* of *Trayodashi.* Now in our example the distance between the Moon and the Sun is 149° and odd. So this falls in the first sector. Now on referring to the relevant page we find that during the first half of *Trayodhashi* as on 1st January 1969 at 5-30 a.m. there is *Kaulava Karana.*

Certain effects due to birth in a particular month on a particular day, when the Moon is in a particular *Tithi* or *Karana* have been given in different texts. It would be too lengthy to go into all these here. So we only give below some particulars of *Tithis, Karanas* and *Nakshatras,* which are not considered good if a birth takes place during them. It is customary for Hindus to perform some *Shanti* or religious propitiation if a child is born during any of these.

Tithis

(i) Religious propitiation is necessary if the birth is during the last 48 minutes or four-fifths of an hour of *Panchami* or fifth lunar day, *Dashami* or tenth lunar day, *Amavasya* or 30th lunar day, *Poornima* or full Moon day or 15th lunar day.

(ii) *Krishna Chaturdashi* on 14th lunar day of the dark fortnight. The entire period is to be divided into six parts; the first one-sixth is auspicious and the rest inauspicious and requires *Shanti* or religious propitiation.

Karanas

If the birth be in the *Bhadra Karana*, as certain evil effects have been ascribed to the same, religious propitiation is necessary. Vishti Karana is also called Bhadra.

Yogas

Birth during any of the following *Yogas* requires religious prayers in the prescribed form: (i) *Yamaganda*, (ii) *Vyatipata*, (iii) *Parigha*, (iv) *Shoola*, (v) *Vaidhriti*.

Nakshatras

(i) Ashwini, (ii) Ashlesha, (iii) Magha, (iv) Jyeshtha, (v) Moola, (vi) Revati. Particularly significant is the commencement of (i), (iii) and (v), and the fag end of (ii), (iv) and (vi), or in other words when the longitude of the Moon is between the following:

(a) 11-26° 40′ to 0-3° 20′ (b) 3-26° 40′ to 4-3° 20′ or

(c) 7-26° 40′ to 8-3° 20′.

It is customary among orthodox Hindus to perform some *Shanti* or religious propitiation if a child is born when the Moon is in any of the above sectors. Similarly if a child is born in a particular *Nakshatra* which happens to be the *Nakshatra* of either parent or a brother or a sister some religious propitiation is made. To know the *Nakshatra* or Moon's position in a particular sector of the parent or brother or sister, his or her birth chart must be studied.

We give below some additional information.

1. If the birth of the child is when the Moon occupies 0° 0′ to 3° 20′ in Sagittarius, this adversely affects the father's health; if the degree occupied is 3° 20′ to 6° 40′ in Sagittarius, it is the mother who suffers. If the degree is between 6° 40′ to 10° there is loss of property and if the degree tenanted by the Moon is 10° to 13° 20′, the child will be prosperous.

2. (a) When the rising sign is Sagittarius and the degree tenanted by the Moon is 13° 20′ to 16° 40′ in Sagittarius there will be trouble to the father.
   (b) When the rising sign is Cancer and the degree tenanted by the Moon is 3° 20′ to 6° 40′ in Cancer the same result as in (a) above.

3. (a) When the rising sign is Sagittarius and the degree tenanted by the Moon is 16° 40′ to 20°, there will be trouble to the mother.
   (b) When Cancer is the ascendant and the degree occupied by Moon is 6° 40′ to 10° in Cancer, the same effect as in (a) above.

4. (a) When the rising sign is Sagittarius and the degree occupied by the Moon 20° to 23° 20′ in Sagittarius, the health of the child is affected adversely.
   (b) When the rising sign is Cancer and Moon tenants any degree from 10° to 13° 20′ the same effect as in (a) above.

5. (a) When the rising sign is Sagittarius and the degree occupied by Moon is 23° 20′ to 26° 40′ in Sagittarius, the health or fortune of the maternal uncle of the child suffers.
   (b) When the rising sign is Cancer and the Moon occupies any degree from 13° 20′ to 16° 40′, the same results as in (a) above.

In Hindu Ephemerides called *Panchangas* the duration of *Tithi, Nakshatra, Karana* and *Yoga* is given for each day. From Ephemerides in English these can be calculated as explained in the earlier pages.

CHAPTER 4

SIGN RISING (ASCENDANT)

AS STATED earlier, in the tropical zodiac the durations of the following signs rising at the eastern horizon at any latitude are equal:

Aries	and	Pisces,
Taurus	and	Aquarius,
Gemini	and	Capricorn,
Cancer	and	Sagittarius,
Leo	and	Scorpio,
Virgo	and	Libra

At the equator, however, the durations of rising, (even among the six signs Aries, Taurus, Gemini, Cancer, Leo and Virgo) of the following pairs of signs are equal:

Aries	and	Virgo,
Taurus	and	Leo,
Gemini	and	Cancer.

So that at the equator the following groups of signs rise for equal periods:

Signs	*Duration* Hr.	Mts.	Secs.
(1) Aries, Virgo, Libra and Pisces	1	51	36
(2) Taurus, Leo, Scorpio and Aquarius	1	59	40
(3) Gemini, Cancer, Sagittarius and Capricorn	2	8	44
	6	00	00

The durations given in Hindu books are in *Asus* or *Ghatis* and *Palas** and they have been converted into hours and minutes for the convenience of readers. In this book of Hindu astrology we are dealing with the basic concepts and practice of Hindu astrology, but have explained all calculations in terms of modern units of time and not the old obsolete ones.

As we go higher up from the equator the durations of Aries, Taurus and Gemini go on diminishing gradually and those of Cancer, Leo and Virgo go on increasing correspondingly.

The decrease in duration of Aries is increase of Virgo. The decrease in Taurus is increase in Leo and the decrease in Gemini is the increase in Cancer.

Since we have stated that at all latitudes Aries and Pisces are of equal duration, loss in duration of Pisces is gain in duration of Libra, loss in duration of Aquarius is gain in duration of Scorpio and loss in duration of Capricorn is gain in duration of Sagittarius.

Due to the shape of the Earth, the obliquity of the Earth's axis and the ecliptic path of the Earth, the decrease or increase in the duration of the rising of signs is not equal, but changes from geographical latitude to latitude on the surface of the Earth. In Hindu astrology very detailed rules are given for calculating the duration of each sign according to the *Palabha* or the geographical latitude by which the degree rising is calculated. The older works of Hindu astrology use *Ghati, Pala* and *Vipala* as units of time.

The use of the hour and the minute, the modern and the current units of time, does not devalue the Hindu system. The principles of Hindu astrology will remain the same, but we have found by experience that it is far easier for the modern educated man to calculate the ascendant and the meridian cusp with this method rather than with the aid of the *Sarinis* given at the end of Hindu *Panchangas*.

The word *Sarini* means a Table. The *Sarini* is found at the end of each *Panchanga*. A Hindu Ephemeris is meant only for the latitude of the place for which the *Panchanga* is published and is strictly correct only for that year, having the *Ayanansha* the precession of equinoxes and nutation for the year noted on the top of the *Sarini*.

* Hindu Units of Time.

The Sun rises according to the Sun's longitude in the tropical zodiac and the rise of signs is also according to their positions in the tropical zodiac. After calculating the degree ascending, the precession of equinoxes and nutation for the day is deducted and the tropical degree is converted into the sidereal degree. Now what the *Sarini* does is to deduct the precession of equinoxes and nutation and give the readymade sidereal degree.

Thus if the *Sarini* is for the latitude of Varanasi and it shows the seventh degree of a sign rising and we calculated the ascendant for the same time in the year seventy-two years after the preparation of the *Sarini*, the ascendant would be 6° only, because the precession or *Ayanansha* will have during the seventy-two years increased by one degree and this has to be deducted from the seventh degree which held good seventy-two years back.

A large number of Hindu horoscopes show the incorrect degree and minute of the ascendant rising due to the following errors which have imperceptibly crept in. It is necessary to invite positive attention to these errors, so that readers may be aware of the pitfalls in the current calculations as generally prevalent and practised by a large number of Hindu astrologers. Those who know take care of the following errors and do not fall into the trap, but the number of really learned astrologers who are well up in calculations and in making predictions is comparatively small. Most astrologers follow their profession as a hereditary vocation, and since most of the Hindu families get a nativity drawn up when a child is born, the mass production of nativities is still in the hands of Hindu astrologers who are not well-educated, weak in mathematics and not conscious of their responsibility in the undertaking. It is for that reason that we advise that before attempting any predictions the rising degree and minute of the ascendant should be checked. The errors which we have found during the last forty-four years of our practice as an astrologer arise out of one or more of the following causes:

(i) The time of birth recorded in Hindu horoscopes is generally indicated as *Ishtam*. The word *Ishtam* in Sanskrit means 'wished for', 'desired for', 'longed for — the objective or the target.' It is expressed in *Ghatis* and *Palas* after sunrise. Now the sunrise for astronomical purposes is the time when the centre of the Sun is on the ecliptic at the eastern horizon. The word sunrise, according to Western astrology, is when the upper limb of the Sun is visible and the word sunset is used when the complete disc of the Sun becomes invisible. Most of the daily newspapers give sunrise and sunset timings according to this Western method. But in Hindu astrology it is the rising or setting of the centre of the Sun's disc which are the corret sunrise and sunset timings. And there is positively some difference between the coincidence, astronomical or truer, of the centre of the Sun with the horizon and the visibility of the upper limb of the Sun. Due to refraction the centre of the Sun becomes visible 2 minutes 15 seconds before the actual centre of the Sun's disc coincides with the eastern horizon. Besides the time between visibility of the Sun's upper limb and the centre is 1 minute 10 seconds approximately. So a total of 3 minutes 25 seconds must be deducted from the time of visibility of the upper limb to arrive at the true or astronomical rise of the Sun's centre. Similarly, to arrive at the correct time of setting of the Sun's centre 3 minutes 25 seconds should be deducted from the generally published sunset time.

(ii) The second error is due to the following factor. In olden days, in most of the Indian cities, local time was used. The local time was calculated by sun-dials and other methods. Even when they started using hours and minutes, 12 noon began to be treated as local mid-noon and 12 o'clock as local midnight. Modern watches, telephones and radios have now a network all over India. The 12 noon by the watch is still erroneously taken by thousands of Hindu astrologers as local mid-noon and 12 at night as midnight. A man goes to the astrologer and tells him that a child was born at 2 p.m. The astrologer opens his *Panchanga* or Ephemeris and finds that the duration of the day, sunrise to sunset, is 33 *Ghatis* 8 *Palas*. Half of it will be 16 *Ghatis* 34 *Palas*. This he takes as the *Ghati* and *Pala* at noon, oblivious of the fact that 12 o'clock. Indian Standard Time is not mid-noon at all longitudes and all latitudes in India. The child is born at 2 p.m., the interval since noon is two hours which when converted into *Ghatis* means five *Ghatis*. The incorrect value for mid-noon arrived at by him for 12 o'clock is 16 *Ghatis* 34 *Palas*. He adds 5 *Ghatis*, i.e. the time elapsed since 12 noon to 16 *Ghatis* 34 *Palas* and writes: *Ishtam* 21 *Ghatis* 34 *Palas*.

Now, since the true noon is not the same at all places, what a blunder he has committed in fixing the time of birth as 21 *Ghatis*

34 *Palas*. Such blunders are very frequent and we have discussed the point here at length so that readers do not fall into the trap.

(iii) Even when the astrologers look up the correct sunrise time in the *Panchanga*, it is not infrequent, for example, that the child is born at Amritsar, but the father of the boy consults an astrologer in Delhi and the *Panchanga* which the astrologer has is for Varanasi alone and not for the whole of India. In olden days astrologers had *Panchangas* calculated for the local longitude and latitude, but now some forty or fifty leading *Panchangas* are popular and some astrologers do not even care to find out the birth place but proceed on the basis of the *Panchanga* available with him. The scruples about longitude or latitude of the place of birth do not worry him. Thus an incorrect *Ishtam* is calculated.

(iv) The *Sarini* or Table of Houses used by him is for a latitude different from the place of birth and the resulting error is obvious. He uses the Table of Houses given as an Appendix in his *Panchanga* though a *Panchanga* gives the Table of Houses for one particular latitude only.

(v) The *Sarinis* are rarely revised and difference arising due to the changing value of precession of equinoxes and nutation is also one of the factors leading to inexactitude as already discussed.

(vi) One of the contributory factors in an incorrect calculation of the rising degree and minute of the ascendant as well as of the longitudes of planets is the incorrect value of the precession of the equinoxes and nutation. This differs from one Hindu *Panchanga* to another.

In order to eliminate all these pitfalls we have given the modern trigonometrical method of finding the ascending degree and minute by calculating the right ascension of the meridian cusp in hours, minutes and seconds. This is very easy. Employing the modern methods and the latest technique does not denigrate in any way the learned principles and practice of Hindu astrology. When we are no longer using *Ghatis* and *Palas* in our routine observations of time, why should we stick to them in matters astronomical? The objective is to calculate the rising degree and the minute of the ascendant at a particular time, date and place and for that the trigonometrical method is by far the most convenient and exact.

HOW TO CALCULATE THE RISING SIGN

A number of persons are interested in astrological readings, i.e., the influence of planets and at what time of life they would be effective; but many of them are reluctant to undertake the mathematical calculations. We have, therefore, in this book on predictive astrology made an attempt to keep the mathematical calculations to the minimum. In fact, there are many detailed ways of interpretation of horoscopes and for which detailed calculations are required, but if we load this book with such diversified and complicated calculations, a large number of readers will be scared away from studying the subject and applying their knowledge. So we shall confine ourselves in these pages to the barest minimum of mathematical calculations.

The first requirement is the calculation of the rising sign, degree and minute on a particular date, at a particular place and at a particular time. For this the following data is essential:

(a) Longitude of birth place
(b) Latitude of birth place
(c) Date of birth
(d) Watch time or the Standard time of the country.

Given these four items, to calculate the rising degree and minute is a very easy and simple matter.

The first two steps are:

(i) To convert the Standard time or watch time into local mean time.

(ii) To look up in the Ephemeris, the sidereal time at preceding noon, i.e., the noon immediately before the birth time and calculate the sidereal time at noon at the place of birth.

We shall explain both of these steps below.

Standard Time and Local Mean Time

The Standard time which the citizens of a place generally use, according to the watch, is the civil time as fixed by the government of the country. This time is used by railways, post and telegraph offices, government offices, business houses and all civil and military personnel and the population at large.

In India the Standard time is 5 hours and 30 minutes ahead of the Greenwich Mean Time. The Standard time in a country is generally fixed according to the central meridian of a country. This central meridian is not the actual centre or the longitude in the exact middle of the country or the political territory it governs, but is generally near about the middle. In India, the central meridián fixed is 82° 30′ East longitude. This was done with effect from 1906. Since from one sunrise to another sunrise or the next day it takes about 24 hours, or 24×60=1440 minutes, and the Earth has been longitudinally demarcated into 360°; the difference in sunrise for one degree of longitude, if the latitude of the two places is the same, is 1440 ÷ 360=4 minutes.

Now 82° 30′ the central meridian of India multipled by 4 would be 330 minutes or 5 hours 30 minutes. Since India is east of Greenwich, this period of 5 hours 30 minutes is added to Greenwich Mean Time and so when it is 6 a.m. at Greenwhich, it will be 11-30 a.m. in India; when it is 12 noon G.M.T., it will be 5-30 p.m. Indian Standard Time, and so on.

Conversion of Standard Time into Local Mean Time

Indian Standard Time is the same throughout the entire political territory of India. If a person at Calcutta speaks on the phone to a person in Bombay and compares the time as shown by his watch with his friend's at Bombay, the two watches should show the same time. But while the Sun may have just risen in Calcutta (because Calcutta is about 15° east of Bombay), it may rise after about 1 hour at Bombay. Thus the local mean time for the two places would be different.

There are two methods of converting Indian Standard Time (and in a similar manner the standard times in other countries) into local mean time. We shall clarify the steps by taking a concrete example.

Suppose we have to find the local mean time for longitude 77° 13′ East, when it is 5-30 a.m. I.S.T.

(i) The first method is to find the difference between 77° 13′ and 82° 30′ (the central meridian of India)

82° 30′
77° 13′
5° 17′

Multiply 5° 17′ by 4 minutes for each degree and we get 21 minutes 8 seconds. Since 77° 13′ is less than 82° 30′, the local mean time will be less. So, when it is 5-30 a.m. Indian Standard Time, it will be 5-8-52 a.m. local mean time at the longitude of 77° 13′ (Delhi).

(ii) The second method is as follows:

(a) Convert 5-30 a.m. Indian Standard Time into G.M.T. by deducting 5 hours 30 minutes. It would be 12 midnight (previous).

(b) Now the longitude for which mean time is required is 77° 13′. Multiply it by 4 minutes for each degree and we get 5 hours 8 minutes 52 seconds. Add this to G.M.T. (12 midnight) and we get 5-8-52 a.m. local mean time.

Whichever method the reader follows he will arrive at the same result.

Sidereal Time

Another data, which one requires for finding the rising sign or ascendant at a particular place is the sidereal time at preceding noon. It is generally given in the Ephemeris for the year. But a small correction is necessary.

Suppose we have to find sidereal time at preceding noon at a particular place. If we use *Raphael's Ephemeris*, the sidereal time given therein is for 0° longitude and if we want the sidereal time for say Delhi on the same noon, we have to deduct 51 seconds (because Delhi is 77° 13′ East of Greenwich) from the sidereal time at Greenwich and we will have the sidereal time at noon at Delhi. We get 51 seconds because 51 is roughly two-thirds of 77° 13′ (Delhi's longitude). We leave out the fraction of seconds.

If we are using *Lahiri's Ephemeris*, the sidereal time given therein is for the meridian 82° 30′ and if we wish to find the sidereal time at noon at Delhi, we will have to add 3 seconds to it. The difference between Delhi's longitude (77° 13′) is about 5° from 82° 30′ and two-thirds of this comes to about 3 seconds. We leave out fractions of seconds. We have added 3 seconds because Delhi is west of 82° 30′ meridian.

Example

Find out the sign, ascending degree and minute at Delhi, at

5-30 a.m. on 1st January 1970. Time and date are already given The longitude of Delhi is 77° 13′ East and latitude 28° 40′ North.

(i) the local mean time at Delhi will be 5 8-52 a.m., in hours, minutes and seconds, as worked out earlier.

(ii) the sidereal time at preceding noon, i.e., on 31st December 1969 as given in *Lahiri's Ephemeris* is 18 hours, 38 minutes, 3 seconds, to which we add 3 seconds, as explained above. So that the sidereal time at Delhi, on preceding noon comes to 18-38-6. Now we proceed to work as follows:

	Hrs.	Mts.	Secs.
Sidereal time at preceding noon	18	38	6
Add time since noon till the local mean time of birth	17	8	52
Add acceleration at 9.8 seconds per hour; 17-8-52×9.8=168 seconds (approx.) or 2 minutes, 48 seconds	0	2	48
	35	49	46
If the hours exceed 24, deduct 24	24	0	0
	11	49	46

The last figure of 11 hours, 49 minutes, 46 seconds is called the right ascension of the meridian cusp or the sidereal time of birth.

Now we require the Table of Houses, which gives the degree ascending according to the right ascension of the meridian cusp. Since Delhi's latitude is 28° 40′, we look up in the Table of Houses that page which gives the ascending degrees for latitude 28° 40′ North. In the Raphael's Table of Houses we find the position as follows:

Right Ascension of the Meridian Cusp			*Sign Rising*		
Hrs.	Mts.	Secs.	S.	D.	M.
11	49	0	8	15	19
11	52	40	8	16	7

Calculating by rule of three we find that our RAMC corresponds to about 8-15-29, i.e., 15 degrees, 29 minutes of sign Sagittarius, since 8 is the number of completed signs, the ninth, Sagittarius, was ascending. But Raphael's Table of Houses gives the positions in the tropical zodiac. We have therefore to deduct the precession of equinoxes and nutation on 1st January 1970. On reference to *Lahiri's Ephemeris* we find that it was 23° 26′ 21″. Deducting this from the tropical longitude.

8-15°	29′	0″
23	26	21
7 22	2	39

We find that the sign ascending was Scorpio (seven completed signs means that eighth was rising) and had risen 22 degrees, 2 minutes, 39 seconds.

If we look up Lahiri's Table of Houses, we will get the degree and minute rising in the sidereal (*Nirayan*) zodiac directly, because Lahiris Table of Houses gives the longitudes in the sidereal zodiac. It would not then be necessary to deduct the precession of equinoxes and nutation.

How to Find Longitudes of Planets

The sign rising is always calculated on the basis of the local mean time. If birth time is specified in standard time it must be converted into local mean time. But the longitudes of planets are always calculated on the basis of standard time (according to which the Ephemeris furnishes longitudes).

On referring to *Lahiri's Ephemeris* again for 1970, we find that the longitudes were as follows:

	S	D	M	
Sun	8	16	43	
Moon	5	17	15	
Mars	10	18	48	
Mercury	9	5	35	
Jupiter	6	8	53	
Venus	8	11	1	
Saturn	0	8	37	R
Rahu	10	20	33	
Ketu	4	20	33	

The Sun's longitude 8-16-43 means 8 completed signs and therefore 16° 43 in Sagittarius. So also with the other planets. When the longitude is given in figures, the first figure refers to the sign completed, the second figure to the degree completed, the third figure to the minute completed, and so on. R indicates that the planet was retrograde.

If we wish to calculate the longitudes from *Raphael's Ephemeris,* first find the longitudes of planets at 12 midnight (on 31st Dec. 1969/1st January 1970) for that will correspond to 5-30 a.m. Indian Standard Time. And since *Raphael's Ephemeris* furnishes tropical longitudes we will have to deduct the precession of equinoxes and nutation to derive the sidereal longitudes.

Now the following chart can be prepared:

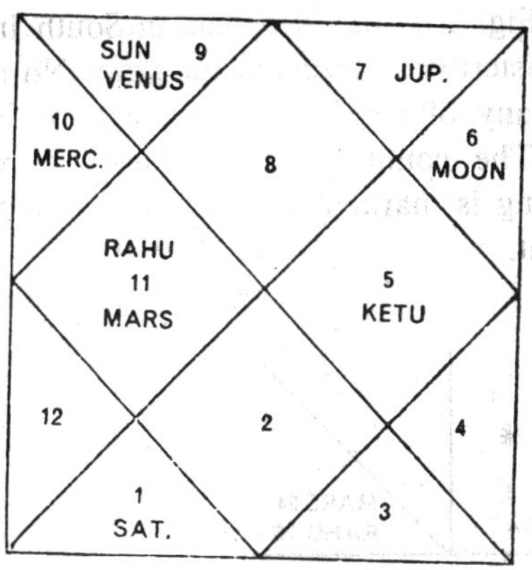

Fig. 1

Here the ascendant is Scorpio, Sun in Sagittarius, Moon in Virgo, Mars in Aquarius, Mercury in Capricorn, Jupiter in Libra, Venus in Sagittarius, Saturn in Aries, Rahu in Aquarius, Ketu in Leo.

Different patterns of charts are made in India. In northern, north-western and central India, the pattern of chart used is shown in Fig. 1. Here the signs are denoted by the numerical figure 1 for Aries, 2 for Taurus and so on. The place at the top centre is reserved for the sign ascending and then other signs are placed in succession anti-clockwise.

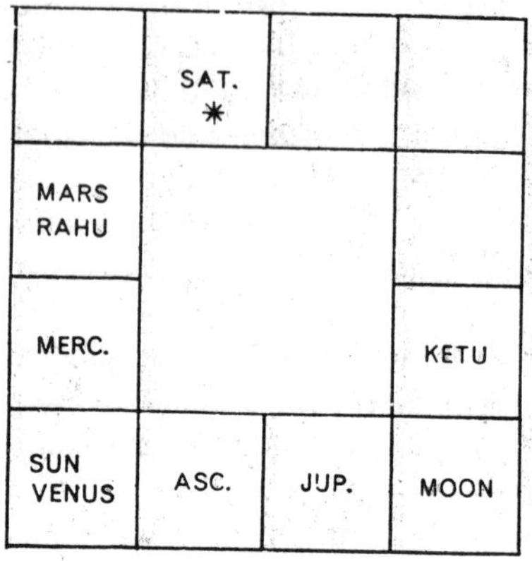

Fig. 2

The chart shown in Fig. 2 is the one made in South India. The place marked with an asterisk is reserved for Aries. No numerical figures are put in for any of the signs. The signs follow Aries, Taurus, Gemini, etc. The count is made clockwise round the rectangle. The sign rising is marked Asc. or by L which denotes *Lagna* or the ascendant.

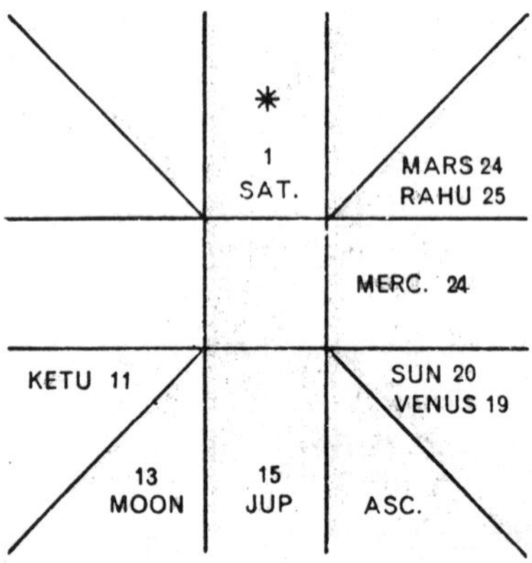

Fig. 3

In eastern India the chart is made as shown in Fig. 3. The place marked with an asterisk is reserved for Aries and the other signs follow in regular order. The count is made anti-clockwise. The sign rising is marked with the letter L. One additional feature is that the location of a planet in a particular constellation is also indicated by a small figure on top of the planet.

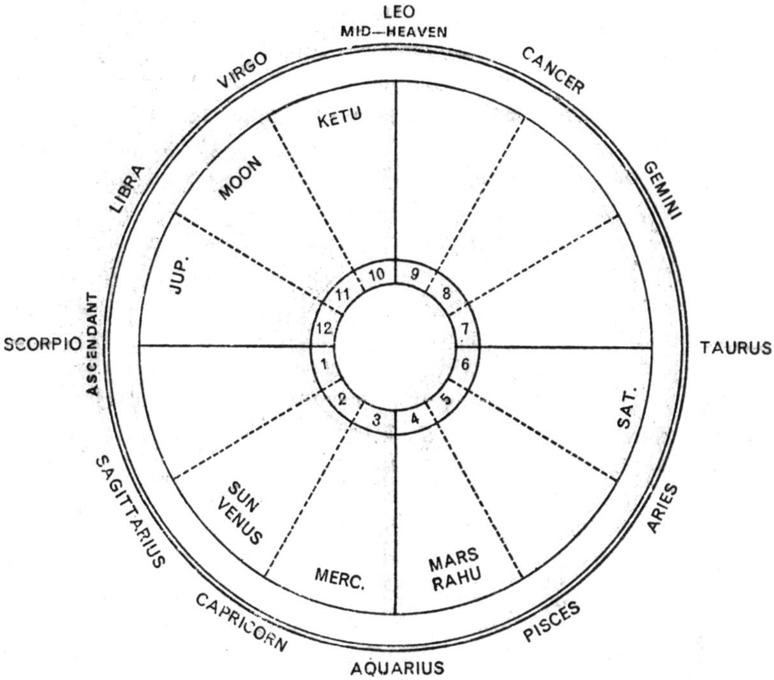

Fig. 4

Many astrologers in India due to close and constant contact with Western astrology have adopted the circular chart as shown in Fig. 4. The sign ascending is placed to the left and the count is made anti-clockwise. So please remember that in the patterns shown in Fig. 1, 3 and 4 the count is made anti-clockwise. Only in Fig. 2 is the counting clockwise.

THE ASCENDING SIGN

The general effects produced when one or the other sign is ascending at the east are as follows: As the effects are modified by the sign and house occupied by the lord of the ascendant and the planets conjoining with him or aspecting him and also according to the planets tenanting or aspecting the ascendant, the following effects will be found to change a little for each birth chart; yet the basic influence of the ascendant according to the sign rising will hold good.

Aries

The native has round eyes, which are slightly copper coloured, and weak knees. He is proud, heroic, active, aggressive and always on the move or fond of walking. He is fond of hot food and vegetables, eats quickly and sparingly, is amorous by disposition and fond of women; prominent veins or marks of wound on body, bad nails; resorts to falsehood in speech; afraid of water; generally he is the eldest brother; prosperity is not constant; he himself is fickle in temperament but proves a good servant. There are sudden outbursts of temper, but he is easily pleased.

It is better if the rising degree is 0° to 3° 20′ and Mars is strong, occupying or aspecting the ascendant.

Taurus

Agreeable appearance; broad face and thighs. There is some mark on the back or sides; walks sportingly; good digestive powers; many have luck in agricultural work, and may possess cows and cattle;* lucky and prosperous; fond of women. The native has a spirit of sacrifice and puts up with hard labour; has more daughters than sons. He is left alone by his previous relations; his sons may forsake him, but the native has permanent friends. The middle and the last one-third parts of life are generally more comfortable.

It is good if the rising degree is between 13° 20′ and 16° 40′ and Venus fully aspects the ascendant or occupies it; Venus in seventh would strengthen the ascendant but would be unfavourable for conjugal matters.

Gemini

Comely appearance, Prominent nose, dark eyes,† curly hair, fond of food; sweet speech, learned, jocular, well up in the art

* Cannot generally apply to town dwellers.

† Cannot always apply to people of Western countries, who generally do not have dark eyes.

of gambling; understands the intentions of others; fond of singing and dancing. Clever in amorous arts, voluptuous, attached to many women; friendship with imbecile and impotent persons; acts as a good ambassador. Such a native prefers to live indoors.

It is better if the rising degree is 26° 40′ to 30° and Mercury occupies the ascendant or aspects it.

Cancer

Not very tall, thick neck, broad waist, walks swiftly and not in a straightline, intelligent, fond of astrology or is an astrologer; likes to live near water; has many friends and is attached to them; owns houses; has a few sons; his fortunes wax and wane like the Moon; he can be brought round by persuasion. He is under the considerable influence of his wife or of women.

It is better if the rising degree is 0° to 3° 20′ and the Moon has good *Pakshabala** and aspects the ascendant or occupies it.

Leo

Yellowish eyeballs, prominent chin, large face, proud; has a few sons. The native has a sacrificing spirit, is of fixed determination, but gets unjustifiably into a temper at the slightest provocation and the anger is not quickly pacified; does not get on well with women; is fond of forests and mountains; is a favourite of his mother. The native is courageous, heroic and capable of prevailing upon others. Suffers from hunger, thirst (or diseases arising therefrom), mental and dental ailments.

It is good if the Sun is strong in the ascendant or tenth house and the rising degree is 13° 20′ to 16° 40′.

Virgo

Drooping shoulders and arms, shy and languid eyes, happy and comfortable life, speaks slowly and truthfully, clever in arts and crafts, enjoys others' wealth and houses, fond of female company; religious, learned, discriminating, with intelligence and good memory; more daughters than sons; lives at a place other

* Waxing Moon is considered stronger than waning Moon. Moon having 8 or more digits is considered as being strong in *Pakshabala*. Author's view is: The Moon having less than 5 digits is weak, with 5 to 10 digits of medium strength and with more than 10 digits strong in *Pakshabala*.

than his homeland.

It is good if the rising degree is 26° 40′ to 30° and Mercury strong in the first house or tenth.

Libra

Tall, lean body, prominent nose, fond of walking or travelling, suffers in some limb, gets setbacks in health due to slight causes but easily recovers; intelligent, clean, very active, devoted to gods and Brahmanas; has two popular names (one of them after a god); a few sons; clever in purchase and sale of goods; acts impartially as an arbitrator; wealthy, skilful and leads a comfortable life. Substantial increase in wealth and status only in the latter part of life.

It is positively good if the rising degree is 0° to 3° 20′ and Venus is strong, tenanting or aspecting Libra.

Scorpio

Big eyes, broad chest, round thighs, knees and calves; sole of feet having fish line on it; cruelly inclined; loses father or a senior member in early period of life; sickly during childhood; occupies a good position in service; respected by the king or government.

It is lucky if the rising degree is between 13° 20′ and 16° 40′ and Mars is strong, aspecting or tenanting Scorpio.

Sagittarius

Large head and neck, prominent nose and ears, bent shoulders, good fleshy arms, big teeth and lower lip; bad nails; active and engaged in work; eloquent in speech; religious and prepared to sacrifice for others; inimical to relations; overpowers enemies; cannot be brought round by force, but can be prevailed upon by persuasion only.

It is better if the degree rising is 26° 40′ to 30° and Jupiter is strong and aspects the ascendant or occupies it.

Capricorn

Good eyes, lower part of the body below the waist under-developed compared to the upper half; thin waist; suffers from diseases arising out of *Vata* (wind); allergic to winter or cold; dotes upon his wife and children; makes a big show of being religious (though in reality he may not be so religious); cruel, avaricious, fortunate and prosperous; accepts advice tendered; has good stamina, fond of walking; indolent; a connoisseur of poetry; devoid of shame, attached to an elderly lady related to the native.

It is better if the degree rising is 0° to 3° 20′ and Saturn is strong and occupies the ascendant or aspects it.

Aquarius

Large face, neck, back, stomach, waist, thighs and feet; ears large and with hair; rough hair* on a large body like that of a pitcher; prominent veins; indulges in sinful acts for the sake of others' wives; fond of good scents and flowers; avaricious; capable of putting up with hard labour or trying journeys; clever in attacking others, not wealthy himself but utilises the wealth of others; his fortunes wax and wane like the Moon.

It is better if the degree occupied is between 13° 20′ and 16° 40′ when the evil influences will be at their minimum and the good ones at their maximum; particularly so, if Saturn is in the ascendant or strong and aspects the rising sign.

Pisces

Lustrous face; fine body, large head, prominent nose; proportionate limbs, beautiful eyes. Attached to wife; fond of good clothes; is under the influence of wife or women; overcomes his enemies, wealthy, gets money connected with water or from goods and men across the seas; may come across buried treasure or may get wealth without much effort; is learned and grateful; drinks water frequently and in large quantities.

The ascendant would become stronger (for the good) if the degree rising is 26° 40′ to 30° and a strong Jupiter occupies the ascendant or aspects it.

Ascendant

Birth at (i) the fag end of Pisces or commencement of Aries, (ii) at the fag end of Cancer or commencement of Leo, (iii) at the fag end of Scorpio or beginning of Sagittarius, is inauspicious and requires sacred prayers (religious propitiation).

The texts state that such a birth curtails longevity of mother

* This will not apply to ladies because they do not have hair on body as men have.

and the child passes a delicate childhood, but if he survives he becomes a very illustrious person.

Note: The effects ascribed above for each of the signs, if rising at the horizon at the time of birth, can be applied also to the Moons' position in the sign, in addition to those described for Moon's location in various signs as given in chapter 8.

CHAPTER 5

THE SIGNS

THERE ARE twelve signs. A sign is called a *Rashi* in Sanskrit. The word *Rashi* literally means a heap, a cluster. As a sign in the zodiac was identified by the characteristic heap or cluster of the stars constituting it, it came to be known as a *Rashi.* This is a general term for a sign, but in Hindu astrology the sign in which the Moon is placed at the time of birth is commonly referred to as *Rashi.* When a brief question is put to a person, "what is your *Rashi*?" it means in which sign the Moon was at the time of your birth?

As we shall have occasion to see, the Moon sign (the sign which was occupied by the Moon at birth) is as important as the sign ascending at birth (the ascendant). Rather, for purposes of transists of planets and their effects the importance given to the Moon sign is even greater than the ascendant. The Moon sign is considered a co-ascendant and we shall in this work refer to it as the lunar ascendant or Moon sign.

In Western astrology, the Sun sign (the sign in the tropical zodiac occupied by the Sun at the time of birth) is of great importance and many books have been written delineating the astrological characteristics peculiar to births according to the Sun sign. A number of newspapers and magazines give weekly predictions on this basis. But in Hindu astrology, the Sun sign or the position of the Sun in a particular sign is not given such overwhelming importance. The Sun's location in a particular sign or house is just a factor like the location in a particular sign or house of Mars or Jupiter or of any other planet. But in case of the Moon, the older Sanskrit works emphasise again and again the importance of judging from the Moon sign (the lunar ascendant) as well as from the ascendant (the rising sign). While taking transits into consideration, the count is always made from the Moon sign. In more detailed consideration of the transits, cognisance is taken of all the seven planets and the ascendant. This is however done only when elaborate calculations are undertaken and the complete details of a birth chart are available; but generally the Moon sign is taken as the centre and predictions based on the Moon's radical position (the sign occupied by the Moon at birth) are published in many Indian newspapers and magazines. For further details in regard to transits and their effects, readers are referred to chapter 16 on Transits. Here it is only necessary to emphasise that the single word *Rashi* is generally interpreted as indicating the Moon sign.

The rising sign is referred to as *Lagna-rashi* or simply as *Lagnam*. The names of the twelve signs have been given before. However some attributes or characteristics of each sign are given below. These characteristics apply to the sign whether they are at the eastern horizon or anywhere else.

(1) The zodiac is taken as representing the body of eternal time. The Sanskrit word used by Hindu astrologers is *Kala-Purusha* and many learned and philosophical dissertations on time find a place in Sanskrit texts. The eternal time which has no beginning and no end is identified as God, the supreme power of the universe; and just as the hour hand, the minute hand and the second hand of the watch are tokens or indicators of time by a watch, so also the Earth's movement on the ecliptic is treated as the hand of eternal time (God). This ecliptic has been referred to mythologically as the *Sudarshan Chakra* (the 'grand splendid wheel') in the hand of God. This zodiac has also been referred to as the 'grand white python' whose hood has a thousand glistening gems, the stars. But we are not concerned here with these philosophical matters. Let us confine ourselves to the ecliptic and the conception that it represents the body of the 'Eternal Time' or *Kala-Purusha*. The various signs constituting his body are as follows:

1. Aries	Head (top portion)
2. Taurus	Face (including the neck)*
3. Gemini	Upper portion of chest and arms
4. Cancer	Heart, breasts, portion above the stomach
5. Leo	Stomach, portion above the navel
6. Virgo	Portion below navel and above *Basti*
7. Libra	*Basti*
8. Scorpio	Genitals, anus
9. Sagittarius	Thighs, hips
10. Capricorn	The two knees, back
11. Aquarius	Calves of legs
12. Pisces	Feet

What is *Basti*? If we take the part of the body commencing from the navel to the genitals and divide it horizontally into two parts, the upper portion represents Virgo and the lower portion Libra. This lower half of the portion (from the navel to the genitals) is called *Basti.*

If any sign is tenanted by a *Papa*§ — malefic or aspected by a *Papa,* the corresponding part of the body suffers from disease.

If any sign is tenanted by a *Shubha* (auspicious) or aspected by *Shubha,* the corresponding parts of the body will be healthy and strong. So it follows that if any sign is strong and its lord is strong, the corresponding part of the body of the person whose nativity is under consideration will be strong and healthy; and if any sign is weak and its lord weak, the corresponding part of the body of the native will be weak or lack in vigour and vitality.

Let us clarify this further. Irrespective of the ascendant (rising sign at birth), i.e., whether Leo be ascending or not, in a nativity in which malefics occupy Leo, the native will have stomach trouble as Leo represents this part of the body. Also Leo as the fifth sign of the *Kala-Purusha* signifies children,† he will not be very fortunate in respect of children if Leo and its lord are weak or tenanted or aspected by malefics.

To take another example, if Sagittarius is strong and favourably tenanted, say, by its lord Jupiter, the native will be religious and

* According to one view the neck is governed by Gemini.

§ *Papa.* This Sanskrit word has been explained in Chapter 6.

† For details See Chapter 7.

devoted to gods. He will have benefits from foreign lands and foreign people, i.e., all matters governed by the ninth sign.

Now the above analogy of the parts of the body (of the *Kala-Purusha*) corresponding to the body of the person whose birth chart is under study, is based on the theory *'yat pinde tat brahmande'* (whatever is in the universe has a replica in the human body). This is one of the cardinal principles of Hindu philosophy. Astrology among Hindus has the status of astral philosophy. Astrology and religion are so closely intertwined that it is difficult to separate the one from the other. The theory of "as above so below" is also well established in other systems of thought, because it is one of the fundamental theories of creation and has been dealt with as microcosm and macrocosm. The entire theory of astrology is based on this principle. If at the time of one's birth, the Sun high above in the heavens was afflicted, one's solar qualities will be of low order and a handicap for one in life; if the Moon was full and tenanting a friends' sign and aspected by benefics and in a good house (the Moon's position in the sky in relation to the longitude and latitude of birth-place on earth), the lunar qualities will be strong and one will achieve laurels in affairs governed by the Moon, and so on.

So if any part of the *Kala-Purusha* was afflicted at birth, the corresponding part of the native's body would be afflicted. Just as the theory is applied to the birth-chart by commencing from Aries, so also is it applied by commencing from the first house or the ascendant (the sign rising). Here the correspondence of various houses to the different parts of the body is as follows:

1.	House	Head
2.	,,	Face (including the neck)
3.	,,	Neck, upper portion of the chest and arms. (some include throat in 3rd house)
4.	,,	Heart, breasts, portion above the stomach
5.	,,	The stomach, portion above the navel
6.	,,	Part below navel and above *Basti*
7.	,,	*Basti*
8.	,,	Genitals, anus
9.	,,	Thighs, hips
10.	,,	The two knees, back
11.	,,	Calves of legs
12.	,,	Feet

If any house is afflicted, the corresponding part of the body will suffer. If any house is strong, the corresponding parts of the body will be strong. We have explained this fully and need not reiterate.

The physical appearance of the tweleve signs is as follows: Aries, a ram; Taurus, a bull; Gemini, a couple of human beings—the male holding a club in his hand and the female holding a Veena*; Cancer, a crab; Leo, a lion; Virgo, a girl in a boat holding a sheaf of corn in one hand and a fire in the other; Libra, a man holding scales in his hand; Scorpio, a scorpion; Sagittarius, a man with a bow and arrow in hand riding a horse or in other words, the first half a man the latter half a horse; Capricorn, the first half representing the head of a deer, the latter half a crocodile; Aquarius, a man holding an empty pitcher on his shoulder; Pisces, two fish with their heads pointing to in opposite directions.

These signs have been classified as living in (i) forest, (ii) village, (iii) water, etc. If a sign in a birth chart shows gain, the benefit should be ascertained from (i) forest, (ii) village, (iii) water, etc., according to the sign. If a sign denotes harm, enmity, loss, death, etc., due to a particular sign, the source of harm should be assigned according to the characteristics of the sign. These characteristics should also be used for determining the property (moveable or immoveable) destroyed, thief, etc. Suppose at the time of a query Taurus rises. The query is 'where is my stolen property kept?' As Taurus represents the fields, the reply would be in the fields. If Cancer rises, as Cancer represents water, the reply would be in the water, and so on. So details regarding each sign are necessary.

Aries—During the day roams in the forest and at night in the village. *Taurus*—A cultivated field. *Gemini*—A village (formerly there were few towns. Now we would include cities also). *Cancer*—Water. *Leo*—Forest. *Virgo*—Boat, field, watery places, where fire or grain is kept. *Libra*—A road, street or a shop. *Scorpio*—A hole. *Sagittarius*—A village (we would now include a city), places where cavalry or contingents of armies are stationed, arsenals, military depots, etc. *Capricorn*—The first half forest, the second half water. *Aquarius*—Village. *Pisces*—watery places.

* Veena is a musical instrument.

During the age, these texts were written, the village, forest and waters were sufficient. Now, we have to include towns and cities under the term village.

Elaborating the above the following has also been allotted to the twelve signs:

Aries. The place of jewels, metals, fire, the earth's surface having jewels and minerals underneath.

Taurus. The forest or field, table-land where cattle or agriculturists reside, field with water where paddy is grown.

Gemini. The places where dancers, singers, artists, women of pleasure reside, a bedroom, the place for sexual enjoyment and indoor sports, where cards or other kinds of betting goes on in rooms, gambling dens, etc.

Cancer. Watery fields where paddy is grown, wells, tanks, banks of river, where there is an abundance of plants, shrubs and trees due to moisture and extra humidity, a chasm with water.

Leo. The regions of deep forest, mountains, hills and hillocks, forts.

Virgo. The place of artisanship, places of enjoyment of women, pasture land, land with corn.

Libra. High land where corn is grown (grain was the chief commodity or merchandise and Libra represents the scales for weighing), streets, shops, a rich man's place of abode (the merchants used to be rich), a merchant's house.

Scorpio. Places having holes or cavities where serpents and others live, poison, crevices in hillocks or mountains, hidden places.

Sagittarius. The places where horses, chariots, elephants live, where *Yajnas* (religious sacrifices) are performed. This is due to the relationship of the ninth sign with religion. The king's residence.

Capricorn. Rivers, forest, watery places, rich or abounding in water, banks or sides of a river or mountain.

Aquarius. Places where water has dried up, where men who manufacture liquors or birds live, gambling dens, place in the house where pots are kept, the place frequented by potters.

Pisces. Religious and holy places (due to Jupiter being the lord of Pisces), rivers where sacred baths are undertaken, seas, oceans, places where there are temples and shrines, where Brahmanas (the first among the four castes of Hindus) live. Traditionally Brahmanas are associated with religion, piety, holiness, etc.

COUNTRIES

Patala	Aries
Karnata the modern karnataka	Taurus
Chera	Gemini
Chola	Cancer
Pandya	Leo
Kerala	Virgo
Kollasa	Libra
Malaya	Scorpio
Saindhava—the modern Sind	Sagittarius
North Panchala	Capricorn
Yavana	Aquarius
Koshala	Pisces

These are the old names of regions as they were known in ancient India.

COLOURS

The colours of the twelve signs are as follows:

Aries—Blood red; *Taurus*—White; *Gemini*—Parrot green; *Cancer*—Whitish red; *Leo*—pale white like smoke; *Virgo*—Variegated or multi-coloured; *Libra*—Black; *Scorpio*—Golden; *Sagittarius*—Brownish; *Capricorn*—Whitish yellow; *Aquarius*—Darkish white; *Pisces*—White. According to one view, Pisces has the colour of a fish but fish are of different colours.

When a planet tenants a sign the planet's colour is also reflected in the sign. If a planet aspects a sign then also its colour is reflected. We may explain this by an example; a bottle may have a distinctive colour of its own but if a liquid of any particular colour is put into it or a coloured light is thrown on the bottle, the colour of the bottle will differ according to the blending of colours — its own natural colour and the colour of the liquid poured into it or the coloured light thrown upon it.

The use of the colours of the signs is to indentify the colour of the lost article or the native whose birth chart is under consideration or to ascertain the complexion of the wife or husband from the seventh house and so on.

CASTES

Aries, Leo, Sagittarius are *Kshatriyas* (the warrior class); Taurus, Virgo and Capricorn are *Vaishyas* (the trading class); Gemini, Libra and Aquarius are *Shudras* (the serving class); Cancer, Scorpio and Pisces are the *Brahmana* caste (the priestly class).

If a particular sign is on the cusp of a good house, gain or benefit from persons of that caste is indicated; if a sign is on the cusp of the sixth house, enmity by persons of corresponding caste is indicated, and so on. Of course, when we come to planets (see Chapter 6), we shall have to take the caste of planets also into account and mark what they indicate according to the caste of the planet, tenanting or aspecting a particular sign which is on the cusp of the house and regarding which judgment is to be had.

MALE AND FEMALE

Aries, Gemini, Leo, Libra, Sagittarius and Aquarius are male signs. Taurus, Cancer, Virgo, Scorpio, Capricorn and Pisces are female signs. The male signs are dominating, active and agresive; the female signs are mild and passive.

If the ascendant, the Moon, the Sun and other planets and particularly the ascendant and the Moon, are in male signs, the native will be pushing and overbearing; conversely if they are in female signs, the native will be passive and accommodating. If the ascendant and the Moon in a woman's nativity are in male signs, her form and temperament will be manly.

ODD AND EVEN SIGNS

Aries, Gemini, Leo, Libra, Sagittarius and Aquarius are odd signs; Taurus, Cancer, Virgo, Scorpio, Capricorn and Pisces are even signs.

When planets are posited in signs, they colour and modify the resulting effects. Thus if Jupiter and Venus are in an odd sign, the natural effect of aggressiveness would be subdued by the benefic influence of Jupiter and Venus. Conversely, if Mars or Saturn tenant an even sign, despite the sign being an even one, the malefic nature of Mars and Saturn would assert itself and the native would be far from being mild or submissive.

In odd signs, even the products or things signified by the signs are rough, rugged and hard, while in even signs the products or material indicated are soft and smooth. Persons born in odd signs have stamina and hardihood; those born in even signs are fickle and have the finer qualities of women. If there are many planets in odd signs, the native will be courageous and dashing; if in even signs, the reverse will be the effect.

WATERY AND WATERLESS SIGNS

Cancer, Scorpio, Capricorn and Pisces are watery signs; Taurus, Gemini, Virgo and Aquarius are *Toyashraya,* i.e., dependant on water. Aries, Leo, Libra and Sagittarius traverse waterless regions.

MOVABLE AND FIXED SIGNS

Aries, Cancer, Libra and Capricorn are movable signs. They are called *Chara.* Taurus, Leo, Scorpio, and Aquarius are fixed. They are called *Sthira.* Gemini, Virgo, Sagittarius and Pisces have the qualities of movable as well as fixed and are called common or *Dwriswabhava.* According to one school, the last fifteen degrees of Gemini, Virgo, Sagittarius and Pisces are movable, while the first fifteen degrees show the characteristics of fixed signs.

Work commenced, such as a journey, when a movable sign is ascending is quickly completed; while matters, such as occupying a house for residence or occupying a chair in the office, commenced when a fixed sign is ascending will last for a long time.

In birth charts, when the ascendant is a movable sign, the native is fond of walking and travelling and particularly so if the lord of the ascendant is also in a movable sign. If a fixed sign be rising, the native would be of sedentary habits, particularly if the lord thereof is also in a fixed sign.

DIRECTIONS

Aries, Leo, Sagittarius	East
Taurus, Virgo, Capricorn	South
Gemini, Libra, Aquarius	West
Cancer, Scorpio, Pisces	North

If a particular sign is strong and occupies the ninth or the eleventh house there may be luck or gain of money in that direction. If a particular sign is weak or afflicted and occupies an adverse place in the birth chart, there may be bodily or mental suffering if the native proceeds to or sets up his business or abode in that direction.

When undertaking a journey, if the ascendant or Moon occupies a sign indicating the direction one is going towards, the journey will be fruitful. If the ascendant or the Moon is on the left, there would only be waste of money; if at the back, the journey will be unsuccessful. If on the right, fairly good results will follow.

BLIND AND DEAF SIGNS

Aries, Taurus and Leo are blind at midnight; Gemini, Cancer and Virgo are blind at noon; Libra and Scorpio are deaf in the fore-noon; Sagittarius and Capricorn are deaf in the afternoon.

If in a nativity, the birth is found to be at midnight and any of the signs Aries, Taurus or Leo be in the second or twelfth houses (or in eighth or sixth) and tenanted by malefics, there are chances of the native becoming blind. If the birth be at noon, judge in a similar manner by reference to Gemini, Cancer and Virgo. Judge similarly in regard to deafness. The third house represents the right ear, the eleventh the left.

LAME SIGNS

Sagittarius and Capricorn are lame and become harmful or fatal during the *Sandhi* at the junction of Sagittarius and Capricorn, i.e., when Saggittarius is ending and Capricorn is commencing. According to another school they show their evil effect at the junction of day and night, i.e., if the birth be during the morning or at twilight.

DIURNAL AND NOCTURNAL SIGNS

Leo, Virgo, Libra, Scorpio, Aquarius and Pisces are diurnal signs. They are strong during the day; Aries, Taurus, Gemini, Cancer, Sagittarius and Capricorn are nocturnal signs and are strong at night. The day is taken as from sunrise to sunset. From sunset to sunrise it is night.

BIPED, QUADRUPED, ETC., SIGNS

Gemini, Virgo, Libra, the first half of Sagittarius and Aquarius are human and biped signs. Aries, Taurus, Leo, and the latter half of Sagittarius and the first half of Capricorn are quadruped signs; the latter half of Capricorn and Pisces are watery signs; Scorpio is reptile or a crawling animal sign. According to one view, Cancer also is a crawling animal sign, but according to others it is a watery sign. The latter half of Capricorn and Pisces are taken as *Keeta* — an insect — crawling animal, but the majority view is that these are watery signs. Human signs are strong if they fall on the cusp of the first house. Quadrupeds are strong if they fall on the tenth cusp. Watery signs are deemed to be endowed with strength if they are on the fourth cusp. Reptile signs are strong on the seventh cusp.

Biped signs are strong during the day. Quadruped signs are strong at night. Reptile signs are strong at dawn and at sunset. As the twelve signs here have been placed in three categories only, Cancer, Scorpio, the latter half of Capricorn and Pisces have to be treated as crawling signs.

If a sign is tenanted or aspected by its lord or Mercury or Jupiter and by no other planet, it is strong. Some texts include Venus also along with Mercury and Jupiter. But according to others, unless Venus is specifically stated for purpose of *Yoga*, his tenancy gives diplomacy but his aspect spoils it.

Conversely, if it is tenanted or aspected by others it would not be strong. The more the malefic tenanting or aspecting, the weaker and worse would be the sign. The Sun is *Krura* (cruel) and imparts heat to the sign it tenants.

It is not good to have the lord of a sign in the 6th, 8th or 12th from the sign.

Signs in angles (*Kendra*) are strong. Those in succedent

(*Panaphar*) are of medium strength. Those in Cadent houses* (*Apoklima*) are weak.

MINERAL VEGETABLE AND ANIMAL SIGNS

The Sanskrit words for the three respectively are (1) *Dhatu,* (2) *Moola,* and (3) *Jeeva. Dhatus* include minerals and metals, and even clay, lime, stone, etc. *Moola* includes all plants, shrubs and trees; and *Jeeva,* all living being down from an insect to a human being.

Aries, Cancer, Libra and Capricorn represent *Dhatu;* Taurus, Leo, Scorpio and Aquarius stand for *Moola;* and Gemini, Virgo, Sagittarius and Pisces for *Jeeva.*

If a malefic planet indicates loss, it may inflict loss of metal (wealth), plants (crop), or of life, according to the characteristic of the sign and the planet. Similarly, if the planet is a benefic, it may cause gain of metal (coins made of metal), crops, life of the native or one of his relations as the case may be.

SHORT AND LONG SIGNS

Aries, Taurus, Aquarius and Pisces are short; Gemini, Cancer, Sagittarius and Capricorn are neither short nor long but are medium; Leo, Virgo, Libra and Scorpio are long.

We have already stated that the twelve houses from the ascendant to the twelfth house correspond to the twelve parts of the body. Now, if a short sign falls on the cusp of a house, the part of the body governed by that house will be short, and particularly so if the lord of the sign also tenants a short sign. For example, if Aries is rising and its lord Mars is in Pisces, as the signs involved are both short, the head will not be large, but small. Conversely, if Scorpio is rising (this is a long sign) and its lord Mars is in Virgo (this also is a long sign), the head would be large.

Of course, planets tenanting a particular house would also accordingly make the part of the body small or large. Besides the general nature of the constitution of the body, whether it is bilious, windy or phlegmatic, has also to be taken into account.

* Ist, 4th, 7th and 10th houses are called angles; 2nd, 5th, 8th and 11th houses are called succedent; 3rd 6th, 9th and 12th houses are called cadent houses.

In horary astrology, if a short sign ascends, the inference drawn is that the article stolen has been taken away a short distance only; if it is of medium size, the article has been removed to a medium distance, and if a long sign ascends, it has been taken to a long distance.

SIGNS RISING WITH HEAD OR BACK OR BOTH WAYS

Certain signs rise with the head first. These are Gemini, Leo, Virgo, Libra, Scorpio, Aquarius. They are called *Shirshodaya* (or rising with head first). Aries, Taurus, Cancer, Sagittarius and Capricorn rise with their hind portion first and they are called *Pristhodaya* (or rising with their hind portion). Pisces rises both ways, that is, it has the characteristics of both types.

The *Shirshodaya* signs are benefic. If benefic planets are posited therein, they become still more benefic. *Pristhodaya* signs are not auspicious. If a *Papa* (malefic) tenants a sign of this group he becomes even more malefic. Pisces has the qualities of *Shirshodaya* as well as *Pristhodaya.* In other words, if a malefic is in *Pristhodaya,* he becomes very malefic; if there is a benefic therein, it does not remain so benefic.

The *Shirshodaya* signs or planets posited therein show their effect in the earlier part of their *Dashas.* The *Pristhodaya* signs or planets posited in them show their effects in the latter part of their *Dashas.* Pisces has characteristics of both and planets posited therein show their effect during the middle portion of the *Dashas.*

SOLAR AND LUNAR SIGNS

The Sun is the lord of Leo and the Moon is the lord of Cancer. But the zodiac itself is divided into two sectors; (1) Leo, Virgo, Libra, Scorpio, Sagittarius and Capricorn — these comprise the solar signs; (2) Cancer, Gemini, Taurus, Aries, Pisces and Aquarius — these comprise the lunar sector.

People born with all planets in the solar sector are brave, courageous and heroic, while those born in the lunar sector are soft and mild and prefer to enjoy life safely.

LORDSHIP OF SIGNS

The names of the lords of the signs are as follows:

Aries	Mars
Taurus	Venus
Gemini	Mercury
Cancer	Moon
Leo	Sun
Virgo	Mercury
Libra	Venus
Scorpio	Mars
Sagittarius	Jupiter
Capricorn	Saturn
Aquarius	Saturn
Pisces	Jupiter

At first glance there appears to be no order in the allotment of the lordship of signs. But, in fact, this superficial view is an erroneous inference. As counted from the Sun, Mercury is nearest to him, then comes Venus, then Mars, then Jupiter, while Saturn is the most distant.

The Moon shines in the reflected light of the Sun. The two are the luminaries. The signs from Leo to Capricorn in order are in the Sun's portfolio, and the other six counted from Cancer backwards up to Aquarius fall in the portfolio of the Moon. Now the sign next to Leo has been allotted to Mercury because Mercury is nearest to the Sun and Gemini, the sign next to Cancer (in the reverse order) is also allotted to Mercury. Then, in point of distance from the Sun is Venus. So the sign next to Virgo, i.e., Libra is allotted to Venus. Similarly, next to Gemini in reverse order is Taurus and its lordship is assigned to Venus. Then comes Mars. He gets one sign next to Libra in the regular order, namely, Scorpio and another sign next to Taurus in reverse order, namely, Aries. After Mars in point of distance from the Sun comes Jupiter. So he gets Sagittarius, the sign next to Scorpio in regular order, and one sign in the reverse order, next to Aries. The most distant, being Saturn he gets the sign next to Jupiter's in the regular order as well as in the reverse order. The sign next to Sagittarius in order is Capricorn. And the sign next to Pisces in the reverse order is Aquarius. So Saturn gets Capricorn and Aquarius.

See chapter 6 on planets for information as to which planet is exalted in which sign and which is the highest exaltation degree or sign of debilitation and deepest debilitation degree. For *Moola Trikona* signs also see chapter 6.

AUSPICIOUS DEGREES OCCUPIED BY THE MOON IN VARIOUS SIGNS

If at the time of birth or when a fresh undertaking is commenced, the Moon occupies the degree noted against each sign, it is auspicious, i.e., the native would do well, the Moon would have a good effect and the undertaking would succeed.

Aries	Moon in	21st	degree
Taurus	,,	14th	,,
Gemini	,,	18th	,,
Cancer	,,	8th	,,
Leo	,,	19th	,,
Virgo	,,	9th	,,
Libra	,,	24th	,,
Scorpio	,,	11th	,,
Sagittarius	,,	23rd	,,
Capricorn	,,	14th	,,
Aquarius	,,	19th	,,
Pisces	,,	9th	,,

INAUSPICIOUS DEGREES FOR MOON TO OCCUPY

It is inauspicious for the native if the Moon occupies the following degrees at birth. If the Moon occupies any of the following degrees, there will be illness or some other trouble at the age indicated by completed degrees.

Aries	8	or	26
Taurus	25	,,	12
Gemini	22	,,	13
Cancer	22	,,	25
Leo	21	,,	24
Virgo	1	,,	11
Libra	4	,,	26
Scorpio	23	,,	14
Sagittarius	18	,,	13

Capricorn	20	„	25
Aquarius	20	„	5
Pisces	10	„	12

THE THREE SECTORS

The twelve signs from Aries to Pisces have been divided into three sectors: (i) Aries to Cancer is called the *Sristhi Khanda* (*Srishti* means "creation" and *Khanda* means 'a portion, a division, a sector'); (ii) Leo to Scorpio comprise the *Sthiti Khanda* (*Sthiti* means 'existence, stability, the state of being'); and (iii) Sagittarius to Pisces comprise *Samhara Khanda* (*Samhara* means 'destruction, annihilation'). In other words, Aries to Cancer represent anabolic activity and Sagittarius to Pisces, the katabolic activity; in between Leo to Scorpio represent equilibrium.

The junction degrees (i) between the fag end of Cancer and beginning of Leo, (ii) between the fag end of Scorpio and beginning of Sagittarius, (iii) between the fag end of Pisces and beginning of Aries are called *Khandanta* or *Gandanta.* If a child is born when a *Gandanta* degree is rising (i.e., is on the ascending degree) or the Moon is therein at any of the junction points, this is inauspicious for the child's longevity or for his mother's. But if the child lives and reaches maturity, he will be extremely wealthy and illustrious.

What is meant by the word fag end of a sign or commencing degrees? How many degrees are to be taken as comprising these? The convention is to take this as 3° 20′ arc. Thus 26° 40′ to 30° 0′ would be the fag end and 0 degree to 3° 20′ would be the commencing degrees. In other words, one-ninth of a sign (30° divided by 9 comes to 3° 20′) is taken as the fag end or commencing degrees.

CHAPTER 6

THE PLANETS

IN HINDU astrology cognisance is taken of nine planets, the Sun, Moon, Mars, Mercury, Jupiter, Venus, Saturn, Rahu and Ketu. The seven planets are the same as in western astrology. In fact, the Sun and the Moon are luminaries and the other five are planets, but for convenience of expression all the seven are referred to as planets. Rahu and Ketu are the special contribution by the Hindus to the principles and practice of astrology.

As we have stated earlier when the Moon in his orbit round the earth goes to the northern latitude, the point where he crosses to the north is called Rahu. Conversely, when the Moon in his orbit round the earth goes to the southern latitude, the point where he crosses to the south is called Ketu. These two points are ever receding in the ecliptic and in about nineteen years one complete circle of the zodiac is completed. Thus while the seven planets have generally a forward motion (except when the five-non-luminaries are retrograde) and proceed from Aries to Taurus, from Taurus to Gemini, and so on, Rahu and Ketu always move backward from Aries to Pisces, from Pisces to Aquarius, and so on.

In Hindu scriptures there exist a large number of mythological stories about Rahu and Ketu who have been described as demons, in contrast to the Sun and the Moon, who are described as gods; but we are not concerned with them here. In astrology they are merely sensitive points, mathematically calculated and inserted in the birth chart.

In western astrology, Rahu is described as the north node of the Moon or Caput Draconis, and Ketu as the south node of the Moon or Cauda Draconis. But as Rahu and Ketu are shorter words, we shall use them throughout this book.

The lordships of signs have already been given.

EXALTATION AND DEBILITATION

The signs of exaltation and debilitation of planets are as follows:

Planet	*Sign of Exaltation*	*Sign of Debilitation*
Sun	Aries	Libra
Moon	Taurus	Scorpio
Mars	Capricorn	Cancer
Mercury	Virgo	Pisces
Jupiter	Cancer	Capricorn
Venus	Pisces	Virgo
Saturn	Libra	Aries

To explain the above, the entire sign Leo is owned by the Sun and if the Sun is in Leo, we say the Sun is strong because he is in his own sign. If the Sun is in Aries, we say that the Sun is in the sign of exaltation and therefore strong or that the Sun is exalted. But if the Sun is in Libra, the Sun is in his sign of debilitation and therefore weak or the Sun is debilitated.

Degree of Highest Exaltation and Deepest Debilitation

The 10th degree of Aries is the highest exaltation degree of the Sun and the 10th degree of Libra, the degree of his deepest debilitation. The 3rd degree of Taurus is the Moon's highest degree of exaltation and the 3rd degree of Scorpio his deepest debilitation point. The degrees are shown below in a tabular form.

Planet	*Sign of Exaltation*	*Degree of Highest Exaltation*	*Sign of Debilitation*	*Degree of Deepest Debilitation*
Sun	Aries	10°	Libra	10°
Moon	Taurus	3°	Scorpio	3°

Mars	Capricorn	28°	Cancer	28°
Mercury	Virgo	15°	Pisces	15°
Jupiter	Cancer	5°	Capricorn	5°
Venus	Pisces	27°	Virgo	27°
Saturn	Libra	20°	Aries	20°

It is necessary to explain in this connection four Sanskrit terms as they will be found to occur often in this book and other texts dealing with Hindu astrology.

AROHA. This means ascending. If a planet has crossed his deepest debilitation point and is proceeding towards his exaltation sign or highest exaltation point, during such a stage the planet is called *Arohi.*

The locations of the planets when they are *Arohi* are as follows:

(1) Sun from 11th degree Libra to 10° Aries.
(2) Moon from 4th degree Scorpio to 3° Taurus.
(3) Mars from 29th degree Cancer to 28° Capricorn.
(4) Mercury from 16th degree Pisces to 15° Virgo.
(5) Jupiter from 6th degree Capricorn to 5° Cancer.
(6) Venus from 28th degree Virgo to 27° Pisces.
(7) Saturn from 21st degree Aries to 20° Libra.

Planets in *Aroha* are considered good.

AVAROHA. When a planet has crossed his highest exaltation point and is proceeding towards his sign of debilitation or towards the deepest debilitation point, he is descending and is called in *Avaroha* or *Avarohi.* Thus the following are the sectors of the zodiac for each planet when he is in *Avaroha*:

(1) Sun from 11th degree Aries to 10° Libra.
(2) Moon from 4th degree of Taurus to 3° Scorpio.
(3) Mars from 29th degree of Capricorn to 28° Cancer.
(4) Mercury from 16th degree Virgo to 15° Pisces.
(5) Jupiter from 6th degree of Cancer to 5° Capricorn.
(6) Venus from 28th degree of Pisces to 27° Virgo.
(7) Saturn from 21st degree Libra to 20° Aries.

Planets in *Avaroha* are called *Avarohi* and are not considered good.

UCHCHABHILASHI. When a planet is in a sign immediately preceding the sign in which he would be exalted, he is called *Uchchabhilashi* or desiring to enter his sign of exaltation. Thus the Sun in Pisces, the Moon in Aries, Mars in Sagittarius, Mercury in Leo, Jupiter in Gemini, Venus in Aquarius and Saturn in Virgo will be respectively in their *Uchchabhilashi* signs. A planet in his *Uchchabhilashi* sign is considered good, for though he has not entered his sign of exaltation yet he is on the threshold.

NEECHABHILASHI. When a planet is in a sign just preceding the sign in which he would be debilitated, he is called *Neechabhilashi.* This position is not so bad as when in the sign of debilitation, yet it is considered unfavourable. Thus Sun in Virgo, Moon in Libra, Mars in Gemini, Mercury in Aquarius, Venus in Leo and Saturn in Pisces are *Neechabhilashi.* Jupiter in Capricorn is in debilitation, the sign just preceding Capricorn is Sagittarius, but Jupiter in Sagittarius is not called *Neechabhilashi* because Sagittarius is his own sign and the goodness due to being in one's own sign far outweighs the disqualification of being in a sign preceding the sign of debilitation.

One's own signs, or the signs of exaltation or debilitation of planets are the same in Hindu astrology as in the Western system. But the conception of the *Moola-Trikona* sign is peculiar to Hindu astrology, as explained below.

MOOLA-TRIKONA. The *Moola-Trikona* signs for the various planets are as follows:

(1) Sun — 0° to 20° in Leo.
(2) Moon — 4° to 30° in Taurus.
(3) Mars — 1° to 12° in Aries.
(4) Mercury — 16° to 20° in Virgo.
(5) Jupiter — 1° to 10° in Sagittarius.
(6) Venus — 0° to 5° in Libra.
(7) Saturn — 1° to 20° in Aquarius.
(8) Rahu — Aquarius.
(9) Ketu — Leo.

A planet in his *Moola-Trikona* is considered good and strong. He is in a better position than in his own sign. Thus, if the Sun is in Leo upto 20° he will be called in *Moola-Trikona;* while the Sun in 21° to 30° will be considered as being in his own sign. The Moon, if located in 0° to 3° of Taurus, is in exaltation, but if he is anywhere from 4° to 30° in Taurus, he is in his *Moola-Trikona* sign. A planet in exaltation is stronger than a planet in *Moola-Trikona;* but as stated earlier a planet in *Moola-Trikona* is stronger and more benefic than when in his own sign.

It will be observed that in discussing own signs or signs of exaltation and debilitation. we have discussed these only in relation to the seven planets, Sun to Saturn, and not Rahu and Ketu, because the ownership of the twelve signs is completed by the set of seven planets. Also in regard to co-ownership by Rahu or Ketu of signs or signs of exaltation and debilitation the various schools of Hindu astrology differ. We can briefly state the positions as follows:

1. Rahu in Aries, Taurus, Cancer, Scorpio and Aquarius is strong; and so also Ketu in Taurus, Virgo, latter half of Sagittarius and Pisces.
2. Some consider Taurus as the exaltation sign of Rahu, while others take Gemini as his sign of exaltation. Ketu would thus be exalted in the seventh, i.e., Scorpio or Sagittarius.

RELATIONSHIP

Having dealt with their relationship with signs, we shall deal with the characteristics of each planet.

Friendship, Neutrality and Enmity between Planets

The following chart makes the natural relationships clear:

Planet	*Friends*	*Enemies*	*Neutrals*
Sun	Moon Mars Jupiter	Venus Saturn	Mercury
Moon	Sun Mercury	—	Mars Jupiter Venus Saturn
Mars	Sun Moon Jupiter	Mercury	Venus Saturn
Mercury	Sun Venus	Moon	Mars Jupiter Saturn

Jupiter	Sun Moon Mars	Mercury Venus	Saturn
Venus	Mercury Saturn	Sun Moon	Mars Jupiter
Saturn	Mercury Venus	Sun Moon Mars	Jupiter

Thus it will be seen that the relationship in all cases is not mutual. The Moon is a friend of the Sun and the Sun is a friend of the Moon. Here the relationship is mutual. Both are friends of each other. But the Sun is a friend of Mercury, while Mercury is neutrâl to the Sun. Here the mutual relationship is not the same. One is a friend of the other, but the other is only neutral. This is the natural relationship or the relationship as applies to all the birth charts.

Temporal Relationship

There is another set of relationship which is special to a particular chart. This is called temporal relationship. Here there is no neutral. There are only friends or enemies. And the relationship is mutually the same. If A is a friend of B, B is also a friend of A or if A is an enemy of B, B is also an enemy of A.

In this, the following rules determine friendship or enmity in temporal relationships:

(1) Planets in the same sign are enemies.

(2) Planets in signs which are fifth and ninth from each other are enemies.

(3) Planets in signs which are sixth and eighth from each other are enemies.

(4) Planets in signs which are seventh to each other are enemies.

(5) Planets in signs second and twelfth from each other are friends.

(6) Planets in signs third and eleventh from each other are friends.

(7) Planets in signs fourth and tenth from each other are friends.

Resultant Relationship

The resultant relationship is based on two factors: (i) natural and (ii) temporal.

(1) Friend in one and friend in the other is a great friend.
(2) Friend in one and an enemy in the other is a neutral.
(3) Neutral in one and a friend in the other is a friend.
(4) Neutral in one and an enemy in the other is an enemy.
(5) Enemy in one and an enemy in the other is a great enemy.

For example, the Sun and the Moon are natural friends. If in a particular nativity the Sun is in Aries and the Moon in Sagittarius, they would temporarily be enemies. So natural friends at one place and temporal enemies at another would make them neutrals in regard to each other. Again, the Sun and Jupiter are natural friends. Suppose in a nativity the Sun is in Aries and Jupiter in Pisces. Being in second and twelfth signs (Sun in second to Jupiter and Jupiter in the twelfth from the Sun) they become temporal friends. So being natural friends and also temporal friends, they become great friends.

PLANETARY ASPECTS

We shall now pass on to another important matter, that of aspects. In Hindu astrology an aspect is counted from sign to sign. All planets have full aspect on the seventh sign as counted from the one tenanted by the planet.

(1) A planet in any degree of Aries will fully aspect the seventh sign, i.e., Libra and so also any planet tenanting any degree of Libra.

(2) All planets except Mars have 75% aspect on the signs which are fourth or eighth from the sign tenanted by the aspecting planet. Mars in such a case has full aspect. Thus, for example, a planet occupying any degree in Taurus will have 75% aspect on Leo and Sagittarius, or on any planet tenanting any degree in Leo or Sagittarius. But if Mars is the aspecting planet and in Taurus from 1° to 30°, he will fully aspect Leo and Sagittarius and the planet anywhere therein.

(3) All planets except Jupiter have 50% aspect on the signs which are fifth or ninth to the sign occupied by the aspecting planet. Jupiter in such a case has full aspect. Thus

Jupiter occupying any degree of Gemini will fully aspect Libra and Aquarius and the planets therein. But any planet other than Jupiter in Gemini will have only 50% aspect on Libra and Aquarius and planets occupying any degree of Libra or Aquarius.

(4) All planets except Saturn have 25% aspect on the signs which are third and tenth from the sign tenanted by the aspecting planet. Thus, if the aspecting planet is in Cancer (any degree—as degrees are not important because the count is made from sign to sign and not from degree to degree), he will have 25% aspect on Virgo and Aries and on planets tenanting Virgo or Aries. But Saturn in such a case will have full aspect, i.e., Saturn in Cancer will fully aspect Virgo and Aries and all planets situated therein. All this can be summarised thus:

Aspecting Planet	*on 7th Sign*	*on 4th & 8th Signs*	*on 5th & 9th Signs*	*on 3rd & 10th Signs*
Sun	100%	75%	50%	25%
Moon	100%	75%	50%	25%
Mars	100%	100%	50%	25%
Mercury	100%	75%	50%	25%
Jupiter	100%	75%	100%	25%
Venus	100%	75%	50%	25%
Saturn	100%	75%	50%	100%

Planets have no aspect on signs which are second, sixth, eleventh or twelfth as counted from the sign occupied by the aspecting planet. Planets in the same sign do not aspect each other. In Western astrology, conjunction is also one of the aspects, but in Hindu astrology conjunction generates effects due to being together, but it is not treated as an aspect.

Rahu and Ketu do not aspect nor are they aspected. But suppose Rahu or Ketu is in a particular sign and that sign is aspected by Jupiter; then due to the quality of the sign being beneficially improved due to Jupiter's aspect, the quality of Rahu or Ketu is also automatically improved and we say that Rahu or Ketu is aspected by a benefic. But strictly speaking Rahu and Ketu are affected by conjunction of benefics or malefics and do not come in the realm of aspects.

It must be emphasised that one great difference between the Western and the Hindu systems in computing the aspect is that in the Western system the count is made from degree to degree, but in the Hindu system the count is made from sign to sign.

Another important difference is that in the Western system the aspect will be mutually the same. Thus if, say, Mars and Jupiter are in trine we can express this by saying Mars Trine Jupiter or Jupiter Trine Mars. But in Hindu astrology, if Jupiter is in say Aries and Mars in Leo, then Jupiter will have full aspect on Mars, but Mars will have only 50% aspect on Jupiter.

The third difference between the Western and the Hindu systems is that in the former certain types of aspects, e.g., sextile or trine are good and certain aspects like square and opposition are evil, but in Hindu system there is no such classification.

In the Hindu system:

(1) Aspects by benefics are always good.

(2) Aspects by malefics are always evil.

(3) Whether a benefic or a malefic if he aspects his own house, he strengthens it and does not harm it.

This is the general principle. But along with this there is also the following special principle:

(1) Aspects of lords of good houses such as fifth and ninth are good.

(2) Aspects of lords of evil houses such as sixth, eighth or twelfth are evil.

Having discussed the quality and the quantity of aspects we shall pass on to other characteristics of the planets.

THE CHARACTERISTICS AND PORTFOLIOS OF PLANETS

In a nativity the Sun represents the soul of the native; the moon, the heart (the emotional mind is referred to as heart; also the physical organ, heart); Mars, stamina—physical as well as mental; Mercury, speech; Jupiter, happiness and knowledge; Venus, pleasures (comforts, as well as pleasure of sex); Saturn, sorrow.

If a planet is strong in the birth chart, he increases the good effects. A strong Sun would give a strong soul. But in case of Saturn it is the opposite: a strong Saturn will lessen sorrow or grief but a weak Saturn would make the native suffer much grief.

Ingredients of the Body. Sun—bones; Moon—blood and flesh; Mars—marrow; Mercury—skin; Jupiter—fat; Venus—semen; Saturn—nerves.

These facts are helpful to determine the cause of disease and death according to the planets afflicted and whose *Dasha* and *Antardasha* are current.

The Sun is the king, the Moon is the queen, Mercury is the prince, Jupiter and Venus are the Ministers, Mars is the commander-in-chief and Saturn is the servant.

In Hindu mythology, Jupiter is described as the religious preceptor of gods, while Venus is the religious preceptor of the demons. This distinction indicates that if Jupiter is strong in a nativity, the native would be good, learned, religious, will be inclined to charity and benevolence; he will be rich and his acts and deeds will be godly and for the good of others. But if Venus is strong, the native will have comforts which give pleasure to the senses, luxuries, erotic pleasures, etc. According to Hindu philosophy the earthly pleasures take a man away from the path of God and so worldly enjoyments have been allotted to the portfolio of Venus who has been described on this principle as the preceptor of the demons.

Complexion

The following are the complexions of planets: Sun—dark red; Moon—very fair; Mars—pinkish fair; Mercury—grass green; Jupiter—pale yellowish fair; Venus—very fair; Saturn—dark; Rahu—black; Ketu—variegated colour. Moon or Venus if in the ascendant makes one fair; in the seventh house they—or one of them—give a fair and a beautiful wife. The purpose of describing the complexion of the planets is this: if a planet is strong in a nativity, it endowes the native with his complexion, and particularly so if he is in the ascendant or if he aspects the ascendant or if he is the strongest planet in the chart.

In horary astrology, the complexion of the planet is also made use of for finding the complexion of a thief and thus identifying him.

Some Physical Characteristics

Sun. Square shaped, honey-eyed, scanty hair on head, illustrious, of good appearance.

Moon. Young, slender and globular body, well shaped limbs, intelligent, good eyes, soft spoken, fond of walking or travelling, having good discrimination, fine (thin) curly hair, fond of middle aged women.

Mars. Cruel glance, young, not very tall, fond of self-praise, inpatient, restless, thin waist, fond of sports (shooting), courageous, commanding influence, sexy.

Mercury. Diplomatic speech or habit of speaking with double meaning; clear pronunciation, spare and thin body, humorous, fond of fun, learned, clever, veins prominent, imitates others in speech and dress.

Jupiter. Big and fat body, prominent belly, brownish eyes and hair, benevolent eyes, very wise, having the voice of a lion, well up in various branches of learning.

Venus. Handsome in appearance, long arms, large thighs, chest and face, having much semen, dark curly and long hair, fond of dress of variegated colour, intelligent, fond of dalliance, big eyes, sexy, wealthy may have come defect in eyes.

Saturn. Indolent or lazy, long and thin body, big or defective teeth, rough hair on body and head, may have hair on the lower part of the ears, lame, hard limbs, inclined to do evil.

This is the appearance of Saturn, if weak. If Saturn be strong the native would be sober, deep, sagacious, fond of mystic and occult sciences, philosophy, etc. Rahu is like Saturn. Ketu is like Mars.

Temperament

The Sun is of fixed or steady temperament; the Moon is fickle; Mars is violent; Mercury has mixed qualities but is generally volatile; Jupiter is mild and soft hearted; Venus is easy going and accommodating; Saturn is harsh, hard-hearted and cruel.

Glance

The Sun and Mars glance upwards; Mercury and Venus side-ways (like a flirting damsel). The Moon and Jupiter glance squarely in front, while Saturn and Rahu look with downcast eyes.

Purpose

When the ascendant is on the border line, one may by tenancy of a particular planet in the ascendant fix the rising sign; or in horary astrology, the planet in the ascendant may describe the person from whom gain may be expected.

Flavour

Sun—bitter; Moon—saltish; Mars—pungent; Mercury—mixed with several tastes; Jupiter—sweet; Venus—sour; Saturn—astringent.

Humours of the Body

According to the Hindu science of medicine all bodily humours have been classified into three categories (i) *Vata* (wind), (ii) *Pitta* (bile), and (iii) *Kapha* (phlegm). All diseases or ailments in the body arise out of the imbalance of one, two or all the three humours. They have been allotted to the seven planets as follows: Sun—bile; Moon—wind and phlegm; Mars—bile; Mercury—wind, bile and phlegm; Jupiter—phlegm; Venus—wind and phlegm; Saturn—wind.

Gunas: Satwika, Rajasika and Tamasika

These are the three qualities which sum up thoughts, deeds and inclinations. Those who are *Satwika* have pure thoughts and are inclined to acts of religious merit. Those who are *Rajasika* are fond of the pleasures of the senses, decoration, fond of money and a gay life. Those who are *Tamasika* are greedy, lustful, of angry temperament and intent upon harming others.

The Sun, Moon and Jupiter are *Satwika,* Mercury and Venus are *Rajasika,* Mars and Saturn are *Tamasika.*

Colours

The colour of the articles or commodities over which each of the planets presides are as follows: Sun—copper coloured; Moon—white; Mars—deep red; Mercury—green; Jupiter—yellow; Venus—of variegated colours; Saturn—black.

If the planet is strong, gain of commodities of above mentioned colour, but if the planet be weak, loss of or through articles of this colour. This is useful in horary astrology to ascertain the colour of things lost or to be gained.

Age

Mars—child; Mercury—boy; Venus—of 16 years; Jupiter—a man aged 30 years. The Sun is a person 50 years old; the Moon of 70 years; Saturn, Rahu and Ketu very old or 100 years old.

This is useful to ascertain the effects of planets. A strong Saturn will indicate wealth and position in old age. A strong Jupiter shows good effect generally after middle age. This principle is recognised in the Western system also. Alan Leo in one of his books states that Jupiter generally shows its good effect after middle age—after the age of 40. In colder climates, the longevity is greater, so he has put middle age at 40.

According to largely practised usage, which is not of Hindu origin but imported from the Middle East, and followed by a large number of Hindu astrologers in the north-western part of India, the age is as follows:

(1) Influence of Moon: from birth to 4 years of age,
(2) Mercury: from 5th year to 14th year,
(3) Venus: from 15th to 22nd year of age,
(4) Sun: from 23rd year to 41st year of age,
(5) Mars: 42nd year to 56th year of age,
(6) Jupiter: 57th year to 68th year of age,
(7) Saturn: 69th year to 108th year of age.

These durations are according to the planetary periods and their distances. However, we are not concerned here with the astronomical basis. A rough and ready way to judge a birth chart on the above basis is as follows. Suppose the Sun in a chart is weak, and ill placed and Mars well placed and strong and the native who comes to an astrologer is aged about 40. On this basis the astrologer would predict that unfortunate conditions of affairs would continue till the age 41 and from the 42nd to the 56th year will be a good period.

According to another astrological usage, the following are the significant years of each planet: Sun 22, Moon 24, Mars 28, Mercury 32, Jupiter 16, Venus 25, Saturn 36, Rahu 48, Ketu 48. If the planet is strong and favourable, good results can be predicted pertaining to the house he is lord of or tenants in that year of age.

Metals

Sun—copper; Moon—silver; Mars—copper, gold; Mercury—alloy of metals; Jupiter—gold; Venus—silver; Saturn—lead, iron.

Jewels

Sun—ruby; Moon—pearl; Mars—coral; Mercury—emerald; Jupiter—topaz; Venus—diamond; Saturn—sapphire; Rahu—gomed (a precious stone of the colour of garnet); Ketu—cat's eye.

If the native is under the unfavourable influence of a planet he should wear the jewel governed by the planet. The evil influence is thus mitigated. Generally the precious stone is wrapped in a silk strip of the same colour as the stone and tied round the arm for a trial period of three days. If it shows a bad effect, it is removed at once. If it shows a good effect, it is studded in a ring or pendant with the underside uncovered, so that it is in direct contact with the skin. The upper surface is also left open to catch the light rays.

Seasons

The Hindu year is divided into six seasons of two months each, beginning from Spring. (i) Spring—Venus, (ii) Summer—Sun and Mars, (iii) Rains—Moon, (iv) Autumn—Mercury, (v) Winter—Jupiter, (vi) Severe Winter—Saturn.

Places

Sun—temple; Moon—tanks, rivers, seas; Mars—kitchens, cremation grounds, where fire is lit (in modern context, factories where fire and electricity are used); Mercury—places for sports, gardens (in modern context, playgrounds, polo-grounds, race courses, clubs); Jupiter—treasuries (in modern context, banks, vaults); Venus—places of pleasure, bedrooms, cinema houses, restaurants; Saturn—where remnants of food are thrown away (in modern context, where low class labour reside or work), burial grounds, gutters, unclean places, forsaken places, etc.

Another classification is as follows: The Moon and Venus reside in water or near water or aquatic regions; Mercury and Jupiter in villages where learned men live; the Sun, Mars, Saturn and Rahu reside in forests and mountains.

Sex

The Sun, Mars and Jupiter are masculine. The Moon and Venus are feminine. Saturn is a male eunuch, Mercury is a female eunuch.

To determine the sex of children and to find out whether more boys or girls would be born remember that Mercury and Saturn indicate female children, for very few eunuchs are born.

Relationships

Sun determines father, Mars brothers, Jupiter sons, Moon mother, Venus wife, Mercury maternal uncle, Saturn servants.

Deities

Here are the names of Hindu gods who preside over each planet.

Sun—Fire and Ṛudra; Moon—Goddess Durga; Mars—Subrahmanya, Hanuman; Mercury—Vishnu; Jupiter—Indra; Venus—Shachi (consort of Indra); Saturn—Brahma; Rahu—Shesha (the celestial python).

Elements

According to Hindu philosophy the entire creation consists of five elements—*Prithvi* (earth), water, fire, air, and ether.

Sun—fire; Moon—water; Mars—fire; Mercury—earth; Jupiter—ether; Venus—water; Saturn—air.

Directions

The planets respectively preside over the directions noted against each of them. East—Sun; South-East—Venus; South—Mars; South-West—Rahu; West—Saturn; North-West—Moon; North—Mercury; North-East—Jupiter.

The above information is for the determination of loss or gain from a particular direction during *Mahadasha* or *Antardasha* of the planet according as he is strong or weak.

Caste

Jupiter and Venus are Brahmanas (priestly class); the Sun and Mars are Kshatriyas (warrior class); the Moon is Vaishya (trading class); Mercury is Shudra (serving class); Saturn is the serving class of mixed caste. According to others, the Moon and Mercury are Vaishyas (trading class), Saturn is Shudra (serving class). Rahu and Ketu are wild tribes or Mlechchas (non-Hindus).

This is used to determine the caste of an enemy or of the person from whom the native is likely to benefit or through whom lose money, or to find the caste of the thief in horary astrology.

Cloth

Sun—thick cloth; Moon—new unused cloth; Mars—cloth, a fringe of which has been burnt away by fire; Mercury—cloth, a portion of which is wet; Jupiter—cloth neither new nor old; Venus—strong, decorated or embroidered cloth; Saturn—old and torn woollen cloth.

The quality of cloth would vary according to the strength of the planet. For example, if Saturn is very strong it may indicate a good blanket or black velvet.

Biped, Quadruped, etc.

Jupiter and Venus are bipeds; Mars and Sun are quadrupeds; Moon is a crawling insect; Mercury and Saturn are birds.

Rising with Front

The Moon, Mercury and Venus rise with the head first; the Sun, Mars, Saturn and Rahu with their hind parts first; Jupiter both ways.

Dhatu, Moola, Jeeva

It has been told already that in Hindu astrology all articles are divided into three categories: (i) inanimate matter—minerals, metals, etc., are covered by the term Dhatu; (ii) plants, trees, grass, creepers are covered by the term *Moola;* (iii) animate creation down from an insect to humans are called *Jeeva* (with life).

The Sun and Mars preside over *Dhatus.* The Moon and Saturn have sway over *Moola,* while Jupiter and Venus represent *Jeeva,* Mercury has a mixed portfolio of all the three.

This information is useful to indicate the source of gain or loss of *Dhatu, Moola* or *Jeeva,* according to the planet in the chart.

Directional Strength

Mercury and Jupiter are strong in the first house or ascendant of a chart; Moon and Venus in the fourth house; Saturn in the seventh, and Sun and Mars in tenth.

Shubha and Papa

Shubha means auspicious or benefic; *Papa* literally means sinful, but in the astrological context, it means extremely harmful and detrimental to the house a *Papa* tenants or aspects.

Mercury if conjoined with a *Papa* acts as a *Papa;* if conjoined with a *Shubha* he acts as a *Shubha,* if conjoined with both types of planets, he shows mixed results. Mercury is the most mutable of planets and most naturally imbibes the quality of the planet he conjoins. If not conjoined with a planet he is a *Shubha.*

Jupiter and Venus are *Shubhas* (natural); Mars, Saturn, Rahu and Ketu are *Papas* (natural).

The Sun if exalted or in own sign is a *Krura* (cruel) but not a *Papa*; otherwise he is a *Papa.* But he has a very light shade of *Papa;* one school would prefer to call him a *Krura* and not a *Papa.*

The Moon is a natural *Shubha* but on the fourteenth and fifteenth days of the dark fortnight he is very weak and is technically called *Ksheenachandra.* To explain this in terms of longitudes, when the Moon is applying to the Sun and the distance between the Moon and the Sun is 24° or less, the Moon is deemed a *Papa.*

The Moon has in the above circumstances been termed a *Papa* not so much because he himself is a *Papa* but because when he is in the above sector (applying and within 24°), all planets do not bestow auspicious effects.

The following are *Papa* in increasing measure: *Ksheena* Moon, Sun, Mars, and Saturn. Ketu has to be bracketed with Mars and Rahu with Saturn.

The *Shubhas* in increasing order are Venus, Mercury conjoined with *Shubha* (and not conjoined with any *Papa*), Jupiter.

Manner of Winning Over

In Hindu polity there are four methods of winning over a recalcitrant, refractory person or an enemy.

Sama (Good Counsel)	By mild approach, request, appeal to reason, good counsel.
Danda (Punishment)	By punishing or threat of punishing or by using physical force or show of physical force.
Dana (Temptation)	By offering monetary or other incentive.
Bheda (Tact)	By tact and diplomacy; by employing spies or secret propaganda.

Jupiter and Venus preside over *Sama;* the Moon over *Dana;* the Sun and Mars over *Danda;* Mercury and Saturn over *Bheda.*

Thus, a man may be brought round by methods and manner indicated above depending on the planets.

Geographical Regions of India

Sun	Kalinga.
Moon	Yavana.
Mars	from Ceylon to Krishna river also Avanti.
Mercury	from Vindhyas to Ganges also Magadha.
Jupiter	from Gautamika to Vindhyas also Sindha.
Venus	from Krishna to Gautamika.
Saturn	from Ganges to Himalayas.
Rahu	Ambara.
Ketu	Parvata.

KARAKA

The word *Karaka* literally means that which does. In the present astrological context it means the matters for which a particular planet is a significator for. While judging the birth chart, besides the house and the house lord which governs a particular matter the *Karaka* is also to be taken into consideration. We give below the several special matters which fall in the portfolio of each planet.

Sun. Soul, self, self-realisation, influence, prestige, power, valour, health, eye, general well being, heat, splendour, father, king, royalty, royal favour.

Moon. The heart, understanding, inclinations, emotions, sleep, happiness, good name and fame, facial lustre, mother, royal favour, affluence (wealth), travel, water reservoirs.

Mars. Stamina, special qualities, such as courage, desire, anger, scandal, diseases, enemies, opposition, controversies, weapons, commander of an army, land, immovable properties, younger brother, relations such as agnate or cognate cousins.

Mercury. Intelligence, discrimination, speech, expression, education, learning, mathematics, logic, astrology, medical knowledge and profession, writing, publishing, acting as a middle man in trade or politics, dancing, drama, mixture of things, leafy trees, testing of precious stones, charms (amulets), maternal uncles, friends.

Jupiter. Wisdom, learning, corpulence or fatness of body, acts of religious merit, devotion to gods, manes and superior persons, holy places, scriptures, proficiency in learning, philosophy, giving alms or donations, benevolence, wealth, respect, sons, religious preceptors, fruit, fruit trees. In female nativities, Jupiter is a *Karaka* for husband, also.

Venus. Wife, marriage, sexual matters, pleasures of the senses (so in a female nativity Venus may be a co-*Karaka* along with Jupiter for the husband), singing, poetry, scents, ornaments, jewellery, all articles of luxury, cooperation from and with others, flowers, flowering trees, beauty, buying and selling, cows, watery places.

Saturn. Longevity, life, death, adversity, calamities, disrespect, diseases, poverty, livelihood, servility, unrighteous conduct, learning of foreign languages and sciences, agricultural pursuits, minerals, oils, things buried deep into the earth and coming out therefrom, maid servants, servants, service, theft, cruel deeds, malice, lameness, very old persons.

Rahu. Paternal grand father, fallacious argument, harsh speech, gambling, movement, travelling, outcastes, foreigners, Mlechchhas (non-Hindus), snake, snake bite, theft, wickedness, widow, intrigue with a widow, skin diseases, itches, eczema, acute or sharp pain in the body, hiccoughs, swelling in the body or any part thereof.

Ketu. Maternal grand father, consumption, pain, fever, wound, witchcraft, causing trouble to enemies, horned animals, dog, cock, birds with spots or of variegated colour, philosophy, salvation.

There is also another rule which is as follows:

As already explained, planets are *Karakas* for certain relations also. The Sun for father, Moon for mother, Mars for brothers (according to one school, Mars for younger brothers, Jupiter for elder brothers), Mercury for friends, maternal uncle and for adopted son, Jupiter for sons, elder brothers, *gurus,* (religious preceptors), and in female nativities for husband, Venus for wife, Saturn for servants, and longevity, Rahu for paternal grandfather; Ketu for maternal grandfather.

According to one school, if the birth or conception be during the day, the Sun is *Karaka* for father, Venus for mother, Saturn for uncle, (father's brother), Moon for mother's sister. If the birth or conception be during the night, Saturn for father, Sun for uncle (father's brother), Moon for mother, Venus for mother's sister.

It is good to have the Sun and Saturn *Karakas* for the above in odd signs. Similarly it is good for the *Karakas*—the Moon and Venus to be in even signs. Some astrologers interpret diurnal birth as birth during the day, in a diurnal sign and odd sign; and a nocturnal birth as birth during night; in a nocturnal and even sign.

Leo, Virgo, Libra, Scorpio, Aquarius and Pisces are diurnal signs, while Aries, Taurus, Gemini, Cancer, Saggittarius and Capricorn are nocturnal.

If the significators for male relations, i.e., the Sun and Saturn, be in even signs and even *Navanshas** the native will be antagonistic to his father or uncle, according to the significator. Similarly, if the Moon and Venus be in odd signs and odd *Navanshas*, the native would be antagonistic to his mother or the mother's sister, according to the significator.

If the above maxim applies and if this *Yoga* is formed in a male nativity having a *Papa* in the ascendant and the lord of the seventh (from which we judge sexual intercourse) is strong, then there is sexual (illicit) intercourse with a relation of the opposite sex.

If the lord of the house governing sisters be conjoined with the Moon and Venus, the native has illicit connection with his sister or some such relation. If the lord of the fifth house be so conjoined, with a daughter or some such relation and if the ninth lord be so conjoined, with maternal uncle's wife and so on.

If in a female nativity if the planet is conjoined with the lord of the fifth house then cohabitation with son or some one closely related like a son is indicated; if conjoined with the lord of ninth then with maternal uncle and so on. If in a female nativity the lord of the third house (governing brother) be conjoined with Sun and Saturn, the female cohabits with her brother or some such close relation. In this manner the person with whom illicit cohabitation takes place has to be determined according to the planet (the houses he rules) conjoined with Moon and Venus if in a male nativity, and Sun and Saturn in a female nativity. But the following ingredients must be present:

* One ninth division of a sign. Odd signs begin with odd *Navansha*, even with even ones.

(a) In male nativities, the ingredients are the placement of the Moon and Venus in odd signs and odd *Navanshas.*

In female nativities placement of the Sun and Saturn in even signs and even *navanshas,*

(b) *Papa* in *Lagna* (ascendant).

(c) Lord of seventh strong.

(d) Conjunction with Sun and Saturn of the lord of a particular house (signifying the relationship of the person) in a female nativity.

(e) Conjunction with Moon and Venus of the lord of a particular house (to denote the illicit relationship) in a male nativity.

We have explained the above to indicate how conclusions are drawn on the basis of significators. This discussion is more with a view to provide a glimpse of the receding horizon of astrology and not for judgment by beginners.

Planets as Karakas for Houses

Besides the planets there are *Karakas* for certain houses also.

The second sense in which the word is used in is as significator for a particular house. Below are given the names of houses and the planets which are respectively significators for them.

I	House	Sun	VII	House	Venus
II	,,	Jupiter	VIII	,,	Saturn
III	,,	Mars	IX	,,	Sun and Jupiter
IV	,,	Moon and Mercury	X	,,	Sun, Mercury, Jupiter, and Saturn
V	,,	Jupiter	XI	,,	Jupiter
VI	,,	Mars and Saturn	XII	,,	Saturn

The above is the view expressed in *Phala Deepika, Sarvartha Chintamani, Jataka, Parijata* and several other standard works. But Parashar who may be described as the father of Hindu astrology, confines the *Karaka* qualities for the fourth house to the Moon, that of the sixth of Mars, that of the ninth to Jupiter, and of the tenth to Mercury. The *Karakas* for the fourth, sixth, ninth and tenth houses will be as given below:

IV House	Moon
VI ,,	Mars
IX ,,	Jupiter
X ,,	Mercury

Thus Parashar recognises only one *Karaka* for each house. In regard to other houses there is an identity of views.

In giving the above outline of *Karakas* of each planet, we cannot claim that we have been exhaustive. In this world there are thousands of things and one or the other planet (or one or more planets jointly) would be *Karaka* for each such item and many a thousand things must fall in the portfolio of each planet. But in a book of this nature, intended for beginners, it would be unwise to load it with too many facts. To give a broad idea, in judging a house or a particular matter governed by a house, we have not only to look at the house and the house lord, but to the *Karaka* also. For example, in a male nativity, if we have to arrive at a judgment in regard to his wife, we must not only look up the seventh house and its lord but also the significator for wife (Venus). Venus may or may not be connected with the seventh house or its lord, but one has, by virtue of the inherent right and significance of Venus, to determine from him also the matters connected with wife. Similarly, if we have to arrive at certain conclusions in regard to son or sons in a particular nativity, we have not only to examine the fifth house and its lord including the planets associated with or aspecting the fifth house and its lord but also Jupiter.

Before concluding this chapter, we would like to emphasise one important point. No planet is always good. No planet is always evil. In some nativities, a strong and well placed Jupiter may give the native wisdom, wealth, sons, and a highly religious conduct; but in another he may cause severe phlegmatic diseases and death. Often in one and the same nativity a planet is good for certain purposes and evil for others. Venus in seventh may give the native a very charming wife, but if aspected by malefics she may be flirtatious. Mercury may make one a good public speaker and author, but, if afflicted may cause some nervous disease or mental derangement. So we should not run away with the idea that any planet is wholly good or wholly evil.

Besides, one and the same planet may show different effects

according to its placement and associations. Mercury if weak may cause the native to indulge in vulgar and foolish jokes; but if the planet is dignified or well aspected, it may produce a rare dramatist with a subtle sense of humour. An afflicted Mars makes one quarrelsome, prone to indulge in quarrels with little provocation or no provocation at all, while a strong and dignified Mars may make one a courageous general. Mars and Mercury if both unfavourable might make one a forger or a cheat—Mercury contributing cleverness and Mars endowing the person with stamina, for even acts of dishonesty, theft, burglary; cheating, smuggling, etc., require stamina and cleverness. The same Mars and Mercury if strong, well placed and well aspected, may endow a general of an army with strategic superiority and logistics. Saturn may produce a mendicant, a shabby beggar or a *yogi* of high order. To repeat; one and the same planet may behave differently though the same streak will be found to run through its effect. Besides a planet cannot act in an isolated manner, insulated completely from the general effects of the nativity, the individual influences generated by other planets and the background of the native.

People educated and belonging to cultured society will not quarrel in the same manner as two vendors in a fish-market, nor will a poor man's inclination towards benevolence and charity find the same expression as similar intentions of a multi-millionaire. While delineating the effects or significance of planets, these basic considerations must not be lost sight of.

PAPAS OR PAPI PLANETS

Papa is a noun and the word *Papi* is an adjective derived from it. *Papa* in Sanskrit means a 'sin' and the word *Papi* means 'sinful'. However, in astrology *Papi* has acquired a particular connotation. There is no single word in English which would convey the idea of '*Papi*'. The word '*Saumya*' can be translated as benefic and '*Krura*' is generally expressed as malefic. We have already explained that the Sun, Moon (on the fourteenth and fifteenth day of the dark fortnight). Mercury conjoined with Mars, Saturn, Rahu or Ketu and Mars, Saturn, Rahu and Ketu are malefics. Moon (except on days already stated), Mercury—not conjoined with Mars, Saturn, Rahu or Ketu—Jupiter and Venus are called benefics or *Shubha.* Mars, Saturn, Rahu and Ketu are in addition to their classification as malefics are also called *Papis.* According to one school the Sun is *Krura* (a malefic) but not a *Papi.* This is one sense in which the word *Papi* is used. Another sense in which the word *Papi* is used is in relation to owning the third, sixth or the eleventh house, i.e., the third, sixth or the eleventh sign as counted from the rising sign. Thus a natural benefic like Jupiter can become a *Papi* due to ownership of the third and sixth or eleventh house. For example, for Libra or Aquarius ascendants Jupiter becomes a *Papi* due to ownership of third and sixth, for Libra and for Aquarius due to ownership of the eleventh.

Similarly, a natural *Papi* can become a *Shubha,* i.e., auspicious, by owning the fifth and ninth houses. Thus for Cancer ascendant, Mars owns the fifth and tenth and becomes a *Shubha* and for Taurus ascendant, Saturn owns the ninth and tenth and becomes a *Shubha.* The word '*Papi*' is used in two senses, (i) to indicate natural *Papa* tendencies; (ii) to indicate the quality arising out of or due to ownership of a particular house in a particular nativity. In the first sense, due to natural propensities, the quality is fixed and immutable, while in the second sense, it is a temporal quality which is mutable and changes from nativity to nativity according to the sign rising.

The *Papa* qualities of the third, sixth, eleventh and eighth houses are in the following proportion:

Lord of third	1 unit
Lord of sixth	2 units
Lord of eleventh	3 units
Lord of eighth	6 units

Thus the lord of the sixth is more *Papi* than the lord of the third. The lord of the eleventh is more *Papi* than the lord of the sixth, and the lord of the eighth is the most *Papi.*

CHAPTER 7

HOUSES

WHAT ARE houses? Every one knows what a house is. But in astrology a house has a special meaning. Generally in Hindu astrology, as explained earlier in Chapter 2, if Aries is the sign ascending, Aries is the first house, Taurus constitutes the second house, Gemini the third, and so on; Pisces constituting the twelfth house. If Taurus is the sign ascending, Taurus will be the first house, Gemini the second, Cancer the third, and Aries the twelfth.

The sign ascending is the first house and any planet therein is deemed to be in the first house. The sign next to the ascendant sign will constitute the second house and any planet therein will be deemed to be in the second house. This is the principle the old Hindu astrologers followed. The sign and the house were deemed synonymous. All the *Yogas* given in ancient Hindu astrological texts are based on this principle. The aspects between planets are also on this basis. So for beginners we suggest that they skip over the subsequent paragraphs dealing with house division. The more serious students of astrology are, however, advised to study what follows.

In Western astrology there are various methods of house division—the Placidian, Campanain or those followed by Porphyry or Regiomontanus. For the last one thousand years or more, due to contacts with Western and Middle Eastern systems of astrology, the method known as Porphyry's system has been in vogue in

India and has become enshrined in Indian texts. This consists of calculating the degree at the meridian and the difference between the meridian degree and the ascendant (ascending degree) is trisected and the cusps of the eleventh and twelfth houses fixed on this basis. Hindu astrologers have now been claiming this as the Hindu method of house division. But this is not so. This is an imported system and not an indigenous one.

The original Hindu method is what is known as the equal house division. Parashar, Jaimini, Mantreshwar, all followed this method. According to this method if the cusps of the 1st house is 7-22° 2′ 39″ (or in Scorpio), the cusps of the other houses will be as follows:

For each house go on adding one full sign, the degrees remaining the same.

		S	*D*	*M*	*S**
The cusp of the	II House	8	22°	2′	39″
,,	III	9	22°	2′	39″
,,	IV	10	22°	2′	39″
,,	V	11	22°	2′	39″
,,	VI	0	22°	2′	39″
,,	VII	1	22°	2′	39″
,,	VIII	2	22°	2′	39″
,,	IX	3	22°	2′	39″
,,	X	4	22°	2′	39″
,,	XI	5	22°	2′	39″
,,	XII	6	22°	2′	39″

A house extends to 15° on either side. Thus adding 15° to the cusp of the first we get:

S	*D*	*M*	*S*
7	22°	2′	39″
0	15°	0′	0″
8	7°	2′	39″

This is the junction point where the first house ends and the second house commences.

* S means completed signs, D indicates completed degree and M means complete minutes of arc. The last S means seconds of arc.

By adding one sign to the junction point we get the following:

Junction point between	S	D	M	S
I and II	8	7°	2′	39″
II and III	9	7°	2′	39″
III and IV	10	7°	2′	39″
IV and V	11	7°	2′	39″
V and VI	0	7°	2′	39″
VI and VII	1	7°	2′	39″
VII and VIII	2	7°	2′	39″
VIII and IX	3	7°	2′	39″
IX and X	4	7°	2′	39″
X and XI	5	7°	2′	39″
XI and XII	6	7°	2′	39″
XII and I	7	7°	2′	39″

So the twelfth house ends with 7-7° 2′ 39″ or the first house commences here. The first house ends at 8-7° 2′ 39″ where the second house commences.

Thus the domains of the twelve houses would be as follows:
First House from

		S	D	M	S		S	D	M	S
First	House from	7	7°	2′	39″	to	8	7°	2′	39″
Second	„ „	8	7°	2′	39″	„	9	7°	2′	39″
Third	„ „	9	7°	2′	39″	„	10	7°	2′	39″
Fourth	„ „	10	7°	2′	39″	„	11	7°	2′	39″
Fifth	„ „	11	7°	2′	39″	„	0	7°	2′	39″
Sixth	„ „	0	7°	2′	39″	„	1	7°	2′	39″
Seventh	„ „	1	7°	2′	39″	„	2	7°	2′	39″
Eighth	„ „	2	7°	2′	39″	„	3	7°	2′	39″
Ninth	„ „	3	7°	2′	39″	„	4	7°	2′	39″
Tenth	„ „	4	7°	2′	39″	„	5	7°	2′	39″
Eleventh	„ „	5	7°	2′	39″	„	6	7°	2′	39″
Twelfth	„ „	6	7°	2′	39″	„	7	7°	2′	39″

Current in India the other system of houses division is in which the tenth cusp is determined trigonometrically and then the distance between the M.C. (Meridian cusp) and the ascending degree is divided into three parts. This is described in *Paddhati* books in

Sanskrit and largely followed in India. But as we consider the equal house division more scientific and the older Hindu method we are using it in this book. More earnest enquirers for the other system may refer to other books on the subject.

Now let us revert to the longitudes of planets which we worked out in the example chart in Chapter 4. They are:

Sun	8	16	43
Moon	5	17	15
Mars	10	18	48
Mercury	9	5	35
Jupiter	6	8	53
Venus	8	11	1
Saturn	0	8	37 R
Rahu	10	20	33
Ketu	4	20	33

Now because the Sun's longitudes is 8° 16′ 43″ (in the domain of the second house which extends from 8-7° 2′ 39″ to 9-7° 2′ 39″), the Sun will be in the second house, the Moon in the eleventh, Mars in the fourth, Mercury in second (because the domain of the second house is from 8-7° 2′ 39″ to 9-7° 2′ 39″), Jupiter in the twelfth, Venus in the second, Saturn in sixth, Rahu in the fourth and Ketu in the tenth.

While counting from sign to sign and treating houses as synonymous with signs, Mercury goes to the third, but in the scheme of house division as explained above, Mercury goes to the second.

We would however recommend that beginners follow the simpler method, which is also followed by the majority, and that is to treat the entire ascending sign as the first house, the next sign the second house, and so on.

In Western astrology the cusps of house is the commencing point and the first house is constituted by space covering about 30° beyond the cusp; but in Hindu astrology the cusp is the mid-point or the centre of the house and extends to 15° on either side. This is the major difference in the Hindu and the Western methods.

It is now necessary to deal with matters which can be judged from each house.

WHAT TO JUDGE FROM EACH HOUSE

In Hindu astrology, certain effects have been described for births according to *Nakshatra* (location of the Moon in a particular constellation), *Tithi* (angular distance between the Sun and the Moon), *Yoga* (sum of the longitudes of the Sun and the Moon), location of planets in signs and houses and mutual disposition or aspects between planets, but the primary judgment of a particular matter or department of life is made from (i) planets and (ii) houses.

Each planet is a significator or *Karaka* for certain matters. For example, the Sun of father, the Moon of mother and so on, or the Sun of the soul and the Moon of the heart (emotional mind), Mercury of intelligence and so on. The significance of each planet has been dealt with in detail in Chapter 6. But over and above this—each planet being the significator for certain matters, affairs, relationships, attributes, etc.—the affairs of a native have been divided as pertaining to one or more houses. There are twelve houses in a nativity because there are twelve signs. So, it would be but logical to assume that all the affairs of the world and hereafter (such as salvation, the state of the native after death) and also his state or condition—the deeds of merit or otherwise he performed in previous births—should be so divided among the twelve houses that no matter or affair is excluded. The logical consequence of this is that each house will have in its portfolio a large number of affairs. It is not possible to cover in this book all the affairs and relationships that a native has or derives pleasure or pain from. So the astrological texts have provided a broad outline and listed certain matters to be judged from each house. This list should, however, be taken as illustrative and not exhaustive; only the important affairs or relationships which each house governs have been stated. Others can be inferred.

For example, the fifth house is the house of children. The fifth from fifth, i.e., the ninth house would represent the children's children (grandchildren). The seventh from the ninth, i.e., the third house would stand for the grandchild's husband or wife as the case may be. Or to take another example, the fifth house stands for children. The eleventh house being the seventh from the fifth would be taken for judgment in respect of the son's wife or daughter's husband. Suppose one's son's wife's younger brother is associated with him or wants to associate with him in business. One has to determine whether he will be a source of happiness and prosperity. Now, since the son is judged from the fifth, the son's wife from the eleventh and the son's wife's brother from the third from eleventh, i.e., the first house, if a malefic enemy of the lord of the first house is in the ascendant, one may pronounce the judgment that the association in business with one's daughter-in-law's younger brother would be a source of trouble. But if instead of a malefic, a benefic is in the first house and he also happens to be a friend of the lord of the first, the business association with him would be a source of pleasure and profit. In this way many corollaries flow from one relationship. Readers will find that certain matters listed by the ancient texts have become obsolete, as for example, elephants, palanquins, forts, etc. For the astrologers of today, enlisting these would be superfluous and redundant; a few persons may keep elephants, but palanquins or forts are no more in vogue. But despite this, they have been added, firstly, to give an insight into the Hindu astrological thought which is of academic interest; and secondly to provide a basis for analogous inferences. The palanquin was an aristocratic and luxurious made of conveyance and we may include in our judgment today Hispanos and Rolls Royces in their place!

Another thing which must be referred to in delineating matters for judgment from each house is that certain matters might appear as duplications. This is true. We have stated hereunder certain matters, the positive side of which is represented by one house and the negative side by another house. For example, the first house stands primarily for the body, health, strength or weakness, the physical constitution, personality, etc., and the sixth stands for ailments, ill health, sickness, wounds and such other matters. In such cases, the judgment has to be arrived at in the following manner. Suppose the first house is strong and the sixth afflicted. The native would have a good constitution and would generally be healthy, but suffer ill health or a particular ailment when the *Dasha, Antardasha* of the planet afflicting the sixth house is acting. On the other hand, let us take a case where the first house is weak and afflicted, but the sixth house is not. In such a case, there would not be a severe bout of illness, but the general constitution of the native would not be strong; he would lack in the energy and enthusiasm required to fight through life and for which his personal constitution and make-up would be the chief determining factor.

Now let us take another example where there does not appear to be duplication, but where there actually is duplication. For example, according to certain authors *Vidya* (education, learning) has to be judged from the second, while according to others from the fifth house and according to the south Indian school from the fourth house. These differences will be discussed later. Now, the second house stands primiarily for speech, while the fifth house stands for intelligence. Suppose the second house is strong and the fifth is not. In such a case, the native would have good powers of speech and if the house and its lord are specially strong he may be able to impress his listeners with his learned discourses and masterful exposition of the *Shastras* (texts of Hindu learning); but he may not be able to write so well or produce a learned work or may not be able to do erudite research work requiring penetrating intelligence, the ability for original enquiry, and profundity of thought. On the other hand, suppose the second house is weak and the fifth house is strong. In such a case, the native would be a profound scholar and may even be an eniment author of learned works, but he would lack the ability of public speaking and oral exposition. He may be able to propound a theory and write a thesis on it which might win the all round approbation of learned men in the line; but if he is asked to propound the theory to an assembly, he would be found utterly lacking in the power of verbal expression. Such learned men are not uncommon.

Or let us take another example. The second house represents wealth. The fourth stands for immovable property, the ninth for *Bhagya* (general prosperity and affluence), and the eleventh is the house of gains. Apparently all these are covered by wealth. But the nicety or distinction is as follows: (i) the second house represents accumulated wealth—movable assets such as money, gold, jewellery; (ii) the fourth house represents immovable properties—houses, landed property, agricultural farms—cattle constitute movable property, but as in the rural economy of ancient India cattle were an adjunct to agriculture, and agriculture and dairy farming were correlated, all these have been taken as pertaining to the fourth house; (iii) the ninth house stands for *Bhagya* a Sanskrit word representing general prosperity, all round happiness in respect of material affairs including domestic felicity, family happiness, respect of others and religious aptitude—a man may have no accumulated wealth, he may own no immovable properties, yet according to Hindu conception he may be described as having good *Bhagya,* if he is happy all round; (iv) the eleventh house represents income—if the eleventh house is strong the native may have plenty of recurring income, but if the second and the twelfth houses are afflicted, the native might not be able to accumulate money or if the fourth house is afflicted, he may have a large income but not own immovable property. If the fourth house is very strong and the eleventh weak, the native may have large properties but inadequate recurring income. Thus, there can be permutations and combinations according to which of the above four houses is strong and which weak. For a really affluent and wealthy person, all the four houses, i.e., the second, fourth, ninth and eleventh, should be strong and the twelfth house should not be stronger than the first or eleventh, otherwise the expenditure would be greater than the income. As the eighth house represents death and things buried in the bowels of the earth, any money incidental to or arising out of or connected with death/longevity would fall in the portfolio of the eighth house. So also would treasure buried underground be governed by the eighth.

Now, let us consider a residential house. It is governed by the fourth house. But Rudra* states that the fourth house stands for a hereditary house and the eighth house for a subsequently acquired one. If the fourth house is weak and the eighth strong, the native would dispose of the old hereditary house and acquire a new one. According to the *Prashna Marga* houses, such as, *Mathas* (monasteries) and secondary residential houses, such as, a country house or a building at a pleasure resort, etc., are to be judged from the eighth. According to Parashar, residential premises are judged from the ninth also, probably on the assumption that for a man to be fortunate (fortune in general is judged from the ninth), it is necessary that he should live in comfortable premises, though he may not own them. Thus there is a subtle distinction in respect of residential premises as judged

* An ancient learned commentator on astrological works.

from the fourth, eighth or ninth houses.

In South India, the father is judged from the ninth, while in North India, he is judged from the tenth. The ninth house is primarily *Dharma Sthana*, i.e., the house of religion, piety, devotion to God, good morals and righteous conduct, and of the *Guru* or the religious preceptor who initiates one into the spiritual life. According to Hindu concepts, a man is born twice, firstly when he is born out of his mother's body, and the second time when he is initiated spiritually during the thread ceremony. This latter ritual is done by the *Guru* and in Brahman families, the father himself generally used to be *Guru*. So, the two offices of father and *Guru* became blended together and judgment used to be made by reference to the ninth house.

Similarly, in South India, *Vidya* (education, learning) is judged from the fourth house, while in the north, it is judged from the fifth. It is not only in regard to this matter but to many others also that there are different schools of Hindu astrology. And this is natural, the continuous process of dynamic activity in a field of learning for many centuries prevented the principles and practice of astrology from becoming static and the divergences of thought in many directions represent the vital growth of the astrological science through the ages. In fact, the concepts of Western astrology as existing today can also be traced through the Greeks and Romans, the Chaldeans and the Arabs, to the parent system of ancient India. A large number of European astrologers subscribe to the view that the Chaldeans were the originators of astrology, but Hindu sources point to the growth and development of the stellar prognostication to times immemorial. However, scholars may differ on this and other points and stick in all sincerity to their own beliefs; differences and distinctions indicate vitality and independent powerful thinking.

We shall now enumerate the various facets of life and matters pertaining to the affairs of man as judged from different houses.

As regards the part of the human body which each house represents, we have dealt with this in the Chapter 5 on signs. Similarly the principle of a particular planet governing specific affairs has been dealt with in the Chapter 6 under *Karakas*. Thus the determination of a matter is dually controlled by the house and the *Karaka*. If we have, for example, to judge the seventh house—the wife in a male nativity, we have to appraise not only the seventh house but Venus also. Thus for judgment we have to examine the two streams, *Karaka* and house, flowing together in one channel. These two component factors have to be examined minutely and thoroughly to arrive at the correct result.

We shall now provide a brief outline of what is to be judged from each house. In doing so, we shall for the interest and enlightenment of serious readers refer at places to the authority advocating the matters of judgment from each house.

I HOUSE

According to Parashar the body, constitution and proportions, appearance, knowledge, complexion, strength or weakness of the native and also of the nativity and the temperament have to be judged from the first house. Among parts of the body the head is governed by this house and according to the *Dreshkana,* also the throat and *Basti.**

According to Rudra, it is the self which experiences health or disease, happiness or sorrow and all this is therefore judged from the first house.

According to Vaidyanatha, fame, personal characteristics, residence abroad, splendour, are also to be judged from the first. According to *Sanketnidhi,* an authoritative text on astrology, a general estimate of the happiness or misery the native is destined to, is also to be guaged from this house; the mother's father (tenth from fourth), father's mother (fourth from tenth) and other relations have also to be determined from this house. The *Prashna Marga,* (written several centuries back) a very authoritative work on astrology, includes good health (a corollary of body), standing in society (status), fame, happiness, and victory over enemies as matters for judgment from the first house. The *Uttarakalamrita* another ancient text-book in Sanskrit, gives a more exhaustive list and though there would be repetition of some of the items already listed, it is worth while to provide a

* A *Dreshkana* means a decanate. A sign is divided into three parts, (i) 0° to 10°, (ii) 11° to 20°, (iii) 21° to 30°.

If the second decanate rises, the first house governs the Throat also. If the third *Dreshkana* rises (i.e., the degree of the rising sign is 21° to 30°), the first house governs basti also. For the meaning of basti, refer to Chapter 5.

translation of the relevant text.

The first house represents the body parts, happiness or misery, old age, knowledge, place of birth, fame, sleep, dreams, strength, dignity, diplomacy or polity, longevity, peace of mind, age, hair, pride, life, gambling or betting on behalf of others, honour, skin, loss of money (being twelfth from second), insult, temperament, illness, asceticism, nature, activity, efforts connected with living beings (such as family members or cattle), loss of respect, blame from others. Thus we find that the main consideration is of 'self' and the various matters arising as corollaries thereof. One point should, however, be clarified: the degrees from 0(zero) of the sign ascending to the degree rising represent the left side of the head, while that from the degree rising to the end of the sign ascending represent the right side of the head. Any malefic, particularly Mars, afflicted in the first house is likely to cause a hurt on the left or the right side of the head according to the degree tenanted by the natal Mars. Sometimes, there is no hurt; but the native suffers from smallpox or similar diseases that might leave permanent marks.

II HOUSE

According to Parashar, wealth, family, the family members, death, enemies, precious metals, jewels, have to be determined from the second house. The eyes are governed by the second and twelfth houses—the right eye by the second. So also according to the *Dreshkana* rising (first, second or third) the eye, the right shoulder and the right portion of genitals and anus. According to Rudra wealth is the source of food, clothes, etc., and therefore the second house determines these. According to Vaidyanath, in addition to the matters referred to above, knowledge, happiness, learning, education, speech, and food are also governed by the second house. In the physical body the second house governs the face, the mouth and tongue, and naturally all food and drinks taken in by the mouth fall in the portfolio of the second house. In ancient India the acquisition of knowledge and learning was primarily oral and the exposition and expression of knowledge was also mainly through speech. When we discuss the fourth and the fifth houses we shall observe that in South India, *Vidya* (education and learning) is judged from the fourth, and in North

India from the fifth; but as far as expression is concerned, the second house is important. According to the *Sanketnidhi,* purchase and sale of goods, which brings in money, are also to be judged from this house. According to the *Prashna Marga,* all who are to be fed or maintained, money, learning, education and speech are to be judged from the second house. The *Uttarakalamrita* gives a long list and it is only right and proper that readers should be acquainted with it. The following are to be determined from the second house: power and quality of speech, wealth, faith in God, maintenance of others, nails, edibles, truth and falsehood which are after all attributes of speech, the tongue, eyes, clothes, diamonds, copper, gold, rubies, pearls, determination, perfumes, family, purchase and sale, soft speech, generosity in giving, efforts for acquisition of wealth, assistance, friends, lustre of the face, miserliness in spending, cheerfulness, good oratory, learning, granaries (this was one of the chief items of wealth in ancient India), courtesy in speech, the nose, fixity of mind as opposed to fickleness of the heart, going out or coming in, the person or persons near the native, life and the state of being wealthy. Thus we find that the various items listed above are all corollaries of wealth or matters connected with the mouth, such as, speech or food. The second house refers to persons close to the native, because the second house is next to the first.

III HOUSE

According to Parashar, valour, brothers, servants and sisters, travelling, advice or learned discourse, death of parents, have to be adjudged from the third house. The right ear is also to be judged from this house, so also the right arm and the right testicle according to the *Dreshkana* rising. Valour means great prowess, physical as well as mental. According to Rudra, companions are also to be judged from the third house.

According to Vaidyanatha, both the elder and the younger brothers are to be judged from the third. Another school however takes the third house as representing younger brothers and the eleventh as governing the elder brothers and sisters, because the first house ('self') would be third from the eleventh.

The throat is according to Vaidyanatha governed by the third;

also what is heard. The ornaments worn in the ear are also governed by this house. This author also includes articles of apparel, steadiness (a corollary of stamina and courage), edible roots and fruit. According to the *Sanketnidhi*, since the first house governs the mother's father, the third governs the mother's father's brother. It also governs slaves of the native, the *Prashna Marga* also includes the right ear and the assistants of the native in his work or undertaking fall in the portfolio of the third house.

Generally speaking, the throat, neck, shoulders, arms and the upper part of the chest fall under the jurisdiction of the third house. Thus, readers will observe that there is a distinction between the second house governing the throat according to Western astrology and the third house governing the throat according to Hindu astrology. The latter makes a distinction between speech where the tongue and the lips are primarily exercised and singing where melody arises in the throat. Let us examine the long list of items that according to *Uttarakalamrita* are to be judged from the third house: patience and perseverance, sisters, fight, ear, leg, place of travel (the distance covered on foot or short travels), perplexity or confusion of mind (the third house being twelfth from fourth), power, stamina, strength, paradise, causing distress to others (an element arising out of fighting), dreams, a fighter, valour, one's relations, friends, walking, the throat, good food, apportionment of property received as legacy (a corollary of brothers, among whom generally the property was partitioned), ornaments, qualities like virtues and vices, education, hobbies which engage the mind, sports, pleasure and vigour, status connected with birth in a good family, servants, the space between the root of the thumb and above the life line (the mount of Mars below the mount of Venus on the palm), female slaves, short travels in a comfortable conveyance, a large undertaking, one's religion (the third house being complementary to the ninth).

IV HOUSE

According to Parashar, coveyances, friends, relatives, maternal as well as paternal, mother, happiness, treasure, fields, agricultural property, dwelling houses, gardens, etc., are to be determined from the fourth house. The holy places of *Dharma* (religion, piety, moral virtues, devotion to God, righteous conduct) have also to be judged from the fourth house. The right portion of the nose is governed by this house, so also the right side of the chest and the right thigh.

According to Rudra, the fourth house represents the hereditary house—the house in which one is born in and the eighth represents the one acquired subsequently. If the fourth house is weak and the lord of the eighth in eighth, the native disposes of his ancestral home and acquires a new house and lives therein.

In regard to matters governed by this house, Vaidyanatha includes education, the welfare of or happiness of mother, sweet smells (because the nose is governed by the fourth), the qualities or inclinations of the heart. Some astrologers also include clothes. According to the *Sanketnidhi,* wells and tanks are also to be judged from this house. According to the *Prashna Marga,* the mother, the maternal uncle, sister's children, delicacy, water, sleeping, increase and cattle are to be included in the fourth house. The *Uttarakalamrita* furnishes the following list:

Vidya (education or erudition), kingdom, residential house, going away from house or leaving the birth place, good conveyances on land or water, anointing the body, mother, *Bandhu* (relations) and friends, caste, clothes, wells and tanks in which water rises from underground), water, milk, perfumes, happiness, good name and reputation, divine herbs used for medication, confidence or belief, false propaganda or uttering a lie, a *Mandapa* (this is a Sanskrit word meaning a canopy or structure of bamboos, grass or a small masonry building under which a religious ceremony is performed), triumph or victory, causing perspiration, agriculture, fields, gardens, digging of wells and tanks and religious ceremonies connected with wells, tanks, etc. and dedication of these to public or private use, relations through mother or other women of the category of mother, diagnosis, intellect, father, wife, placing wealth in safe custody (the fourth house deals with the underground and money and precious metals which used to be consigned to underground pits or vaults for safety) a beautiful mansion, architecture (because it pertains to houses), buildings, entry into a house, ultimate results, temperament, loss of house (this is the negative aspect), ancestral property or what is one's own, feeding of gods, indication of place where stolen property has been consigned, an ant-hill, knowledge of the Vedas and

Shastras—the sacred books of the Hindus, buffaloes, cows, horses, elephants, good yields of crops. All these are to be judged from the fourth house.

V HOUSE

According to Parashar, *Yantras* (charms engraved on metal plates), *Mantras* (religious incantations in prescribed manner for fulfilment of a particular objective), progeny (sons and daughters), fall from kingship or high office (because it is eighth from tenth) have to be adjudged from the fifth house. The right cheek is governed by this house, as also the right side of the heart and the right knee according to whether the first, second or the third *Dreshkana* rises, i.e., is the ascending degree.

According to Rudra, intelligence and discretion—what to do and what not to do and good counsel—are to be judged from the fifth house.

Vaidyanatha includes the following under the fifth house, called the house of sons or children: native's family deity, sovereign, sons and daughters, father (though father is primarily judged from the ninth in South India and from the tenth in North India), intelligence, religion, legacy of good actions due to good actions in previous birth, a pilgrimage should be judged from the second, fifth, seventh and tenth. According to the *Sanketnidhi,* intelligence, inclination, production of works including books and authorship, disciples, are also judged from this house. According to *Prashna Marga,* intelligence, talent, memory, discretion, *Mantras,* ministership, sons and good inclinations are to be judged from this house. The *Uttarkalamrita* gives the following long list of affairs which fall in the portfolio of the fifth: children, virtuous acts, giving rise to religious merit, ministers of a king or ministers and the king, good behaviour and a good heart, artisanship, inclinations of the mind, education, conception leading to the birth of a child, discrimination, the umbrella which was the ancient insignia of royalty, good stores, auspicious letters like invitations to religious or social ceremonies and functions, the various desired objectives and actions in pursuance thereof, father's money, anxiety of a distant matter or far-sightedness, gain of money or fortune arising out of or connected with wife or husband (the fifth house being eleventh from the seventh), embrace of a prostitute, depth of mind, sobriety, intensity or gravity, mystery, courtesy, descriptive writing of long articles or books, business, affection, literary productions or works of poetry, entering into an undertaking, stomach, *Mantras*, and realisation thereof, devotion to God, cheerfulness, affluence, giving of grain in charity, the goodness (*Punya*) arising out of good actions of religious merit, intelligence, review of matter, good thoughts, efforts for earning money, musical instruments and auspicious occasions for music and singing, good deed, erudition, contentment, and a hereditary post of a minister in a state.

These items give an insight into the logic of arriving at matters which should be judged from a particular house.

VI HOUSE

According to Parashar, the sixth house governs maternal uncle (mother's brother), god of death, worries and anxieties, fear of calamities, enemies, wounds, and step-mother. The right portion of the chin is governed by this house as also the right portion of the stomach and the right calf of the leg, according to the *Dreshkana* rising.

According to Rudra, all diseases arising out of one or more of the three humours-*Vata, Pitta* and *Kapha* (wind, bile and phlegm) and hurts, whether due to assault or due to falls, etc., are to be judged from the sixth, Vaidyanatha includes vices or vicious habits in the portfolio of the sixth house, probably because the sixth governs enemies and forces which pull down and one's own vices and vicious habits are one's worst enemies and the most important factor which works to the detriment of the native and brings him distress by undermining him. The *Jatakaratna,* a standard work in Sanskrit, while enumerating matters to be judged from the sixth, includes thieves also and all handicaps or obstructions in the path of progress of the native as well as distress.

In addition to the above, the *Sanketnidhi* states that battles, maternal uncle and cruel acts are also to be judged from this house. According to the *Prashna Marga,* thieves enemies, obstacles, mental and physical diseases and death at an enemy's hands are also to be judged from the sixth house.

In addition to the matters already enumerated above, the

Uttarakalamrita also includes the following in the portfolio of the sixth house: fighting in a battle or combat, phlegm (i.e. diseases arising of the maladjustment of *Kapha* or phlegm, one of the three humours regulating health in human body), dysentery, swelling of any part of the body, insanity, wounds, boils, sickness, eye troubles, urinary and venereal diseases, gout, severe colicky pain, phthisis, exertion, weariness, fall from a boat, mental worry, intense anguish of mind, severe reproach, miserliness, cruel deeds, debt, enmity, receiving charity or alms, troubles, untimely meals, poison, guarding of one's credit, theft, calamity, imprisonment, or prison house, misunderstanding with brothers. Thus we see that all the above are only details of suffering, physical or mental, which have been pithily referred to by other writers. The only additional points worthy of our attention are (i) gain, and (ii) service which this Sanskrit text includes. In Western and Middle Eastern astrology the sixth house includes 'service' as falling in the jurisdiction of the sixth. But other writers have not included gain under the sixth house. However Kalidas appears to have done so for three reasons. Firstly, 'gain' is the positive side of loss, debts, etc; and secondly, the sixth house is an *Upachaya* house (*Upachaya* means 'increase'); thirdly, the sixth house is ninth from tenth and tenth from ninth and by the theory of *Bhavat Bhavah,* he judges the *Bhava* (house) from the Bhava, on which principle the eighth being the house of longevity, the eighth from eighth, that is, the third from the ascendant is also called the house of longevity.

VII HOUSE

Parashar states that wife or husband, journeys, expenditure at night, and one's own death must be looked up from the seventh house. The face is also governed by this house and so also the navel and the feet according to whether the first, second or third *Dreshkana* is rising. According to Rudra the seventh house stands for sexual desires, enjoyment of women (by analogy enjoyment of men in female nativities).

Vaidyanatha states that from the seventh house, an astrologer can ascertain everything about a journey, the native's sons, wife and enjoyment. What has been stated earlier about happiness or misery in respect of sons in relation to the fifth house may also be predicted from the seventh. It is true, wife and children are co-related and children are a corollary of wife. According to ancient Hindu thought, the chief object of having a wife was to beget children. But to include all affairs of the children seems to be inexplicable unless we reconcile it in the following manner: one cannot beget children unilaterally. A second party is required to bear children. Children are as much the product of the first party as of the second and so if we take the seventh house as co-ascendant (ascendant of the second party) and the fifth from it also into consideration, it may reveal the state of affairs in regard to the children (of the wife and also the native's children). Dhundhiraja, the author of *Jatakabharana*, a standard text in Sanskrit, includes the battle-field and trading (commercial business) in this house. According to the *Sanketnidhi*, controversies and litigation, water-houses (for serving free drinking water), conveyances and trade and commerce must also be included in matters to be judged from the seventh. According to the *Prashna Marga*, marriage, sexual affairs including extra marital connections, bed, house and lost wealth are to be judged from this house.

We give below from the *Uttarakalamrita* a list of matters to be judged from the seventh house: marriage, sexual union, adultery, success in love affairs, enmity with an unchaste woman (and in female nativities enmity with an adulterous person), semen, adulterous nature or otherwise, deviation from moral conduct, losing the right track in travelling, break in a journey, loss of memory, money placed elsewhere, good scents, betel leaf, partaking of delicious food, curds, sweet drinks, acquisition of apparel, a couple of wives, genitals, urine, anus, gift or giving in charity, trade, victory over enemy, litigation, adopted son, foreign place, theft. It will be observed, while going through matters falling in the portfolio of the eighth house that the genitals are included by many authors under the eighth house also. In fact, in the physical body also, the regions governed by the two houses, the seventh and the eighth, are so inter-related and overlapping that it is difficult to place them in water-tight compartments. This difficulty has confronted authors of Western astrology also. For example, Alan Leo writes: "We must carefully distinguish between the part ruled by Libra and those by Scorpio. An apparent Libran disorder may be actually due to

Scorpionic influence. For instance, suppression of urine and retention of urine are different things; the former is a true Libran complaint occuring when the kidneys for some reason or other do not secrete the urine; the latter is Scorpionic, the urine being duly secreted by the kidneys, but retained for some reason in the bladder."

Such modern minute analytical details have not been gone into by the ancient authors and so at times we find the boundaries overlapping.

VIII HOUSE

Parashara says that this house governs the genitals and anus, incurring debts, giving of loans, piles, fistulas, prolapsus and other diseases of the rectum motion, gait, that which is not stated (that is, what we mean by the English expression 'reading between the lines'), has to be judged from the eighth house. A synonym for the eighth house is a 'hole' or a 'cavity.' So also the left part of the chin, the left region of the stomach and the left calf of the leg, according to the decanate rising.

According to Rudra, all kinds of *Adhi* (mental distress) and *Vyadhi* (physical pain ailments, agony and diseases) and calamities are to be judged from the eighth house.

The eighth is called the house of longevity; so also the third house which is eighth from eighth. But primarily, longevity, the genitals and excretory organs, milk, honey, urinary diseases, splitting of partnership or split between friends, defeat by diplomatic strategy, death—its cause, the month, the day of the week, the asterism in which the moon will be at the time of death —all are to be ascertained from the eighth. According to the *Jatakabharana* going across the rivers and things across the rivers and by analogy things across the seas and oceans, severe difficulties or path through rough mountainous regions or through wild dense forests, weapons, calamities, are also to be judged from this house. According to the *Sanketnidhi,* fear of enemies, boats, arrest, detention, crossing a river, theft, going astray down the wrong path, literally as well as symbolically, etc., are also to be judged from the eighth house. The author adds that all matters such as wealth, which are judged from the second house, must be judged from the eighth also, because this house is directly opposite to the second and thus complementary to the latter and any planets herein will fully aspect and influence the second house. He states that malefics in the eighth house destroy wealth, but benefics in the eighth bring wealth. According to the *Prashna Marga,* total destruction, calamities, bad name and ill fame, the cause and place of death, slaves, acquisition or construction of religious properties, house, impediments, and ailments are to be judged from the eighth house. The *Uttarakalamrita* includes the following among matters to be judged from the eighth house; longevity, death, cause of death, mutilation of a limb, happiness, defeat, fear, calamity, quarrels due to grain, punishment inflicted by government, great mental distress, legacy or the wealth of the dead repaying a debt, loss of money, money deposited or kept at a place permanently, money of others received inadvertantly, facial disease (the eighth being in opposition to the second house), urinary diseases, fatigue, brother's enemy (the eighth house being sixth from third), trouble to wife (being second, a *Maraka* place from seventh), enemy's fort, battle, hazardous paths, evil news, causing or death of animals by the native.

Apparently contradictory matters, such as longevity and death, happiness and mental distress, etc., are really not contradictory but represent the positive and the negative aspects of the same content.

IX HOUSE

Parashar states that a residential house, *Dharma* (religion piety, good morals, righteous conduct, devotion to gods and manes), wife's brothers (by analogy husband's brothers also), brother's wife (because it is seventh from third), by analogy sisters' husbands also, visiting of holy rivers, sacred baths, worshipping at temples and religious shrines—all these must be looked up from the ninth house. So also the left cheek, the left portion of the heart and the left knee, according to the *Dreshkana* rising.

According to Rudra, the ninth house stands for the religious preceptor, one who counsels, directs and guides in all matters that bring happiness in this world and the next. The Hindus believe in a life after death and the transmigration of souls. The eighth house stands for death or the destruction of this physical body and so no wonder the ninth house, i.e., next to eighth, stands for the next world. According to Vaidyanatha, prosperity in general, and religious austerities are included. According to the *Jatakaratna*, money given in alms and charities, people who dine with the native, and sons' sons, are also to be judged from the ninth. According to the *Sanketnidhi*, religious and charitable properties are also to be judged from this house, which is complementary to the third and judgment in respect of brothers and sisters should also be made from it. Benefic male planets here aspecting the third, the native would have brothers; if benefic female planets tenant the ninth the native will have sisters. Malefics would cause illness to or premature death of brothers or sisters. According to the *Prashna Marga*, general prosperity, fortune, *Dharma* (religion), benevolence, acts of religious merit, austerities, penances, father, sons' children, charity, devotion to God, goodness of heart, and religious preceptors, are to be judged from the ninth.

The *Uttarakalamrita* also refers to the above matters. The following additional matters are also listed:

Medicines, efforts for acquisition of learning, conveyance, travelling, all kinds of wealth, place of coronation, investment of money. Being fifth from fifth, this house also stands for grandchildren.

X HOUSE

According to Parashar, the kingdom (it can apply to the nativities of kings or members of the royal family who are or can be heirs to a kingdom) and so by analogy, in the nativities of common men, it should refer to rank and status, position and authority to give orders, command, ruling powers, the sky, means of livelihood and all actions and dealings in pursuance thereof, respect, honour, father, living abroad, debts, have to be judged from the tenth house. So also the left portion of the nose, the left side of the chest and the left thigh according to the decanate rising. According to Rudra, the word 'respect' connotes all sentiments and experiences which elevate and uplift the feeling of self-gratification and the honour and homage paid by others—whether by the members of a clan or community or government must be judged from the tenth. Also from the tenth is to be judged whether the native would be able to retain his position or topple down as a result of opposition and enmities.

According to Vaidyanatha, in addition to the matters stated above, the native's actions or activities, ornaments, sleep, agriculture, renunciation of worldly life and taking to asceticism, means of livelihood, are to be judged from the tenth. According to the *Sanketnidhi*, the tenth house includes the backbone, trade and commerce, seal of authority, position, etc. If malefics tenant the tenth house there may be pain in the knees, the back, etc. According to the *Prashna Marga*, temples, the city, municipal, legislative or administrative council, rest houses where free lodging and boardings used to be provided for travellers, commonly known in India as *Dharmashalas*, slaves, all activity, authority, and support, are to be judged from the tenth house.

Kalidasa in his *Uttarakalamrita* includes trade, depositing of a treasure, riding a horse, road or track for a journey, athletics, teaching, supremacy, fame, elders, talismans, mother, adopted son, as in matters to be judged from the tenth house.

XI HOUSE

According to Parashar, gain of money, things or miscellaneous articles, son's wife, enemies and matters pertaining to them, should be judged from the eleventh house. So also the left ear, the left arm and the left testicle, according to the *Dreshkana* rising. According to Rudra, all gains are to be judged from the eleventh. According to *Jatakaratna*, the elders (brothers and sisters), wealth and hopes, should also be judged from this house. According to *Jatakabharana*, gain or acquisition of elephants, gold, cloth, jewels, palanquins and all the paraphernalia of luxury, are to be judged from here. According to the *Sanketnidhi*, gain of knowledge like learning and education, elephants, horses, conveyances, palanquins, gold ornaments, apparel and auspicious events are to be judged from this house. This house, being opposite to the fifth, should also be consulted for judgment in regard to affairs pertaining to the fifth house according to the nature of the planets—benefics or malefics—in the eleventh house. According to the *Prashna Marga*, all desired or cherished objectives like hopes and aspirations and the fulfilment thereof, the elder brother, all sons already born (those who are to be born have to be judged from the fifth), the left ear and gain of money are to be judged from the eleventh house.

The *Uttarakalamrita* repeats some of the affairs already given above. In addition, according to this text, wicked desires, subservience, paternal uncle (being third from ninth; according to the south Indian school of Hindu astrology, father is judged from the ninth), paternal property, ministership, the master's wealth, lost wealth, cooking, lovely paintings and skill in practical arts, gain from father-in-law, rise in prosperity, mother's longevity (eleventh being eighth from fourth) are to be judged from the eleventh house.

XII HOUSE

According to Parashar, expenditure, and by analogy, financial loss, tidings about an enemy and the end have to be judged from the twelfth house. Also, the left eye, the left shoulder, and the left portion of the genitals and anus, according to the *Dreshkaṇa* rising. According to Vaidyanatha, a person's wandering far away from his home-land, misfortune, giving away in charity, loss or purchase of luxury, comforts of the bed (sexual pleasures), and the waste of wealth are to be judged from this house. According to the *Jatakaratna,* all kinds of expenditure of bodily vigour as well as of wealth, fall, hell (the native's going to hell after this life), infirmity of a limb, are to be judged from the twelfth. According to *Jatakabharana,* losses, charity, expenditure, punishment, confinement, arrest—all these are to be judged from this house. According to the *Sanketnidhi,* imprisonment, acceptance (such as of wife or husband, i.e., marriage), punishment, are to be judged from here. According to the *Prashna Marga,* sins, expenditure, fall (physically while on the road or from a house top and also figuratively from a high office or fall into hell), the left eye, affliction of a limb, are to be judged from the twelfth house.

Among matters falling in the portfolio of the twelfth house included in the *Uttarakalamrita,* are break in sleep, adultery, loss of wife, impediment in sexual enjoyment, mental distress, enemy, fear of enemy, paternal wealth, discharge of debts, going to foreign lands, going to heaven, gallantry, humility, brother or sister of father (being third from tenth), fall in this house.

We have referred in detail to the matters which are to be judged from each house and provided a cross section of view as held by various eminent ancient authors. Matters of the world are inexhaustible and corollaries flowing out of each of the items may cover a wide network. No book can exhaustively enumerate all these matters, much less a text-book of this type. But the general canons of Hindu astrology have been succinctly stated above.

SUMMARY

The list of matters to be judged from each house is long and may appear formidable. Beginners are likely to be frightened by the long array. But that has been done to provide a glimpse of the wide horizons of Hindu astrology. They need not take into account all the matters given above for judgment from each of the twelve houses. For their benefit, we are giving below a short and condensed list of matters which should be judged from each house.

First house: self, head, body, personality, mental temperament, health.

Second house: eyes, face, upper part of the throat, speech, wealth, family.

Third house: arms, lower part of the throat, shoulders, brothers, sisters, valour.

Fourth house: chest, heart, mother, landed property, friends, conveyances, happiness.

Fifth house: stomach, education, intelligence, sons, daughters.

Sixth house: the region of navel, illness, enemies, debts, distress.

Seventh house: partnership, sexual relations, husband or wife, the part of the body below the waist and up to the genitals.

Eighth house: genitals, anus, death, legacies.

Ninth house: hips, thighs, religion, devotion to God, prosperity, religious preceptor.

Tenth house: knees, back, father, position in life, activity, status, honour from government.

Eleventh house: calves of legs, income.

Twelfth house: expenditure, loss, sexual enjoyment, left eye, teeth, confinement.

It will be found quite sufficient for beginners to confine their attention to judgment of the above matters only from each house.

CHAPTER 8

PLANETS IN SIGNS

Given below are the effects of planets in the different signs. First we give the influence which the planet would exert anywhere in the sign, occupying any degree from 1 to 30. Then will be described the effects if the planet occupies a particular degree or sets of degrees. One important principle of astrology should not be lost sight of. And that is that for certain purposes the first sign, Aries, corresponds to the first house; the second sign, Taurus would correspond to the second house, and so on. Thus a malefic in Aries would affect adversely the head or brain, a malefic in Virgo the intenstines, and so on. Benefics in Taurus would improve wealth, in Libra conjugal happiness, and so on.

SUN IN THE TWELVE SIGNS

Sun in Aries

If the Sun is in the 10th degree of Aries, it makes the native famous, fond of travelling and connected with manufacture of or trade in arms. But the native will not be rich. Such a person is capable of rising to the highest pinnacle of leadership. It is better to have the Sun from 1° to 10° than from 10° to 30°. The Sun anywhere in Aries makes the native courageous; he has strong bones but the health may cause trouble due to too much heat, excess of bile or blood disorders. If the Sun is from 0° to 30° 20′ or from 13° 20′ to 16° 40′, it will have very good effects during his *Dasha* or *Antardasha*. But if the Sun is between 20° to 23° 20′, all good effects due to sign position are completely devalued. The native is indolent, timid, unreliable and suffers disappointments and frustrations in his career.*

Sun in Taurus

The native will succeed in buying, selling or trading in cloth and scented things. He is a connoisseur of music and singing. But he is not an ardent lover of his wife or may have enmity with a barren woman. He is capable of bearing much physical stress and strain like a bull; suffers from the diseases of the mouth and the eyes. He is clever in dealing with others; does not have many enemies; is afraid of water.

The Sun will show much better effect during his *Dasha* and *Antardasha* if between 10° and 16° 40′ or between 23° 20′ and 26° 40′.

Sun in Gemini

The native receives good education, is learned and fond of astrology. He is intelligent, clever, wealthy and liberal in dealing with others. His memory is good; he is courteous and speaks in an agreeable manner. He may be brought up by a woman other than his mother or may have two mothers.

If the Sun occupies any degree from 20° to 23° 20′ or 26° 40′ to 30°, he will have much better effects during his *Dasha* and *Antardasha*, but if in 0° to 3° 20′, much of the good effects described above will be devalued and the *Dasha* and *Antardasha* will cause setbacks in health and give rise to mental worries.

Sun in Cancer

The native has a good appearance; is fond of wine; he is not capable of continuous hard work and is easily tired; he acts quickly; is engaged in the work of others; has a sharp temper and opposes his own people, particularly his father, uncle, etc.

* Two sets of views have been described for each planet in each sign. If the planet is in the special degrees as stated to be good, the maximum good effects come to pass and the evil ones are not felt or are at their minimum. Conversely, if the planet occupies the unfavourable degrees, as stated for each planet under each sign or the planet is combust, the good effects are felt at their minimum and unfavourable ones are at their maximum.

He has to maintain a large family; has many servants, but is usually worried. He is not rich and does not have a very agreeable wife. The native suffers from imbalance of bile and phlegm in the body.

If the Sun occupies any longitude between 0° and 6° 40′, his *Dasha* and *Antardasha* would be comparatively better, but if between 10° and 13° 20′, much of the good influences described above will be devalued and the evil effects delineated above will be more prominent.

Sun in Leo

The native is proud, courageous, enthusiastic, famous; at times violent in temper. If a non-vegetarian, fond of meat dishes. He has qualities of leadership; is deep and has much stamina. The native is rich and has commanding manners and generally occupies a good position in life. He is endowed with intelligence; annihilates his enemies. The native is fond of forests, mountains, cows and cattle.

The Sun shows better results if therein from 0° to 20° than in the remaining ten degrees. Much of the good influences are devalued if between 20° to 23° 20′ and the *Dasha* of the planet proves unfavourable. If however the longitude, occupied is between 0° to 3° 20′ or 13° 20′ to 16° 40′, the good effects described show very good results and the *Dasha* and the *Antardasha* are beneficial.

Sun in Virgo

The native is shy and has a feminine appearance. He is clever in writing, painting, poetry, and mathematics; has a good memory; his speech is endearing, soft and humble; he is generally intelligent and good in education. He has not much physical or mental stamina; pays homage to religious preceptors and is efficient in serving others. The native is fond of literature, songs and music.

The planet will show very good results if the longitude tenanted is between 10° and 13° 20′ or between 23° 20′ and 30°.

Sun in Libra

The planet would be debilitated here and as such weak. The soul would not be strong and matters governed by the Sun would not show very good results. From 0° to 10° is worse, than from

10° to 30° when the position is slightly improved.

If the native engages in trade pertaining to elephants or liquor, intoxicants, etc., it will bring money. He resorts to all kinds of low and underhand dealings, such as smuggling of gold, or other unfair practices for earning money. Unless other planets are strong, he does not get name and fame. He lacks in enthusiasm but talks volubly. The native may meet many frustrations in life; he travels much; his expenditure is heavy; is in the company of low people. He earns a living by dealing in base materials, such as iron; is envied by others; attached to other's wives; is not very clean; is hostile and suffers at the hands of the government.

If the Sun is exact in 10th degree, this is a strong argument for indigent circumstances and the evil influences are at their peak; but if the longitude occupied is 0° to 3° 20′, the evil influence is mitigated in some measure. If, however, the Sun tenants any degree from 20° to 23° 20′, the evil influences described for the Sun in Libra are not felt and the Sun's *Dasha* and *Antardasha* yield good results.

Sun in Scorpio

The native has success in the latter half of life. There is no achievement of ambitions in the first half, when the pace of progress is very slow. The native is very learned, but there is a streak of cruelty in him. He is courageous; does not stick to truth; may earn from poison or poisonous drugs. The native has a fiery temper; does not have much conjugal happiness. If other indications confirm, there is premature loss of his wife. The native himself is likely to be hurt by fire, weapons or poison. The native is avaricious and quarrelsome; very vindictive; strikes his opponent in a subtle and secret manner like the scorpion which stings with its tail.

If the Sun occupies any degree between 3° 20′ and 6° 40′ or 13° 20′ to 16° 40′, the *Dasha* and *Antardasha* of the Sun are much better. If the degree occupied is 10° to 13° 20′, the result of the *Sun's Dasha* or *Antardasha* is evil.

Sun in Sagittarius

The native has a broad chest, a fully developed body and much stamina. He is intelligent, devoted to gods and Brahmans. He obliges his kith and kin. He is wealthy, respected by the clans, unions of people and also by the government. The native can be clever in the use of arms and in training elephants. He may be a good physician or artisan or well up in arts and crafts. The native is very wealthy. The above good effects are felt in greater measure, if the longitude of the Sun is 0° to 3° 20′ or 13° 20′ to 16° 40′ or 26° 40′ to 30°, in which case the *Dasha* and *Antardasha* also show very good results. But if the degree tenanted is 20° to 23° 20′, much of the good effects described for the Sun in this sign are devalued and the *Dasha* or *Antardasha* also proves unfavourable.

Sun in Capricorn

The native indulges in low acts; he proves a bad tradesman; is not very learned nor rich; avaricious; wants to appropriate other people's money by unfair means; is unhappy when other people get, success and prosper.

The native is timid and has not much stamina; is fond of walking and travelling; is devoid of help and support from his relations; is of a fickle mind. His digestive powers are good; he engages in a variety of work and earns by means not very commendable.

The above unfavourable effects are greatly lessened if the longitude of the Sun is 0° to 3° 20′. If the planet is between 23° 20′ and 26° 40′ of the sign it is still better and shows markedly good results. If the longitude tenanted is 10° to 13° 20′, most of the ill effects do not manifest themselves and the results as well as the *Dasha* and *Antardasha* prove positively beneficial.

Sun in Aquarius

The native resorts to low acts; has no happiness from his sons; does not prosper and is devoid of wealth; is liable to heart troubles, particularly if Aquarius be the rising sign (ascendant). The native is not even-tempered; is a back-biter; is not very straight forward in his dealings. His friendship is fickle and he proves an unreliable friend; is not very comely. But the native has great stamina and is also voluble in irrelevant talk. The native does not feel happy.

The above effects will be worse if the Sun occupies any longitude between 0° and 3° 20, but the position is much improved if the Sun is between 13° 20′ and 16° 40′. If the Sun tenants any degree between 20° and 23° 20′, the planet's general effects are positively good. So also his *Dasha* and *Antardasha*.

Sun in Pisces

The native has good friends and is loyal to them; gains money and comforts due to love with ladies by whom the native is favoured; is intelligent; annihilates a host of enemies; is wealthy and earns name and fame. He has good sons and servants, but diseases of the private part; has brothers. The native can earn much money by dealing in aqueous products or goods across the water or anything connected with water. There is liability to scandal.

The good effects are maximum and the *Dasha* and *Antardasha* yield good results if the longitude of the Sun is 3° 20′ to 6° 40′ or between 26° 40′ to 30°. If, however, the Sun occupies any degree between 10° and 13° 20′, much of the good effects described are devalued and the planet's periods also prove unfavourable.

MOON IN THE TWELVE SIGNS

Before describing the effect of the Moon in various signs, we must emphasise that in case of the Moon, the *Pakshabala,* which is a Sanskrit word, is very important and this must first be explained.

Pakshabala. A month is divided into two fortnights—the bright half of the month, when the Moon is waxing, and the dark half of the month when the Moon is waning.

(i) The Moon is considered strong when he is 90° or more away from the Sun on either side.

He is considered weak if the distance of Moon from the Sun, on either side, is less than 90°.

A waxing Moon is considered auspicious and strong. A waning Moon is weak, malefic and inauspicious.

Other writers divide the influence into three categories as counted from the Sun.

(1) If the Moon is beyond 120° on either side of the Sun, he is ordinarily good.

(2) If the Moon is from 120° to 180°, he is very good and strong.

(3) If the Moon is within 0° to 60° on either side of the Sun; he is weak.

Moon in Association with Other Planets

There is a certain element of give and take when two planets combine in a sign or aspect each other. It is common experience that if two vessels one containing hot water and the other cold are placed in close contact, the hot water does not remain so hot and the cold water not so cold. When two chemicals are mixed, at times a new chemical is formed. So it is with planetary influences.

But of all the planets, the Moon and the Mercury are most receptive and the Moon very easily absorbs the qualities of other planets and so the results described below may be modified favourably or adversely according as this planet is associated with or aspected by benefics or malefics. This principle applies to all the planets, but as stated above, applies to the Moon in greater measure.

High and Low Tide

When the Moon occupies any degree between the ascendant and the cusp of the fourth house or between the cups of the seventh and the tenth, there is low tide; but when the Moon is located between the cusps of the fourth and the seventh, or between the cusps of the tenth and the ascendant, there is high tide. The Moon at high tide is strong. The Moon at low tide is weak.

Moon in Aries

Good complexion, wealthy, devoid of happiness from brothers, courageous, voluptuous, weak knees, bad nails, hair not good, several children, round eyes, loving, afraid of water, veins prominent, marks of wounds or boils on the body; under the influence of his wife.

If the longitude of the Moon is between 0° to 6° 40′ or 10° to 13° 20′, he shows good results and if the *Pakshabala** is also good, he will show better results and his *Dasha* and *Antardasha* will show good effect. If the longitude tenanted is 23° 20′ to

* *Pakshabala* is the over-riding factor to determine the strength of the Moon.

26° 40′, much of the good results will be devalued; the native will be timid and the *Dasha* and *Antardasha* will also be unfavourable if the *Pakshabala* is also weak.

Moon in Taurus

Broad chest, generous in giving, plenty of curly hair, voluptuous, famous, adorable looks, enjoys well, has more daughters than sons; eyes like those of a bull; gait like that of a goose, is happy during the middle one-third and last one-third of life; the waist, feet, shoulders, knees and face are broad with a thick neck; some mark on one side of the body; has the quality of forbearance.

Obviously it is better to have the Moon from 0° to 3° than in the rest of the sign. If however the Moon is between 13° 20′ to 16° 40′ or 20° to 23° 20′, then also the planet shows excellent results.

Moon in Gemini

Broad limbs; prominent nose; dark eyes (obviously this would not apply to people of the West), well up in amorous arts, poetic, enjoys luxuries; attractive looks, adorable, with humorous speech, intelligent; prominent veins on the body; over-sexed; under the influence of his wife; is brought up by a lady other than his mother or may have two mothers, has friends among impotent or imbecile persons.

Many of the good qualities described above are devalued if the degree tenanted is 3° 20′ to 6° 40′; but the *Dasha* or *Antardasha* proves good if the Moon is from 23° 20′ to 30°

Moon in Cancer

Prosperous; comfortable house; fond of walking and travelling; having a love for astrology; amorous; grateful; minister of a king, lives at a place other than his native home-land; too much imagination running riot, thick neck, fond of good dwelling places and tanks, rivers, sea-side and flowers. There is a cycle of waxing and waning in his career.

The Moon would show particularly good results if between 0° to 3°, 20′. If between 13° 20′ and 16° 40′, the good effects are at their minimum; the native will be timid and the *Dasha* or *Antardasha* does not prove so effective.

Moon in Leo

Broad chest; thick bones; very light and scanty hair on the body; large face and throat, eyes with yellowish tinge and not very large; does not get on well with women, if a non-vegetarian, is fond of meat; suffers from hunger, thirst, stomach troubles and pain in the teeth; generous in giving; sharp tempered; has a few sons; fond of towns and forests; under the influence of his mother; has a dignified look; is courageous; engages in varied work.

If the Moon occupies 10° to 16° 40′, it shows better results; but if the longitude tenanted is 23° 20′ to 26° 40′, much of the good results described above are devalued. The *Dasha* and *Antardasha* show the same difference in quality.

Moon in Virgo

Flirtatious, long arms; soft and adorable body and face; good eyes, ears and teeth; learned; sweet speech; sticks to truth and purity; persevering; engaged in other people's work; forbearing; prosperous; compassionate; has more daughters than sons.

It is better to have the Moon between 13° 20′ to 16° 40′ or between 20° to 23° 20′ or between 26° 40′ to 30° when better results are obtained.

Moon in Libra

Broad chest; prominent nose; lean body and face; attached to more than one woman; benefit from cattle and land; very wealthy; valorous; active in work; devoted to gods and Brahmans; sticks to purity; generous in giving; does good to relations.

The results are better if the longitude tenanted by Moon is 0° to 3° 20′ or 23° 20′ to 26° 40′; so judge the *Dasha* and *Antardasha* on similar basis. If between 3° 20′ and 6° 40′, good effects are devalued, particularly if the *Pakshabala** is lacking.

Moon in Scorpio

Avaricious; round thighs and calves; hard body; small chin and nails; beautiful eyes; prominent veins; big belly; does not have much faith in religion; inclined to acts of cruelty; thievish disposition; engaged in work; clever and capable; probable liaisons with wives of others; proud or intoxicated; over-bearing;

* Never ignore *Pakshabala*, when judging Moon.

prosperous; devoid of relations or not on good terms with them; suffers financial penalty at the hands of the Government.

It is better to have Moon from 0° to 3° 20′ when good effects are augmented and unfavourable owners mitigated. If the longitude tenanted is 13° 20′ to 16° 40′, then also the position is improved. Keep this also in mind when judging the *Dasha* and *Antardasha.*

Moon in Sagittarius

Bent body; round eyes; broad chest and waist; long arms; high shoulders; large neck, strong body; prominent throat and nose; well built body; courageous; grateful; eloquent in speech; well up in artisan's work; likes to stay near sea-coast, river or water; affectionate with relations.

The Moon shows much better results if the longitude occupied is 3° 20′ to 6° 40′ or 10° to 13° 20′ or 26° 40′ to 30°. Much of the good effects are devalued if the Moon is between 23° 20′ and 26° 40′, so judge the *Dasha* and *Antardasha.*

Moon in Capricorn

Prominent veins; tallish; lean body; good eyes; round calves; large neck; prominent ears; poetic; connoisseur of singing; afraid of cold; cool tempered; religious; sticks to truth; famous; cruel hearted; shameless; probable liaison with an elder's wife (look to other indications as well); not very enthusiastic.

The Moon would show comparatively better results if occuping any degree between 0° to 3° 20′ or 13° 20′ to 16° 40′ or 20° to 23° 20′. Judge the *Dasha* and *Antardasha accordingly.*

Moon in Aquarius

Prominent nose; dry skin; large hands and feet; large head; large face and waist; poor eyes; fond of and clever in artisanship; ill-tempered; inclined to drink; devoid of religion; may produce sons by wives of others; incurs enmity with good people; wicked; indolent; suffers from sorrows and is poor.

It is better to have the Moon between 13° 20′ and 16° 40′ or 23° 20′ to 26° 40′ when the evil would in some measure be mitigated and the *Dasha* and *Antardasha* would also show comparatively better results. But if the longitude tenanted is 3° 20′ to 6° 40′, the Moon will be weaker and as such, more adverse.

Moon in Pisces

Handsome body; large head; gets authority if engaged in works of arts, artisanship or crafts; inclined to get into a temper though generally good tempered; learned; connoisseur of singing; has a religious bent of mind; attached to many young women; under the influence of his wife; serves the Government; leads a comfortable life; happy; may get sudden or buried wealth or treasure or inherits; inclined to travel by water; interested in countries and products beyond the seas; generous in giving.

The Moon between 0° and 3° 20′ or 26° 40′ to 30° will be stronger for the good and show better results radically as well as during his periods. If the planet occupies a degree between 13° 20′ and 16° 40′, much of the good effects described above will be devalued.

MARS IN THE TWELVE SIGNS

Mars in Aries

Liable to hurt in the body or wounds; courageous; having much stamina; fond of battle; truthful; fond of walking or travelling; strongly sexed; having thievish tendencies; generous in giving; respected by the king, government; leader of a section of the army or head of an institution; wealthy; owner of cattle; if engaged in trade, success therein. This is an excellent position by sign endowing the native with heroic spirit and fine martial qualities.

Even in Aries it is better if the planet is between 0° to 10° Mars would be particularly strong if occupying any degree between 0° to 3° 20′ or 23° 20′ to 26° 40′ where he shows excellent results. Despite being in Aries, if he occupies a degree between 10° and 13° 20′, many of the fine qualities would become grosser, e.g., instead of being a hero, the native may be quarrelsome.

Mars in Taurus

Fond of songs and music; is not self-confident; apprehensive; does not have a stable position in life; well-dressed; well-groomed; cruel; talkative; speaks harshly; does not have several sons; not wealthy; envied by many. The native is under the influence of women; attached to the wives of others; antagonistic to friends;

sinful and cunning; maintains a large family, but creates split in the family.

If Mars occupies 0° to 3° 20′ the native will have minimum of bad qualities and maximum of good ones. So also tenancy of any degree between 10° and 16° 40′ is good. But if the planet is any where between 20° and 23° 20′, the disqualifications are more marked and the good qualities at the lowest ebb. Judge the *Dasha* and *Antardasha* accordingly.*

Mars in Gemini

Attractive appearance; has much bodily vigour and strength; can put up with severe strain, has several sons; without friends; grateful; clever in poetry, dancing, singing and music or is a connoisseur of these and artisanship requiring mechanical dexterity; fearless; miserly; wealthy; fond of travelling abroad. The native engages in a variety of work; obliges sons and friends. Such a native can be clever in military strategy as well.

The planet is stronger for the good if occupying a degree between 3° 20′ and 6° 40′ or 10° to 13° 20′ or 20° to 23° 20′ or 26° 40′ to 30° and shows much better results in his *Dasha* and *Antardasha*.

Mars in Cancer

Intelligent; restless and worried due to some chronic ailment. The native is soft and can be prevailed upon; wicked; gain from agriculture; inclined to live in others' houses.

Grateful; without friends and wealth; earns through boats and ships or goods transported by them; may get a government scholarship in boyhood or be supported by some one other than his family. There is a cycle of wealth and lack of luck; good health and ailments alternate.

Evil influences would be mitigated in great measure and good ones augmented if the longitude occupied is between 0° and 3° 20′ or 13° 20′ and 16° 40′ or 20° to 23° 20′. On this basis judge the *Dasha* and *Antardasha* also.

* At places, it has not been stated that *Dasha* and *Antardasha* should be judged accordingly. But where location between certain degrees has been stated to be good or evil, it has to be taken into consideration in delineating the *Dasha* or *Antardasha* effects.

Mars in Leo

Strong body; fearless; has great stamina; overbearing and intolerable of others; fond of roaming in forests and of hunting; capable of putting up with hard labour; devoid of wealth; little happiness from wife (or premature death of wife); has only a few sons, inclined to appropriate other people's wealth; affectionate to sons of others; persevering in work.

If Mars is between 0° to 3° 20′ or 13° 20′ to 16° 40′ or 23° 20′ to 26° 40′, the good effects are increased and the evil ones mitigated, but if between 10° to 13° 20′, the reverse is the case.

Mars in Virgo

Not courageous; learned; fears opponents; respected by gentlemen; very wealthy; fond of sex and singing; speaks softly and pleasingly; incurs heavy expenditure; clever in artisanship; religious; fond of baths and fragrant applications; wealthy and with many sons.

It is better to have Mars between 0° to 3° 20′ or 10° to 13° 20′ or 26° 40′ to 30° where he is strong and the influence is improved for the good; but if between 20° and 23° 20′, the good influences are devalued in some measure and evil ones augmented.

Mars in Libra

Good appearance; talkative; timid, cunning; harsh; antagonistic to friends; liaisons with women; liking for drink; wastes money over wine and women and is under their influence; defective in some limb; fond of fight; likelihood of premature death of first wife (look to other indications also in the nativity and also wife's horoscope).

If the planet occupies 0° to 6° 40′ or 10° to 13° 20′ or 20° to 23° 20′ good effects predominate and the evil ones are at their minimum.

Mars in Scorpio

Marks of wounds or those caused by fire on the body; the native is the head of some department or institution or a businessman with a flourishing trade of his own; rich; respected by the government; may suffer from poison (like food poisoning); clever; fond of giving a fight; vindictive; indulges in sinful acts; intent on harming his opponents; may gain money by underhand means.

If the planet occupies 0° to 3° 20′ the good effects are devalued greatly, but if the planet is between any of the following degrees, more good effects are felt and the evil ones show the least results: 13° to 16° 40 or 20° to 23° 20′.

Mars in Sagittarius

Harsh speech; dependence on others; may bear marks of wounds on the body; evil intentions; fearless; a good fighter; has many enemies; occupies a high position in government or large institutions; famous; a few sons; wealth and happiness lessened due to the native's uncontrolled temper; attains happiness and comfort only after hard labour.

The best degrees for the planet to occupy are 0° to 3° 20′ or 23° 20′ to 30°, when the good effects will be predominant. If the planet tenants any degree between 10° to 13° 20′, the good effect will be at the minimum and the unfavourable ones will be stronger.

Mars in Capricorn

Plenty of wealth; several sons; a king* or equal to a king; healthy; wise; famous; head of a section of an army or a department or institution; independent; victorious in undertakings; patronises his relations; courteous; has much paraphernalia.

Very good results are felt if the planet occupies any degree

* When these texts were written there were thousands of rajas (kings) in India. Some of them had only a hundred acres of land or an income of one thousand rupees per month, which is now the income of a labourer in the U.S.A. Millions of people are born when Mars is in Capricorn and surely now millions cannot become kings or equal to kings. But these are the actual expressions used by Varaha Mihir. While aware of the poetic way of expression, we have made an effort to give a gist of the ancient texts throughout this book so that readers can get a taste of the actual ancient recipe and not the modern cooked up version. We want the readers who do not know Sanskrit to have an insight into the original.

Nor have we hesitated to call a spade a spade. Many writers convey the same meaning in sophisticated terms. If the texts say poor, say poor, and not describe this saying 'not wealthy' so, also, if the texts describe as 'attached to many women and having liaisons with them' why say 'fond of female company'? To interpret these texts against the background of a native and to edit the views has been left to the reader himself. One sparrow does not make a spring nor is one influence a deciding factor. All the influences latent and patent have to be synthesised to arrive at the true results.

between 10° to 13° 20′, and most excellent results if the planet occupies 0° to 3° 20′. But good results are at their minimum if the degree occupied is 20° to 23° 20′.

Mars in Aquarius

Rough hair on body; not pleasing in appearance; cruel; not wealthy; afflicted with sorrows; wanders aimlessly; untruthful; earns livelihood with difficulty; may lose money by gambling in races or speculation or due to the native's own malice and dishonesty; devoid of respect for and courtesy towards others; envious; fond of drinking.

The evil effects will be mitigated in some measure if the degree occupied is 3° 20′ to 6° 40′ or 10° to 16° 40′ or 20° to 23° 20′.

Mars in Pisces

Fearless; has many enemies; occupies a good position in life; well-known; suffers deep sorrows; ailments of the body; crooked in views; sharp tempered; insults seniors and Brahmans; has a few sons who are not intelligent or do not progress well in life; suffers loss of wealth due to his own deceitful conduct; lives at a place other than his homeland.

The worst side of the effects will be felt if the planet occupies any degree from 0° to 3° 20′. If the planet tenants any degree from 13° 20′ to 16° 40′ or 20° to 23° 20′ or 26° 40′ to 30°, the evil effects will be mitigated considerably.

MERCURY IN THE TWELVE SIGNS

Mercury in Aries

Lean body; fond of gambling, food and drinks; also of music and dance; thievish tendencies; has not much faith in gods; cunning; given to untruth; does not have a good wife; diplomatic; of a quarrelling disposition; well up in cartography, drawing or painting; labours hard but loses wealth; devoid of wealth; may incur debts; may have to live in confinement.

If the planet tenants any of the following degrees much of the evil influence described above is mitigated:* 0° to 3° 20′; 6° 40′ to 10°; 16° 40′ to 20°

* The Planets for which good effects have been described show good effects during their *Mahadashas* or *Antardashas* and vice versa. But the

Mercury in Taurus

Respects teachers or his religious preceptors, father, etc.; several sons; plenty of money; good conjugal happiness; generous in giving; clever; famous; learned; of fixed determination; jocular; fond of physical exercises, dress, ornaments and flowers; talks endearingly; accepts advice.

The best effects are shown if the planet occupies any degree between 13° 20′ to 20° or 26° 40′ to 30°. Least good effects come to pass if the degree occupied is 6° 40′ to 10°

Mercury in Gemini

Very eloquent and good at narration; at times argumentative; learned and clever in the fine arts; speaks sweetly; humorous; dresses well; independent; wealthy; generous; actively engaged in work; leads a happy and comfortable life; may have two wives or twin sons.

The best degrees for Mercury to occupy are 26° 40′ to 30° when the qualities will show at their best. If the degrees tenanted are 16° 40′ to 20° a great deal of the good effects will be devalued.

Mercury in Cancer

Intelligent, very active and talkative; lives at a place other than his homeland; fond of women and songs; loss of money due to enmity with wife or other women; not good tempered; engaged in various works; antagonistic to his own people; gain from water and also products of water or connected with water or goods across the seas; famous due to his family.

The best degrees for the planet to occupy are 0° to 3° 20′ or 6° 40′ to 10°, where he will show the maximum good effects. If the planet occupies a degree between 26° 40′ to 30°, he will be less good and show more unfavourable trends.

Mercury in Leo

A wanderer; not truthful; devoid of wisdom and dexterity in the fine arts; does not have a good memory; devoid of good actions;

sign position is only one factor. A *Dasha* or *Antardasha* shows its effects according to the position of the planet in the sign, house, lordship of the house, aspect of or conjunction with the planet. The same principles apply to Sun, Moon and all other planets.

an unfavourable factor for longevity of brother (or the native may be antagonistic to his brothers and family); an adverse factor for issues; does not have a good wife or happiness through her; desirous of female company; independent, famous and if Mercury is strong and well aspected then wealthy, otherwise poor.

The best degrees for Mercury to occupy are 6° 40′ to 10°, and 13° 20′ to 20° when most of the unfavourable features will not be felt or very feebly felt.

Mercury in Virgo

Religious; of a forgiving nature; endowed with many good qualities; happy; clever; well mannered; sweet in speech; eloquent; good logical or argumentative abilities; fearless in debates; a literary critic; proficient in the sciences, arts and crafts; earns the respect of friends; occupies a senior position; sexual vigour less than normal.

Even in this sign, Mercury will show better effects if occupying any degree between 16° 40′ and 20° and the best result if between 26° 40′ to 30°. The poorest effects will be shown if between 6° 40′ to 10°.

Mercury in Libra

Generous; clever in speech; devoted to God; respectful to seniors; hospitable as a host; displays much pretended love for friends; spends discriminately on projects for gain of wealth; inclined to have businesses at various places in different directions; intent upon earning money; attached to wife and sons.

In this sign, Mercury will show least good effects if tenanting any degree from 16° 40′ to 20°; the maximum favourable results will occur if occupying 0° to 3° 20′ or 26° 40′ to 30°.

Mercury in Scorpio

Not truthful; not wise; avaricious; having thievish tendencies; without wealth; indebted; materialistic in outlook; not much faith in God; fond of good food, drinks and betting. He does not have a good wife or is attached to an unworthy woman. Generally his friends are of a lower rank. The native is harsh in dealing with others and may indulge in unfair practices. The financial returns are not in proportion to the labour and effort put in. He does not win approbation of good people.

In this sign, the worst effects will be felt if the degrees occupied by the planet are 26° 40′ to 30°. But if the degree occupied is 6° 40′ to 10° or 13° 20′ to 16° 40′ the least evil results will be experienced.

Mercury in Sagittarius

Very intelligent; well informed; famous; endowed with many good qualities; generous; courteous and courageous; clever in speech; may occupy an emiment position; may become a royal priest or a minister; well versed in writing and penmanship. The native is liked by the king or government. He may devote his time to religious affairs or teaching.

Very good results will be felt if the degree tenanted is 6° 40′ to 10° or 16° 40′ to 20° or 26° 40′ to 30° and the least good effects will result if the degree tenanted is 23° 20′ to 26° 40′.

Mercury in Capricorn

Poor; indebted; not intelligent; not endowed with outstanding qualities; serves others; good in crafts; does not dress well; has to put in much physical labour; various difficulties oppress him; he may not stick to truth; be a back biter; may be separated from Bandhus (relations); is always apprehensive; his mind feels cramped; may have dreams of pleasure and enjoyment.

The worst effects will be felt if the degree occupied is 6° 40′ to 10° and the evil effects will be at their minimum if the degree occupied is 0° to 3° 20′ or 16° 40′ to 20° or 26° 40′ to 30°

Mercury in Aquarius

Not fortunate; career of employment; his duties involve a heavy load of work; not clean; may acquire some wealth by means not above-board, but incurs debts; not very eloquent or intelligent but proficient in inferior artsmanship; very timid; has little enjoyment in life; oppressed by enemies; does not have a congenial wife.

The worst effects will be felt if the degree tenanted is between 3° 20′ to 6° 40′ or 16° 40′ to 20° and the least unfavourable results will be experienced if the degree tenanted is between 13° 20′ to 16° 40′ or 26° 40′ to 30°.

Mercury in Pisces

Excels his colleagues in rendering service to his master; not very learned in the arts or literature; clever in menial artsmanship; good deeds liked by gentry; not firm in matters religious; poor; not happy in respect of children (at least for some time); has a good wife.

The least good effects will be felt if the degree occupied is between 13° 20′ to 16° 40′, but the good results described will be felt if the planet tenants any degree from 6° 40′ to 10° or 26° 40′ to 30°.

JUPITER IN THE TWELVE SIGNS

Jupiter in Aries

Head of an army or section of an army; blessed with wife and several sons; generous; has good servants; forgiving; overcomes others with his valour; endowed with many qualities; heavy expenditure; many enemies; his body may bear scars of wounds—in other words, he may be a hero of many battle—literally or figuratively speaking. The native has much stamina and is daring in deeds which bring him name and fame. If not in the army, he may command a dominating position in an institution. He would be a strict disciplinarian.

The good effects will be felt at their maximum if the degree occupied is between 0° to 3° 20′ or 10° to 13° 20′ or 26° 40′ to 30°.

Jupiter in Taurus

Stout and large body; handsome; intelligent and wise; good health; sweet speech; happy; wealthy; dresses well; is courteous and popular; diplomatic; endowed with a sacrificing spirit; has good sons; attached to his own wife; owns cattle; gains from agriculture; has valuable possessions. The native is diplomatic; pays homage to gods, Brahmans and cows.

Poorest effects will be felt if the planet occupies 0° to 3° 20′. The good effects described will be at their maximum if the degree tenanted is between 6° 40′ to 10° or 13° 20′ to 16° 40′ or 20° to 23° 20′.

Jupiter in Gemini

Learned; very intelligent; good memory; a poet; clever in arts and sciences; religious; respected by seniors as well as relations; happy; has sons and friends; gets good food and good clothes and has the necessities for comfortable living; keeps part of his money in deposit; has many auspicious celebrations in the family; may become a minister or counsellor or adviser. The native is very active and diligently engages in work.

In this sign, Jupiter will be at his best if occupying any degree between 6° 40′ to 10° or 16° 40′ to 20° or 26° 40′ to 30°, but the least good will ensue if between 10° to 13° 20′.

Jupiter in Cancer

Handsome, wise and learned; sweet temperament; religious; strong; very wealthy; possesses precious jewellery; has a good wife and good sons; well endowed with the comforts of life. The native obliges a host of good people and is noted for truth and righteous conduct and earns a good name and fame for his magnificent deeds.

In this sign, the planet will show the maximum good effects if occupying any degree between 0° to 3° 20′ or 16° 40′ to 20° or 26° 40′ to 30°, and the worst effects if tenanting any degree between 20° to 23° 20′.

Jupiter in Leo

Good personality; strong and compact body; intelligent; learned; virtuous; having good qualities of head and heart; famous; devoted to gods; happiness from wife and sons; noted for good acts; head of an army or section of an army or institution. The native has much stamina and the enmities incurred last long. He is a loving friend. Fond of forts, forests and mountainous regions.

The planet will show maximum good results if occupying any degree between 10° and 16° 40′ or 26° 40′ to 30°.

Jupiter in Virgo

Good memory; of fixed determination; courteous; inclined to virtues; religious; generous; clever in execution of work; fond of scents and flowers, has all the comforts of life; has good sons and friends; gains money by his erudition, arts and crafts or work connected with them. The native may rise to a high position in life, such as that of a minister or counsellor.

The planet will show the least good effects if tenanting a degree from 0° to 3° 20′. If, however, occupying a degree between 6° 40′ to 10° or 20° to 23° 20′ or 26° 40′ to 30° he will show maximum good effects.

Jupiter in Libra

Good memory; good actions; pleasing personality; engaged in pursuit of learning; fond of good clothes; comfortable living; very wealthy; happy; liked by others; has several good sons and good friends. The native himself is a friend of businessmen, lives at a place other than his homeland; may gain money connected with jugglery, dance, etc. (in the present context, theatres, films, etc.). The native attains a high position in life. He is religious, and devoted to gods; is a hospitable host.

The planet will be at its best if occupying a degree between 0° and 3° 20′ or 6° 40′ to 10° or 16° 40′ to 20° and will show the least good effect if between 10° and 13° 20′.

Jupiter in Scorpio

Strong and overpowering personality; of a forgiving temperament; generous; happiness from wife, but the native may not have many sons. He helps in the construction of a temple or charitable or benevolent institution, but there is an element of show or pretensions in matters religious. The moral conduct may not be of high order. He occupies a respectable position but has to labour hard and has also some chronic ailment. If following the literary line, he would be a scholar and an author, clever but with a streak of vindictiveness.

The best degrees to occupy in the sign are 0° to 3° 20′ or 13° 20′ to 20° or 26° 40′ to 30°, when the good qualities will show their best effects and the evil trails their least. But if the degree occupied is 20° to 23° 20′, the reverse will be the case.

Jupiter in Sagittarius

Very intelligent; learned; wealthy; has good friends; generous; obliges others; will live at many places other than his homeland; visits holy places; will have good houses; occupies a high position such as a chieftain or a minister of a king.

May be a professor or religious preceptor. In short, very good results have been described for this and therefore the texts have not dilated upon the many happy effects that will be experienced.

The best degrees for the planet to occupy will be 10° to 13° 20′ or 26° 40′ to 30°, where the maximum good effects would result.

Jupiter in Capricorn

A weak body; not intelligent. The native would have little money and little happiness; not much stamina or virility; will have to put in much hard labour for low financial returns; he has to run errands for others. He has several low traits of character; will have little sense of cleanliness, or love for his people, or compassion and his religious conduct will be at its lowest ebb; he lives at places other than his native one and is timid and melancholy.

If occupying any degree between 0° to 3° 20′ or 6° 40′ to 10° or 20° to 23° 20′, the effects will not be so bad.

Jupiter in Aquarius

One ancient text states that Jupiter in Aquarius will show the same results as in Cancer, but according to another, the native is hard hearted, a back-biter, avaricious, not of noble temperament, puts in much unproductive labour in works connected with water or artisanship. He is not intelligent, suffers from a chronic ailment and destroys his wealth or lessens his income by his speech. He prefers the company of low people but becomes the head of his group. He may have liaison with a female related to the native.

If Jupiter occupies any degree between 13° 20′ to 20°, the position would be improved, but if he tenants a degree from 10° to 13° 20′, the effects described will be at their worst.

Jupiter in Pisces

The native is learned and is not vain; he is respected by his friends; he cannot be overpowered by others; is of a fixed determination in the execution of work; he has much quiet stamina; earns praise, name and fame for his work and conduct. He is very wealthy or the minister of a king or the head of a section of the army. In other words, he occupies a good position in life and is well off. The native is good in dealing with others and or with matters of educational and military strategy.

If the planet occupies any degree between 0° to 3° 20′ or 16° 40′ to 20° or 26° 40′ to 30°, the good effects will be at their maximum, but if the degree tenanted is 20° to 23° 20′, the reverse will be the case.

VENUS IN THE TWELVE SIGNS

Venus in Aries

Having many vices or bad qualities; liaisons with other's wife; fond of prostitutes, forests and mountains; may be confined due to a woman; not large hearted; cruel at heart; voluble in speech but not reliable; quarrels or enters into litigations on account of attachment to a woman and loses wealth as a result thereof; brings discredit to one's family. The native has a thievish mental aptitude but occupies a good position in life all the same; in old age may become night blind.

If the planet occupies any degree between 0° and 6° 40′ or 20° to 23° 20′, the evil influence will be mitigated in some measure. The reverse will be the case if occupying a degree between 16° 40′ to 20°.

Venus in Taurus

Comely appearance; strong; has the company of a large number of women; gains from agriculture; fond of good clothes, scents and flowers; gains from cows; fearless; generous; helps and maintains his relations; wealthy; learned; noted for his many virtues; famous; obliges good people; respected by the king or government and his own group of people, whom he heads.

The planet shows better results if tenanting any degree between 6° 40′ to 10° or 13° 20′ to 16° 40′ and not such good results if between 26° 40′ and 30°.

Venus in Gemini

Handsome; over-sexed; loved by others; a gentleman; fond of music and dance; well up in the arts and sciences; clever at writing and painting; sincerely affectionate; wealthy; engages in government work; devoted to gods and Brahmans.

The planet shows very good effects if between 0° to 3° 20′ or 16° 40′ to 20° or 23° 20′ to 30°,

Venus in Cancer

Good looking, strong; amorous; may have two wives; tactful; intelligent; a chief person in his group; having all the desirable necessities for comfort; religiously inclined; suffers from chronic ailments caused by excessive indulgence with women and drinks; is at a disadvantage on account of some blemish in the family. The native is soft and does not have much stamina or powers of resistance; is timid and inclined to seek favours or money from others; takes sorrows deeply to heart.

If the planet tenants any degrees between 0° to 3° 20′ or 10° to 13° 20′ or 26° 40′ to 30°, the results will be good, if it occupies a degree between 6° 40′ and 10°, the good effects are at their lowest.

Venus in Leo

Not much stamina; fond of Bandhus (relations); has unusual happiness; also sorrows; does good to and obliges others; liked by his religious preceptors and Brahmans; not much worried; adores ladies and derives pleasure, happiness and money from them; married in a high family; has a few sons.

The planet shows good effects if occupying any degree between 3° 20′ to 6° 40′ or 13° 20′ to 16° 40′ or 20° to 23° 20′, but if it occupies degrees between 16° 40′ and 20°, the good effects will be at their lowest ebb.

Venus in Virgo

Poor, humble, low acts, not wise, soft, clever, serves others; connoisseur of the arts; speaks sweetly like a damsel; longs for love affairs, loves wicked women; does not have much happiness or luxuries; is taken as a scholar in religious congresses at holy places.

In this sign the best degrees to tenant are 6° 40′ to 10° or 13° 20′ to 16° 40′ or 26° 40′ to 30° when the evil effects will be mitigated and the good ones augmented.

Venus in Libra

Handsome, courageous, learned, strong and fearless; clever in defending and protecting his interests; active in work even in difficult ones; very wealthy; fond of flowers and clothes; gets a good name due to devotion to gods and Brahmans; inclined to live at a place other than his native land; earns money by hard labour. The native is well liked in society and the state and becomes famous.

In this sign, the planet will produce better results if tenanting any degree between 0° to 3° 20′ or 16° 40′ to 20° or 23° 20′ to 26° 40′.

Venus in Scorpio

Very cruel and envious; irreligious; very talkative and wicked; devoid of brothers; attains good position; enmity with a woman of loose character; clever in damaging the names of others; indebted; poor; not good tempered; suffers from disease of the private part or from some hidden disease. Such a native succeeds in defeating his opponent. He may, by favouring a lady, oppose or enter into litigation with another party and thereby damage his own prosperity. The cumulative effect of this is that the native brings discredit to his own family.

If the planet occupies any degree between 10° to 16° 40′ or 26° 40′ to 30°, many of the evil effects described above will be at their minimum, but if the degree tenanted is 6° 40′ to 10°, the native will be poor, but his temperament will be better and he will feel the worst effects described for the planet in the sign.

Venus in Sagittarius

Tall; well developed body; handsome; loved by all; learned; very clever; fond of dressing up; earns wealth and has the necessities for comfort due to righteous and good actions; rises to an eminent position, such as, that of a minister; possesses cows; very wealthy; is respected by people and society.

If the planet occupies any degree between 3° 20′ to 6° 40′ or 20° to 23° 20′ or 26° 40′ to 30°, the good effects described above will be at their maximum, but if the degree occupied is any degree from 0° to 3° 20′ or 16° 40′ to 20° or 23° 20′ to 26° 40′, much of the good effects due to the position of the planet in the sign will be devalued.

Venus in Capricorn

Weak body, but good looking; may suffer from heart disease; not wise; always apprehensive; very sorrowful; avaricious; cunning in deceiving others by speaking lies for gain of money;

industrious but not sexually virile; his efforts end in frustration; sweats for others. The native is attached to an unworthy or elderly female; he is under considerable influence of his wife or other women.

If the planet occupies any degree from 0° to 3° 20′ or 6° 40′ to 10° or 13° 20′ to 16° 40′, the evil effects described above will be appreciably reduced, but if the planet tenants any degree between 10° to 13° 20′ or 26° 40′ to 30°, the worst effects will come into force.

Venus in Aquarius

Good appearance; antagonistic to his sons and seniors (father, etc.); agitated in mind; uneasy due to ailments; persistently engages in work which does not yield the desired results; attached to another woman; irreligious; unclean; does not like baths; does not care for a well-groomed appearance; attached to an unworthy woman; under considerable influence of his wife or other women.

If the planet occupies any degree from 0° to 3° 20′ or 13° 20′ to 20° or 23° 20′ to 26° 40′, the evil effects will be mitigated in some measure, but if the planet occupies any of the following degrees, the worst side of the influence will be experienced: 3° 20′ to 6° 40′ or 10° to 13° 20′ or 20° to 23° 20′.

Venus in Pisces

Eloquent and very wise; sweet in speech; generous; clever; endowed with many good qualities; very famous; engages in big projects; very wealthy, defeats his opponents; a favourite of the king; occupies an eminent position; gains money from and the respect of good folk.

The planet will show very good results if occupying any degree from 10° to 13° 20′ or 26° 40′ to 30°, but much of the good effects described will be devalued, if the degree tenanted is 6° 40′ to 10° or 13° 20′ to 16° 40′.

SATURN IN THE TWELVE SIGNS

Saturn in Aries

Cruel, sharp tempered, not wise but garrulous; fiery; uses harsh language; impudent, envious, deceitful; poor and ill-dressed; has to labour hard; inclined to damage the interests of his relations;

fond of quarrelling. The native does not perform good acts but rather commits sinful acts, gets blamed for them and is condemned by others. He has no friends; wanders aimlessly.

The planet will shed much of his evil qualities if occupying any degree between 0° to 3° 20′ or 26° 40′ to 30°. If tenanting any degree between 20° to 23° 20′, he may actually show good results; the latent evil traits will be sublimed. But if tenanting any degree between 23° 20′ to 26° 40′, he will evince the maximum evil traits.

Saturn in Taurus

Devoid of wealth; unrighteous conduct; his arguments are not logical; has bad friends; follows a career of service; constantly attached to women; a favourite of undesirable or elderly women and runs errands for them. He is not wise; is insulted; engaged in a variety of work.

If the planet occupies any degree between 0° to 6° 40′ or 13° 20′ to 16° 40′, the evil qualities will be much less pronounced. But if the plânet tenants a degree between 10° and 13° 20′ the worst effects will be felt.

Saturn in Gemini

Industrious; secretive; wicked; cruel; not good tempered; a hypocrite; not benevolently inclined; very active; may become accused in a criminal case; voluptuous; deceives others. The native at times receives insulting treatment; harbours ill feelings; fond of outdoor sports. He exceeds his sphere of work and may incur debts; occupies a good position with a large staff under him; not much happiness from sons.

The planet shows good results if occupying any degree from 0° to 3° 20′ or 10° to 16° 40′ or 26° 40′ to 30°; the reverse is the case if the degree occupied is 3° 20′ to 6° 40′ or 20° to 23° 20.′

Saturn in Cancer

Good looking, but space in between teeth; poor; suffers sickness in childhood; intelligent; very soft; associates with important people; always restless; opposed to his relations; attains a good position in life; not good tempered, loses mother early in life; not much happiness from sons; impedes progress of others; enjoy luxuries at the cost of others. The middle part of life is better than the first one-third or the last one-third.

The planet shows comparatively better results if occupying the following degrees: 0° to 3° 20′ or 10° to 13° 20′ or 20° to 26° 40.′ Mostly evil results are felt if the degree occupied is 13° 20′ to 16° 40′.

Saturn in Leo

Not noble; condemned for evil actions; not good tempered; without happiness; without relations (or not on loving terms with them); clever in reading and writing; (without wife or lacking in conjugal happiness); earns by service; given to a career of low acts; full of latent anger; dispersed body due to putting in hard labour; sons a source of trouble to the native.

The worst degrees for the planet to occupy in the sign are those between 0° to 3° 20′ and 23° 20′ to 26° 40′, when the evil results felt will be at their maximum. But if the planet tenants any degree from 13° 20′ to 16° 40′ or 20° to 23° 20′, most of the evil traits will not be felt or felt very feebly.

Saturn in Virgo

Very wicked; little hair on chin and cheeks; not wealthy; inclined to enjoy the hospitality of others; without shame; liaisons; not clever as an artisan; does not engage in productive work. The native is far-sighted and obliges others by doing good to them; little happiness from sons; heads an institution with a large staff, such as a police officer or works in the defence department.

The best degrees for the planet to occupy are 0° to 6° 40′ or 26° 40′ to 30°, where the good effects are predominant. If the planet occupies 10° to 13° 20′, mostly evil results will be experienced.

Saturn in Libra

Endearing speech; intelligent; occupies a senior position among groups of people and respected in the village or town he resides in; very rich—equal to a king; earns money and respect by touring or contacts with foreign countries; can bank upon hoarded money; rises in life as age advances. The native is fond of associating with women of loose morals.

Saturn if occupying any of the following degrees will show excellent results: 0° to 3° 20′, 10° to 16° 40′. But if the planet tenants a degree from 20° to 23° 20′, much of the good effects described above will be devalued.

Saturn in Scorpio

Vain, cruel, envious, opposed to others, avaricious, fiery temper, very active; suffers from fire or poison; rich; inclined to appropriate other persons' property; suffers many sorrows but outwardly appears as if enjoying life. Liability to suffer confinement or physical chastisement or reprimands; may suffer heavy expenditure; depletion of energies arising out of a chronic ailment.

If the planet occupies any degree from 10° to 16° 40′ or 20° to 26° 40′, the evil effects will be mitigated, but if in any of the other degrees, there will be no such mitigation.

Saturn in Sagittarius

Religious; righteous conduct; not talkative; soft; very intelligent; learned, good knowledge of the *Shastras* (Standard Hindu Books), clever in dealing with others; illustrious sons who bring credit to the father; enjoys wealth particularly in the last one-third part of life when he is much respected. The native may become head or leader of a village, town, section of army or have many employees under him; peaceful death.

Excellent results will be produced if the planet occupies any degree from 20° to 23° 20′ or 26° 40′ to 30°, but much of the good effects described for the planet in this sign will be devalued if he occupies any degree from 0° to 3° 20′ or 23° 20′ to 26° 40′

Saturn in Capricorn

Learned; valorous; languid eyes; unclean body; famous; clever in execution of work; proficient in artisanship; occupies an eminent position in his own clan or family and respected by other groups also; generally lives at a place other than his native land; derives financial benefit from other person's wife; dotes upon his children. The native is wealthy and leads a comfortable life.

The best degrees for the planet to occupy in this sign are between 0° to 6° 40′ when the good effects will be at their maximum, and the worst degrees to tenant are 10° to 13° 20′ where the good effects will be at their minimum and the unfavourable ones at their maximum.

Saturn in Aquarius

Very untruthful; harsh in speech; indolent eyes; strong; fiery tempered; outwardly talks of philosophy and religion; gain from another person's wife; addicted to wine and women; tendency to deceive others; has bad friends; initiates a variety of work. The native is wealthy and occupies a good position in life.

If Saturn occupies any degree from 0° to 3° 20′ or 10° to 16° 40′, he will show comparatively better results, but if tenanting a degree between 20° and 23° 20′, only evil results will follow.

Saturn in Pisces

Sober; a good diplomat; the native can be a good jeweller; chief among friends and relations; good wife, good sons; head of an institution, village or town; commands, respect and trust in government; wealthy; engaged in religious conduct; well-mannered; endowed with many good qualities. A good end to life and peaceful death.

If occupying any degree between 10° to 13° 20′ or 20° to 26° 40′, very good results will be felt. The worst degrees to occupy are those between 13° 20′ to 16° 40′ when much of the good effects described will be devalued.*

Rahu and Ketu

The effects of Rahu and Ketu in the different signs need not be described in detail. They imbibe the characteristics of Saturn and Mars respectively, i.e., Rahu is like Saturn and Ketu like Mars. Rahu in Aries, Taurus, Gemini, Cancer, Virgo Sagittarius and Pisces is favourable.

Rahu and Ketu generally bestow the effects of the planets they are conjoined with.

We shall now close this chapter with some concluding remarks on the mode of interpretation of the influence of the planets in the different signs.

* As stated earlier, never forget that signs correspond to houses; Aries to first, Taurus to second and so on. Thus, benefics in Taurus would increase wealth, in Libra give a good wife, in Sagittarius religiousness, prosperity and wealth and benefits connected with foreign lands and people. Saturn or Mars in Leo would give trouble from children or stomach ailments, in Capricorn, they would curtail happiness in respect of father, etc. A malefic in his own sign would however not cause detriment to the house he tenants but promotes its affairs.

HOW TO INTERPRET THE INFLUENCES IN SIGNS

Certain effects of planets caused by their occupying particular signs have been described in the preceding paragraphs. These traits, trends and probabilities have been described in standard Sanskrit texts on the subject and as far as possible we have given here a faithful rendering of the original to provide an insight into the ancient dicta.

Some of the crude descriptions, such as those described for Saturn in Aries, would probably not be liked by those who or whose friends or relations have Saturn in Aries. They may well point out a million persons, who have Saturn in Aries and yet who are scholars and rich, have friends and lead a comfortable life; nor do they lack in the milk of human kindness. There are professors, scholars, engineers, good lawyers, judges, efficient executives, well-to-do businessmen who have Saturn in Aries. The critic might with justification ask why if the description does not fit in with realities, has it been given in here.

Saturn stays in Aries for two and a half years. And every thirtieth year, he comes back to Aries and is there for two and a half years. How can millions and millions of persons born during this two and a half years have the same traits or characteristics? The point raised is very relevant. The explanation is that there is a set of planetary influences working for each individual and that set can be analysed as follows:

(i) The rising sign, (ii) the degree rising in the sign, (iii) planets in signs, (iv) the degree occupied by a planet in the sign, (v) the house position of the planet, (vi) the aspect on the rising sign, (vii) the aspect of planets on planets, (viii) the pattern of distribution of planets in the chart; the combination of planets interse, (ix) the strength of the planets and their dispositors. For example, Saturn in Aries will show twelve kinds of influences according as Mars, lord of Aries is in Aries, Taurus, Gemini or Cancer and so on. If Mars is exalted in Capricorn, Saturn in Aries, due to his occupying sign of Mars, will not show such evil results; but if Mars is debililated in Cancer, Saturn in Aries would produce the worse effects and several other factors, which can not be gone in to in an elementary textbook, modify the effects. So, the sign position is only one factor out of many. And though detailed descriptions have been given in the ancient texts of the aspects of other planets modifying the influences due to occupation in a particular sign by a particular planet space does not permit going into them here and we shall content ourselves by stating that the aspect of benefics, Jupiter, Mercury, Venus or the Moon with *Pakshabala* on another planet tones down the evil influence and at times makes it positively good. The converse is also the case, when the benefic results described for a planet are pulled down if aspected by a malefic like Saturn, Mars or the Sun. The conjunction also acts in a similar manner. If Jupiter and Saturn are conjoined, then some of the good qualities of Jupiter are minimised, while the evil ones of Saturn are mitigated.

Another principle should also never be lost sight of. The inherent vices of wickedness, meanness, dishonesty, treachery, quarrelsomeness, adulterous conduct, sinful acts, selfishness, lust and greed, are deep rooted at all levels of society. Foolishness and stupidity are also found in educated people. What is folly? The *Oxford Dictionary* describes it as being 'foolish, want of good sense, unwise conduct; foolish act, idea or practice.' And the word stupid, is defined as 'in a state of stupor or lethargy, dull by nature, slow witted, lacking in sensibility, obtuse. . . .'

So we find these qualities in all ranks of people, but the wickedness or dishonesty of a cooly who may pilfer a passenger's luggage will be different from the wickedness or dishonesty of a businessman, who gradually eats up the funds of a joint stock company and ultimately brings about its liquidation to the detriment of the share-holders, or the wickedness or dishonesty of the politician who resorts to all kinds of practices. fair and unfair, to keep himself in power.

Hindu astrologers have stated time and again that in making predictions the setting or the background of an individual is an important factor. They say, "Take into consideration the country, he belongs to, the times and the individual." We shall explain this further, for this is the cardinal principle of astrological interpretation. Let us take the country first. How would the physical characteristics, the complexion particularly, of a child born of Anglo-Saxon parents agree with those born of Negro parents?

Next let us take the time factor. Conditions of living and social circumstances differ from time to time. One hundred years back, if a lady in India knew the three R's she was called educated.

Today girls in millions are receiving higher education. Then comes the third factor—the person whose nativity is under consideration. If the person is born in a rich and affluent family that purchases one or two new cars every year, acquisition of a vehicle would be no astrological prediction; while to a labourer or a clerk, even the purchase of a scooter would be a red letter day in his life.

In writing this our purpose is to apply the principles of astrology with due consideration of all the factors. We have given in the next chapter the influences of planets in different houses. The influence due to (i) sign position and (ii) house position, should be blended and the result arrived at after noting the conjunctions or aspects they form with other planets.

CHAPTER 9

PLANETS IN HOUSES

SUN IN THE TWELVE HOUSES

Sun in First House. If the Sun is in the first house, the native is chivalrous; he is not easily moved from his resolve by others; suffers from eye-disease and is without mercy. If the Sun in the first house be in Aries, he is learned, wealthy and independent, but may suffer in respect of eye-sight; if it be in Leo, he is liable to suffer from night blindness; if it be in Libra, he will be in indigent circumstances, a son or sons may die prematurely; eye-sight is also likely to suffer; if it be in Cancer, some white film or speck will be formed in the eye. If the Sun be in Pisces, the native will be waited upon and served by ladies.

The Sun here inclines to baldness; the native is of angry temperament, impatient and lazy but proud; he is not of a forgiving disposition. The native is not fat, may have some ailment in the head due to *pitta* (bile); spends on benefic objects; has average matrimonial happiness; gains from cattle. According to one view, the health is indifferent during boyhood.

Sun in Second House. Very wealthy, but if the Sun is weak, liable to financial penalty or confiscation of property by the government; suffers from diseases of the mouth; devoid of learning, defective or of harsh speech but eloquent; fair chance of gain from copper, gold and metals; not a good position for happiness in respect of wife or children.

Sun in Third House. Endowed with valour and intelligence; the native will be wealthy but inimical towards his relations, particularly brothers and sisters, or one of them might prematurely die; illness of mother or inharmonious relations with her; travels much; has good servants; happy but his companions are rough or undesirable persons.

Sun in Fourth House. If the Sun is weak, devoid of happiness, suffers from mental distress; has no property nor friends. He serves the government and spends away his paternal property; liable to suffer from heart disease; illness of mother; opposition from *Bandhus* (agnates and cognates). If the Sun is strong, respect from the government and acquisition of landed property and friends.

Sun in Fifth House. Premature death or illness of a son; devoid of wealth; not very long lived. The native will be intelligent and learned and will travel over mountainous regions. He is courageous and vanquishes his enemies; gain of money; suffers from stomach diseases. According to one view, the native is cruel, hard-hearted, suffers during childhood, and suffers from stomach disorders during youth or middle age.

Sun in Sixth House. Proud, strong, worried by enemies but vanquishes them; will rise high in life; will be wealthy; have good digestive power; strongly sexed; will occupy a position of authority; respected by government. The wife's health is not very good; performs good deeds; heavy expenditure due to government or friends.

Sun in Seventh House. Suffers insult, injury, humiliation due to women; acts in a manner to arouse the opposition of the government; health suffers; remains worried; matrimonial happiness suffers; wife may not keep good health; not strongly sexed; visits abroad; business does not thrive well.

Sun in Eighth House. Few sons; eye-sight suffers; loses wealth; not long lived; also suffers in respect of friends; inimical towards women; separation from one's own people; apprehension of diseases due to imperfect secretion of bile. Sun herein causes worry; ailments of private parts; heavy expenditure but elevates the native in matters religious. The native is discontented.

Sun in Ninth House. Has sons, wealth and happiness; not good for the longevity of father or may be inimical towards father or religious preceptor; religiously inclined; lacks harmonious relations with wife; much travelling; intelligence; chivalry; comfort of servants and conveyance. The native is long lived but health may be indifferent during childhood.

Sun in Tenth House. Valorous, learned, will have sons, conveyances; will be wealthy; will be very intelligent and accomplishes projects taken in hand; cannot be subdued by rivals or opponents; the native's business expands; suffers in respect of happiness from mother; may live at a place other than his native place; inherits wealth and fame.

Sun in Eleventh House. Very wealthy; will be long lived; has a good position; strong; has good servants; others are jealous of him; devoid of friends or if the Sun is strong may have one powerful friend; an evil influence in respect of the eldest child/son; gain from several sources; stomach troubles; gain from government service; enjoyment of wife.

Sun in Twelfth House. Fallen, i.e., unsuccessful in work or fall in career. The native will be inimical towards his father; bereft of wealth and happiness in respect of children also suffers; has not a liberal outlook; devoid of strength; spends money on benefic objects; troubled by enemies but vanquishes them; impediments in work connected with government. Sun herein elevates in matters religious. The native travels much.

MOON IN THE TWELVE HOUSES

Moon in the First House. When at birth the Moon is in the first house in Aries, Taurus or Cancer, the native is very clever, wealthy and of good personality; but in other signs, it damages the sense of sight, hearing or speech or intelligence and the native follows a career of service. The ill effects described for Moon's location generally manifest themselves when the Moon is waning and is weak particularly when aspected by malefics. On the other hand, if the Moon is waxing, i.e., the birth is in the bright half of the month with good *Pakshabala,* the native has a strong constitution and is long lived. According to one school, if the Moon is debilitated or in the house of a malefic, then only the evil effects take place, otherwise the native has a good body and is wealthy. The Moon being generally a benefic, the native is cheerful, fond of aesthetic pleasures, travels much or has a passion for walking, particularly if the Moon be in a moveable or dual sign. The native has good conjugal happiness.

Moon in Second House. Endowed with wealth; the native has a large family; is sensuous and of agreeable speech. If the Moon is full, the native is very wealthy and does not speak much. The Moon herein gives more sisters than brothers; the native enjoys good food. A strong moon will give a beautiful face to the native and good name and fame. The native is clever in understanding the ideas of others and fond of learning. A weak Moon in second, fully aspected by Mercury, makes the native spend away his wealth. The Moon in the dark fortnight and with little *Pakshabala* is deemed a malefic and retards accumulation of wealth and particularly so if aspected by a malefic. Also, the Moon herein causes apprehension from water.

Moon in Third House. The native is strong, powerful and courageous; has brothers and patronises them; is of lascivious inclinations. He is learned but miserly. He has a cheerful temperament; engages in business; is fond of travelling. This is a good position for having conveyances. If the Moon is in a malefic's sign, it is adverse for happiness in respect of brothers and sisters; the native does not speak much and is of an aggressive temperament.

Moon in Fourth House. Endowed with happiness, landed property, friends, etc.; prospers well in respect of matters pertaining to the fourth house; amorous; enjoys life. The native is also generous in giving to others. He is fond of travelling by water or likes to live near the sea, rivers or lakes. He obliges his friends; is intelligent and of a cool temper.

Moon in Fifth House. Endowed with intelligence, sons and daughters and happiness in respect of the affairs of the fifth house; rises to a high position in life. He has good friends and is of a forgiving temperament. The native walks gently. The Moon in the fifth gives good fecundity but if the Moon is weak (in *Pakshabala*) and in a *Papa's* sign, trouble on account of children is to be expected. The native is inclined towards occult and religious practices. A very weak Moon unaspected by male planets may give him only daughters.

Moon in Sixth House. The native has a large number of enemies; digestive powers are sluggish or he may suffer from stomach trouble; sexual urge also below par; he is indolent but aggressive. If the Moon is weak (in *Pakshabala*) he will suffer humiliation at the hands of others. This is also an adverse factor for good longevity. But a full Moon bestows long life. The Moon in the sixth gives unhappiness during childhood, impairs eyesight and inflicts trouble from enemies. The native has good servants and cattle. But if there be full Moon or he be in his own sign or exalted, the native is generous and leads a luxurious life.

Moon in Seventh House. The native is jealous; is attached to women; is very intelligent; strongly sexed and of comely appearance. He has a wife with a good personality. He is fond of travelling and is of soft speech. He engages steadfastly in business. If the birth be during the dark half of the month and the Moon is weak (in *Pakshabala*) the native has health troubles and is humble. If the Moon be weak and aspected by malefics, even his wife would be sickly. The Moon in the seventh in a male nativity makes him subservient to his wife's wishes.

Moon in Eighth House. Very intelligent and valorous; suffers from *Vyadhis* (physical ailments); not long lived. If the birth be during day time and during the dark half of the month, i.e., when the Moon is waning, such a Moon is not detrimental to longevity, rather it protects the child. Similarly, if the birth be during night and during the bright half of the month, it is not unfavourable for longevity—the native will have a good span of life.

The Moon in the eighth makes the native jealous, fickle minded and keeps the mind worried. He is generous, but does not have a large family, unless the second house is very strong. If the Moon be in Taurus, Gemini, Cancer, Virgo, Libra, Sagittarius or Pisces or there be a full Moon, the native suffers from respiratory troubles, asthma, etc. The Moon herein gives love for learning. Again, a strong Moon herein, as in the second house, makes one rich and bestow overlordship.

Moon in Ninth House. Endowed with wealth, prosperity, sons, friends and *Bandhus** (relations). He is very popular with ladies. The native is religiously inclined. He is very active, fond of foreign places, is intelligent, a lover of learning, of good temper, pays homage to elderly people, and is courageous. He does not have many brothers. If the Moon be a weak one, then the native is not very intelligent nor rich.

Moon in Tenth House. Highly religious; valorous; endowed

* *Bandhus* include relations through father as well as through mother.

with wealth; successful in his undertakings; performs good deeds and obliges others. He will triumph over others. He is generous in giving. The native is optimistic and pushes on ahead successfully. He has maternal happiness, has friends, is long-lived, industrious and leads a comfortable and luxurious life. He may be connected with governmental work. This position is good for name and fame.

Moon in Eleventh House. Famous, prospers well in respect of eleventh house affairs. He will apply his mind closely and perseveringly to work in hand; will have wealth, sons and daughters, servants, and will be long-lived. He is clever in governmental work. He is very fond of his sons and has a great yearning for foreign lands. But if the Moon be weak, debilitated or in the sign of a *Papa,* he does not enjoy the good effects described above; will not be intelligent; also suffers from matters of health.

Moon in Twelfth House. Does not have a liberal outlook; suffers from infirmity of some limb or in respect of eye-sight; has an undignified position in life. People will be jealous of him. He will be indolent and will suffer misery and humiliation. The native will be much worried, will spend much; speak softly; will be proud and of good appearance. According to one school, the Moon in Gemini, Cancer, Virgo, Sagittarius and Pisces, shows good effects; the native is merciful and has control over his senses, but his company consists of low class persons. The Moon herein generally takes one abroad or the person lives in a region other than his native place.

Thus it will be seen that in delineating the influence of the Moon in the twelve houses, great emphasis has been laid on the strength of the Moon. A planet has twenty-four kinds of strength, but here cognisance has primarily been taken of two kinds: (i) position in sign, and (ii) the *Pakshabala.* A waning moon is considered weak. A waxing Moon is considered strong. The greater the number of bright digits, the stronger the Moon. Thus when there is conjunction of the Sun and Moon, the Moon has no *Pakshabala* and as it proceeds away from the Sun, the number of bright digits commence to increase, so that on a full Moon day, the Moon has the greatest strength. A full Moon is good, but this position of the Moon is likely to affect adversely the eye-sight if the Moon is in second, sixth, eighth or the twelfth house. Barring this aspect, the full Moon being a strong benefic enhances the good effects of the house he tenants.

MARS IN THE TWELVE HOUSES

Mars in First House. Gets hurt in the body, generally the head or the part of the body representing the sign on the ascendant; or instead of the hurt, there might be a boil or operation. The native is hard-hearted and unless Mars be in his own sign or exalted, a malefic in the first house is instrumental in affecting longevity adversely. The native is very courageous and active. Trouble to the mother; the early part of the life — the childhood years — is not happy; diseases of stomach and teeth likely; impaired matrimonial happiness also and unless Mars is strong, it is an adverse factor for accumulation of wealth. Mars in the first house gives a youthful appearance, i.e., even in old age the native appears younger than his actual age.

Mars in Second House. The native commits sinful acts; not eloquent in speech or speaks harshly. This location of Mars is an impediment to learning and wealth; but not so if Mars is in Aries, Scorpio or Capricorn. The native has to be dependant on undesirable people; trouble in eye or ear; loss by theft; disharmony in family. This is a good location for business in metals or manufacturing where fire is used. The native generally settles down at a place other than his homeland. If Mars be weak or afflicted by aspect of *Papas,* loss of wealth may be expected.

Mars in Third House. Intelligent, wealthy and happy; has much resistance and fighting stamina, but an adverse factor for longevity of a younger brother or relations with brothers may not be cordial; also an adverse factor for happiness in respect of mother. If Mars is exalted, the native leads a luxurious life, but Mars in debilitation or in an enemy's sign or in that of a *Papa* curtails wealth and happiness. Mars in third, if aspected by Saturn, is likely to cause a fracture of the arm, thigh or hip. But if benefics tenant or aspect the third house, this disaster may be averted.

Mars in Fourth House. Unless Mars is in his own sign, the native will have much distress of mind; will be bereft of friends, happiness from mother, landed property and conveyances. The fourth is the house of comforts and happiness. An ill-placed Mars curtails these. But if Mars is strong and aspected by benefics, gain of landed property is likely. It is an adverse factor for matrimonial happiness for Mars herein will aspect the seventh house; also affects adversely the house of children, the fourth house being twelfth from fifth; the native lives at a place other than his homeland. He is sensuous and inclined to have liaisons with women. Mars in the fourth, if aspected by malefics, will cause disease in the region of the chest or in the part of the body governed by the sign on the cusp of the fourth house.

Mars in Fifth House. Unless in his own sign or Mars be the lord of the first house, happiness in respect of children is curtailed; causes sickness to children or premature death of a child. It is an impediment to accumulation of money. The native will be a back-biter and suffer reverses in career. This location has an unfavourable impact on intelligence also. There is trouble from enemies; loss of cattle; the native eats much and there is likelihood of stomach troubles. Disease also likely in private parts.

Mars in Sixth House. The native is strong and vanquishes his enemies; but if Mars be weak, the native is much troubled by his enemies. He is oversexed. He has a good digestive power. He is wealthy and famous. But there is likelihood of boils and wounds and disease due to impurity of blood. Causes trouble to maternal uncle (mother's brothers and sisters — the sixth being third from fourth). The native is religious and his powers and prestige increase. But there is heavy expenditure of money; this location also causes an impediment in the conception of children. An exalted Mars would bestow very good results, but an afflicted one will produce constant pinpricks from enemies. Mars in Aries or Scorpio make one generally follow a service career.

Mars in Seventh House. A very disturbing factor for matrimonial happiness, but if Mars be in his own sign or lord of the first, not so evil. The native suffers humiliation on account of women; also liable to contract diseases from women. The native travels much. His actions are not commendable. This location is also not good for wealth or the native's own health. His temper is fiery. This position also curtails happiness in respect of father. Mars herein generally gives an aggressive and combative wife.

Mars in Eighth House. Few sons; eye-sight suffers; liability to have piles or fistula, as also diseases arising out of impurity of blood. Generally gets indebted and runs overdraft account. This location of Mars curtails longevity. It also brings infamy, and also causes mental distress. Happiness in respect of brother is impaired; brings fear from thieves and enemies; the native is constantly worried on account of financial matters.

Mars in Ninth House. Endowed with sons, wealth and happiness, but curtailed happiness in respect of father; the native performs cruel acts; has powerful supporters. The ninth being the house of piety and religion, a malefic therein, unless exalted or in own sign, drags down the nativity in respect of good actions. From the ninth, Mars fully aspects the third, and unless the sign on the third is Mars' own, either there is premature death of a brother or relations with brothers are not harmonious. If Mars and Moon are both together in the ninth, this is not good for longevity of mother.

Mars in Tenth House. Learned and famous; a leader of men; occupies good position in life; not good for father's longevity or relations with him may not be very cordial; generally gains from fire, copper, factories, or red things and commodities falling in the group of Mars; enters military or police service; generous and praised by eminent persons; very active and dashing; triumphs over enemies; trouble from brothers. Mars in the tenth house, opposed by Sun from fourth, may cause heart disease to the father of the native.

Mars in Eleventh House. Very wealthy, courageous and happy. The native will be of good temper, but the adverse aspect on the fifth house will spoil the prospects of that house. The native will be religious but of an angry temper. If Mars is exalted, the native will be very wealthy and pushing, and there will be much inflow of money. But this location curtails matrimonial happiness and simultaneously with good income, there is heavy expenditure also.

Mars in Twelfth House. Falls from grace; eye-sight, especially the left eye, suffers; ear trouble; premature decay of teeth and dental diseases; gets indebted and generally runs an overdraft account; if very much afflicted, liable to be accused in a criminal case or suffers confinement. The native is evil-minded. This location also affects matrimonial happiness adversely. Mars in twelfth if conjoined with a female planet may cause loss of money due to dancing girls, etc.

MERCURY IN THE TWELVE HOUSES

Mercury in First House. The native is learned, intelligent, clever in speech and of sweet tongue. He will be well versed in general knowledge of lands and people and well up in poetry and mathematics. Mercury in the first house endowes the native with a good body, much physical activity and a long life. The native is fond of friends and supports his relations. He is also attached to his wife. He is economical and prudent. He may live and prosper at a place other than his native land.

Mercury in Second House. The native is wealthy, and earns money by dint of his intelligence. He is truthful and his speech is sweet, clear and unambiguous. He is diplomatic. Unless Mercury is conjoined with or aspected by Saturn, Rahu or Ketu, the native is devoted to his father. His actions are good. He partakes of dainty dishes, i.e., gets sumptuous food. As the second house pertains to family, Mercury which is a natural benefic herein, gives a large family.

Mercury in Third House. The native is brave and powerful. He lives up to the age of 72. He will have good brothers and sisters. If the lord of the third and Mars are strong and well placed and if the third house is beneficially aspected, the number of brothers and sisters will be large. But if the reverse be the case, the number of brothers and sisters will be limited. The native will suffer fatigue due to hard work and he may also have to suffer humiliation. He is clever in keeping his thoughts concealed from others. He is always on the move, and particularly so if in a moveable sign. The native is religious and does good deeds. He has a knack for trade and commerce and is respected by his relations.

Mercury in the Fourth House. The native is learned. He will win the favour of others with his pleasing speech. He has friends, conveyances, lands, money and granaries. He has a number of people around him and has good *Bandhus* (strictly speaking '*Bandhus*' mean persons by cognate relationship. But here the term may be taken to include agnates as well as cognates). The native is devoted to his mother.

Mercury is a natural benefic and he provides abundance of material comforts and happiness from relations as judged from the fourth house. The rule that a *Karaka* if tenanting the house for which he is a *Karaka,* spoils the house tenanted does not appear to apply to Mercury.

Mercury is a volatile planet and attracts in greater measure the qualities of the sign he is in and of the planets he is associated with; so if he is in a malefic's sign in the fourth, the number of relations will be curtailed, and the native will make money by dubious and underhand means; if Mercury be exalted, good conjugal happiness may be expected. Mercury weak and aspected by malefics, keeps the native sickly in boyhood.

Mercury in Fifth House. The native will be a good counsellor or secretary, and if the nativity is strong, he may occupy the elevated position of an ambassador or adviser or minister. He has a thirst for knowledge and love for poetry and may be humorous also if Moon and Mercury conjoin. He will command respect due to his power of delicate discrimination and will be initiated into the incantation of *Mantras* (divine spells). The native will be religiously inclined and devoted to gods and Brahmans. The native will have a large progeny. He will be optimistic and happy. This is a good position for conjugal happiness also.

Mercury in Sixth House. The native will have no enemies, but there will be many occasions to cause ire on account of disputes. The native will use sharp speech, i.e., he will be harsh and incisive in speaking. He will, however, be a little lazy. But *Saravali,* a standard work in Sanskrit, advances an apparently contrary view in regard to disputes and enmities. According to *Kalyanvarma,* the author of *Saravali,* the native will be much oppressed by his enemies and will also suffer from physical ailments, which would be a source of constant trouble. The fact is that there is no contradiction. If Mercury is strong, in a benefic's sign and aspected by benefics, good results will follow; but if the planet is in a malefic's sign and aspected by malefics, evil influence described above will be felt. An afflicted Mercury in the sixth gives an unhappy boyhood. Mercury herein makes the native industrious and fond of his wife.

Mercury in Seventh House. The native will be intelligent, learned and well up in the amorous arts. He will wear fine clothes, will attain grandeur and marry a rich lady. The native's wife will be intelligent and comely in appearance, but if Mercury be weak or in a malefic's sign, she may not come from a high family and may have a long tongue. The native himself attains good status in life and is long-lived. He has a knack for trade and commerce, but unless the planet is strong and well aspected, being a male eunuch, he curtails the potency and virility in a male nativity.

Mercury in Eighth House. The native will attain a high position in life and will be well renowned and long-lived. He will be the head of a large family and will occupy a position where he can inflict penalty on others. He is industrious, wealthy and religiously inclined. But if the planet is in a malefic's sign and aspected by malefics, the native's actions will not be good and he will earn infamy thereby. An afflicted Mercury herein also gives a troublesome period in boyhood.

Mercury in Ninth House. The native is happy, endowed with wealth and sons. He will be learned, very clever, eloquent in speech and religious. He engages in trade and commerce or is an author of books or in diplomatic service. Mercury is primarily the planet governing intelligence, expression, diplomacy and tact and the native will be successful in all kinds of work where he is an intermediary between two parties. But if Mercury is associated with malefics, the native will no doubt be industrious but his actions will not be commendable.

Mercury in Tenth House. The native is valorous, intelligent and well informed. He will be learned and stick to the path of truth. He will be devoted to his parents and earn respect of the people and the government. His actions will be above blemish. He will have much physical and mental stamina and will engage himself in large undertakings, in which he will be successful. The native will be wealthy, possesses property and household goods.

Mercury in Eleventh House. The native is very wealthy, famous and longlived. He will be truthful and have a number of obedient servants. He will be fond of female company and will be endowed with various worldly comforts. This is a good position for happiness in respect of children. The native triumphs over his enemies.

Mercury in Twelfth House. The native will fall from a high position or his enterprises end in frustration. He is listless, devoid of learning, hard-hearted and indolent and will suffer humiliation. He will be intent upon following advice offered by others, but success will not be achieved. The above ill effects are felt if Mercury is weak and afflicted by malefics, but if the planet be strong and well aspected, the native has a pleasing personality, is religiously inclined, speaks sweetly and spends on good deeds.

JUPITER IN THE TWELVE HOUSES

Jupiter in First House. If Jupiter is in the first house, the native is learned, long-lived and has a pleasing personality. He will have a good body and abundant life force. He will be free from fear. His execution of work is after mature deliberation, i.e., after considering all the pros and cons. He will be wise, persevering and of good conduct. He will command wealth and respect and will have sons.

Jupiter in Second House. If Jupiter is in the second house, the native will be learned and eloquent in speech. He gets sumptuous food and has an adorable face. The native is inclined to sacrifice his money for the good of others. The first part of his life is not happy or prosperous. If Jupiter herein be in Sagittarius or Pisces, the native is wealthy and overcomes his enemies, he engages in trade and commerce; but Jupiter in second in any other sign keeps the finances at a low ebb and disturbs family happiness also.

Jupiter in Third House. If Jupiter is in the third, the native is miserly. He however spends on a good cause, is religious and learned, fond of his wife or women, is inclined to travel and may be an author. The native will have confidence in his brothers or his brothers will have confidence in him. He will be maliciously inclined; his actions will not be commendable and he will not command much respect. Jupiter herein brings occasions when the native is put to humiliation. His digestive power is not good. He will have an overbearing wife. He will feel the pinch of money at critical times.

Jupiter in Fourth House. If Jupiter is in the fourth, the native leads a comfortable life. He will have happiness in respect of mother, friends, servants, wife and agricultural produce. He will be eminent, but will have distress due to enemies. He is long-lived and earns respect, spends on a good cause, but unless the fifth house and the lord thereof are strong and well aspected, this location of Jupiter may cause an impediment or delay in the birth of sons.

Jupiter in Fifth House. If Jupiter is in the fifth, the native is intelligent and may occupy a high position in life. He will have wealth and will be happy and have friends. The *Phala Deepika*, a standard work in Sanskrit, states that the native will suffer on account of, or want of, sons, but according to *Kalyan Varma*, an ancient writer, the native will have sons and happiness thereby. The two views have to be reconciled thus. Jupiter unconjoined with any benefic or aspected by malefics shows unfavourable trends in regard to sons. But if Jupiter is strong and beneficially conjoined or aspected, good results in respect of children are to be predicted. Generally speaking, Jupiter by himself in the fifth house, causes unhappiness in regard to sons and gives stomach troubles also.

Jupiter in Sixth House. If Jupiter is in the sixth, the native is free from enemies or overpowers his enemies, but he will be indolent and suffer disrespect also. He is well up in the use of charms and divine spells. He is weak and lacks in vitality and potency; the digestive power is low. The native, however, becomes famous; he earns a name and fame through his wife also (the natives' wife may be an important person). But if Jupiter is retrograde, however high a position the native might have, he will suffer distress on account of his enemies.

Jupiter in Seventh House. If Jupiter is in the seventh, the native rises to a position higher than that of his father. He will have a good wife, good speech and a pleasing personality. He will be rich and more generous than his father. The native is wise and holds an important position. He may be a poet. He is very famous but is lustful and inclined to have liaisons.

Jupiter in Eighth House. If Jupiter is in eighth, the natives' actions are not commendable. He will be humble and earn his livelihood by service; he runs errands for others. The native visits holy places and is fond of the mystic and occult traditions. He has a slovenly wife (look for other indications also). He is dissatisfied with his wife and with his financial circumstances, but is long-lived. The native is put to financial loss by his friends and is worried. He may also suffer from some undiagnosed or concealed disease.

Jupiter in Ninth House. If Jupiter is in the ninth, the native is given to performing religious austerities. He becomes famous and may occupy a high position in life and if the nativity is strong, he may become a minister or a leader. He worships gods and

Brahmans and is endowed with learning, sons and wealth, but is miserly.

Jupiter in Tenth House. If Jupiter is in the tenth, the native is very rich. He receives favours from the government. He follows the path of righteous conduct and is devoted to his parents. The native is clever and prosperous and is successful in all his undertakings. This is a very good location of the planet for happiness, wealth, attendants, conveyances, name and fame. The native leads a chaste life.

Jupiter in Eleventh House. If Jupiter is in the eleventh, the native has a large income. He is wealthy and long-lived. He will have servants and conveyances, but a limited number of children. His education will also not be very high. He will be bold and fearless. Generally Jupiter alone in the eleventh house obstructs the inflow of wealth, but when conjoined with another planet he brings in much money.

Jupiter in Twelfth House. If Jupiter is in the twelfth, the native is devoid of attachment. People will harbour enmity towards him. He is not eloquent in speech, nor will there be happiness on account of sons. He will be sinful in conduct, indolent and engage in the service of others. He travels a lot. If Jupiter is in the sign of a malefic, the native makes a hypocritical show of religious fervour. Jupiter in Sagittarius or Pisces in the twelfth does not show the evil traits described for his location in the twelfth house; the native is religious and inclined to charity and benevolence and accumulates money.

VENUS IN THE TWELVE HOUSES

Venus in First House. When Venus is in the first house, the native leads a comfortable life and is long-lived. He has a pleasing personality, but is not courageous. He is well up in the amorous arts. The native speaks well and is generally liked. This is a good position for female company.

Venus in Second House. If Venus is in second, the native's speech is sweet. He is learned and if other indications confirm he may be a poet. He gets sumptuous food throughout his life. The native is courageous and fortunate. He has a good family. The native may gain from metals (silver and lead) and other people's wealth. Venus herein makes one wealthy.

Venus in Third House. If Venus is in third, the native is miserly and is not liked much. He lacks enthusiasm. He is fond of travelling and is fortunate; he has good servants. The native is devoted to his mother; lives at a place other than his homeland. His eye-sight may suffer. If Venus is strong and well aspected, the native will be wealthy and have conjugal happiness; but if Venus be weak and aspected by malefics, he will be devoid of wealth and conjugal happiness, but the native's wife will have considerable influence over him.

Venus in Fourth House. If Venus is in the fourth, the native leads a comfortable life; has a good house, conveyances, good clothes and ornaments. He has an amiable personality and an enthusiastic frame of mind. He has good friends and relations. He is devoted to his father and eldery people. The native is wealthy and generally fortunate.

Venus in Fifth House. If Venus is in the fifth, the native is wealthy. He is amorous and leads a comfortable life. He has sons and good friends. He is learned and very intelligent and speaks well. He may engage in trade and commerce. He annihilates his enemies. If Venus is strong, he may occupy a good position as a secretary, counsellor, minister, magistrate or a judge. This location of the planet indicates more daughters than sons and the native is attached to his sons-in-law.

Venus in Sixth House. If Venus is in the sixth, the native resorts to low acts, but is without wealth. He spends economically and to good purpose. The native suffers from secret ailments or ulcers. He will be corrupted by young women and will have no peace of mind. Venus herein gives rise to enmities with women. If Venus is exalted or strong, the native will have no enemies or will overpower them, but if the planet is weak, the native will have a number of enemies.

Venus in Seventh House. If Venus is in the seventh, the native has a good personality and is over-sexed. He will have a good and beautiful wife, but will have liaisons with other women of loose morals and if other indications confirm, he may lose his wife prematurely, particularly if Venus herein be in Scorpio. This is on the principle that the location of the *Karaka* in the house for which he is a *Karaka,* is not good.

Venus herein makes the native wealthy. He would be of an amiable disposition and will avoid frictions, but if Venus be afflicted by malefics he will be quarrelsome. The native will generally be fortunate and have sons, but he will suffer from diseases of the urinary tract.

Venus in Eighth House. If Venus is in the eighth, the native resorts to low acts. He is persevering and fond of travelling and is religious. This is a good location for longevity, the owning of immovable property and for service with the government. The native is prosperous and leads a comfortable life. In a male nativity, a weak Venus may cause diseases of the urinary tract or spermatorrhea.

Venus in Ninth House. If Venus is in the ninth, the native is religious, worships gods and manes and is hospitable to guests and Brahmans. He is learned and sticks to truth; he will have happiness in respect of wife, sons and friends. He will be wealthy and lead a comfortable life. The native is optimistic and rises in life by dint of his own efforts. He commands respect and receives favours from the government.

Venus in Tenth House. If Venus is in the tenth, the native is wealthy and possesses property. He will earn name and fame. He will have friends and a regular income for a comfortable life. He will be very intelligent. In any contest or competition with others, he will come out with flying colours and each of these occasions will add to his rise in life.

Venus in Eleventh House. If Venus is in the eleventh, there is good gain of money, pleasures of the bed and the requisites of comfort. The native has good servants and leads a comfortable life.

Venus in Twelfth House. If Venus is in the twelfth, the native is wealthy, economical and saves money. Health during childhood may suffer. The native is well up in the amorous arts, but indolent and leads life in a happy-go-lucky fashion. He, however, triumphs over his enemies. The native's wife has considerable influence over him. The planet's location herein is good for pleasures but not so for a career.

Note: Venus in Pisces, in any house, will make one wealthy,

SATURN IN THE TWELVE HOUSES

Saturn in First House. The native leads a life of poverty; he is indolent, melancholy, sickly, unclean, and resorts to low acts.

He has dissatisfied lust; speaks slowly; suffers in health during childhood. If the planet herein is in an enemy's sign, the native quarrels with his friends. But if Saturn be in Libra, Sagittarius or Pisces, the native is good-looking and learned; he is the head of an institution and equal to a king. Saturn in Capricorn or Aquarius shows the same effects as in Libra, Sagittarius or Pisces, but in lesser measure. According to one school, the planet here in Taurus is also good.

Saturn in Second House. The native suffers from facial disease or a disease of the mouth. He has plenty of money, but suffers financial penalty at the hands of the government. According to the *Phala Deepika,* the native would be poor, but at a later age he would live at a place other than his native home and will have wealth, vehicles and pleasures. The native is devoted to his mother, but it is in an adverse location for happiness in respect of brothers.

Saturn in Third House. The native will be intelligent, wise and valorous; he will be indolent and have no peace of mind; he spends much and will be inclined to give in charity, though generally speaking, his actions will not be commendable. He will have happiness from his wife, but suffer in respect of children. Saturn herein also causes damage to younger brothers and sisters. He generally lives at a place other than his homeland.

Saturn in Fourth House. The native is devoid of happiness; has no peace of mind; is constantly worried; ill health during childhood; separation from mother; suffers in respect of happiness pertaining to father; bereft of property and conveyance; liable to heart disease, and also to suffer from ailments of the stomach. If Saturn is retrograde, there is distress due to wife, children and servants, also distress at places other than the homeland. But if Saturn is strong, the native is prosperous and has conveyances also.

Saturn in Fifth House. The native may suffer for want of sons or there might be premature death of a child or trouble connected with children. He is also devoid of wealth, happiness and knowledge and oppressed by enemies. The native has an evil bent of mind; his way of thinking is not straightforward. Liability to mental diseases, as also ailments of the stomach. The native has an appearance of humility; he leads an humble role in life. But if the planet be exalted or in his own sign, the evil effects are minimised and the good ones felt.

Saturn in Sixth House. If the planet is strong, the native triumphs over his enemies, but if he be weak, the native himself suffers at the hands of his enemies. The planet afflicted or in an enemy's sign or in debilitation brings about annihilation of the native's own family. The native is impudent, proud, and wealthy. He is over-sexed; has good digestive powers. But this is an evil location for happiness pertaining to mother, to whom he is the source of distress. Liability to suffer from ulcers and wounds and diseases arising out of imbalance of 'wind'. He is strong, but does not follow a righteous conduct.

Saturn in Seventh House. The native's teeth are prominent. He is indolent and restless. He is put to distress and humiliation on account of women. He is without wealth and travels much; is attached to an unworthy or unseemly woman. The native resorts to low acts. Probability of a sickly wife or her premature death.

Saturn in Eighth House. The number of children is limited. Eye-sight suffers; he also suffers from diseases of the stomach; liability to some undiagnosed disease or diseases of the private parts or piles. The native has good digestive powers. He is not wealthy; is disrespected by people. He serves others; lacks in the ability to take the initiative in new projects. The native will not be happy during the early years of life. Death due to ailments connected with *Vata* (wind) or at the hands of a ruffian. *Kalyan Varma* says that the native will not be long-lived, but other standard texts state that Saturn herein bestows long life. We agree with the latter view.

Saturn in Ninth House. If the planet is strong, the native is rich and happy; happiness also from sons. The planet gives the native a philosophical turn of mind; he is fond of occult studies. But if the planet be weak, he is bereft of good fortune, wealth and father or no happiness in respect of them. The native will then have a malicious bent of mind and will cause distress to others. The native suffers in respect of brothers. He is courageous but oppressed by enemies; lives at a place other than his homeland.

Saturn in Tenth House. There is gain from agriculture or products derived from the bowels of the earth, such as, minerals, oils, etc. The native has much knowledge of the *Shastras* (scriptures), i.e., he is learned; brave and famous. He is wealthy and occupies a high position in life. He is the head of an institution or at the helm of affairs in his sphere of activity. This is an unfavourable location in respect of happiness pertaining to mother, but not evil in respect of father, unless Saturn is lord of the eighth house. The native generally lives at a place other than his home-land.

Saturn in Eleventh House. The native has plenty of wealth, and is possessed of property; good income. He is courageous, has good health, but suffers ill health during childhood. He is strong, industrious and engages in trade or commerce. He may earn from artisanship or from products in Saturn's portfolio. But Saturn in this house is an adverse factor for happiness in respect of brothers, sons or wife. The native may have more daughters and a few sons or no son.

Saturn in Twelfth House. The native is 'fallen'; i.e., suffers in public estimation due to low conduct or demoted in career or meets frustration in business enterprises. There is heavy expenditure. Eye-sight suffers; premature decay of teeth; not good for maternal uncle. The native is impudent and indigent; suffers from infirmity of a limb, is devoid of intelligence and is oppressed by enemies.

RAHU IN THE TWELVE HOUSES

Rahu and Ketu have no physical bodies. They are merely sensitive points. They, therefore, imbibe the qualities of the planets they are conjoined with. If any of the nodes tenants a trine (the fifth or the ninth house) and is conjoined with the lord of an angle, it bestows excellent results. Similarly, if a node tenants an angle (the first, fourth, seventh or tenth house) and is conjoined with the lord of a trine, it is considered a very good combination.

So let us not forget that Rahu or Ketu if conjoined with any planet in any house, will imbibe the qualities of the planet conjoined with it. If the house tenanted is good and the planet also good (inherently, as well as by ownership), the results will be excellent. But if the house tenanted is evil and the planet conjoining also evil, unfavourable results will follow.

Another important feature about Rahu and Ketu is that if they are not conjoined with any planet, or even if they are conjoined with any planet, they take up the qualities and attributes of the house they tenant.

According to one school, they also reflect the quality of their dispositor. For example, a node in Cancer will reflect in some measure the effect of the Moon; the node in Leo will show some attributes of the Sun; in Virgo, he will behave in a manner similar to Mercury, and so on, according to the lordship of the sign he is in.

Hindu astrologers regard Rahu as having the qualities of Saturn and Ketu those of Mars. The third, sixth and the eleventh houses are considered the best for them to occupy; but when Rahu is in the third, Ketu will be in ninth; when Rahu is in sixth, Ketu will be in the twelfth — not a happy position; and when Rahu will be in eleventh, the corresponding position of the other node will be in the fifth — an evil location for affairs of the fifth house.

We shall, however, briefly give below the effects of Rahu and Ketu in the twelve houses.

Rahu in First House. Rahu in the first house endows one with the qualities of a serpent. He is cruel, devoid of mercy, inclined to be irreligious, maliciously inclined and over-sexed. He practices deception on his own people and resorts to low acts. The native is sickly, suffers from diseases of the head or in the upper part of the body. But he is strong and wealthy, triumphs in disputes with others. This is, however, not a good location for promoting conjugal happiness. The number of the native's sons is limited. He generally shines by reflected light, i.e., in the glory of others or by deriving authority from others and enjoys wealth also in a similar manner. He is amorous and fond of the company of women; engages in strife with others. If other indications confirm, likelihood of two marriages.

Rahu in Aries, Taurus or Cancer in the ascendant, protects the native from all kinds of troubles of health or enemies. Rahu herein in Leo makes the native wealthy. He enjoys many luxuries.

Rahu in Second House. The native is talkative but not truthful in speech; his speech may be dubious, insincere, misleading or factually incorrect. The native suffers from diseases of the mouth. He is malicious and of an angry temperament and does not accept the good advice of well wishers; opposes others. The native oppresses his brothers and is also oppressed by them. He tries to save money but is not rich. Although of a fearless frame of mind, he apprehends danger or assaults from enemies. He has to work in a subordinate position and may suffer at the hands of the government on account of intrigues against him by low people. The early period of life is not happy. Gains from government sources, are likely.

Rahu in Third House. The native has fixity of purpose; is proud and courageous like a lion. He is strong, has sisters; few brothers or the relations with his brothers are not harmonious. The native is very intelligent, optimistic and valorous and engages in profitable work or business. He is friendly with people but not prompt in doing good to others. He attains good fortune, is rich and is long-lived.

Rahu in Fourth House. Not very intelligent; no happiness from brothers or friends. This location is also adverse in respect of happiness from mother, father and wife or the native is hard-hearted and deceptive and is constantly worried. Little happiness; suffers from diseases of the stomach. Not very eloquent; untruthful in speech. But if Rahu be in Aries, Taurus, Gemini or Virgo, he gains from the government.

Rahu in Fifth House. The native is timid but hard-hearted. He is intelligent and fond of learning. He speaks with a nasal accent and suffers from diseases of the stomach, abdomen, or either side of the belly; a female may have health troubles connected with the uterus. The native will pass an anxious time in expectation of a son and may have one or two sons late in life. The native is worried; does not have peace of mind. He engages in work and is fortunate. He does not gain from government sources. His wife may suffer from stomach troubles.

Rahu in Sixth House. The native is very valorous and long lived but is oppressed by enemies and evil planetary influences. He, however, overcomes his enemies and is happy. Suffers from teeth troubles, ulcers and wounds and also from anal diseases. The early period of life is not happy, but later, he is rich and strong, does not have happiness in respect of brothers, paternal or maternal uncles. On the whole, this is deemed a good location for the node, because it increases the physical as well as the mental stamina of the native and he comes out victorious, after struggles and strife.

Rahu in Seventh House. The native is self-willed, proud and independent, but not very intelligent. He is clever, fickle and avaricious; is inclined to have liaisons, but in a male nativity it may be adverse for virility. In nativities of either sex it impairs conjugal happiness; the partner may be lost or be sickly or non-co-operative. The native may lose money through contact or liaisons with women. His conduct is not commendable; he engages in disputes, suffers in family affairs and separation from Bandhus (relations). There is no peace of mind.

Rahu in Eighth House. This is an evil position both for mental aptitude and physical health. The native is dilatory in work, resorts to unholy acts, is weak but inclined to much sexual activity. He may suffer from diseases arising out of imbalance of wind, ailments of the stomach, enlargement of glands or their imperfect functioning, is sickly and may have an undiagnosed disease of the private regions, or may have infirmity of a limb. He has few sons. This location is adverse for a long life. He earns name and respect but his reputation is blemished. Friends forsake him. For financial prospects, the blessings are mixed; some times the native gains money, at others there is loss. He is oppressed by enemies.

Rahu in Ninth House. The native is retaliatory in speech. He is evil-minded but intelligent; opposes his father or may not have much happiness in that respect. But he is firm and if benefics aspect the ninth house he may perform acts of religious merit. The native has fixity of purpose and does not abandon work once undertaken or lose determination. He has love for his brothers but is not fortunate in respect of sons. For worldly prospects of name, fame, wealth and splendour, this is an excellent position.

Rahu in the Tenth House. The native is proud and fearless, fond of struggle and strife, but is engaged in work for others and does not have reliable friends. He is economical but this is not a factor for much wealth. The native has powerful enemies. The happiness in respect of parents is also impaired. He may have a few sons. The mind is constantly worried. In male nativities there is probability of liaisons with widows; gain from *Mlechchhas* (non-Hindus).

Rahu in Eleventh House. The native is wealthy and long-lived. He is intelligent, has good children, but the number of sons is limited. He travels a lot and has a large retinue. He is famous both in his own and the opposite camp. The native is industrious, engages in trade and business or perseveringly applies himself to work undertaken. Gain from *Mlechchhas.* (non-Hindus). The native is courageous, avaricious, and has an inclination to appropriate other people's wealth. He gains from good advice tendered by others. He is heroic in strife and overcomes his enemies. The health is generally good but diseases of the ear or deafness in advanced age are likely.

Rahu in Twelfth House. This is an adverse location for health; the native is weak; eye-sight suffers, also trouble in the region of the heart or sides due to imbalance of 'wind'; may also suffer from diseases such as oedema. The native is inclined to commit uncommendable acts in a secret manner, gains from secret financial dealings but there is heavy expenditure, at times through undesirable channels. His undertakings initially bring frustration but become successful finally. The native has an appearance of humility but is courageous; he is friendly with the wicked and antagonistic to gentlemen. If an agriculturist he has a large herd of cattle. The native wanders a great deal and falls from high position. This is an unfavourable position for the pleasures of the bed.

Note: The above are the effects of Rahu, if not conjoined with another planet in the house. The effects would be coloured correspondingly according to the attributes of the planet associating. If Rahu and Ketu are in Aries, Taurus, Gemini, Cancer, Virgo, Sagittarius or Pisces, the evil effects shown are less. It is good to have a node conjoined with a planet and particularly so if (i) Rahu is in an angle with the lord of a trine, (ii) Rahu is in a trine with the lord of an angle, (iii) in any other house with a benefic, (iv) in third, sixth or eleventh, with a malefic or a benefic. This applies to Ketu also.

KETU IN THE TWELVE HOUSES

Ketu in First House. The native is devoid of happiness, is a back-biter, avaricious, suffers some physical ailment or nervousness which keeps him restless and worried. He loses good positions. He is industrious, voluptuous, performs uncommendable acts. This location also impairs conjugal happiness. The native has few sons, no happiness from maternal uncle; trouble from relations, fear from opponents, ailment of the stomach. But Ketu in Capricorn or Aquarius mitigates evil influences.

Ketu in Second House. An adverse factor for learning and wealth. The native's tongue is incisive and sharp and he may even use foul language. There is loss of money due to government; opposition from relations, inharmonious relations with brothers. He likes to depend upon food of others or does not partake of wholesome food. He has an evil eye (a superstition current in olden times). There are diseases of the mouth. The native opposes others due to his malicious criticism of them. But if Ketu be in his own or exalted sign or in a benefic's sign, the rigour of the evil influences is much relaxed. The native then accumulates money and is happy.

Ketu in Third House. The native is intelligent, strong and courageous. He has much fighting stamina and crushes his enemies. This location increases wealth, luxuries and strength, but the native is mentally much agitated due to disputes. He has little happiness from brothers, there may be premature death of a brother or no love last between the native and his brothers. The native applies industriously to work and is long-lived. There may however be pain in the arms.

Ketu in Fourth House. An adverse factor for all fourth house affairs — land, fields, mother. The native fritters away paternal property due to bad friends. He is cruel, malicious and hypocrite; talks ill of others; does not live at his ancestral home. If Ketu be in his own house or exalted, then happiness pertaining to home is foretold.

Ketu in Fifth House. The native has an evil nature, has malicious intentions, ailments of the stomach, trouble from *Pishachas* (evil spirits). The native's brothers are liable to get hurt; few sons and little happiness from them; afraid of water. But the native is fond of learning, engages perseveringly in work and is intelligent. Gain from cows. The mind is constantly worried.

Ketu in Sixth House. The native is strong, famous and has fixity of purpose. He is oppressed by opponents but overpowers his enemies and achieves his objectives. The node herein generally bestows good health but there is trouble in the eye; also anal diseases. The teeth are weak. There is loss of wealth. The native is much liked by his relations, but does not fare well with his maternal uncles. A good position for general stamina and gain from cattle, but the period of boyhood is not happy.

Ketu in Seventh House. This is an adverse position. There is much wandering and fear arising during travels and from water.

The native is attached to an unworthy woman; suffers separation from his wife or the wife may be sickly or not even tempered. Suffers from intestinal troubles or hernia. The native is avaricious and his conduct is low; heavy expenditure, mental worries, loss of vitality, fear from thieves; but if Ketu is in Scorpio the effects are in a great measure mitigated and the native makes money.

Ketu in Eighth House. An adverse factor for longevity; piles and anal diseases, wounds, separation from dear ones, quarrels, opposition from all quarters. General effect of Ketu in eighth is poor but if aspected by benefics the native accumulates money and is long-lived. Also if the node be in Aries or Taurus, there is gain of money and of sons. If in Gemini, Virgo or Scorpio, then also gain of money after obstruction. Generally it is an unfavourable position for wealth. The native suffers from diseases of the stomach. He is oppressed by enemies; fear from cattle. The native covets others' money and wives.

Ketu in Ninth House. The native is religious but has malicious inclinations and an uneven temper. He may be a religious hypocrite; is intelligent, proud, courageous and wealthy. He suffers in respect of father; there is pain in the body particularly in the arms. Visits holy places. Gain from Mlechchhas (non-Hindus). An adverse factor in respect of happiness from brothers. The ninth house is a good one but Ketu being a malefic mixed results follow. But if Ketu is conjoined with a benefic, the evil influences will be minimised.

Ketu in Tenth House. The native is very courageous, pushing, popular and brilliant. He has knowledge of the Self and has a philosophical bent of mind; but affects happiness pertaining to both the parents, particularly from the father is adversely affected. The native causes distress to the father or vice versa, or the father may not be long-lived. The native's conduct is not always of a high order; he meets many obstacles, but overcomes them. He is good in mechanics; has little happiness from sons. The native is always on the move; travels much. The body shows excess of phlegm. There is fear from quadrupeds and conveyances. If the node be in Aries, Taurus, Virgo or Scorpio, the native crushes his enemies. The native is economical and accumulates money.

Ketu in Eleventh House. An excellent position for the inflow of money, luxuries, good learning, popularity, authority, gain and success. The native speaks well, is contented, performs good deeds and commands respect. But the native does not have good sons, and their number may also be limited. They are a source of worry to him. The native himself suffers from ailments of the stomach and anal disease. He is avaricious, industrious and engages perseveringly in work.

Ketu in Twelfth House. This is an adverse location. The native indulges secretly in sinful acts. There is expenditure on unwholesome objects and the native spends away money saved. He acts contrary to good advice, but is victorious in disputes. He is worried; there is no happiness from the maternal uncle. There are ailments of the feet, in the regions of the navel and anus and in the eye. He is weak but voluptuous and conjugal happiness is impaired.

* * * *

The above delineation of the effects of the nine planets in the twelve houses is general, and is given here for a general understanding of the individual influences and to arrive at the resultant effects after weighing the favourable and unfavourable factors of all the nine planets as distributed in the birth chart. The judgment, however, has to be applied against the background of the native. In India there are many crores of people whose income is only a few annas per day or less than one rupee per day and so how would effects pertaining to the inflow of money or wealth apply to them? Similarly, some of the planets in some houses have been described as making the native learned; half the population in India is illiterate. How will these effects apply to them? What we wish to emphasise is that the general principle of weighing the planetary effects against the background of the native should always be kept in mind.

We would also sound a note of warning against judging loose moral conduct or sex-aberrations in the case of women. Extra-marital relations have been a feature of society since creation. But the moral and social values differ from society to society, and while in certain countries flirtation is the rule, in a place like India where the religious and moral fibre in this regard is strong, in many a hearts there might be a lurking desire which is kept unfulfilled due to self-control. Besides other mitigating astrological factors may set at naught one single factor due to the location of one planet. Beginners are therefore warned not to wreck family happiness by pronouncing judgments on such a delicate issue.

Again, reverting to the astrological principles, the following general rules should be kept in mind:

(i) A planet in exaltation or own house shows the good effects fully.

(ii) A planet in a friend's house shows three-fourths of the good effects.

(iii) A planet in an enemy's house shows half of the good effects.

(iv) A planet in debilitation shows one-quarter of the good effects.

Conversely:

(i) A planet in exaltation or own house shows only a quarter of the evil effects.

(ii) A planet in a friend's sign shows half of the evil effects.

(iii) A planet in an enemy's sign shows three-fourth of the evil effects.

(iv) A planet in debilitation shows the evil effects fully.

An additional rule which the readers will do well to bear in mind is that conjunctions or aspects of benefics increase the good effects and mitigate the evil ones. Conversely, the aspects or conjunctions of malefics decrease the good effects and increase the evil ones.

CHAPTER 10

GENERAL PRINCIPLES OF JUDGMENT

IN THE PREVIOUS chapters we have provided an outline of influences and trends in character according to the sign rising and the placement of planets in signs and houses. Over and above these it should always be kept in mind that if a planet or a house is aspected by benefics, its quality improves. On the other hand, if the house or any planet is aspected by malefics, it is devalued.

In the case of a house, if it is tenanted or aspected by its lord even though he be a malefic, he only strengthens the house and does not damage it. Jupiter, Mercury, Venus and Moon are benefics. Saturn, Mars, Rahu, Ketu and Sun are malefics. If a malefic tenants a house and is aspected by another malefic, it causes more damage to the house. For example, if Mars tenants the third house, it is evil for the native's brothers—either, a brother or sister may die prematurely or the native's relations with brothers will not be cordial. If under the circumstances, Saturn from the sixth house (by its tenth aspect) or from the ninth (by its seventh aspect) or from the ascendant (by its third aspect) fully aspects Mars, the results would be worse. On the other hand, if a benefic in a house is fully aspected by another benefic, the quality of the house tenanting the aspected planet is improved. For example, suppose Mercury is in the eleventh. Here Mercury improves the eleventh (house of gains). Now, suppose, Jupiter tenanting the third house fully aspects Mercury by its ninth aspect or Jupiter in the fifth fully aspects the eleventh (Mercury therein) by its seventh aspect or Jupiter from seventh fully aspects Mercury by its fifth aspect, then Mercury's wealth giving powers in the eleventh are still further augmented.

This principle of receiving malefic and benefic aspects should be applied to all the houses and planets. In Western astrology square or opposition aspects are considered evil, conjunction with a benefic is deemed good, while with a malefic, evil. But that is not so in Hindu astrology.

A planet if exalted increases the good effects of the house he owns. Similarly if a planet occupies his own sign, he increases the good effects of the house he occupies and also of the other house he owns. The Sun and Moon however own only one house each. Some of these points have been referred to at the end of Chapter 6 and the attention of readers is invited to the principles stated there.

As regards the location of planets in houses, it is good to have benefics in the angles and trines and malefics in third and sixth. All planets, benefics as well as malefics, are good in the eleventh. Benefics are good in the second also, provided they are not lords of the seventh. It is best to have no planets in the eighth or the twelfth, but of the two sets of planets, benefics and malefics—the benefics in the eighth and the twelfth do not do as much harm as malefics. If the birth be during day time and the Moon is waxing and is in the eighth, it poses a danger to the longevity of the child. Similarly, if the birth be at night and the Moon is waning and occupies the eighth, there is danger of severe illness during childhood. But if the birth is at night and the Moon is waxing, it preserves the child; and if the Moon is waning and in the eighth and the birth is during day time, the child does not die at a young age unless other detrimental factors are present.

Some general principles as laid down by Sanskrit texts are given below:

1. If there be at least one planet exalted or in his own sign, and that planet is conjoined or aspected by a benefic, the native leads a comfortable life, is rich and occupies a good position in life.

2. When a planet instead of having a direct forward motion appears to recede in the zodiac, i.e., has a backward motion, it is called retrograde; this state is indicated by the letter R in the Ephemeris. A planet when retrograde, if not combust, is deemed

strong. He is considered strong, though he be in his debilitation or in an enemy's house.

Planets in retrogression become strong, but if a planet is in his sign of exaltation and retrograde also, the efficacy of his being in his exalted sign is impaired.

3. A planet in an angle is stronger than in a succedent house. The position in a succedent house is stronger than in a cadent house.

4. Of the two kinds of friendship and enmity, natural and temporal, the natural is stronger than the temporal.

5. In the elimination of *dosha** and in adding beneficence, Jupiter is the most powerful. Venus has half the strength of Jupiter and Mercury one-fourth. But the Moon's strength serves as the basis of all strengths. The principle is that the Moon presides over the heart. A man who has a strong Moon has undaunted courage and courage is the secret of success.

We now give below some additional principles, which should generally be applied in evaluating nativities.

1. The 6th, 8th and 12th houses are known as *Trik* or *Dusthanas*. If the lord of any house tenants one of these houses, the efficacy of the house of which he is the lord, is impaired. For example, if the lord of the first house occupies the 6th, 8th or 12th house from the ascendant, the health and personality, individual efforts, pushing power (all these are judged from the first house) are impaired.

If the lord of the sixth, eighth or twelfth house occupies any house, it impairs the house occupied. For example, if the lord of the eighth occupies the tenth, the father's longevity would be curtailed because the father is judged from the tenth. This will be particularly so if it is a malefic planet.

An exception to the above rule is —

(i) Lord of sixth in eighth or twelfth.
(ii) Lord of eighth in sixth or twelfth.
(iii) Lord of twelfth in sixth or eighth.

These positions are not considered evil.

2. The first, fourth, seventh and tenth houses are called angles. These are good places. Herein a planet is strong. If movable signs are on the cusps of fourth, seventh and tenth also, (Aries, Cancer, Libra and Capricorn are movable signs, so if movable signs

* The word has been explained on a subsequent page in this chapter

are in angles), the native would be active, pushing and dynamic; particularly so, if there are some planets therein also. If fixed signs are on the cusp of the angles, the native would be more fixed in his idea; will be thoughtful; he would not be inclined to move about much, would not like to travel, prefer to stick to the home and desire intellectual occupation or a profession where there is not much movement. Taurus, Leo, Scorpio and Aquarius are fixed signs. If the signs on the cusps of angles are common, i.e., having the qualities of both movable and fixed signs, the native has some qualities of both the groups. Gemini, Virgo, Sagittarius and Pisces are common signs. One view is that the first fifteen degrees are of the nature of fixed signs and the latter fifteen degrees have the qualities of movable signs.

Also examine whether the lord of the first occupies a movable, fixed or common sign and the inference drawn from the above should be drawn from this also.

3. Each planet is a *Karaka* for some relation, matter or affair (see Chapter 6 on planets). While judging the house or house lord also examine the *Karaka*. For example, if we have to judge about the father, we should not only take into account the tenth house and the lord of the tenth house, but the Sun also, who is *Karaka* for father. If we want to arrive at a judgment in regard to the mother, we should not only take into account the fourth house and its lord but also the Moon—*Karaka* for the mother also, and so on.

4. There are twin principles for judgment. One is from the house and the other from *Karaka*. For example, judge the father from the tenth; judge father's wealth from the eleventh (second from the tenth), the father's brothers and sisters from the twelfth (third from the tenth), the father's mother from the first, and so on. Similarly, judge the father from the Sun, the father's wealth from the second from the Sun (the sign next to that occupied by the Sun), the father's brothers and sisters from the third from the Sun, the father's mother and landed properties from the fourth from the Sun, and so on.

To take another example, judge the wife from the seventh, the wife's wealth from the eight (second from the seventh), the wife's brothers and sister from ninth (third from the seventh), and so on. Similarly, judge the wife from Venus, the wife's wealth from the second from Venus (i.e., the sign next to that tenanted by Venus), the wife's brothers and sisters from third from Venus, and so on.

5. The effect of good or bad *Yogas* is felt during the *Dasha* and *Antardasha* of planets forming the *Yoga*.

6. In the judgment of a house, the following factors must be taken into account.

A. (i) Whether benefics or malefics tenant the house.

(ii) Whether lords of benefic or malefic houses tenant the house.

(iii) Whether the house is hemmed in by benefics or malefics. For example, if we have to judge about the fourth house, and if there are benefics in the third and the fifth on both sides of the fourth, the fourth house will be deemed to be hemmed in by benefics. If, however, there are malefics in the third and the fifth houses, the fourth house will be hemmed in by malefics.

(iv) Whether the house receives the aspects of benefics or malefics, if of both types of planets, examine which is stronger and in greater measure.

(v) Whether the house receives the aspect of lords of good houses or evil houses.

B. (i) Whether the lord of the house is well placed from the ascendant.

(ii) Whether the lord of the house is well placed from the house he is the owner of, and which is under judgment.

(iii) Whether the lord of the house is hemmed in by benefics or malefics. Suppose the Sun is at 26° of Scorpio and Mars is tenanting 20° of Scorpio and Saturn 29° of Scorpio, the Sun will be deemed to be hemmed in by malefics. If instead of the Mars and Saturn, there are Jupiter and Mercury on the two sides of the Sun, he will be deemed to be hemmed in by benefics. If there are no planets in the sign, judge from the planets in adjacent houses, that is, from the second and the twelfth signs, counted from the sign tenanted by the house lord. For judging the hemmed in position, we never go beyond the adjacent signs.

(iv) Whether the house lord is combust. A planet is deemed combust when due to his nearness to the Sun he is not visible. For determining whether a planet is combust, refer to the end of this Chapter.

(v) Whether the house lord aspects the house he is lord of and which is under judgment.

(vi) Whether the house lord is conjoined with malefics or benefics.

(vii) Whether the house lord is conjoined with lords of good houses or evil houses.

(viii) Whether the house lord is aspected by benefics or malefics.

(ix) Whether the house lord is aspected by lords of good houses or evil houses.

(x) Whether the house lord occupies his own house or is in exaltation or in a great friend's sign, a friend's sign or an enemy's sign or a great enemy's sign.

C. (i) Whether the *Karaka* is well placed as counted from the ascendant. It is generally not considered good if the Jupiter *Karaka* for the second — is in the second, or the Mars *Karaka* for the third is in the third, or the Jupiter *Karaka* for the fifth is in the fifth, or the Venus *Karaka* for the seventh is in the seventh.

(ii) Whether the *Karaka* is conjoined with benefics or malefics.

(iii) Whether the *Karaka* is conjoined with lords of good or evil houses.

(iv) Whether the *Karaka* is combust or with brilliant rays.

(v) Whether the *Karaka* is aspected by benefics or malefics,— their strength and measure.

(vi) Whether the *Karaka* is aspected by lords of good or evil houses.

(vii) Whether the *Karaka* is hemmed in by benefics or malefics.

7. Aspects of planets differ in strength and measure. This expression may not convey its exact meaning to beginners and is therefore explained below.

(i) Jupiter's aspect is good. But his 50% aspect would be greater in measure than a 25% aspect; similarly a 75% aspect would be greater in measure than a 50%, and a full (100%) aspect would be the greatest in measure.

(ii) As regards strength, if Jupiter is in Cancer in his sign of exaltation, then the strength of his aspect would be greater than if Jupiter were in debilitation in Capricorn. The strength of aspect is proportionate to the strength of the planet aspecting, in the following decreasing order: (i) exaltation, (ii) own sign, (iii) great friend's sign, (iv) friend's sign, (v) neutral's sign, (vi) enemy's sign, (vii) great enemy's sign, (viii) in a debilitated sign.

(iii) There is also difference in the qualitative strength according to whether a planet is lord of good houses or evil houses.

For example, aspect of Mars in birth charts with Virgo ascendant, will be very evil—his tenancy will also be very evil because he will be the lord of the third and eighth houses. But in birth charts with Cancer as the rising sign, the aspect of Mars would not be so damning because he would be the lord of the fifth and the tenth—both good houses.

(iv) In judging a house lord conjoined with or aspected by a benefic or malefic, due regard should be paid to the house lordship of the planet conjoining or aspecting. For example, for a person with Cancer rising, if Mars conjoins or aspects Jupiter with his seventh aspect, it will be a *Sambandha* of lord of the tenth (an angle). Mars, with Jupiter lord of the ninth (a trine) and will be a positive *Rajayoga* due to mutual *Sambandha* between the lords of an angle and trine and will be extremely good. On the other hand, if Taurus is rising and Jupiter and Saturn conjoin or have a full mutual aspect, it will have a dragging down effect on status and position, because the lord of the tenth (Saturn) will have *Sambandha* with the lord of the eighth and the eleventh (Jupiter). These subtleties have to be borne in mind.

8. In judging a chart, keep in mind the *Yogas* given in the next Chapter. These *Yogas* are exceptions to the general rule.

9. (a) If a planet is owner of one good house and one evil, if he is strong he will show more good effects than evil ones; but if he is weak he will show more evil effects than good ones.

(b) Excepting the Sun and the Moon, each of the other five planets is lord of two houses. If out of the two—one good and one evil—he occupies the good house, he does not show the evil effect of ownership of the other evil house. For example, if Virgo is rising, Saturn will be the lord of the fifth (Capricorn) and the sixth (Aquarius). If he occupies the fifth house (Capricorn), his own sign, he does not damage the fifth house due to his evil lordship of the other house (sixth).

10. Whether a benefic or malefic, if he is the lord of the ascendant, he does not damage the house he tenants or aspects. For example, if Aries is rising, Mars who is a natural malefic would be the lord of the first and the eighth and if he occupies the fifth house, he does not damage the fifth house due to his inherent malefic nature or due to his evil house lordship. Or if Scorpio is rising, Mars becomes the lord of the first and the sixth, an evil, house. But if

he tenants the fifth he does not damage the fifth house.

11. All houses, first, second, third and so on, should be judged not only as counted from the ascendant but from the Moon sign also. In fact, some astrologers go to the extent of declaring that if the Moon is stronger than the ascendant, then the Moon sign should be given preference over the ascendant. In counting from the Moon sign, the sign occupied by the Moon will be the first house, the next sign would be the second house, the third sign, as counted from the Moon sign, would be the third house, and so on. Suppose a person has a strong Moon in Cancer; he is born at night in the bright fortnight of the month and the Moon is fully aspected by benefics. Now since the Moon occupies Cancer, Cancer will be the first house, Leo the second, Virgo the third, Libra the fourth, Scorpio the fifth, Sagittarius the sixth, Capricorn the seventh, Aquarius the eighth, Pisces the ninth, Aries the tenth, Taurus the eleventh, and Gemini the twelfth. In such a case we shall judge wealth from Leo (second from Moon), children from Scorpio (fifth from Moon), and so on.

But even when the first preference is given to the rising sign or ascendant, the twelve houses from the Moon sign should be judged and the results arrived at by blending the influences pertaining to a house as counted from the ascendant as well as from the Moon.

12. (a) If a malefic planet is in a benefic's sign and is aspected by benefics, his malignancy is softened, that is, he does not prove so evil.

(b) If a benefic planet occupies a malefic's sign and is aspected by a malefic, his benefic powers are curtailed.

13. We have discussed above that it is not good for any house lord to be in the sixth, eighth or the twelfth house, which are called *Dusthanas* or evil houses. We have also discussed that a planet should not be in his sign of debilitation. Now a relevant point for enquiry arises: suppose (a) the lord of a house or *Karaka* is in a good sign but in an evil place; alternatively suppose (b) the lord of a sign or *Karaka* is weak by sign position but well placed by house, say in the eleventh. Now of the two disqualifications (a) good by sign but evil by house position, and (b) evil by sign position but good by house position, which is preferable? Our experience is that if we have to choose between the two evils (b) is better than (a).

This book is written with a view to be self-sufficient in regard to the subject matter dealt herein. A glossary of technical words with their English equivalents has been given at the end, but certain terms are so technical that no single word or phrase can describe the meaning of the Sanskrit word and while dealing with a point, if we explain the Sanskrit word at every stage, it would mean deviating too far and too frequently from the context.

Besides, it is expected that readers of this volume will have occasion to study other works on Hindu astrology; readers may also have occasion to refer to the English translations of Sanskrit works on the subject. So, it becomes necessary to explain here some important terms, that are of a fundamentally important character. We have arranged them alphabetically for convenience of reference.

SANSKRIT TERMS AND THEIR MEANINGS

APACHAYA. The first, second, fourth, fifth, seventh, eighth, ninth and twelfth houses.

ASTA (combust). The Moon is combust when it is within 12° of the Sun. Mars is combust when within 17° from the Sun. If Mercury is direct, it becomes combust within 14° from the Sun; but when Mercury is retrograde, it is combust within 12° from the Sun. Jupiter becomes combust when within 11° from the Sun. If Venus is direct, it becomes combust when within 10° from the Sun; but if Venus be retrograde, he becomes combust when within 8° from the Sun. Saturn becomes combust when within 15° from the Sun. These are the normal distances. If planets have very wide latitudes at the moment they would not become combust at the exact degrees specified above. But for practical purposes the above distances may be taken as correct.

DOSHA. This is a Sanskrit word and used frequently in astrological literature. Literally it means a blemish, a disqualification, a pulling down weight, want of perfection, intermixture of unfavourable factors with favourable ones, a factor impeding good effects, an obstructing influence, a weakness to achieve and such other attributes on the negative side. Let us consider some of the *Doshas*.

We shall first deal with those connected with signs.

A planet in his sign of debilitation or in an enemy's or great enemy's sign is considered weak and yields unfavourable results.

Now we shall deal with a *Dosha* connected with houses.

A planet in the sixth, eighth or twelfth house has *Dosha* because these three houses are considered evil. A malefic in the sixth is, however, not considered unfavourable. Under certain other circumstances, for example, when a planet in the eighth forms a *Yoga,* he is not considered evil. But these are exceptions. Generally speaking, planets in *Trik* are considered as occupying unfavourable positions.

Let us now deal with the *Dosha* arising out of ownership of houses.

(i) Lords of angles are considered good particularly when they do not own an evil house also; they bestow good results during their *Dashas* and *Antardashas*. Lords of triangles, whether benefics or malefics, are always considered good.

(ii) The lord of the eighth house is considered very evil. The two exceptions are when the sign Aries is on the ascendant or when Libra is rising, the lord of the eighth house is not considered evil. Also the Sun when Capricorn is rising or the Moon when Sagittarius is ascending are not considered as having *Dosha,* but the convention is that they are not altogether free from *Dosha,* but do have slight *Dosha.* In all other charts, i.e., when a sign other than Aries, Libra, Sagittarius or Capricorn is rising, the planet owning the eighth is deemed to have great *Dosha.* The Sun in Leo in eighth or the Moon in Cancer in eighth has no *Dosha.*

(iii) Lords of the third, sixth and eleventh houses are called *Papis* and as such have *Dosha.*

(iv) Lord of the twelfth, according to one school, has *Dosha;* but according to another school, if he is placed in a good house owns another good house or is conjoined with the lord of a good house, he has no *Dosha.*

(v) Lord of the second owns the *Maraka Sthana* (death inflicting house). But when he is in company of the lord of a good house and situated in a good house, or owns another good house, he has no *Dosha* to spoil another planet's good prospects, though he himself might inflict harm.

(vi) When the lord of a good house, say of an angle or a trine is also the owner of the third, sixth, eighth or eleventh house, though he is good due to lordship of a good house, yet he also becomes evil due to owning a bad house and as such a good planet is considered as having a *Dosha*.

The following are other factors which cause *Dosha*:

(i) A planet who is combust is considered powerless or having very little power to do good. If a malefic, he becomes more evil.

(ii) Planets having crossed their lowest debilitation points and proceeding towards their highest exaltation points are considered good, while planets having crossed their highest exaltation points and proceeding towards their deepest debilitation points are considered as having *Dosha* of *Avaroha*.

(iii) A planet conjoined with *Papas* or aspected by *Papas* is considered as having *Dosha*.

(iv) A planet conjoined with a planet who is debilitated or who is a *Papa*, or who is his enemy or great enemy is also considered as having *Dosha*.

(v) The *Dosha* ascribed to conjunction in (iv) above is also produced if instead of conjunction there is aspect of the planet, who by conjunction would have caused *Dosha*.

DUSTHANA. The sixth, eighth and twelfth houses are called *Dusthanas* or evil houses. Thus, it will be seen that the sixth house is both an *Upachaya* as well as *Dusthana*. For which purposes it is good and for which others it is evil is indicated in the context it is used.

KARAKA. This is again a Sanskrit word frequently used in Hindu astrology and which cannot be adequately translated into English. Nor can the full connotation or complete meaning be conveyed in a single phrase or even a sentence. It can only be explained by bringing out the various meanings in all their aspects. The word *Karaka* is used in three senses: (i) as opposed to *Maraka*, (ii) significator of particular matters, (iii) significator of certain houses. Let us take these one by one. It is only after one has fully understood each of the meanings that one will be able to decide by the context in which the word occurs as to the sense which this word is expected to convey in that particular context.

(i) One of the meaning of the word is 'that which does.' Its meaning in this sense is just opposite of *Maraka*. *Karaka* and *Maraka* are the two extreme points of an axis. One is good, the other is evil. If *Karaka* represents the positive, additive or benefic nature, the *Maraka* stands for negative, subtractive and malefic nature. *Karaka* does good, accomplishes, increases, brings about fruition of efforts, produces good tangible results. *Maraka* on the other hand annihilates, frustrates, decreases, brings failure and does evil, kills, lowers the prestige, brings about illness, loss of prestige, etc.

The lord of the first, fourth, fifth, ninth and the tenth houses are generally called *Karakas*. But when the lord of the third, sixth or eleventh house is in his own sign in the third, sixth or eleventh house respectively, it can also prove a *Karaka*. So also the lord of the twelfth and the eighth can also prove *Karakas* if the lords are benefic and strong and occupy their own signs; but generally speaking the lords of angles (except the seventh) and the trines are called *Karakas*.

(ii) The second sense in which the word *Karaka* is used is as significator for particular matters or houses. For this readers are referred to Chapter 6 on planets.

(iii) The third sense in which the word *Karaka* is used is that each planet signifies certain matters, things, functions, aptitudes. The various constituents of the body, professions, tastes, learning, the functioning of the body, birds, beasts, metals, alphabet, kinds of cloth, merchandise, etc., have been divided and allotted to different planets. They have been given in Chapter 6 in detail. A planet is *Karaka* for the matters assigned to his portfolio.

MARAKA. The word *Maraka* is a word in Hindu astrology the sense of which cannot be conveyed by a single word or phrase in English. *Maraka* literally means a killer, but a *Maraka* does not always kill. The planet described as a *Maraka* has a propensity to kill. The words 'to kill' are used to indicate extreme detriment physically, mentally, or financially, substantial lowering of status, political defeat, marked insult, conviction in a criminal case, mutinuous disturbance in the domestic sphere and such other evil effects.

(i) The planets who are lords of the second or the seventh are *Marakas* particularly if they occupy the second or the seventh house. If a planet owns the seventh and the second—both, as for Aries and Libra, ascendants—he becomes a strong *Maraka*.

(ii) The lord of the third, the sixth and the eleventh are *Papis*. Their relative strengths are as follows: lord of the third, one unit; lord of the sixth, two units; lord of the eleventh, three units. Being *Papis*, they have also *Maraka* qualities, but these three, if in their own houses in the third, sixth or eleventh, will not be *Papis*. An eleventh lord, being the owner of the eleventh, would not bring financial loss, unless he is adversely placed, i.e., in a debilitated sign, in the eighth or the twelfth house, aspected by the lord of the eighth or the twelfth, or a *Papi* planet. The lord of the eleventh if in own house may produce *Maraka* effects in spheres other than financial, such as the father's death.

(iii) The lord of the eighth, unless he is the owner of the first house also, proves a *Maraka,* but for Aries and Libra—as one and the same planet owns the first and the eighth—he is not a *Maraka.* For Sagittarius and Capricorn, the Moon and the Sun are the respective owners of the eighth, but they are not *Marakas.*

(iv) The lord of the twelfth if conjoined with or aspected by a *Maraka* may evince *Maraka* propensities.

(v) When a benefic owns an angle, if he be a *Maraka* on any of the above counts, e.g., lordship of seventh, his *Maraka* qualities are enhanced. The order in which the *Maraka* qualities are enhanced in increasing measure are the Moon, Mercury, Venus, Jupiter. Thus if Moon be the lord of the seventh, he will be a *Maraka;* if Mercury be the lord of the seventh, his *Maraka* qualities will be more than that of the Moon. If Venus owns the seventh, his *Maraka* propensities would in such circumstance be greater than those of the Moon and Mercury; and if Jupiter owns the seventh, his *Maraka* propensities would be the maximum.

(vi) The *Maraka* propensities of planets are enhanced if they occupy the second or the seventh, which are called *Maraka* places; particularly so, if the lord of the second or the seventh is in the second or the seventh. Of the two houses, the second and the seventh, the second is more powerful in *Maraka* propensities and thus it follows that the second lord is a stronger *Maraka* than the seventh lord and the second house is more fraught with *Maraka* propensities than the seventh.

RAJAYOGA. A good indication for a good position in life, money, success, etc.

SAMBANDHA. Sambandha is a Sanskrit word and in the general sense, it means connection, relationship; but in Hindu astrology the word has acquired a special meaning. There is no single word in English which can convey the full meaning of the astrological definition of *Sambandha* and it must therefore be explained. There may be *Sambandha* between two planets and therefore also between the houses they own, in one of the following ways:

(a) If the two planets are in the same sign.

(b) If the two planets, say A and B, so occupy the signs that A is in B's sign and B in A's sign.

(c) If A fully aspects B and B fully aspects A. This mutual full aspect is possible only if they are in signs which are seventh to each other or if Mars is in the tenth from Saturn, when both will fully aspect each other. The opposite signs are:

(i) Aries, Libra; (ii) Taurus, Scorpio; (iii) Gemini, Sagittarius; (iv) Cancer, Capricorn; (v) Leo, Aquarius and (vi) Virgo, Pisces.

(d) There can be *Sambandha* between:

(i) Sun and Mars: if Mars is in Leo (Sun's sign) and fully aspects the Sun in Pisces.

(ii) Sun and Jupiter: if Jupiter is in Leo (Sun' sign) and the Sun is in Aries.

(iii) Sun and Saturn: if Saturn is in Leo (Sun's sign) and the Sun is in Libra or Taurus.

(iv) Moon and Mars: if Mars is in Cancer (Moon's sign) and the Moon is in Libra or Aquarius.

(v) Moon and Jupiter: if Jupiter is in Cancer (Moon's sign), and the Moon is in Scorpio.

(vi) Moon and Saturn: if Saturn is in Cancer (Moon's sign) and the Moon is in Virgo or Aries.

(vii) Mars and Jupiter: (a) if Jupiter is in Aries and Mars in Leo; (b) if Jupiter is in Scorpio and Mars in Cancer.

(viii) Mars and Jupiter: (a) if Mars is in Sagittarius, Jupiter, in Cancer or Pisces; (b) Mars is in Pisces and Jupiter in Gemini or Libra.

(ix) Mars and Saturn: (a) if Mars is in Capricorn and Saturn in Leo; (b) Mars in Aquarius and Saturn in Taurus or Virgo.

(x) Mars and Saturn: (a) if Saturn is in Aries and Mars in Gemini; (b) Saturn in Scorpio and Mars in Leo.

(xi) Jupiter and Saturn: (a) if Jupiter is in Capricorn, and Saturn in Taurus or Virgo; (b) Jupiter in Aquarius and Saturn in Gemini or Libra.

(xii) Jupiter and Saturn: (a) if Saturn is in Sagittarius and Jupiter in Aquarius or Virgo; (b) if Saturn is in Pisces and Jupiter in Taurus or Sagittarius.

(xiii) Mercury and Mars: (a) if Mars is in Gemini and Mercury in Virgo or Capricorn; (b) if Mars is in Virgo and Mercury in Sagittarius.

(xiv) Mercury and Jupiter: (a) if Jupiter is in Gemini and Mercury in Libra or Aquarius; (b) if Jupiter is in Virgo and Mercury in Taurus or Capricorn.

(xv) Mercury and Saturn: (a) if Saturn is in Gemini and Mercury in Leo or Pisces; (b) Saturn is in Virgo and Mercury in Scorpio or Gemini.

(xvi) Venus and Mars: (a) if Mars is in Libra and Venus in Capricorn or Taurus; (b) Mars in Taurus and Venus in Leo or Sagittarius.

(xvii) Venus and Jupiter: (a) if Jupiter is in Taurus and Venus in Virgo or Capricorn; (b) Jupiter is in Libra and Venus in Gemini or Aquarius.

(xviii) Venus and Saturn: (a) if Saturn is in Taurus and Venus in Cancer; (b) if Saturn is in Libra and Venus in Cancer or Sagittarius.

We have described above *sambandha* between two planets, where the planet A occupies the sign owned by planet B and A fully aspects the planet B. There is another variation of this, in which the planet A fully aspects B, where the B tenants the sign owned by planet A. The examples of this second category would be as follows:

(1) Mars in Virgo or Capricorn and any planet in Aries; Mars will have *sambandha* with the planet in Aries.

(2) Mars in Leo or Aries and any planet in Scorpio: Mars will have *Sambandha* with the planet in Scorpio.

(3) Jupiter in Aries or Leo and any planet in Sagittarius; Jupiter will have *sambandha* with the planet in Sagittarius.

(4) Jupiter in Cancer or Scorpio and any planet in Pisces; Jupiter will have *sambandha* with the planet in Pisces.

(5) Saturn in Aries or Scorpio and any planet in Capricorn; Saturn will have *sambandha* with the planet in Capricorn.

(6) Saturn in Taurus or Sagittarius and any planet in Aquarius; Saturn will have *sambandha* with the planet in Aquarius.

In these examples from (i) to (xviii) the principle underlying is that the planet A should occupy a sign owned by planet B and should fully aspect the planet B.

In the examples (1) to (6) given after the first set of examples, the principle is that planet A should fully aspect the planet B and the latter should tenant the sign owned by planet A.

To put it succinctly there is *sambandha* between two planets

A and B if :

(i) A occupies the sign owned by B and fully aspects B.

(ii) A fully aspects B and B occupies the sign owned by A.

Sambandha is a special feature of Hindu astrology and must be fully understood, because it is an important consideration in Hindu predictive astrology.

TRIK. The sixth, eighth and twelfth houses. Each of these three is a *Trik*. The cumulative reference to *Trik* includes all the three houses, viz., the sixth, eighth and twelfth. The location of a planet in *Trik* is generally considered adverse. Malefics in the sixth are however not so bad. Benefics in the eighth or twelfth are not so bad. According to one school, benefics in the sixth may produce enemies, but as it is an *Upachaya* house, the ultimate result is good. See also *Dusthana*.

UPACHAYA. The third, sixth, tenth and eleventh houses are called *Upachaya*. A planet in *Upachaya* is considered strong, and particularly so, if it is not aspected by *Papas* or by planets who are enemies of the lord of the sign. See also *Dusthana*.

YOGA. The word *Yoga* in Sanskrit means a combination: (i) a combination of two or more planets or a *Sambandha* between two or more planets, (ii) combination of a planet and a sign, (iii) combination of a planet and a house, (iv) location of planet in a particular sign or house and aspect over it of any particular planet and so on. Sometimes more than two ingredients qualify for a particular *Yoga*. But the minimum requisite is that two ingredients must be present to justify the use of the word *Yoga*.

A *Yoga* may be good or bad. Sometimes the astrologers describe an evil *Yoga* as an *Avayoga* or an *Ashubha Yoga* and a good *Yoga as a Shubha Yoga*, or just as a *Yoga*.

YOGA KARAKA. Five out of the seven planets own two houses. Generally one of them is good, the other evil. When a planet owns both good houses, one angle and one trine, he is called *Yoga Karaka* for a particular ascendant. Thus Saturn for Taurus and Libra ascendants, Mars for Cancer and Leo ascendants, Venus for Capricorn and Aquarius ascendants, would be *Yoga Karaka*.

For Aries, the Sun and the Moon; for Scorpio also, the Sun and the Moon. For Gemini and Virgo, Mercury, and for Sagittarius and Pisces, Jupiter would be as good as *Yoga Karaka* for they two own good houses.

CHAPTER 11

YOGAS—COMBINATIONS OF PLANETS

SOME important *Yogas* are given in this Chapter. This is with a view to cultivate the faculty of astrological appraisal and discrimination and also to examine the birth chart with reference to *Yogas* in a particular nativity.

In ancient India, when texts on astrology were written, owners of large areas of land were common and the number of feudal lords who were called Rajas and Maharajas ran into tens of thousand. The number of armies was equally large and thousands of people were kings and commanders-in-chief. We have at places allowed the phraseology to remain as in the original texts. It is left to the readers to interpret them against the prevailing political and social background of the country in which the native is born and brought up, or lives.

The *Yogas* have been grouped under certain heads, but no strict arrangement has been followed with in the group, because each Yoga is independent of the other.

I. YOGAS BASED ON ASCENDANT AS A FACTOR

(1) If benefics occupy the second and twelfth houses as counted from the ascendant, it is called *Shubha Kartari* — *kartari* means a pair of scissors; here the second and the twelfth houses are analogous to the two blades. If malefics occupy the second and twelfth houses, as counted from the ascendant, it constitutes

Papa Kartari. The result of *Shubha Kartari* is good health and accumulation of money. The *Papa Kartari* makes the native sickly and poor.

(2) If benefics occupy the second house from the ascendant and are not aspected by malefics, it makes *Shubha Yoga*. The native has a good face and is wealthy.

(3) If Mercury, Jupiter or Venus occupy any of the three houses, namely, the sixth, seventh and eighth, as counted from the ascendant, it constitutes *Adhi Yoga*. The native is wealthy and occupies a good position; if less than three are present the *Yoga* will not be so strong.

(4) If all the three benefics, Mercury, Jupiter and Venus are in *Upachaya* houses (i.e., the third, sixth, tenth and eleventh from the ascendant), the *Yoga* is called *Ati-vasuman*. The native is very wealthy.

If instead of the three benefics, only two benefics are present, the *Yoga* formed is less powerful and would be the least powerful if only one benefic is in *Upachaya*. The *Yoga* is not marred if along with benefics, a malefic or malefics are also present.

(5) If the ascendant occupies any degree from 0 to 3° 20′ in Aries, Cancer, Libra or Capricorn or any degree from 13° 20′ to 16° 40′ in Taurus, Leo, Scorpio or Aquarius or any degree from 26° 40′ to 30° in Gemini, Virgo, Sagittarius and Pisces, and is fully aspected by four planets other than the Moon, it constitutes a *Raja Yoga*.

(6) If Capricorn be the rising sign, with Mars and Saturn therein, and the Sun and Moon are in Sagittarius, it constitutes a *Raj Yoga* of a high order.

(7) If Capricorn be the rising sign with the Moon and Mars therein and the Sun is in Sagittarius, it is a good *Raj Yoga*.

(8) If Aries be the rising sign with the Sun therein, Jupiter in Sagittarius and the Moon and Saturn are together in Libra, it constitutes a good *Raj Yoga*.

(9) If Mercury, Jupiter and Venus be in the ascendant and Saturn in the seventh, the native is very rich and leads a very luxurious life.

(10) If Jupiter is in the ascendant, Saturn in the seventh and Sun in the tenth, the same results as in (9) above may be foretold.

(11) If Jupiter be in the ascendant, Mars in the second, Venus and Sun in the fourth, the Moon in the tenth and Saturn in the

eleventh, the native become a ruler. Planets should not be in their signs of debilitation.

(12) If Mars and Saturn are in the ascendant, the Moon in the fourth, Jupiter in the seventh, Venus in the ninth, the Sun in the tenth and Mercury in the eleventh, the native becomes a mighty ruler.

(13) If a strong Mercury is in the ascendant, a powerful benefic in the ninth and the other planets in the second, third, sixth, ninth, tenth and eleventh houses (distributed in one or more) the native becomes a ruler.

(14) If the longitude of Venus is in the initial 13° 20′ of the sign Aries, and the sign Aries is rising and Venus is fully aspected by the Moon, Mars, Jupiter and Saturn, the native occupies an outstanding and high position.

(15) If the rising sign is Pisces and the rising degree is between 26° 40′ to 30° and Venus also occupies a degree between 26° 40′ to 30° in Pisces, the native occupies a very high position in life. He may be equal to a king.

(16) When Rahu is in the ascendant and the Moon, Mercury and Venus are in angles, the native's action are of a low order.

(17) If Mars and Saturn together occupy the ascendant and the lord of the ascendant is in the second, eighth or the twelfth house and if the benefics do not occupy angles, the native will be sickly throughout his life.

(18) Jupiter in ascendant, except in Capricorn, confers a good *Yoga*.

(19) If Mars is in Aries, Leo or Sagittarius in the ascendant and is aspected by a friend, the native owns large properties and occupies a good rank.

II LORD OF ASCENDANT AS A FACTOR

(1) If the lord of the ascendant, the Sun and Moon are in angle or a trine (it is not necessary that they be together) in their respective signs of exaltation or own signs or in friendly signs, the *Yoga* is called *Shri Kantha*. The native would be a devotee of lord Shiva, highly religious, magnanimous and very illustrious.

(2) If the lord of the ascendant is strong and the lords of the fourth and the ninth are in angles from each other, i.e., the lord of the fourth is conjoined with the lord of the ninth or in fourth,

seventh or tenth from the lord of the ninth, the native is learned and wealthy and commands a good position and lives a luxurious life.

(3) If Venus is not in Virgo or in an enemy's sign and occupies the second house and the lord of the ascendant is strong, the native is very wealthy and occupies a very eminent position.

(4) If the lord of the ascendant is strong and conjoined with the dispositor of the Moon (the lord of the sign in which Moon is posited) and aspects the ascendant, he will occupy an eminent and powerful place in life. He will be of a pushing temperament and achieve success in life.

(5) If the lord of the ascendant is in his sign of exaltation and aspects the Moon, the native acquires much wealth and the requisites for comfort and crushes his enemies.

(6) If the lord of the ascendant is strong and the lord of the ninth is not only in his sign of exaltation but in the highest exaltation degree the native is of handsome appearance, very learned and famous, and blessed in respect of wife and sons. He owns large properties.

(7) If the lord of the ascendant is weak and aspects the Moon which has no *Pakshabala,* the native is poor and leads a religious mendicant's life.

(8) If the lord of the ascendant is in the second (in a sign which is not his sign of debilitation or his enemy's sign) and is conjoined with Venus, the native is very wealthy with various luxuries at his command.

III SUN AS A FACTOR

(1) If the lord of the fifth, Jupiter and Saturn are in their respective signs of exaltation, own signs or in friends' signs and occupy an angle or trine, the resultant *Yoga* is called *Viranchi.* The native will have knowledge of the 'self,' will be highly devoted and long lived, learned, much respected and will lead a happy life. If the Sun is also strong, there will be still better results.

(2) If at birth the Sun is in the tenth degree of Libra, the native though born a king's son, lives on alms and charity.

(3) If Sun is in Leo, except in 3° 20′ to 6° 40′ or 20° to

23° 20′, and Mercury is in Virgo, the native though born in an humble position rises very high in life.

(4) (i) If the Sun occupies any of the following degrees
13° 20′ to 16° 40′ in Aries, Leo and Sagittarius
23° 20′ to 26° 40′ in Taurus, Virgo and Capricorn
3° 20′ to 6° 40′ in Cancer, Scorpio and Pisces

(ii) and Moon is in Cancer, it is a good *Raja Yoga.*

(5) If the Sun is in Aries in the ascendant, Jupiter and Venus in Pisces, Saturn in Libra and full Moon is aspected by Mars, the native will be a king commanding a large army.

(6) If the Sun and the Moon are in the first half of Sagittarius, Saturn in the ascendant and a strong Mars exalted in Capricorn, the native becomes a mighty king of whom his enemies are always afraid.

(7) If there is a benefic planet, other than the Moon, in second from the Sun, it constitutes *Veshi Yoga,* if there is a benefic planet, other than the Moon, in twelfth from the Sun it constitutes *Vashi Yoga;* if there are benefic planets in both adjacent signs to the one occupied by the Sun, it gives to *Ubhayachari Yoga.* All these three *Yogas* if formed by benefics are good foı wealth and status. The converse is the case if formed by malefics.

IV. MOON AS A FACTOR

(1) If any planet other than the Sun occupies the second sign as counted from the sign occupied by the Moon it constitutes *Sunapha Yoga.* If any planet other than the Sun occupies the sign twelfth from that occupied by the Moon, this is called *Anapha Yoga.* If there are planets other than the Sun in signs, i.e., adjacent to the sign tenanted by the Moon, it is called *Durudhara Yoga.* The Sun in second or twelfth from the Moon does not mar the *Yoga,* but is not taken into consideration for constituting the *Yoga.* All these three *Yogas* are good for wealth and prosperity.

(2) If there is no planet (Sun, Rahu and Ketu are not taken into account in *Yogas* 1 and 2) on either side (adjacent to the Moon sign), it is called *Kemadruma Yoga* and the result is poverty. There is one exception to this *Yoga.* If Jupiter is in the first, fourth, seventh or tenth house from the Moon, it cancels the *Kemadruma Yoga.*

(3) *Adhi Yoga* is also formed if instead of counting from he ascendant, the three benefics occupy the three houses — the sixth, seventh and eighth as counted from the Moon.

In I(3) and IV(3) above it is not necessary that Mercury, Jupiter and Venus be in the sixth, seventh or eighth house in regular order. They can all be in one house, or in any two houses or in three different houses; but these houses must be sixth, seventh and eighth. Nor is the *Yoga* cancelled if along with benefics there are malefics, though the power is impaired. If instead of the three benefics only one is present, 33% of the good effects will be felt; if there are two benefics, the good effects will be 66%, while if all the above three are present, good results will be obtained in full. Such a native is wealthy and occupies a good position in life.

One point must be clarified. In considering this *Yoga* it has to be judged from the ascendant (See I(3) above) or independently from the Moon. We cannot mix up the two by saying Mercury is in the sixth from the Moon and Jupiter seventh or sixth from the ascendant and so an *Adhi Yoga* is formed. If however the Moon is in the ascendant, the *Adhi Yoga* will be formed by benefics in the sixth, seventh and eighth from the ascendant. This will be one *Adhi Yoga*. Another *Adhi Yoga* will be formed from the Moon. And thus a double set of *Adhi Yoga* will be formed which will be doubly good.

(4) If all the three benefics, Mercury, Jupiter and Venus, are in the third sixth, tenth or eleventh house from the Moon, the *Vasuman Yoga* is formed. For result and other particulars see *Yoga* I(4).

(5) If the Moon is in the third, sixth, ninth or twelfth house from the Sun, the native is courteous, intelligent, learned, wealthy and clever. If the Moon is in the second, fifth, eighth or eleventh from the Sun, the above qualities are of medium order. If the Moon is in the first, fourth, seventh or tenth from the Sun, the above good qualities are at their minimum.

(6) If the Moon occupies the degrees stated in No. I(5) above and is fully aspected by four or more planets, the same results as stated in I(5) above may be foretold.

Note: By permutation and combination, this will give rise to 44 patterns of charts.

(7) If the Moon is in an angle from Jupiter it constitutes *Gaja*

Kesari Yoga. The native is long-lived, wealthy and prosperous. If both the planets are in angles from the ascendant also, it is a more powerful *Yoga.*

(8) If the Moon is in the sixth, eighth or twelfth house from Jupiter, it constitutes *Shakata Yoga.* The native undergoes a cycle of prosperity and adversity like a wheel: for a period he is prosperous and this is followed by a period of adversity, then again a prosperous period, and so on. If the Moon is in angle from the ascendant the above *Yoga* is not formed.

(9) If the Moon and Jupiter are in their own signs or in their respective signs of exaltation and posited in the first, fourth, fifth, seventh, ninth or tenth house the resultant *Yoga* is called *Gauri.* The native leads a comfortable life and is well honoured by the government.

(10) If the Moon and Mars are together, the native is always rich; of course the effects would differ in intensity according to the sign and house position and according to the houses these planets are lords of.

(11) If a full Moon occupies the fourth, seventh or tenth house and is aspected by Jupiter and Venus, the native verily occupies a very high position and has real splendour.

(12) If the full Moon is in the ascendant in Taurus, Venus in Libra and Mercury in the fourth house, the native occupies a very high rank.

(13) (i) If a strong Moon is in Cancer, and two planets occupy the ascendant, which is the own sign of one of the two planets and the exaltation sign of the other, the native occupies a position equal to a king.

(ii) If a strong Moon is in Cancer and only one planet in his own sign, or exalted sign tenants the first house, the same results as in (i) above but in less measure.

(14) If the Moon and Venus are in angles and *Papas* tenant the eighth or ninth house, the native suffers from epilepsy.

(15) If a full Moon in the fourth, seventh or tenth house is fully aspected by an exalted planet or a planet in his own sign, even one born in a low family attains a kingly position.

(16) If out of the three lords—lord of second or ninth or eleventh—any one is in an angle as counted from the Moon and if Jupiter be the lord of the second, fifth or eleventh, the native is wealthy and owns large properties. He also holds an

eminent position in life.

(17) Full Moon in Pisces if aspected by a friendly planet confers *Raja Yoga.*

(18) Full Moon in Taurus confers *Raja Yoga.*

(19) If a white Moon (by inference full Moon) occupies any of the following degrees;

(i) 13° 20′ to 16° 40′ in Aries, Leo or Sagittarius,

(ii) 23° 20′ to 26° 40′ in Taurus, Virgo or Capricorn,

(iii) 3° 20 ′to 6° 40′ in Cancer, or Pisces, and all the benefics—not conjoined with malefics are in angles, the native becomes a king or occupies an equally eminent position.

(20) If the dispositor of the Moon (the lord of the sign which is occupied by the Moon) is in conjunction with the lord of the ascendant and occupies an angle (as counted from the ascendant) or tenants a great friend's sign, and secondly if a strong benefic aspects the ascendant the above setting of planets constitutes *Pushkala Yoga.* The native having this *Yoga* will be wealthy and earn name and fame for himself and will be honoured by the government.

V. DAY AND NIGHT BIRTHS

(1) If the Moon is strong in his own sign or in his sign of exaltation and (i) the birth be during day and if the Moon be fully aspected by Jupiter, the native will be wealthy; (ii) if the birth be at night and the Moon in his own sign or in exaltation is fully aspected by Venus, similar results may be expected.

(2) If the birth be of a male, during daytime, and the ascen dant, the Sun and the Moon, all three are in odd signs, it constitutes *Mahabhaghya Yoga.* The native is wealthy and prosperous and occupies a good position in life.

(3) If the birth be of a female, during night, and the ascendant, the Sun and the Moon be in even signs, it also constitutes *Mahabhagya Yoga* and the lady has long life and conjugal happiness. She is fortunate and prosperous and has sons and grand sons.

(4) If the Moon in Aries is in the ascendant and the time of birth be when half of the Sun's disc has risen at the eastern horizon, i.e., the longitude of the sign, degree and minute of the Sun coincides with the rising sign, degree and minute and if

Mars is in Capricorn, Jupiter in Sagittarius and Saturn in Aquarius, the native becomes a mighty ruler.

(5) (a) If in a male nativity, the birth is during day and the longitudes of the ascendant, the Sun and the Moon fall in any of the male *Nakshatras* (constellations), the native is much respected and is very fortunate, learned and has sons and grandsons.

(b) If in a female nativity the birth is during night and the longitudes of the ascendant, the Sun and the Moon are in female *Nakshatras,* the same results as in (a) above may be expected. The longitudes comprising each constellation are given in Chapter 1.

Ashwini, Punarvasu, Pushya, Hasta, Anuradha, Sharavana, Poorvabhadra and Uttarabhadra are male constellations; (ii) Mrigashira, Moola and Shatabhisha are eunuchs; (iii) the rest of the constellations are female.

(6) If the birth be during day, during the bright fortnight (when the Moon occupies 0° to 180° as counted from the Sun's longitude) and the lord of the first occupies his sign of exaltation, the native is learned, religious, long-lived, happy and owns large properties. He occupies an eminent position in life.

VI. SIGN POSITIONS

(1) If all the seven planets are posited in Leo, Virgo, Libra, Scorpio, Sagittarius and Capricorn, the native has push. He is courageous and is dynamic. All the six signs referred to need not be tenanted.

(2) If all the seven planets are in Aquarius, Pisces, Aries, Taurus, Gemini and Cancer, the native is mild, prosperous and fortunate. All the six signs need not be tenanted.

(3) If the benefics occupy angles and tenant the signs owned by benefics and the malefics occupy the signs owned by malefics, the native is wealthy and is a leader of daring people.

(4) If Mercury is fully aspected by Jupiter, the native is very intelligent and wise and even eminent people abide by his advice.

(5) (1) If one planet is in his own sign, the native's status will be in keeping with his family status; (ii) if the number of planets in own signs is two, he will be the head of the family; (iii) if three planets are in own signs, the native will command

respect from the whole of his clan; (iv) if four planets are so placed, he will be very wealthy; (v) if the number of planets in own signs is five, he will lead a happy life; (vi) if six planets are so placed he will have all comforts and luxuries at his command and enjoy them; (vii) if seven planets occupy their own signs, he will be a king or equal to one and occupy an eminent position and have all the paraphernalia of royalty.

(6) (i) If the number of planets in great friend's house is one, the native enjoys hospitality and food at other's cost; (ii) if the number of planets is two, the native is helped financially by his friends; (iii) if such planets are three, he will have the patronage of his kinsmen; (iv) if there are four such planets, he will receive help and assistance from his *Bandhus* (relations); (v) if five planets are in their respective great friend's signs, he will be the head of a tribe or institution; (vi) if there are six such planets, he will be the head of an army or a section of an army; (vii) and if all the seven planets are so placed, he will be a king or equal to one.

(7) (i) If malefics are in the first fifteen degrees of odd signs or in the last fifteen degrees of even signs, the native is strong, pushing, industrious, very courageous and wealthy.

(ii) If benefics are in the last fifteen degrees of odd signs or in the first fifteen degrees of even signs, the native is handsome, soft, benevolent and fortunate. His speech is sweet and manners endearing.

(8) Venus aspected by Jupiter confers wealth.

VII. EXALTATION OR OWN SIGNS

(1) Mars or Mercury or Jupiter or Venus or Saturn, any of these five planets in his own sign or in his sign of exaltation, if occupying the first, fourth, seventh or tenth house from the ascendant or the Moon constitutes a *Mahapurusha Yoga*. *Mahapurusha* means a great man and the angular position of any of these five non-luminaries in an angle, as described above, ensures wealth and a good position in life.

Thus Mars in Aries, Scorpio or Capricorn in an angle constitutes *Ruchaka Yoga;* Mercury in Gemini or Virgo in an angle constitutes *Bhadra Yoga;* Jupiter in an angle in Cancer, Sagittarius or Pisces constitutes *Hansa Yoga;* Venus in Taurus, Libra or Pisces in an angle constitutes *Malavya Yoga;* Saturn in Libra, Capricorn or Aquarius constitutes *Shasha Yoga.* These are five independent *Yogas* comprised by *Mahapurusha Yoga.*

(2) If three or more planets are in exaltation, the native becomes a king. Similar is the result if five planets are in their own signs. But if the malefics are strong, the native would be cruel; if benefics are strong, the native would be of a benevolent nature.

(3) If the Sun is in Aries, Moon in Taurus and Saturn in Aquarius and one of these in the ascendant, it is a *Raja Yoga.* The native occupies a high position.

(4) If Mercury is in Gemini, Jupiter in Leo, and Mars in Scorpio and one of them is in the ascendant, the same effects as in (3) above.

(5) If Saturn and Moon be exalted and one of them is in the ascendant, and the Sun and Mercury are in Virgo, Mars in Aries, Jupiter in Cancer and Venus in Libra, this combination constitutes a powerful *Raja Yoga.*

(6) If the Sun, Mars, Jupiter and Saturn, all the four are in their respective signs of exaltation and one of these four is in the ascendant, it constitutes a *Raja Yoga* of a high order.

(7) The *Yoga* given in (6) above is also caused when instead of the four planets above named, only three are in their respective signs of exaltation and one of them is in the ascendant. Same results as in (6) above but in lesser measure.

(8) The *Yoga* in (6) above is also formed if instead of the four planets above-named, only two are in their respective signs of exaltation and one of them is in the ascendant and the Moon is in Cancer. Same results as in (5) above materialise.

Note: By permutation and combination, (6), (7) and (8) will give rise to sixteen types of birth charts.

(9) If the lord of the ninth and Venus be in their own signs or in their respective signs of exaltation and posited in the first, fourth, fifth, seventh, ninth or tenth house, it is called *Lakshmi Yoga.* The native is wealthy and enjoys a luxurious life.

(10) If the lord of the sign, occupied by the lord of the ascendant is in his own sign or sign of exaltation in an angle or trine from the ascendant it constitutes a *Yoga.* The native is powerful, rich and owns lands. He is much respected.

(11) Suppose X is the sign on the ascendant and A is the lord

of the sign. Now A is posited in sign Y and B is the lord of sign Y. Now suppose B occupies the sign Z and C is the lord of sign Z. Then if the planet C is in an angle or trine from the ascendant, in his own sign or sign of exaltation, the resultant *Yoga* is called *Kahala*. The native is very rich, benevolent, and wealthy.

(12) If exalted Moon is in the ascendant and the Sun, Jupiter and Saturn are respectively in the fourth, seventh and tenth houses the native will no doubt becomes a king.

(13) If Saturn in Capricorn is in the ascendant, the Moon in Pisces, Mars in Gemini, Mercury in Virgo, Jupter in Sagittarius, the native becomes a king.

(14) If Mars be in Capricorn, Jupiter in Sagittarius and if Mercury in Virgo is in the ascendant, or if Venus in Pisces is in the ascendant, the native becomes a king.

(15) If exalted Jupiter is in the ascendant, the Moon, Mercury and Venus are in Taurus, and the Sun in Aries, the native is very courageous and becomes a king.

(16) If the Moon in Pisces is in the ascendant, Saturn in Aquarius, Mars in Capricorn, and the Sun in Leo, the native becomes a ruler.

(17) If Mars in Aries is in the ascendant and Jupiter in Cancer, the native is endowed with many qualities and becomes a ruler.

(18) If exalted Jupiter is in the ascendant and Mars in Aries is in the tenth, same results as in (17) above are expected.

(19) If Saturn in Capricorn is in the ascendant, Mars in Aries, the Moon in Cancer, Sun in Leo, Mercury in Virgo, and Venus in Libra, the native becomes a mighty king.

(20) If Mercury in Virgo is in the ascendant, the Sun in Leo, Venus in Gemini, Moon and Jupiter in the seventh, Mars and Saturn in the fifth, the native becomes a king.

(21) If the lord of the tenth house is exalted, the native will be a minister to the king or occupy an equally eminent position. If the lord of the tenth is in his own sign or in a friend's sign, the effect is not so powerful as in the case of exaltation, but still the native commands good respect and position.

(22) Even one planet exalted in the ascendant conjoined with a friend and aspected by a friend, makes one wealthy.

(23) If three or more planets are exalted or in their own signs, and are in angles, the native becomes a renowned king if the native is born in a royal family.

(24) If five or more planets are exalted or in their own signs and are in angles, the native though born in an ordinary family becomes a king or equal to a king or holds an equally eminent position.

Note: While judging 15 and 16 above please examine that there is no evil *Yoga* or *Yogas* and the planets are not combust

VIII. HOUSE POSITIONS

(1) If benefics are in the tenth house from the Moon, it constitutes *Amla Yoga*. The native will be of righteous conduct, benevolently inclined, wealthy and prosperous and will occupy a good position in life.

(2) If benefics occupy the tenth house from the ascendant then also *Amla Yoga* is caused and the result will be the same as in (1) above.

(3) (a) If Mercury, Jupiter and Venus occupy any of the following houses, first, second, fourth, fifth, seventh, ninth, or tenth, and (b) if Jupiter is in his exaltation or occupies his own or a friend's sign, *Saraswati Yoga* is formed. The native will be very intelligent, learned, famous, and fortunate. He may be a good poet.

(4) If Mercury, Jupiter and Venus or the Moon occupy the ninth house and are with bright rays, i.e., not combust, and are conjoined or aspected by friends, the native rises to a very exalted position.

(5) If all the seven planets* occupy one sign, it is called *Gola Yoga*. The native would be poor and associate with low people. He will be devoid of wealth. His actions will be sinful. He will be indolent and will have a short life.

(6) If all the seven planets occupy two signs, it constitutes *Yuga Yoga*. The native will be poor and a hypocrite.

(7) If all the seven planets occupy three signs, it constitutes *Shoola Yoga*. The native will be cruel, ill-tempered and lead an indigent life.

(8) If the seven planets occupy four signs, it is called *Kedara Yoga*. The native will own agricultural lands and will be rich.

(9) If all the seven planets are in five signs, the *Yoga* is called

* Whenever there is reference to seven planets, it means Sun, Moon, Mars, Mercury, Jupiter, Venus & Saturn.

Pasha. The native will have financial affluence, good relatives, will be of good conduct, and enjoy life.

(10) If the seven planets occupy six signs, the *Yoga* is called *Dama*. The native will be benevolently inclined, generous, and occupy a good position in life.

(11) If the seven planets occupy seven signs, it constitutes *Veena Yoga*. It is also called *Vallaki Yoga*. The native will be fond of singing, dancing, and all arts and will be rich.

(12) In *Yogas* (5) to (11) above, the locations of planets need not be in contiguous signs. We are now describing twelve *Yogas* in which the seven planets occupy seven contiguous signs. If all the seven planets occupy seven contiguous signs and no sign in between is untenanted by a planet, then:

(i) from the first to the seventh house, the native occupies a kingly position and has a host of conveyances.

(ii) from the second to the eighth house, the native is good-looking, very wealthy, persevering, endowed with many virtues, occupies a very high position, and is devoted to his father;

(iii) from the third to the ninth house, the native is very courageous and wealthy. He occupies a high rank but is sickly;

(iv) from the fourth to the tenth house, the native enjoys the luxuries of many kinds, is very generous, and occupies a kingly position;

(v) from the fifth to the eleventh house, the native performs *Yajnas* (religious sacrificial worship according to religious codes), he earns name and fame and occupies an outstandingly respected position;

(vi) from the sixth to the twelfth house, the native is generally very poor; only occasionally he will have a little money or comforts;

(vii) from the seventh to the first house, the native is the darling of many damsels and occupies a good rank in life;

(viii) from the eighth to the second house, the native will be long-lived, but without wealth; he will be henpecked or under the influence of women;

(ix) from the ninth to the third house, the native is devoted to religious austerities and worship. He is endowed with many qualities and occupies a good position in life. He is wealthy and prosperous;

(x) from the tenth to the fourth house, the native pursues

useful activities. He is devout and religious and is respected by gentle folk;

(xi) from the eleventh to the fifth house, he has a good woman as his wife, possesses precious jewellery and is a capable administrator;

(xii) from the twelfth to the sixth house, the native spends very heavily; is respected everywhere.

In these twelve kinds of *Malika Yogas*, also called *Ekavali*, one planet in each sign successively—consideration has to be paid whether the signs occupied are signs of exaltation, own signs or signs of friends or enemies or signs of debilitation. For example, if the Moon is in Cancer, the Sun in Leo, Mercury in Virgo, Venus in Libra, Mars in Scorpio, Jupiter in Sagittarius, and Saturn in Capricorn it will be a powerful *Malika Yoga*. Conversely, if the planets are in their signs of debilitation or in enemies' signs, this will not be able to do much good.

The placement of lords of houses and other features also form important factors on which astrological delineations are based and naturally different shades of effects will be produced according to the blending of influences.

(13) If all the benefics occupy the fifth, sixth and seventh houses from the ascendant, this constitutes *Shubha Mala Yoga*. The native will be wealthy and occupy a good position in life.

(14) If all the benefics occupy the sixth, eighth and twelfth houses from the ascendant, it is called *Ashubha Mala Yoga* and the result is evil. There will be heavy expenses and the native will not be happy.

(15) If Venus in Taurus or Libra is in the fourth, the Moon in the ninth and other planets in the third, sixth and eleventh, the native owns land and rules over it.

(16) If the Moon, Venus and Saturn are in angles, Mars in the eighth and the Sun in the twelfth (or both Sun and Mars in the eighth or twelfth), the native does not stick to one place and has to face adversities in life.

(17) If there are planets in the ascendant, fourth, seventh, ninth and tenth houses and no planets occupy the eighth and twelfth, it is a very good *Yoga*. The native occupies an important position, has religious and benevolent inclinations, is courteous, learned and wealthy.

(18) If all the planets are in the first, fourth, seventh and

tenth houses, the native is very fortunate and occupies a prominent position. This *Yoga* is called *Mangal.*

(19) If all the planets are in the second, fifth, eighth and eleventh houses, it is called *Madhya Yoga.* The effect is moderate wealth and position. Sometimes the native accumulates money; at othertimes he is poor.

(20) If all the planets are in the third, sixth, ninth and twelfth houses, the *Yoga* is called *Kleeva* (literally, the word means impotent, but in this context it means powerless). The native does not succeed in attaining a high position or accumulating wealth. He generally leads a static existence and happiness and comforts are not his.

(21) If the Moon and Mars are together in the ascendant and Jupiter is in the ninth or tenth house from the ascendant and the Sun is strong, the native will be wealthy and occupy a high position in life.

(22) If Mars and Saturn be in the first, fifth or tenth house and the full Moon occupies the ninth house, the native occupies a very high rank.

(23) If all the planets occupy angles and trines and any of them is in his sign of exaltation, the native becomes a king or equal to a king; is very generous and leads a luxurious life.

(24) (i) If the native is born on a Tuesday or Saturday and if the Sun and the Moon are in the first, fifth or ninth house and if Jupiter is in the third, or in an angle from the ascendant, the native will be fickle-minded like an insane person.

(25) If the Moon and Mercury are in angles from the ascendant and are not aspected by their dispositors nor are they conjoined with other planets, the native may suffer from schizophrenia or insanity.

(26) If the Moon and Jupiter together are in an angle and aspected by Venus, this confers great wealth and a good position provided that there is no planet in debilitation.

IX. LORD OF FIRST TO TWELFTH HOUSES

(1) (a) If the lord of the first, second, fourth, fifth, seventh, ninth, tenth or the eleventh house mutually changes place with any of the lords of houses grouped above, it is a *Maha Yoga.* For example, the lord of the first in the eleventh and the lord of the

eleventh in first or lord of the second in the eleventh and lord of the eleventh in the second; or lord of the fourth in the tenth and lord of the tenth in the fourth, and so on. There is increase in respect of good luck pertaining to the houses involved.

(b) If any lord of the first, second, fourth, fifth, seventh, ninth, tenth or the eleventh house changes place with the lord of the third, it is called *Khala Yoga*. For example, the lord of the tenth is in the third and the lord of the third in the tenth; or the lord of the third in the fourth and the lord of the fourth in the third. This is a bad *Yoga* called *Khala*.

(c) If the lord of a house stated in clause (a) above changes place with the lord of the sixth, eighth or twelfth house, it is called *Dainya Yoga.*

The sixth, eighth and twelfth houses are called *Trik*. They are also called *Dusthanas*. So if the lord of the first, second, fourth, fifth, seventh, ninth, tenth or the eleventh house exchanges place with the lord of a *Trik*, it will constitute *Dainya Yoga*, a pulling down weight for luck and prosperity. *Dainya Yoga* is worse than *Khala Yoga*.

Thus by permutation and combination there will be 66 *yogas*.

(i) Lord of the first, second, fourth, fifth, seventh, ninth, tenth or eleventh house mutually changing places: 28 *Yogas* (*Maha Yoga*).

(ii) Lord of the twelfth changing places with lords of the remaining eleven houses: 11 *Yogas* (*Dainya Yoga*).

(iii) Lord of the eighth changing places with lords of houses from first to eleventh: 10 *Yogas* (*Dainya Yoga*).

(iv) Lord of the sixth changing places with lords of any house from first to eleventh (except 8th covered by (iii) above): 9 *Yogas* (*Dainya Yoga*).

(v) Lord of the third changing place with lords of the first, second, fourth, fifth, seventh, ninth, tenth or eleventh: 8 *Yogas* (*Khala Yoga*).

Thus we get 28 *Maha Yogas*, 8 *Khala Yogas* and 30 *Dainya Yogas*. In the delineation of effects, the sign positions, whether by changing places a planet will be occupying his sign of exaltation or own sign or a sign of debilitation should be attached due weight.

For example, if the rising sign is Scorpio, the lord of the first (Mars) occupies the ninth (Cancer, the sign of debilitation of

Mars) and the ninth lord (Moon) occupies the first (Scorpio, the sign in which the Moon is debilitated). This cannot be so powerful a combination for good as when Leo is rising and the lord of the ninth (Mars) is in Leo in the first and the lord of the first exalted in Aries in the ninth.

This principle has also to be applied to *Dainya Yogas*. Suppose Libra is the rising sign and the lord of the first (Venus) is exalted in the sixth and the sixth lord (Jupiter) is in the first. This will not be so evil. All these different shades arising out of sign positions must be taken into account. Here we have stated the goodness or otherwise arising out of a mutual exchange of places between house lords.

(2) If a house is tenanted by a benefic or aspected by benefics and the lord of the house is well placed and in his own sign or sign of exaltation and not combust, twelve *Yogas* (one pertaining to each house respectively) are formed. If the house and house lord fulfil the conditions laid down above and it is the —

(i) *first house*: the *Yoga* is *Chamar*. One born in this *Yoga* gains eminence and prosperity like a waxing moon. He is wealthy, long-lived, famous and occupies a high position.

(ii) *second house*: the *Yoga* is *Dhenu*. The native will have delicious food and drinks and be learned, and wealthy, and have a large family.

(iii) *third house*: the *Yoga* formed is *Shourya*. The native's younger brothers will be famous and respect the native; he will himself be very courageous, earn name and fame and will engage in governmental work.

(iv) *fourth house*: the *Yoga* constituted is *Jaladhi*. The native has agricultural lands, cattle, property, conveyances, a good wife and home comforts. He will engage in governmental work; will also be inclined to construct wells and tanks. He holds a good position in life.

(v) *fifth house*: the *Yoga* formed is *Chhatra*. The native will have a happy home life, a good wife and children. He will speak sweetly; be intelligent and learned. The native earns a good name and fame and will be a minister, counseller or adviser to the government or hold an equally eminent position.

(vi) *sixth house*: the *Yoga* is called *Astra*. The native is strong, proud and powerful. He subdues his opponents by sheer force. He has undaunted courage and a combative spirit and may have scars of wounds on his body.

(vii) *seventh house*: the *Yoga* constituted is *Kama*. He will have a good wife and children and will be attached to his own wife. He will rise to a rank higher than that of his father, and will be prosperous and happy.

(viii) *eighth house*: the *Yoga* is called *Asura*. The native is selfish, a back-biter and malevolent, always causing harm to others. He is poor and commits low acts and has to face trouble due to them. In short, the temperament, the inclination and behaviour are malevolent and he suffers in life.

(ix) *ninth house*: the *Yoga* formed is *Bhagya* because the ninth house is called *Bhagya*—which means good luck and prosperity of all kinds. The native will be lucky and prosperous in all respects, wealthy, command respect and occupy a good position in life. He will be religious and devoted to God.

(x) *tenth house*: the *Yoga* constituted is *Khyati*, which in Sanskrit means fame. The native will be wealthy and prove a good ruler or administrator. He will be renowned.

(xi) *eleventh house*: the *Yoga* is called *Suparijata*. The native will have a good income and will be wealthy; he will have a large family and there will be a chain of auspicious festivities. He will be learned, fond of hearing religious discourses and be of a righteous conduct.

(xii) *twelfth house*: the *Yoga* formed is called *Musala*, which in Sanskrit means a big pestle. The native will become wealthy by earning money through much hard labour and difficulties, he will spend money only on worthy objects; he will be very active and talkative; will be over-powered by his opponents. After death he attains heaven.

Note: For judging the effects of a house, how far the *Yoga* is fulfilled, five factors must be present: (i) the house should be tenanted by a benefic; (ii) the house should be aspected by a benefic or benefics; (iii) the house lord should not be combust; (iv) the house lord should be in an angle or trine or in a good place; (v) the house lord should be in his own sign or sign of exaltation. Though it has not been stated in the text, yet if any of the following adverse factors are present, the *Yoga* will be tarnished and will be incapable of giving rise to the full effects of the *Yoga*: (i) If malefics tenant the house; in this the connection it has to be borne in mind is that a malefic in his own sign is not evil;

but a malefic in his own house, if it is in the twelfth house from the ascendant it will give rise to heavy expenditure. (ii) The house is aspected by malefics. (iii) The house lord is in undesirable degrees. For undesirable degrees for each planet in each sign readers are referred to Chapter 8. (iv) If the house lord is conjoined with or aspected by malefics.

Again, all benefics will not behave equally. Jupiter is a benefic but he will have different shades of effects, (i) according to the sign he is in, as for example, Jupiter in Cancer will be far different from Jupiter in Capricorn; (ii) according to the house of which the planet is the lord, as for example, Jupiter as lord of the first and the fourth house will have effects which Jupiter as lord of the third and the sixth cannot have.

Therefore, readers are requested to develop their own faculties of discrimination and judgment which is necessary to appraise an individual chart. No set of rules can provide for all contingencies and all the permutations and combinations possible.

(3) If the lord of a house is in an evil place* or the house tenants or is aspected by a malefic, twelve *Yogas*—one for each house—arise: if the house affected is the—

(i) *first house*: the *Yoga* is called *Avayoga*, which in Sanskrit means a bad *Yoga*. The native has an uneventful life of poverty. He will suffer many humiliations; his company will be of low and wicked people. This *Yoga* impairs health and longevity is curtailed.

(ii) *second house*: the *Yoga* constituted is known as *Niswa*, which in Sanskrit means without wealth. The native has bad teeth, poor eye-sight or the eyes may have some defects; his power of speech is not good; his enemies appropriate his wealth; he is neither intelligent nor learned.

(iii) *third house*: the *Yoga* formed is *Mriti*. The native is without brothers or there is no happiness from them. His wealth and strength are undermined; he is not even tempered; his efforts are misdirected and end in failure and frustration. The native lacks in courage and there is a latent feeling of timidity or an inferiority complex.

(iv) *fourth house*: the *Yoga* is known as *Kuhu*. The native suffers in respect of his mother, conveyances, friends, relations,

* The 6th, 8th and 12th are called evil places. This group of houses is called *Trik* or *Dusthana*.

apparel and happiness. The fourth house is the house of ease, comfort, mental tranquillity and happiness and all these are curtailed. He suffers in respect of his position and property also. He is attached to an unworthy woman who may be his own wife or some other woman.

(v) *fifth house*: the *Yoga* so formed is called *Pamara*. The native tells lies; he lacks in the finer sense of discrimination, cheats others, does not believe in God or religion; has evil company. He may have no sons or there may be premature death of sons or no happiness from them.

(vi) *sixth house*: the *Yoga* is called *Harsha*, which in Sanskrit means happiness or delight. If the sixth lord is placed in a *Dusthana*, it gives rise to happy circumstances. The native has a strong body; he does not indulge in evil acts and has no evil intentions; he enjoys happiness, luxuries and good fortune; overcomes his enemies; is a favourite of eminent people; has wealth, good friends and sons and earns name and fame for himself.

(vii) *seventh house*: the *Yoga* has been named *Dushkrit* (which literally means evil actions). The result is separation, inclination for liaisons with others' wives, wandering aimlessly, venereal or urinary diseases such as spermatorrhoea, diabetes; trouble from government. The native is despised by his relations and suffers.

(viii) *eighth house*: the *Yoga* is called *Sarala*, which means easy. It is good to have the eighth lord in the sixth or eighth or twelfth house. If a malefic, he would spoil the twelfth, but whether a benefic or malefic, if the lord of the eighth is in a *Dusthana* it fortifies the eighth house. The native is long-lived, of a strong mind, fearless, learned, wealthy, blessed with sons. He overcomes his enemies, is famous and the work he undertakes is accomplished successfully.

(ix) *ninth house*: the *Yoga* is called *Nirbhagya* which means luckless. He brings about ruin of immoveable ancestral property by neglect, or by mortgaging or selling it away under financial pressure; is irreligious, talks ill of and does not respect his religious preceptors and ascetics; is poorly dressed, and suffers much distress.

(x) *tenth house*: the *Yoga* is known as *Duryoga*. Whatever the native undertakes, despite his strenuous efforts, ends in frustration and disappointment. He suffers humiliation in society, lives at a place other than his homeland and leads an unhappy life. The native is antagonistic to others and suffers distress.

(xi) *eleventh house*: this *Yoga* is known as *Daridra,* which means poverty. The native incurs heavy debts and is poor. He is not good tempered; has no good brothers; may suffer from diseases of the ear. He runs errands for others, i.e., occupies a subordinate position. His speech is not good and his actions are not commendable.

(xiii) *twelfth house*: the *Yoga* is called *Vimala,* which means free from blemish. Like the lords of the sixth and the eighth, it is good for the lord of the twelfth to be in *Trik* or *Dusthana.* The native does not spend much and accumulates wealth; is agreeable to all people and is liked by them. He leads an independent life and is happy. He follows an honourable profession and is known for his good qualities.

X. LORDS OF HOUSES

(1) If the lord of the second is in the eleventh and the lord of the eleventh in the second or both of them are in angles from the ascendant, there is good gain of money.

(2) If the lord of the ninth, Mercury and Venus be in their respective signs of exaltation or in own signs or in their friends' signs and occupy an angle or a trine, though all the three need not be together, it is called *Shrinatha Yoga.* The native would be a devotee of lord *Vishnu,* highly religious, learned, free from malice, rich and lead a happy and comfortable life. He will command much respect and will have a good wife and sons.

(3) If the lord of the ninth house is strong in own sign or exaltation in the ascendant, the third or the ninth, the native is powerful and influential.

(4) If the lords of the ninth and tenth are together in a good house (i.e., other than 6th, 8th, 12th and 3rd), it is a powerful *Raja Yoga.* The native is fortunate and occupies a high position.

(5) If in (4) above, if the combination occurs in an angle or trine it is called *Shankha Yoga.* The same results as in (4) above but in greater measure.

(6) If the lord of the tenth is in the ninth and the lord of the ninth in the tenth, the native occupies a high position and is in

the good books of the government.

(7) If the lords of the sixth, eighth and the twelfth are strong and occupy angles or trines and if the lords of the first, fourth, ninth and tenth are in the sixth, eighth and twelfth, and if the planets are without strength or are combust, then there is *Duryoga* or evil *Yoga* leading to all kinds of evil results. But if the reverse is the case, that is, if the lords of *Trik* are in any of the *Dusthanas* and the lords of the first, fourth, ninth and tenth are strong and occupy good houses and if the planets are strong and not combust, the nativity becomes a good one for long life, happiness, prosperity and good position in life.

(8) If the lord of the ninth is in the twelfth, a weak lord of the twelfth is in the second and *Papas* in the third, the native is licentious, indulges in evil acts, incurs debts and procures enjoyment thereby; he is always in need of favours and money from his friends.

XI. DIRECTIONAL STRENGTH

(1) If two or more planets have directional strength and the native is born in a royal family he becomes a king.

(2) If out of Sun, Moon, Mars, Mercury, Jupiter and Venus, five have directional strength or even four, a person born even in an ordinary family becomes a king or occupies an equally eminent position, such as, the head of a large institution, a minister in the Union or State cabinet.

XII. PLANETS IN DEBILITATED SIGNS

(1) If a planet is in debilitation and if the lord of the sign in which the debilitated planet is or the lord of the sign in which the debilitated planet would be exalted is in an angle from the ascendant or the Moon the evil effect of debilitation is cancelled and the native prospers.

(2) If a planet is debilitated but is retrograde, it becomes powerful. This applies to Mars, Mercury, Jupiter, Venus and Saturn.

(3) When planets occupy their signs of debilitation or are in an enemy's house, the native leads a life of poverty and distress. He is not intelligent or learned and his actions are bad. (Refer to Chapter 8, Planets in signs). If the planet occupies the good

degrees stated therein, the evil is mitigated.

(4) If a planet is in his sign of debilitation and if he is fully aspected by his dispositor (the lord of the sign in which the planet is), the debilitation is cancelled and good effects follow.

(5) If a planet is debilitated and if the lord of the sign the planet is in, and the lord of the sign in which the debilitated planet would be exalted, are together or in opposite signs or in the fourth and tenth from each other, the debilitation is cancelled and a good *Yoga* is formed.

XIII. RETROGRADE PLANETS

Even a single planet, though he be debilitated, if occupying a good house is retrograde and not combust, it raises high the native's status. Should there be two or three such planets, the native attains a very high rank and position in life.

KENDRA TRIKONA YOGA

The *Kendra-Trikona Yoga* is abbreviated to as *K.T. Yoga.* The first, fourth, seventh and tenth houses are called *Kendras* or angles. The fifth and the ninth houses are called *Trikonas* or trines. The first house is both a *Kendra* and a *Trikona.* This *K. T. Yoga* means any of the following *Yogas*:
Sambandha between,

(i) lords of the first and fifth
(ii) lords of the first and ninth
(iii) lords of the fourth and fifth
(iv) lords of the fourth and ninth
(v) lords of the seventh and fifth
(vi) lords of the seventh and ninth
(vii) lords of the tenth and fifth
(viii) lords of the tenth and ninth

For certain purposes the first house is considered as a *Trikona* also, but the convention is not to call the *Sambandha* between (i) lords of the first and fourth, (ii) lords of the first and seventh, (iii) lords of the first and tenth a *K. T. Yoga,* although a *Sambandha* between (i) lords of the first, and fourth, and (ii) the first and tenth is considered a *Raja Yoga*—a very good *Yoga.*

For understanding the full meaning of *Sambandha* refer to Chapter 10.

The *K.T. Yoga* is really efficacious in full measure when the lord of an angle has *Sambandha* with the lord of a trine, but does not have *Sambandha* with the lord of the third, sixth, eighth or the eleventh house, but where the lord of a trine is also the lord of these houses (3rd, 6th, 8th, 11th), the full efficacy of the *K.T. Yoga* is marred; the power to do good is lessened, but not completely wiped out. Even among the angles, the strength of the four lords of angles is in the following proportions:

Lord of the first	1 unit
Lord of the fourth	2 units
Lord of the seventh	3 units
Lord of the tenth	4 units

Thus the lord of the fourth is stronger than the lord of the first, and the lord of seventh stronger than the lord of the fourth, and the lord of the tenth is the strongest of them all.

As stated earlier, the lords of the first (the first is both a *Kendra* and a *Trikona*), the fifth and the ninth are lords of *Trikonas.* They are powerful for the good in the following order:

Lord of first	1 unit
Lord of fifth	2 units
Lord of ninth	4 units

The strength ot the lords of the third, sixth, eleventh and the eighth houses, in regard to their *Papa* qualities has been stated in Chapter 6 under 'Papi' to which please refer. Also refer to '*Maraka*' in Chapter 10.

To ascertain the efficacy of the *K.T. Yoga,* proceed in the following manner. The units of lords of trines and angles to do good is positive, additive or plus. The units of lords of 3, 6, 11 and 8 to do evil is represented as negative, subtractive or minus.

Now we shall work out some examples to demonstrate how the resultant is arrived at after making due allowance for the lordship of good and evil houses.

Example 1: *Sambandha* between lords of the first, fifth and third

Lord of first	1	
Lord of fifth	2	
Lord of third	—1	
Net	2	Good

Example 2: *Sambandha* of lord of the seventh, ninth and eighth

Lord of seventh	2
Lord of ninth	4
Lord of eighth	—6
Net	0

Example 3: *Sambandha* between lords of the ninth, tenth and eleventh

Lord of ninth	4	
Lord of tenth	4	
Lord of eleventh	—3	
Net	5	Good

Example 4: *Sambandha* between lords of the fourth, ninth, sixth and eighth

Lord of fourth	2	
Lord of ninth	4	
Lords of sixth	—2	
Lord of eighth	—6	
Net	—2	Evil

In all these *K. T. Yogas,* at least one planet should be lord of a *Trikona,* i.e., lord of the fifth or the ninth and at least one planet, the lord of the first, fourth, seventh or the tenth. It follows that if the lord of an angle has *Sambandha* with both the lord of the fifth and the ninth it will be very powerful to do good, and particularly so if the *Sambandha* is unsullied by *Sambandha* of any planet who is lord to 3, 6, 8 or 11.

Example 5: Lords of the fifth, ninth and tenth

Lord of fifth	2	
Lord of ninth	4	
Lord of tenth	4	
No other *Sambandha*	—0	
Net	10	Very Good

K. T. Yoga however differs in strength according to the strength of the planets constituting the *Yoga* and the house they occupy. For example, for Sagittarius, Sun and Mercury together in the tenth will be very powerful because the lord of the tenth would be in a good house (tenth), in an angle (tenth) and Mercury would be exalted in Virgo. The same *K. T. Yoga* can be formed by Mercury and the Sun tenanting either the eighth or the twelfth house or even the eleventh house where the Sun would be debilitated. Thus the effects differ according as the planets are strong or weak in a good house or evil houses.

CHAPTER 12

JUDGMENT OF THE TWELVE HOUSES

SOME GENERAL principles for judgment of each house have been given in Chapter 10. They should be applied to each of the twelve houses. We shall not repeat them here or when we take up each of the houses one after the other.

Judgment of each house can be divided into four parts: (i) the house, the planets posited therein, and the aspects which the house and the planets therein receive from other planets; (ii) the position of the lord of the house in sign and the house and the aspects such lord receives from other planets, or his conjunction with other planets; (iii) the *Karaka* or the significator, his position by sign and house and the aspects he receives from other planets or his conjunction with other planets; (iv) good or bad *Yogas* affecting a house, as given in Chapter 11.

For example, from the second house we judge accumulated wealth; from the fourth immovable property and happiness; from the eighth legacy; from the ninth prosperity and fortune, and from the eleventh income. Even eliminating the eighth for judging finances, we have to take stock of the cumulative effects of the second, fourth, ninth and the eleventh. If one of the houses does not promise good results, but the other houses are fairly good and there are *Yogas* for wealth, even the house which does not hold out bright results may not fare so badly. This is what we imply by other *Yogas* or prospects in the rest of the chart. The following points have to be reiterated even at the cost of repetition:

(i) In *Yogas* where there is reference to aspect, only the full aspect should be considered. But in the matter of judgment of each house, the quarter aspect, the half aspect, the three-quarter aspect, and the full aspect, are all effective in an increasing order, i.e., the 50% aspect is more powerful than the 25% aspect, and the 75% aspect is more powerful than the 50% aspect; the 100% or full aspect is the most powerful of them all.

(ii) Conjunction, according to old masters of Hindu astrology, occurs when two planets are in the same sign, irrespective of the distance between them or whether they are applying or separating. The orb of aspects and whether they are applying or separating are alien to Hindu astrology. These principles originated in the Middle-East and the West, but are not found in the older Hindu texts. So, if a planet A is, say, in the 1st degree of Aries and a planet B is in the 29th degree of Aries, still they are treated as being in conjunction, provided both are in the same sidereal sign. Suppose two planets are in the same tropical sign, but after deducting the precession of the equinoxes and nutation from the tropical longitudes, if the sidereal longitudes fall into two different sidereal signs, there will be no conjunction. We shall illustrate this by a concrete example. Suppose Mars occupies the 29th degree in the tropical Aries and the Moon occupies 1°; also in tropical Aries, and suppose the precession of the equinoxes is 23°, then deducting 23° from the tropical longitudes of Mars and Moon, the longitude of Mars will be 6° in Aries and of the Moon 8° in Pisces in the sidereal zodiac. Since one falls in sidereal Aries, and the other in sidereal Pisces, Mars and Moon will not be treated as being in conjunction, but as in the second and the twelfth from each other.

(iii) The third point which we want to reiterate is that the houses should be counted from sign to sign. For example, if Leo is rising, Pisces would be the eighth sign and any planet in Pisces occupying any degree therein, should be treated as in the eighth house.

After emphasising these points, it is now necessary to deal with each house individually.

First House

Judge the house, house lord and the *Karaka*—Sun. Then take the following into consideration.

If the lord of the first house is conjoined with a malefic (Sun, Mars, Saturn or Rahu or Ketu) and occupies the sixth, eighth or twelfth house, he impairs health. If the lord of the first is himself a malefic and occupies the above position, even then the health is not so good. But (a) for Scorpio ascendant Mars is the lord of the first and the sixth and if he is in Aries in sixth, or (b) for Aries, Mars is the lord of the first and the eighth and if he is in Scorpio in the eighth, or (c) for Aquarius ascendant, Saturn is the lord of the first and the twelfth and if he is in Capricorn, it is not so evil. If in the above cases (a), (b) and (c), the lord of the ascendant (owning 6th, 8th or 12th respectively) is in the ascendant, it is not bad for health.

If the lord of the ascendant is in an angle or trine, it is good for bodily happiness and particularly so if aspected by benefics.

If there is a *Papa* (malefic) in the ascendant and the lord of the first is weak, the native suffers from diseases and mental anxieties. The native is under constant dread or apprehension and there is nervous tension. But if the lord of the ascendant is himself a *Papa* and occupies the first house, it does not cause the ill-effects stated above.

If the lord of the first is in the sixth, the native has constant worries and suffers mental distress due to them. If the lord of the first is posited in a sign owned by a *Papa,* the native is not so intelligent. This does not apply if the lord of the ascendant is in his own sign.

If the Sun and the Moon are hemmed in by malefics, the native's actions are not good but rather evil. He is malevolently inclined. If Mars is in the seventh from the Sun, the Moon or the lord of the ascendant, the native is attached to other peoples' wives. If Gemini or Virgo is rising and Mercury is in Aries, Taurus, Cancer, Sagittarius or Capricorn, the native has a weak body.

If a malefic is in the first house, he generally causes hurt in the head. If he is posited in the first 15°, the hurt will be on the left side of the head; if in the latter 15° on the right side of the head. Mars in the ascendant gives a youthful appearance and even in old age the native looks young. Saturn on the other hand will cause the native to appear older than his age. Mercury herein makes the native quick and nimble like a boy. Venus imparts refinement in appearance, and Jupiter makes one deep and wise.

The Moon herein makes one restless unless he travels about. For detailed effects of planets in the ascendant refer to Chapter 9.

If there is a movable sign on the cusp of the first house, the native is fond of action, walking, moving about or travelling. If the lord of the ascendant is also in a movable sign, the above effects are reinforced. If there is a fixed sign on the cusp of the first house, the native's temperament in respect of walking, moving about or travelling is just the reverse of that described for a movable sign; more so particularly if the lord of the first is also in a fixed sign. If a common sign is rising, that is, it is the ascendant, and its lord is also in a common sign, mixed results will result as shown above.

If the lord of the first occupies a good house and has *Sambandha* with a benefic planet, he lives in a good place; conversely, if the lord of the ascendant occupies an evil house or *Dusthana* and is conjoined with or has *Sambandha* with a malefic the reverse is the case. If Saturn, unless exalted or in own house, or Rahu has *Sambandha* with the first house or its lord, the native keeps company with low people. If benefics have the above *Sambandha,* instead of Saturn or Rahu, the reverse is the case. Look to the quality and inherent nature and attributes of the various planets as given in Chapters 6, 8 and 9. The native's companions and environment will be according to the planets which tenant the first house or aspect it or conjoin the lord of the ascendant or aspect him.

The health, bodily vigour, mental energy, daring, push, optimism, capacity — all such qualities will be according to the strength or weakness of the first house and its lord. However, the actual temperament will also depend upon the nature of the planet owning the first or occupying the house. A benefic in the above set-up would make the native good and kind. A malefic in the ascendant, would make him hard-hearted but industrious.

Readers are referred to Chapter 4, which gives the general summing up according to the sign rising. If a long sign is on the cusp of the first house and the lord of the first also occupies a long sign, the head would be large. If a short sign be ascending and the lord thereof be also in a short sign, the size of the head would not be large.* The complexion will be modified according

* This principle should be applied to ascertain all parts of the body. Each house governs a part of the body.

to the colour of the planet owning, occupying or aspecting the first house.

Of all the houses, the ascendant is the most important. The natives who have a strong first house and a strong lord thereof are generally successful in life.

If the lord of the ascendant is not combust and is in his own sign or exalted and occupies an angle or trine and if a benefic is posited in the ascendant and the lord of the eighth is in a house other than an angle, the native is long lived, wealthy and maintains good health.

Second House

Judge from the second house, the planets tenanting or aspecting it, from the lord of the second house his location and planets conjoining or aspecting him, and *Karaka* for the second house, viz., Jupiter. We judge the family, speech, eyes, and wealtn from this house. Benefics augment the good effects by location as well as by aspect; while a malefic, unless he be the lord of second, would do the reverse. Since Mercury is primarily the planet governing speech, due attention should be paid to him also. The second house governs the eyes and malefics herein or a combination of the Sun and Moon herein or in the eighth house impairs the right eye. The left eye is judged from the twelfth house. The Sun and Moon together, the Sun and Venus together in the second or the eighth impair the eye-sight. Mars frequently gives granules in the eye or trouble from sore eyes, and also impairs the eye-sight.

If the lord of the second and the twelfth are conjoined with or aspected by malefics and posited in *Trik*,' then the eye-sight suffers. Similarly, if the lords of the second and twelfth are conjoined with *Papas* (malefics) there is eye trouble. We also judge speech from this house. If benefics tenant or aspect it, the speech would be sweet, but if malefics do so instead, the speech would be harsh. Mars gives anger in speech, while Ketu makes it abusive. Rahu imparts falsehood and slyness. Saturn does the same, the Sun herein may make the speech sound proud if the planet is strong; but if the Sun is weak, it will be arrogant. Mercury, Jupiter, Venus and Moon with good *Pakshabala*, would make it logical, sweet, poetic and attractive respectively. These attributes of planets should also be applied according as one or the other planet conjoins or aspects the lord of the second.

Some astrological principles governing eloquence have been given under the fifth house also because that house governs education and learning. The second house governs the mouth and also food. Each planet governs a taste (of food). If Jupiter is in the second, the native would be fond of sweet dishes; if Venus is present there, he would like sour ones, and so on. Refer to Chapter 6 on planets to determine which kind of taste is governed by each planet.

If the lord of the second is conjoined with Mercury, Jupiter and Venus and posited in an angle or trine from the ascendant, it confers wealth; but if the lord of the second is conjoined with the above-named planets and occupies the sixth, eighth or the twelfth house, the native suffers in respect of wealth.

The conjunction of the lords of the first and second or their mutual exchange of places—the lord of the first in the second and the lord of the second in the first, makes one earn money with little effort.

Generally benefics augment the good effects of the house they tenant. But there is another rule also that the *Karaka* tenanting the house for which he is a *Karaka* is not good, except for Saturn in the eighth. If Jupiter is conjoined with another planet and is in the second, it is good; but if Jupiter alone occupies the second house, it does not let the native accumulate wealth; it also curtails family happiness.

The Sun and Moon together in the second are adverse for accumulation of wealth; also the native's speech is harsh; the Sun and Mercury together in the second produce the same effect.

If a Moon weak in *Pakshabala* is in the second and fully aspected by Mercury, he causes loss of wealth; or if Mercury in the second is aspected by the Moon, the native is without wealth. Venus in the second confers wealth.

If the Sun in the second is conjoined with a planet, say A, the native's wealth will remain in the custody of the native's relation as signified by A. We shall clarify this by two examples. Suppose Taurus is rising and the Sun and Mercury are in the second. Here Mercury will be the lord of the fifth also. The fifth signifies children. The question now arises as to whether the children will be sons or daughters. Since Mercury is not a male planet, he will not signify sons but daughters and so the native's wealth will be in the custody of his daughter or daughters.

Suppose the Sun and Jupiter are in Pisces in the second. When Pisces is in the second, Aquarius will be the ascendant. Jupiter will be the lord of the eleventh also. The eleventh signifies elder brother, also friends. So the native's wealth will be in the custody of his elder brother or friends. Why an elder brother and not an elder sister? Because Jupiter is a male planet.

Rahu in the second causes disease of the mouth or teeth, the Moon means trouble for the eyes, Venus to eyes or ears, Mars to ears; Mercury or Jupiter in own sign or exalted makes one deliver learned discourses in the congress of scholars. If Rahu or Saturn are conjoined with a female planet in the second, the native loses money through undesirable women.

Third House

If the lord of the third and Mars are in the sixth, eighth or the twelfth house (not necessarily together), there is no happiness in relation to younger brothers. If the lord of the eleventh and Jupiter are in the abovementioned houses, there is no happiness in respect of the elder brothers.

If the lord of the third, conjoined with a benefic, is in the third house there is happiness from younger brothers. If the lord of the ascendant, conjoined with a benefic, is in the eleventh, there will be happiness from elder brothers. If Mars alone is in the third or if Jupiter alone is in the eleventh, there is no happiness from younger and elder brothers respectively.

If Saturn in the third is aspected by Mars, there is loss of brothers; but if aspected by Jupiter or Venus, the house yields good results in respect of brothers. Jupiter in Sagittarius or Pisces in the third is good for brothers. Saturn herein increases the native's fortune and prosperity. But if Saturn and Rahu are together in the third, there may be hurt from wood, in the right arm or pain due to *Vata* (wind). If the Sun and Mars together are in the third, there may be fracture of the right arm. If the Sun is in Leo in the ninth, there is loss of brothers; if a brother survives, he will attain a very high position in life. The Moon in the third, fully aspected by *Papa,* leads to loss of brothers. Mars in the third causes loss of younger brothers; the Sun herein causes loss of elder brothers. Saturn and Rahu together in the third cause loss of younger as well as elder brothers.

Mars in the third house, aspected by a malefic, causes hurt in the arm from a weapon. If Saturn is in the seventh, Rahu in the ninth and Mars in the eleventh, there is loss of brothers. Saturn in the third also causes loss of brothers. Mercury, Jupiter or Venus (one or more of them) in the third, is good in respect of brothers.

In the above, where the word brother or brothers has been used, sister should be included. A female planet in the third gives more sisters, a male planet more brothers. Aspects of male or female planets on the third house should also be taken into account.

Fourth House

Apply the general principles regarding planets in the fourth house and the sign therein and those enunciated in Chapter 10. If the lord of the first and the fourth are conjoined together in the fourth, there is sudden gain of immovable property. If the lord conjoined with Mercury, Jupiter, Venus or lord of the fifth or the ninth, is in the fourth, it is an exceptionally good combination for acquisition of immovable properties and conveyances. If the lord of the fourth has *Sambandha* with Jupiter and the lords of the first and the ninth and is posited in the ascendant, it is a very good *Yoga* for position. The native is much honoured by the government.

If the lord of the fourth is conjoined with the lord of the fifth or the ninth and is posited in the eleventh, it is a very good *Yoga* for acquisition of conveyances. Or if the lord of the fourth conjoined with the lord of the fifth or the ninth fully aspects the fourth, then also it is a good *Yoga* for conveyances. If the lord of the fourth is in the fourth, the native has a good house to live in and has good friends. Malefics in the fourth house, unless he be the lord of the first or the fourth, impair happiness in respect of the fourth house affairs. Saturn herein gives immovable property after thirty-five years of age; but the property acquired will not be new. This will however be so if Saturn is the lord of good houses. Malefics, whether in the fourth, eighth or the twelfth house, lead to annihilation of comforts in respect of conveyances.

The *Karaka* for mother is the Moon. All about the mother — happiness or otherwise — should be ascertained from the Moon, the fourth house and its lord and also from the fourth house as counted from the sign tenanted by the Moon.

The Sun and Mars in the fourth cause trouble in the region of the chest, due to imbalance of *Pitta* (bile). The fourth house governs the whole of the chest and the heart also. Malefics herein would cause diseases in the region and particularly so if they are lord of evil houses. If the lord of the fourth is weak or ill-placed by sign and house and if malefics tenant or aspect the fourth house, the native will not feel happy.

If the native belongs to a class or community owning agricultural lands, the kind of land should be determined from the nature of the sign on the cusp of the fourth house and the planet or planets tenanting or aspecting the house.

Fifth House

If the lord of the fifth house from the ascendant and the lord of the fifth counted from the sign tenanted by the Moon, along with Mercury, Jupiter and Venus, are in *Trik*, the native does not receive higher education. On the other hand, if the lord of the fifth from the ascendant and from the Moon and Mercury, Jupiter and Venus are in angles, trines or the eleventh house, the native is highly educated and learned. If some of the good features enumerated above are present along with some adverse placements, the native has moderately good education.

If the lord of the fifth, as counted from the radical* Mercury is well-placed† the native's logical and reasoning power is well developed; if the lord of the fifth as counted from the radical Jupiter is well-placed, the native has a good memory; if the lord of the fifth as counted from Venus is well placed in angles or trines, conjoined with a benefic, the native has good understanding of texts and good grasping power. If the lords of the fifth as counted from the ascendant and the Moon are combust, or in the initial five degrees or the last five degrees of a sign, then the intellect is not sharp. So will also be the case if the combinations stated above are present in respect of Mercury, Jupiter and Venus.

The fifth house is studied for education and learning; the second house determines speech. But the two are inter-related. If the

*Radical means the sign occupied by a planet in the radix, i.e., nativity or birthchart.

† Well-placed means well placed by sign and house and conjoined with or receiving aspect of benefics.

lord of the second and the fifth and Jupiter are not well-placed and are in the sixth, eighth or the twelth house, or they have *Sambandha* with the lord of the eighth, then the power of speech is not good. Mercury also represents power of speech and if he is well-placed and has *Sambandha* with benefics, speech will be good. The reverse will be the case if this planet is weak, ill-placed and has *Sambandha* with *Papas.*

If the second house tenants *Papas,* eloquence is impaired. Saturn in the second house is a great handicap for public speech. If Virgo is the sign ascending or if the Moon or the Sun occupy the sign, the native is a very good drawing-room conversationalist, but is shy in the matter of public speaking.

Children are judged from the fifth house and Jupiter. In additon to the general principles stated in Chapter 10, the birth chart should be screened to find out if any of the following *Yogas,* which curtail the prospects of the birth of children or their living to a mature age, are present.

(i) The lords of the ascendant, the fifth and the ninth and the lord of the fifth from Jupiter, if in *Trik.*

(ii) *Papas* in the fifth and the eleventh or in either of these two houses.

(iii) Malefics in the third.

(iv) The Sun and Mercury both together in the first, second, fifth, tenth or the eleventh house.

(v) Malefics in the fifth from the radical Moon and Jupiter.

(vi) *Papas* in the first, fourth, fifth, eighth, ninth, eleventh and the twelfth. The larger the number of houses tenanted by *Papas,* the greater the impediment to happiness in respect of children.

(vii) *Papas,* the Moon and Jupiter in the fourth and the eighth.

(viii) Rahu not conjoined with any planet, in the tenth.

(ix) *Papa* in the fourth, Venus in the seventh and the Moon in the tenth.

(x) *Papas* in the ninth, Venus in the seventh and the Moon in tenth.

(xi)The Moon and Jupiter in the ascendant and Saturn in the seventh.

(xii) Venus and Saturn in the seventh.

(xiii) The Sun in the ascendant, and Saturn in the seventh.

(xiv) The Sun and Saturn in the seventh, and the Moon in the tenth.

(xv) The lord of the sixth conjoined with the Sun and Saturn in the sixth and the Moon in the seventh.

(xvi) Mars in the fifth or the eleventh particularly destroys children. If Mars in the fifth is in his own sign or Mars is the lord of the ascendant, he does not destroy.

(xvii) The Sun in the eleventh or the fifth destroys the eldest child or eldest son. But the Sun in Leo does not do so.

(xviii) *Yogas* which involve ill health or premature death of wife or husband also impair longevity of children.

(xix) If *Papas* are in the ascendant, the seventh or the twelfth and a weak Moon (in *Pakshabala*) in the fifth, this combination destroys children.

(xx) Mars and Saturn in a watery sign in the sixth.

(xxi) Saturn in the fifth, Venus in the seventh.

(xxii) The lord of the seventh conjoined with a *Papa* in the fifth.

(xxiii) Rahu in Virgo in the ascendant.

(xxiv) Sagittarius or Pisces on the cusp of the fifth house and the fifth not aspected by Mars or Jupiter.

(xxv) Jupiter not conjoined with any planet in the fifth or the seventh.

Papas in the fifth house destroy children after birth; but if aspected by Jupiter, subsequent children will survive. If Rahu or Ketu is in Aries, Taurus or Cancer in the fifth, they do not obstruct children. Saturn in Aquarius in the fifth gives five sons; Saturn in Capricorn in the fifth three daughters.

Saturn in Taurus or Gemini in the fifth gives one son. The lord of the fifth in an odd sign gives more sons, but in an even sign more daughters. The female planets in the fifth give more daughters; male planets more sons.

We shall examine the fifth house from one more point of view and conclude with discussion pertaining to this house. The fifth governs the stomach. Malefics herein impair the digestive power. The Sun gives pain in the stomach; Mars may give peptic ulcers; Saturn, Rahu and Ketu may impair digestion due to wind, gas, etc. The aspects of malefics act similarly.

Sixth House

Apply the general principles to this house. But it is not good to have the lord of the sixth stronger than the lord of the first.

The first house represents the self and the sixth represents the enemy. If, therefore the lord of the first is stronger than the sixth, the native would overpower his opponents and enemies, but if the converse be the case, the native's opponents and enemies will vanquish him. Similarly, the first is the body and the sixth governs diseases and so quite naturally if the sixth is stronger, the factors of illness and ill-health will overpower the body; but if the first house and its lord are stronger, the native would overcome the adverse factors of health.

If the lord of the sixth is conjoined with a malefic and is posited in the ascendant or the eighth, it causes a wound. If it be the Sun, he causes an ailment or wound in the head; the Moon in the mouth, Mars in the neck or throat, Mercury in the region of the heart, Jupiter in or near the navel, Venus in the eye, and Saturn or Rahu or Ketu in the legs, feet or lips.

If the lord of the ascendant is in Aries, Gemini, Virgo or Scorpio or in any other sign, if he is aspected by Mars and Mercury, there is some defect in the eye.

If the lord of the sixth is in the ascendant sixth, seventh or the eighth, he causes destruction of enemies. If the lord of the sixth is in the fifth or the ninth, the son of the native is antagonistic to him. If the lord of the sixth is in the second or the twelfth, the native is very malevolent. If the lord of the sixth is in the third or the eleventh, the native is strong and puts others to distress. If the lord of the sixth is in the fourth or the tenth, there is some ailment in the region of the navel, or the lower part of the stomach.

The lord of the first or the eighth in the sixth causes trouble in the left eye, Venus and Saturn together in the sixth cause ailments in the left eye, leg or foot. If the lord of the ascendant is in Aries, Gemini, Virgo or Scorpio in the sixth, the native does not enjoy good health and is sickly. Even if he is in the above signs in any other house, if he is aspected by his enemy, the native has poor health.

Rahu or Ketu in the sixth or the eighth cause trouble in the teeth. If the Moon, conjoined with a *Papa*, is in the sixth, he causes sickness or physical ailments. The Moon conjoined with a malefic in the ascendant also makes the native sickly. If the lord of the ascendant is conjoined with a *Papa*, the native does not keep good health. Similarly, if the Moon in any sign of house is conjoined with a *Papa*, the native does not keep good health. If *Papas* are in angles and are not aspected by benefics, the same result is to be expected. If the lord of the sixth is conjoined with the Sun or Rahu and tenants the twelfth house, the native lives in another man's house at the latter's cost and resorts to low acts. If the lord of the first or the eighth, Venus or Saturn occupy the sixth house, the native suffers from wounds or ailments during their *Dasha* (periods). If the lord of the eighth is in the eighth conjoined with a *Papa*, the native's acts are of a low order.

The Sun or Moon together or the Sun and Venus together or the Moon and Venus together or Mars and Saturn together in the sixth cause trouble in the left eye.

Seventh House

Apply the general principles to the seventh house, the lord of the seventh and to Venus who is significator for wife. In female horoscope, Jupiter should also be considered as significator for husband. Since Venus represents all kinds of sensuous pleasures, such as good food, good clothes, a good house, comforts, conveyances, etc., and as the pleasures of sex are included as an integral part of enjoyment, Venus in male nativities is considered the significator for wife. But Venus being a female planet, his counterpart Jupiter is taken by one school of Hindu astrologers as the significator for husband. We recommend that Jupiter as well as Venus be taken into account in female charts.

If the house tenants its lord or a benefic and is aspected by benefics and if the lord of the seventh does not occupy the sixth, eighth or the twelth house from the ascendant and is not conjoined with a malefic, and if Venus is also in a good house and neither conjoined with a malefic nor aspected by a malefic, prospects for matrimonial life and conjugal happiness are good. If the planetary position is otherwise, the reverse is the case. If some good features are present and others are unfavourable, there would be neither conjugal bliss nor complete happiness.

The appearance and temperament of the wife will be according to the lord of the seventh and if there is a planet in the seventh, according to his traits. This has also to be judged from the seventh from the radical Moon.

The state of married happiness and the longevity of the

marriage partner also depend upon the following two factors:

(i) The *Nakshatra* (constellation) in which the native has his radical Moon and the *Nakshatra* tenanted by the Moon of the marriage partner.

A Table or chart is generally given as an Appendix in the Hindu *Panchangas* (Ephemerides), which gives the harmonious points between two birth charts, depending upon the location of the Moon in the husband's chart as well as the longitude of Moon in the wife's chart. The maximum number of harmonious points is 36. If on the basis of the two longitudes of Moon in the two charts, the harmonious points are 18, the two charts are considered as being in agreement. The greater the number of harmonious points the greater the harmony. If the number of harmonious points is less than 18, the pandits do not declare that the pair should be matched, because there would be no harmony between the couple. The smaller the number of harmonious points the lesser the conjugal happiness.

(ii) Mars, Saturn, Rahu, Ketu and the Sun are the five malefics which should not be (a) in the first or the seventh or the eighth, (b) in the second, or the fourth or the twelfth.

The position in group (a) of houses is worse than in group (b). Even among the five planets named above, as regards malignancy they are not rated equally.

In regard to matrimonial happiness and longevity of the marriage partner, Mars is considered the worst — the most baneful. Then comes Saturn a close second. Then Rahu and Ketu and then the Sun.

As regards the Sun in the seventh from the ascendant, unless he be in his sign Leo, in a female nativity he leads to a separation. Whether the separation will be temporary or permanent can however be determined by examining the over-all picture, and the strength or weakness of the seventh house and its lord from the ascendant as well as from the Moon. But barring location in the seventh, the Sun is not considered so baneful for matrimonial happiness in the first, second, fourth, eighth or the twelfth house.

As regards each of the five planets (malefics) stated above, the malignancy decreases in the following order:

(i) In debilitation
(ii) In great enemy's house

(iii) In enemy's house
(iv) In neutral's house
(v) In friend's house
(vi) In great friend's house
(vii) In own house
(viii) In exaltation

Let us illustrate this; suppose Mars is in his great enemy's house. This will be very evil. But Mars in his own house in the first will not be so bad. The same applies to Saturn, Rahu, Ketu and the Sun.

Just as we examine (a) the first, seventh and eighth houses, or (b) the second, fourth or twelfth houses from the ascendant or the rising sign, so also we have to examine from the radical Moon; Malefics in (a) first, seventh and eighth or (b) second, fourth or twelfth from him also damage matrimonial happiness.

Similarly, the above houses from the radical Venus, if tenanted by one or more of the five malefics, will be harmful for conjugal happiness and damage matrimonial life. Since we have enumerated six houses out of twelve where malefics are harmful and we have advised counting of these houses not only from the radical ascendant but from the natal Moon and natal Venus also, a doubt will arise that there are bound to be one or more houses (from the ascendant, Moon or Venus), tenanted by malefics. Then, is the matrimonial happiness sure to be damaged? The reply is 'No.'

Malefics in the above places in one birth chart (husbands' or wife's) act as an antidote to the evil effects (if there are malefics in any of the above places) in the other nativity. For example, suppose there is Mars in the seventh in the male chart and Mars in the ascendant in the female chart. No more will Mars thwart married happiness in either chart. These influences are referred to in Hindu astrology as *Mangalika.* The world literally means pertaining to Mars; but Mars being the commander-in-chief of malefics for matrimonial purposes, includes in its connotation Saturn, Rahu, Ketu and Sun also. And so the collective term goes under the nomenclature of *Mangalika.*

In order to assess whether there is a complete balancing of malefic influences in one chart by the malefics in the other, all the houses where malefics act evilly have to be tabulated and then compared.

Apart from these, suppose the man or the girl is unmarried or if married the birth chart of the partner is not available, then how is matrimonial happiness to be astrologically judged. When only one party's chart is available the following rules should be followed:

Influences which Mar Matrimonial Happiness

(i) Malefics in second and seventh.

(ii) The lord of the second or seventh house conjoined with a malefic.

(iii) (a) Venus conjoined with a *Papa;* (b) Venus hemmed in between *Papas;* (c) *Papas* in the fourth or eighth from Venus.

(iv) Malefics in the first, fourth, seventh, eighth or the twelfth from the ascendant.

(v) The lord of the seventh in the eighth or the lord of the eighth in the seventh, or the lord of the sixth in the seventh or the lord of the seventh in the sixth.

(vi) (a) Jupiter alone in the seventh, or (b) Jupiter conjoined with a *Papa* in the seventh.

(vii) Influences which have been described under the fifth house, curtailing longevity of children also act as impediments to matrimonial happiness.

(viii) The lord of the seventh in the fifth.

(ix) The lord of the fifth in the seventh.

(x) The Sun and Rahu together in the seventh means loss of wealth through women.

(xi) Venus in Scorpio in the seventh.

((xii) Mercury in Taurus in the seventh.

(xiii) Jupiter in Capricorn in the seventh.

(xiv) Saturn in Pisces in the seventh; particularly so, if the Sun is also in Virgo in the ascendant.

(xv) The lord of the seventh combust or hemmed in by malefics or debilitated or conjoined with *Papas.*

(xvi) Venus and Moon in opposition to Mars and Saturn.

(xvii) Ketu in the seventh gives a sickly wife.

If any of the above are present, matrimonial happiness would be curtailed in any of the following manners:

(1) Delayed marriage.

(2) Incompatibility of temperament.

(3) Separation due to inability to pull on together or one living away from his wife due to economic or other reasons.

(4) Illhealth of the partner.

(5) Premature demise of the partner.

Eighth House

From the eighth house we judge longevity. For judgment of longevity, the span of life has been divided into three sectors: (i) upto the age of 36 years; (ii) from the 37th to the 72nd year; (iii) from the 73rd to the 108th year or beyond. These three sectors are referred to in Hindu astrology as (i) short life, (ii) medium life, and (iii) long life.

Whenever the *Mahadasha or Antardasha* (how to calculate the *Mahadasha* and *Antardasha* and when it will be operative has been explained in a subsequent chapter) of a *Maraka* planet is operative, there is danger to the life of the native. If by calculations which we shall explain below, the native is assigned a short life, the relevant period has to be looked up during the sector of age upto 36 years. If he is assigned medium life, we look up to the fatal period (*Dasha*) and sub-period (*Antardasha*) during the age of 37 to 72. If the calculations show that he has long life, we look to such periods beyond the age of 72.

For judging short, medium or long life we base our calculations on the following data:

(i) Location of the lord of the ascendant.
(ii) Location of the lord of the eighth house.
(iii) The sign occupied by Saturn.
(iv) The sign occupied by the Moon.
(v) The sign rising (ascendant).
(vi) *Hora-lagna.*

Readers are familiar with (i) to (v) above but ingredient (vi) will be new to them. So we shall first explain how to calculate it.

The word '*Lagna*' means ascendant and the word '*Hora*' means hour. So the expression *Hora-lagna* means hour-ascendant; but we shall refer to it as *Hora-lagna* because that is the technical word which occurs in all the old texts on the subject. It is calculated as shown below.

The longitude of the Sun at sunrise and one sign for each hour since sunrise, give the longitude of *Hora-lagna.*

Example: To find the *Hora-lagna* for 4 P.M. I.S.T. (time of birth) on 2nd October 1969 at Delhi. Look up the Ephemeris and find sunrise at Delhi on 2nd October.

The sunrise at Delhi was at 6-14 A.M. (Indian Standard Time). On looking up the Ephemeris and calculating the longitude of the Sun at sunrise, we find that it was 5-15-12-58.

The hours elapsed from sunrise to 4 P.M. will be:

	16- 0 hours (4 P.M.)
deduct	6-14
	9-46

Nine completed hours come to 9 signs and since 1 hour is equal to 1 sign or 30° and 46′ = 23″; so 9 hours 46 minutes equal to 9 signs 23 degrees.

	S.	D.	M.	S.
	5	15	12	58
Add the two	9	23	0	0
Deduct if the	15	8	12	58
Sum exceeds 12	12	0	0	0
	3	8	12	58

So the *Hora-lagna* is 8° 12′ 58″ in Cancer.

Having explained the calculation of *Hora-lagna,* we give the principles of judging whether the life would be short, medium or long. Three sets of principles are given below. If the same inference is derived from any of the two sets, it should be accepted as the resultant inference.

Readers will in the following lines come across the expression—movable, fixed and common signs. They have been specified in Chapter 5 dealing with signs. The same are given below for easy reference.

(1) Aries, Cancer, Libra and Capricorn are movable.

(2) Taurus, Leo, Scorpio and Aquarius are fixed.

(3) Gemini, Virgo, Sagattarius and Pisces are common.

A. (i) If the lord of the first is in a movable sign and the lord of the eighth also in a movable sign or one of them in fixed and the other in common sign: long life.

(ii) If the lord of the first is in a common sign and the lord of the eighth also in a common sign or one of them in a movable and the other in a fixed sign: medium life.

(iii) If the lord of the first is in a fixed sign and the lord of the eighth also in a fixed sign or one of them in a movable sign and the other in a common sign: short life.

B. Look to the sign tenanted by Saturn and the sign tenanted by Moon.

(i) If both are in movable signs or one in a fixed and the other in a common sign: long life.

(ii) If both are in common signs or one in a movable and the other in a fixed sign: medium life.

(iii) If both are in fixed signs or one in a movable and the other in a common sign: short life.

Note: If the Moon occupies the ascendant or the seventh house, instead of judging from Saturn and the Moon as described above, judge from the sign on the cusp of the ascendant, instead of the sign occupied by Saturn, and the sign tenanted by Moon.

C. Look to the sign on the cusp of the ascendant and also the sign in which the *Hora-lagna* falls. How to calculate the *Hora-lagna* for a birth chart has been explained above.

(i) If both of them fall in movable signs or one in a fixed and the other in a common sign: long life.

(ii) If both of them occupy common signs or one in a fixed and the other in a movable sign: medium life.

(iii) If both of them are in fixed signs or one in a movable and the other in a common sign: short life.

The same inference arrived at by any two of the above (A), (B) and (C) is taken as the resultant inference. Suppose the three inferences are all different, i.e., from one set we get long life, from the other medium life and from the third short life, what should be done under such a circumstance?

In such a case, the inference drawn from (C), that is, the *Lagna* (ascendant) and the *Hora-lagna* prevails. There is one more proviso to the general rule. If Jupiter occupies the first or the seventh house and if he is not aspected by malefics, then if the resultant inference denotes short life, it should be raised to medium life; if it denotes medium life, this should be raised to long life.

Despite the above rules, it must be admitted that the determination of longevity is a very difficult matter for the Hindu texts state that the conclusion arrived at from these rules will be true only if the native leads a pious and moderate life. They add that gluttony, drinking, smoking, addiction to drugs—in short leading an intemperate life will curtail longevity. Similarly, vicious thoughts and malevolent inclinations harden the arteries and weaken the heart and the native dies earlier than expected. Hindu texts lay down specifically that envy and enmity weaken the heart, and that is perhaps the single largest factor for cardiac insufficiency or weakness. This has not been realised fully by our heart specialists, but this rule has been laid down by the ancients with their wise and watchful experience of humanity

To revert to the astrological rules, we give below some more principles. Apply the general principles laid down in Chapter 10. The strength of the ascendant and the ascendant lord is the most important factor. To give good longevity, the lord of the ascendant should be stronger than the lord of the eighth and the latter should preferably not occupy an angle as counted from the ascendant.

The location of Saturn in the eighth house confers longevity. The general rule is that a *Karaka* spoils the house if he tenants the house for which he is a *Karaka*. But there is an exception to this general rule for Saturn occupying the eighth house. Saturn is the *Karaka* for the eighth house, but his occupation of the eighth confers longevity.

If benefics occupy the eighth, the native has an unhappy childhood, but he is very courageous and achieves success in very difficult projects. Jupiter in the eighth causes undiagnosed diseases. If the lord of the eighth is in the eleventh, the native leads a happy life in old age.

If a *Papa* is lord of the eighth, it does not promise a very long span of life unless conjoined with a benefic. Similarly, the lord of the eighth, if conjoined with a *Papa* and occupying the sixth or the twelfth house from the ascendant curtails longevity; the native has thievish inclinations and is troubled by enemies. The lord of the eighth in the eighth augurs long life. So also the lord of the third in the third and the lord of the eighth in the third are considered good for longevity.

From the eighth, we also judge legacy. If the lord of the eighth is strong and the house beneficially tenanted and aspected and the lord of the eighth house is also aspected by benefics, the native may gain a legacy. The question of legacy has, however, to be judged against the family background and the circumstances, for a legacy presupposes affluent but old relations.

Ninth House

The ninth house primarily refers to fortune and prosperity, while the tenth to actions and position in life. The two are allied but if we have to make a distinction we would explain it as follows.

A man may be rich and prosperous and may lead a comfortable life, but have no status in life. Let us take the example of a villager who migrates to a large town like Delhi or Bombay and sells Pan (betel-leaf) and earns a thousand or fifteen hundred rupees per month; or a villager owning fields, a granary and cattle. Their ninth house is strong. On the other hand let us take the example of a professor, earning only a few hundred rupees a month but hundreds of students bowing down to him every day. Or a newly appointed magistrate, with hardly enough of a salary to make two ends meet, but hundreds of people salaaming him. Their tenth house is strong.

But though the above distinction can be made, it is the general practice to take the two houses, the ninth and the tenth, together because one determines vocation or self efforts and the other predicts prosperity.

Judge the ninth house according to the general principles in relation to the house, its lord and the *Karakas*—the Sun and Jupiter for the ninth house. It is not good to have the lord of the ninth in the sixth, eighth or the twelfth. Nor is it desirable to have a lord of any of these houses in the ninth.

From the ninth we judge religiousness and also benevolent or malevolent intentions of the native, since benevolence has been preached by all religions and malevolence graded as irreligiousness. Mars, Saturn or Rahu in the ninth make one untruthful. These malefics also make one hard-hearted and malevolent.

Jupiter, the Sun, the Moon, Mercury, Venus or Ketu incline one to much religiousness and dogmatic worship in the traditional orthodox manner. Mars, Saturn and Rahu — particularly the last two—make one a free thinker not bound by rituals. If only Saturn and Rahu are present without the aspects of benefics or Saturn aspects the ninth, the native may not have much faith in religion. But Saturn or Rahu in the ninth fully aspected by a strong Jupiter, would make one philosophical with a mystic approach, caring more for the true religious spirit than for rituals. A strong Saturn tenanting or fully aspecting the ninth house develops an inner feeling of renunciation and we do not infrequently come across a strong Saturn in the ninth or aspecting it in the charts of ascetics.

To revert to the material side of life, we can provide the following criteria for judgment of fortune and prosperity (ninth house) and rank and prosperity (tenth house).

(i) If the lord of the ascendant has *Sambandha* with the lord of the ninth and the latter along with Jupiter tenants the ascendant, the native is greatly respected by the people and the government. Even if the lord of the ninth is in the ascendant and is fully aspected by Jupiter, the native is well respected.

(ii) If the lords of the first, fourth and the ninth houses have *Sambandha* and the three lords aspects their houses, the native is fortunate and long-lived.

(iii) The *Sambandha* between the lord of an angle and the lord of a trine is a contributory factor for good luck. For details refer to *Kendra—Trikona Yogas* in Chapter 11.

(iv) The following are the great years for each planet:

Sun 22, Moon 24, Mars 28, Mercury 32, Jupiter 16, Venus 25 Saturn 36, Rahu 42 and Ketu 48. How to predict from these years is described below.

Suppose a well-placed Sun is in the ninth house or the lord of the ninth house. Then the native's fortune would escalate when he completes 21 years of age and from his 22nd year onwards, he will rise in life. Suppose it is the Moon who is the lord of the ninth house and well placed in the chart or a strong Moon occupies the ninth. Then as the Moon's great year is 24, we predict escalation in fortune from the 24th year onwards. And so with other planets according to the year ear-marked for each.

This principle is also applied in the case of other houses. Suppose for a Gemini ascendant lord of fifth, Venus is exalted in the tenth. Then we may predict in the 25th year the birth of a son (fifth house) or rise in position (tenth house) or sudden gain of money (fifth house) according to the background and circumstances of the native. We have generally observed that if a strong

Saturn is lord of good houses and strong by sign and is in the fourth house, the native starts acquiring immovable properties after he completes 35 years of age and from the 36th year onwards. This is a rough and ready way of prediction without calculating the *Dashas* and *Antardashas* which we shall deal with in a subsequent chapter.

In South India, the astrologers judge the father from the ninth house, but in northern India the judgment is made from the tenth.

Tenth House

The *Karakas* for the tenth house are four: Sun, Mercury, Jupiter and Saturn. This is the house of personal efforts, of action, achievements of success or otherwise, trade and commerce, rank and status in service, political power, the respect one commands and the position in life. For all these, we have to judge the tenth house, its lord and the *Karakas*. If the tenth lord is relegated to the third, sixth, eighth or the twelfth, it is generally an argument against the achievement of a very high rank in life. But if the lord of the tenth is Mars, from the third house he will fully aspect the tenth house (the aspect of Mars, on the eighth house from the one occupied by him is full) it is not bad. Similarly, if Saturn is the lord of the tenth and occupies the eighth house, he will fully aspect his own house—the tenth, because Saturn has full aspect on the third house as counted from the one occupied by him, and this is not so bad; for the general principle is that if the lord of a house fully aspects his house it is very good; whether the planet be a malefic or a benefic it is good for him, to occupy his own house or fully aspect it.

(i) The lord of the first in the tenth is a strong argument for enhancing the general prestige of the native and giving him success in his projects. If the lord of the tenth also occupies the first, the prospects will be still better.

(ii) Similarly, the lord of the tenth in the ninth or the lord of the ninth in the tenth is a very good argument for good luck and eminent position. If the lord of the ninth and the tenth are together in the ninth or the tenth, it is still better. Or if the lord of the tenth is in the ninth and the lord of the ninth in the tenth, the mutual exchange of houses is considered a good *Raja Yoga*. Or if both the lords combine in any house, in an angle or trine, it promotes prosperity and improves the position in life.

(iii) The placement of the lord of the fifth in the tenth or the lord of the tenth in the fifth is very good. If they mutually exchange places, it is still better. So also if both the lords are conjoined and together occupy any house, preferably an angle or trine; this is considered a very good *Raja Yoga*.

We have referred to the conjunction or mutual exchange between (i) the lords of the ninth and the tenth, and (ii) the lords of the fifth and the tenth. In fact, any kind of *Sambandha* between the lord of an angle and that of a trine causes *Raja Yoga* (see *Kendra-Trikona Yogas* at the end of Chapter 11).

A large number of *Yogas* have been given in Chapter 11. They should be screened to see if any of them are found in the birth chart under examination and the results predicted according to the effects given therein. Some other rules for judging the tenth house are given below.

If a benefic planet occupies the tenth house and the lord of the latter is strong in his own house or his sign of exaltation in an angle or trine, the native occupies a high position and is long-lived.

If the Sun or Mars occupies the tenth house and the lord of the tenth house is well placed, the native commands great respect and is daring and pushing. He is also popular.

It may however be added that though the Sun and Mars in the tenth will escalate the native's own position, they would curtail the father's longevity and particularly so if they are aspected by or conjoined with malefics. Saturn in the tenth is not considered bad in Hindu astrology, though according to some leading Western astrologers, Saturn in the tenth raises the native very high and then his career crashes to the ground. In Hindu astrology no such stigma or prejudice is attached to Saturn. On the other hand, the lord of the sixth, eighth or the twelfth in the tenth is considered a pulling down force for career and rise in life. The lord of the eighth in the tenth is considered particularly evil, both in regard to curtailing longevity of the father and in respect of the native's career. For judging longevity of the father, consider also whether the Sun is strong and well placed or otherwise because the Sun is *Karaka* for the father.

Since the tenth house also governs trade and commerce and business activities and most businessmen carry on trade and commerce in partnership with one or more partners, due thought should be bestowed to the seventh house and its lord also. The natives who have malefics in the seventh or whose seventh lord tenants the sixth, eighth or the twelfth house as counted from the ascendant should not carry on partnership business. Either the partner will let him down or the partnership will be broken or there will be a financial loss.

The four *Karakas* for the tenth house—the Sun, Mercury, Jupiter and Saturn—each represents one or more features. The Sun represents the self and health. If the self is strong physically and mentally, the native will be vigorous in pushing ahead and mentally alert. Mercury governs speech, nimbleness activity, quick disposal, dealings with others, expression, correspondence, etc. Besides, it presides over nerves and a person has to be good in all these to achieve success in his efforts and be diplomatic in his dealings with others. Jupiter represents wealth and also wisdom. If our personal efforts are to result in an increasing bank balance, Jupiter has to be strong and well placed. Besides a shallow mind may emit a flitting light but cannot be a permanent source of illumination. It is the deep seated wisdom of Jupiter which is always necessary for arriving at sound judgment. And lastly, a good Saturn bestows the quality of patience and perseverance, hard work and laborious application to work. A rolling stone gathers no moss and a person who is impatient or does not have enough perseverance leaves the task in hand incompleted. As the wise proverb goes, success is one per cent inspiration and ninety-nine per cent perspiration. Saturn stands for hard and persistent application and those who lack in labour are unsuccessful.

We have emphasised the role of *Karakas* so that the readers while judging the tenth house may not overlook them. We have seen even some good astrologers devoting time and attention exclusively to the tenth house and its lord and ignoring the *Karakas* altogether with the result that their judgments miscarry. One word more and we shall finish with the judgment of this house. Do not ignore the Moon. Look to the sign occupied by the Moon and the tenth house from it.

A planet in the tenth from the ascendant or the Moon gives an indication of the type of work a man is destined to do. For the type of work governed by each planet, readers are referred to Chapters 6, 8 and 9.

Eleventh House

The eleventh house is primarily the house of gain and income. This is the only house where all planets, whether benefics or malefics are considered good for they add to the native's income. But *Papas* here, while good for the native's own income cause ill-health or premature death of the father and the elder brother of the native; they are also adverse for children.

Note the two houses, (i) the house or houses owned by the planet tenanting the eleventh, (ii) the house tenanted by the lord of the eleventh. The gain of money or acquisition will be governed by the matters and affairs of these two houses. For example, if the lord of the eleventh is in the fifth, there may be sudden gains through learning or authorship or from sons—all matters governed by the fifth house. Or take the example of the lord of the seventh in the eleventh when there may be gain through the wife or father-in-law, in partnership, business, etc.

The income or money is one of the chief points of enquiry in every birth chart. The second is the house of accumulated money, the fourth of landed properties, the eighth of money or properties received through legacy, the ninth of general good luck and fortune, the tenth of personal efforts and success in endeavours and the eleventh of income. In fact, we should look to all these houses, if we wish to arrive at a balanced judgment in regard to wealth and affluence of the native. We therefore provide below some general rules which will touch on one or more of these houses.

The *Sambandha* between the lords of the following houses is good for wealth: (i) first and second, (2) first and fourth, (3) first and fifth, (4) first and ninth, (5) first and tenth, (6) first and eleventh, (7) second and fourth, (8) second and fifth, (9) second and ninth, (10) second and tenth, (11) second and eleventh, (12) fourth and fifth, (13) fourth and ninth, (14) fourth and tenth, (15) fourth and eleventh, (16) fifth and ninth, (17) fifth and tenth, (18) fifth and eleventh, (19) ninth and tenth, (20) ninth and eleventh, (21) tenth and eleventh. This last Yoga is good for wealth but a pulling down force for rank and status. Some other planetary settings propitious for wealth are:

(i) The lord of the second strong in the tenth. (ii) The lords of the fourth and the ninth together in second. (iii) The lord of the eleventh in the second and the lord of the second in the eleventh or both strong in an angle from the ascendant.

The good *Yogas* given in Chapter 11 should also be examined. Now, here are some combinations which cause poverty. It is only after examining the two sets of combinations—for wealth and for poverty—that one should arrive at any inference.

The *Sambandha* between the following lords causes poverty:

(1) sixth and first, (2) sixth and second, (3) sixth and third, (4) sixth and fourth, (5) sixth and fifth, (6) sixth and seventh, (7) sixth and eighth, (8) sixth and ninth, (9) sixth and tenth, (10) sixth and eleventh, (11) sixth and twelfth, (12) eighth and twelfth, (13) twelfth and first, (14) twelfth and second, (15) twelfth and third, (16) twelfth and fourth, (17) twelfth and fifth, (18) twelfth and seventh, (19) twelfth and ninth, (20) twelfth and tenth, (21) twelfth and eleventh.

Some other planetary combinations which cause poverty are given below:

(1) If the lord of the first or the eighth be Jupiter and the lord of the ninth is weaker than Jupiter or combust and the lord of the eleventh is weak and does not tenant an angle from the ascendant.

(2) Mars, Mercury, Jupiter or Saturn, if combust or debilitated in the fifth, sixth, eighth, eleventh or the twelfth.

(3) If Mars, Mercury, Jupiter, Venus and Saturn occupy the fifth, sixth, eighth, tenth and the twelfth, in any order, and the lord of the twelfth is combust or debilitated and stronger than the lord of the first.

(4) If Virgo or Capricorn be the rising sign and the Moon, Mars, Jupiter and Venus are debilitated and occupy any of the following houses: 1st, 5th, 7th, 9th, 10th and 11th.

(5) If a fixed sign is rising and *Papas* are in angles or trine and there is no benefic in an angle or trine.

(6) If the birth is at night, the Moon very weak and the eighth from Moon is tenanted or aspected by *Papas*.

(7) Rahu or Ketu conjoined with the Moon cause poverty. This is one factor; other factors must also be looked into.

(8) *Papas* in the fourth from the ascendant or Moon cause poverty.

(9) If the lord of the ascendant is weak and is aspected by the lord of eighth.

(10) If the lord of the fourth is aspected by the lord of the sixth,

the lords of the eighth and the ninth are in the fifth and the lord of the first is debilitated.

(11) If benefics occupy the sixth, eighth, and the twelfth, malefics occupy the fifth and ninth and the lord of the eleventh is weak.

(12) If the lord of the ascendant is conjoined with a *Papa,* Jupiter and Venus are combust, the lord of the fourth is conjoined with a *Papa* and combust.

(13) *Papas* in any of the following houses, aspected by *Papas,* enemies or debilitated planets, cause poverty: 1st, 2nd, 3rd, 4th, 5th, 7th, 9th, 10th, 11th.

If there is one *Papa* fulfilling the above condition, the native is poor during childhood; if there are two such *Papas,* he experiences poverty in middle age, if there are three such *Papas,* there is poverty in old age.

These rules have been given to provoke thought in regard to the principles underlying the *Yogas* and help develop a sense of discrimination as to how the distribution of planets by sign and house or their combination or aspects cause good or evil effects.

Twelfth House

If the lord of the twelfth is in the ascendant, the native is good looking and has good powers of speech. If the lord of the twelfth is in the twelfth, the native spends generously and owns cattle. The lord of the twelfth in the ninth makes one religious. He visits holy places, but if the lord of the twelfth is in the ninth conjoined with a malefic, the native commits sinful acts instead.

If benefics occupy the twelfth, the native is philanthropic and spends on charity or auspicious celebrations, purchase of property etc., and generally his money is well spent. Jupiter herein inclines one to benevolence and to give in charity for the education of others and such other good objects. Venus herein inclines one to spend on luxuries, pleasures and women. Benefics make one save money also. Malefics herein cause heavy expenditure on unworthy objects such as, litigation and also loss in business, speculation, etc. It is generally not good if the lord of a house occupies *Trik,* but if the lord of the twelfth occupies the sixth or the eighth, it is considered good. If a male planet occupies twelfth, the native spends more on males; if a female planet tenants the twelfth, he spends more on females.

Mark the house tenanted by the lord of the twelfth and the houses he aspects. The expenses will mostly be on objects and affairs governed by this house, tenanted or aspected. If the lord of the twelfth is conjoined with a benefic, the money will be well spent and on a good cause connected with the house tenanted or aspected; if the twelfth lord is conjoined with a *Papa*, the money will be ill spent in connection with the houses whose lord conjoins or which the lord of the twelfth tenants or aspects.

Similarly, judge according to the *Karaka* conjoined with the lord of the twelfth. There will be expenditure on illness, treatment or due to enmity if conjoined with the lord of the sixth. If the lord of the twelfth is conjoined with Jupiter, then on sons or religious acts. If with Venus on wife or women, with Moon on the mother, with Sun on the father or in connection with the government, with Mercury on friends or in dealings with others, with Mars on brothers and quarrels, with Saturn on servants and low people. If the lord of the eighth is conjoined with the lord of the twelfth, there will be expenses connected with death.

If there is a benefic in the ninth and the lords of the first and the twelfth are conjoined or mutually aspect each other, there is expenditure on pilgrimages.

If the lords of the fifth, ninth, and the twelfth and Jupiter are beneficially conjoined, there is expenditure on good objects, such as, sons, education, religious and benevolent undertakings, etc.

If the lord of the ascendant, the Sun or Venus is in the twelfth, there is trouble to the left eye. Mars or Saturn in the twelfth causes premature teeth troubles. They also impair eyesight. Mars causes heavy over-draft accounts and indebtedness. We have observed in many birth charts that Mars in the eighth or the twelfth also leads to hospitalisation, living abroad or imprisonment.

If Jupiter is in the twelfth, the native becomes clever in his work, whether domestic or business, at a comparatively young age.

The above rules in regard to judging each house provide certain guide lines to help develop the powers of discrimination and judgment. Each birth chart is different from the other. All charts have different patterns and no rules could be wide enough to cover all the permutations and combinations possible. In the texts on Hindu astrology, many thousands of such rules have been given and it is not possible to reproduce them in a text-book for beginners. So readers are expected to take a clue from the rules and general observations made in this chapter and proceed with the examination of the chart and the patent or latent possibilities. Each placement by sign and house, the conjunction of planets benefics or malefics, or their aspects, have to be taken into account in arriving at the resultant inference.

CHAPTER 13

CALCULATION OF MAHADASHAS AND ANTARDASHAS

SO FAR we have been dealing with what astrology is and what effects the planets produce according to their placement by sign, house, combinations or aspects. Now we shall tackle the problem of "when" — that is, when the good or bad effects reflected in the radix (birth chart) will be felt.

Pandit Jawaharlal Nehru spent some of his time in prison; the same man became the Prime Minister of India and almost reigned for seventeen years. When the timings of evil planets were current, it was a period of struggle, strife and suffering for him, when the timings were for the blessed planets to shed their benefic light, he was surrounded with all possible luxuries and enjoyed virtually the powers and privileges of a king.

In smaller or greater measure, we all have such cycles of fortune and misfortune. There are very few people who do not suffer these alternate cycles. But there is a difference: those in whose charts planets for riches and wealth are strong, do not suffer and go down financially to the same extent as do those who have unfavourable planetary positions in regard to money. That is why all these chapters have been written to enable the readers to judge the radix. If the birth chart is strong for wealth, even under adverse periods, the native would not be reduced to dismal poverty. Conversely, if it is a poor horoscope for money, the native will not, even during the brightest periods — rise to dizzy heights. The influences operative at birth do not affect the monetary matters alone, but all departments of life.

These timings, good or bad, are referred to as periods. They are called in Sanskrit *Mahadasha* or simply *Dasha*. Some astrologers describe them as major periods because the prefix *'Maha'* in Sanskrit means great or major. If a planet is good and strong, his period would be beneficial; the converse will be the case if the planet is afflicted in the radix and portends evil.

The first point, therefore, is to calculate when a particular period, i.e., period of a particular planet, will be operative. This is described below.

In Hindu astrology, the seven planets and Rahu and Ketu are taken into account. Other planets, such as Herschel, Neptune or Pluto are not at all taken cognisance of.

(a) The maximum duration of life an individual is expected to live is taken as 120 years. Each of the planets has his period for the number of years as noted below:

Sun 6, Moon 10, Mars 7, Mercury 17, Jupiter 16, Venus 20, Saturn 19, Rahu 18 and Ketu 7.

(b) We have given the above list in the order of planets presiding over the week days and the nodes in the end. But their periods do not follow the above order. The order of periods of the nine planets (we have referred to Rahu and Ketu also as planets only for convenience of expression, though we are aware that these two are only nodes) is as follows:

Ketu, Venus, Sun, Moon, Mars, Rahu, Jupiter, Saturn, Mercury.

Why the order is as above and why the number of years allotted to each planet varies is a big question mark in Hindu astrology. Some authors have tried to explain this, but the reasoning is far fetched and not convincing. As regards the order in which these planets operate, the following explanation has been offered.

The following sets of constellations are presided over by planets noted against each.

	Constellations		*Planet*
Ashwini	Magha	Moola	Ketu
Bharani	P. Phalguni	P. Ashadha	Venus
Krittika	U. Phalguni	U. Ashadha	Sun
Rohini	Hasta	Shrawan	Moon
Mrigshira	Chitra	Dhanishtha	Mars

Ardra	Swati	Shatabhisha	Rahu
Punarvasu	Vishakha	P. Bhadra	Jupiter
Pushya	Anuradha	U. Bhadra	Saturn
Ashlesha	Jyeshtha	Revati	Mercury

The longitudes in each sign, covered by each of the constellations, have been given earlier and readers are referred to Chapter 1. Each of the planets presides over three constellations; thus Ketu presides over Ashwini, Magha and Moola; Venus presides over Bharani, P. Phalguni, and P. Ashadha, and on.

The first *Mahadasha* at birth is that of the planet which presides over the constellation occupied by the Moon at the time of birth and other *Mahadashas* follow in the order given in (b) above.

For example, if the Moon is at birth in Ashwini, the order of the *Mahadashas* will be Ketu, Venus, Sun, Moon, Mars, Rahu Jupiter, Saturn, Mercury. If at birth the Moon is in Pushya, the order of the *Mahadashas* will be Saturn, Mercury, Ketu, Venus, Sun, Moon, Mars, Rahu and Jupiter. Again, if the Moon was at birth in Revati, the order of *Mahadashas* will be Mercury, Ketu, Venus, Sun, Moon, Mars, Rahu, Jupiter and Saturn.

Few persons are however lucky enough to have all the nine *Mahadashas,* for their total extends to 120 years. How many people live upto that age? Some have two or three, others four or five and yet others six or seven *Mahadashas* and then life comes to an end. A few die in their first *Dasha* only.

One more point needs explaining. The duration of initial *Mahadasha* depends upon the distance covered by the Moon in the particular constellation. Suppose the Moon has just entered Aswini, then the native will have full quota of the Ketu *Mahadasha* comprising seven years. But if the Moon has covered one-fourth of Aswini, say 3° 20′ of Aswani (the total span of each constellation in space is 13° 20′), then one-quarter of 7 years, i.e., one year nine months should be deducted out of 7 years and the balance of Ketu *Mahadasha* at birth will then be 5 years 3 months after birth; then Venus for 20 years; then Sun for 6 years and so on.

Let us take another example. Suppose the longitude of the Moon at birth is 23° 20′ in Pisces. Reference to an earlier chapter will show that Revati extends from 16° 40′ to 30° Pisces. Now 23° 20′ is just the mid-point between 16° 40′ and 30°. So the native will have half of the full quota of 17 years of Mercury, i. e., a balance of 8 years 6 months of Mercury *Mahadasha,* then 7 years of Ketu, then 20 years of Venus, and so on.

The balance is calculated on the basis of the rule of three only in case of the first *Mahadasha.* The subsequent *Mahadashas* have their full quota.

A ready reckoner to ascertain the balance *Mahadasha* at birth, on the basis of the Moon's longitude at birth, has been given on the next pages which will save readers the inconvenience of calculating by rule of three.

Table I

BALANCE OF VINSHOTTARI MAHADASHA BY LONGITUDE OF MOON

Long. of Moon		Moon in Aries, Leo, Sagitt. — Balance of Mahadasha				Moon in Taurus, Virgo, Capri. — Balance of Mahadasha				Moon in Gemini, Libra, Aquar. — Balance of Mahadasha				Moon in Cancer, Scorpio, Pisces. — Balance of Mahadasha			
			y	m	d		y	m	d		y	m	d		y	m	d
0	0	Ketu	7	0	0	Sun	4	6	0	Mars	3	6	0	Jup	4	0	0
0	20		6	9	27		4	4	6		3	3	27		3	7	6
0	40		6	7	24		4	2	12		3	1	24		3	2	12
1	0		6	5	21		4	0	18		2	11	21		2	9	18
1	20		6	3	18		3	10	24		2	9	18		2	4	24
1	40		6	1	15		3	9	0		2	7	15		2	0	0
2	0		5	11	12		3	7	6		2	5	12		1	7	6
2	20		5	9	9		3	5	12		2	3	9		1	2	12
2	40		5	7	6		3	3	18		2	1	6		0	9	18
3	0		5	5	3		3	1	24		1	11	3		0	4	24
3	20		5	3	0		3	0	0		1	9	0	Sat	19	0	0
3	40		5	0	27		2	10	6		1	6	27		18	6	9
4	0		4	10	24		2	8	12		1	4	24		18	0	18
4	20		4	8	21		2	6	18		1	2	21		17	6	27
4	40		4	6	18		2	4	24		1	0	18		17	1	6
5	0		4	4	15		2	3	0		0	10	15		16	7	15
5	20		4	2	12		2	1	6		0	8	12		16	1	24
5	40		4	0	9		1	11	12		0	6	9		15	8	3
6	0		3	10	6		1	9	18		0	4	6		15	2	12
6	20		3	8	3		1	7	24		0	2	3		14	8	21

			y	m	d		y	m	d		y	m	d		y	m	d
6	40	Ketu	3	6	0	Sun	1	6	0	Rahu	18	0	0	Sat	14	3	0
7	0		3	3	27		1	4	6		17	6	18		13	9	9
7	20		3	1	24		1	2	12		17	1	6		13	3	18
7	40		2	11	21		1	0	18		16	7	24		12	9	27
8	0		2	9	18		0	10	24		16	2	12		12	4	6
8	20		2	7	15		0	9	0		15	9	0		11	10	15
8	40		2	5	12		0	7	6		15	3	18		11	4	24
9	0		2	3	9		0	5	12		14	10	6		10	11	3
9	20		2	1	6		0	3	18		14	4	24		10	5	12
9	40		1	11	3		0	1	24		13	11	12		9	11	21
10	0		1	9	0	Moon	10	0	0		13	6	0		9	6	0
10	20		1	6	27		9	9	0		13	0	18		9	0	9
10	40		1	4	24		9	6	0		12	7	6		8	6	18
11	0		1	2	21		9	3	0		12	1	24		8	0	27
11	20		1	0	18		9	0	0		11	8	12		7	7	6
11	40		0	10	15		8	9	0		11	3	0		7	1	15
12	0		0	8	12		8	6	0		10	9	18		6	7	24
12	20		0	6	9		8	3	0		10	4	6		6	2	3
12	40		0	4	6		8	0	0		9	10	24		5	8	12
13	0		0	2	3		7	9	0		9	5	12		5	2	21
13	20	Ven	20	0	0		7	6	0		9	0	0		4	9	0
13	40		19	6	0		7	3	0		8	6	18		4	3	9
14	0		19	0	0		7	0	0		8	1	6		3	9	18
14	20		18	6	0		6	9	0		7	7	24		3	3	27
14	40		18	0	0		6	6	0		7	2	12		2	10	6
15	0		17	6	0		6	3	0		6	9	0		2	4	15
15	20		17	0	0		6	0	0		6	3	18		1	10	24
15	40		16	6	0		5	9	0		5	10	6		1	5	3
16	0		16	0	0		5	6	0		5	4	24		0	11	12
16	20		15	6	0		5	3	0		4	11	12		0	5	21
16	40		15	0	0		5	0	0		4	6	0	Mer	17	0	0
17	0		14	6	0		4	9	0		4	0	18		16	6	27
17	20		14	0	0		4	6	0		3	7	6		16	1	24
17	40		13	6	0		4	3	0		3	1	24		15	8	21
18	0		13	0	0		4	0	0		2	8	12		15	3	18
18	20		12	6	0		3	9	0		2	3	0		14	10	15
18	40		12	0	0		3	6	0		1	9	18		14	5	12
19	0		11	6	0		3	3	0		1	4	6		14	0	9
19	0	Ven	11	6	0	Moon	3	3	0	Rahu	1	4	6	Mer	14	0	9
19	20		11	0	0		3	0	0		0	10	24		13	7	6
19	40		10	6	0		2	9	0		0	5	12		13	2	3
20	0		10	0	0		2	6	0	Jup	16	0	0		12	9	0
20	20		9	6	0		2	3	0		15	7	6		12	3	27

Deg	Min		Y	M	D		Y	M	D		Y	M	D		Y	M	D
20	40	Ven.	9	0	0	Moon	2	0	0	Jup	15	2	12	Mer	11	10	24
21	0		8	6	0		1	9	0		14	9	18		11	5	21
21	20		8	0	0		1	6	0		14	4	24		11	0	18
21	40		7	6	0		1	3	0		14	0	0		10	7	15
22	0		7	0	0		1	0	0		13	7	6		10	2	12
22	20		6	6	0		0	9	0		13	2	12		9	9	9
22	40		6	0	0		0	6	0		12	9	18		9	4	6
23	0		5	6	0		0	3	0		12	4	24		8	11	3
23	20		5	0	0	Mars	7	0	0		12	0	0		8	6	0
23	40		4	6	0		6	9	27		11	7	6		8	0	27
24	0		4	0	0		6	7	24		11	2	12		7	7	24
24	20		3	6	0		6	5	21		10	9	18		7	2	21
24	40		3	0	0		6	3	18		10	4	24		6	9	18
25	0		2	6	0		6	1	15		10	0	0		6	4	15
25	20		2	0	0		5	11	12		9	7	6		5	11	12
25	40		1	6	0		5	9	9		9	2	12		5	6	9
26	0		1	0	0		5	7	6		8	9	18		5	1	6
26	20		0	6	0		5	5	3		8	4	24		4	8	3
26	40	Sun	6	0	0		5	3	0		8	0	0		4	3	0
27	0		5	10	6		5	0	27		7	7	6		3	9	27
27	20		5	8	12		4	10	24		7	2	12		3	4	24
27	40		5	6	18		4	8	21		6	9	18		2	11	21
28	0		5	4	24		4	6	18		6	4	24		2	6	18
28	20		5	3	0		4	4	15		6	0	0		2	1	15
28	40		5	1	6		4	2	12		5	7	6		1	8	12
29	0		4	11	12		4	0	9		5	2	12		1	3	9
29	20		4	9	18		3	10	6		4	9	18		0	10	6
29	40		4	7	24		3	8	3		4	4	24		0	5	3
30	0		4	6	0		3	6	0		4	0	0		0	0	0

TABLE II

PROPORTIONAL PARTS FOR MAHADASHA OF PLANETS

(To be subtracted from the balance of *Dasha* for increase by minutes of the longitude of moon)

	1′	2′	3′	4′	5′	10′	20′	
Ketu or Mars	3.15	6.3	9.45	12.6	15.75	31.5	63	Days
Venus	9	18	27	36	45	90	180	,,
Sun	2.7	5.4	8.1	10.8	13.5	27	54	,,
Moon	4.5	9	13.5	18	22.5	45	90	,,
Rahu	8.1	16.2	24.3	32.4	40.5	81	162	,,
Jupiter	7.2	14.4	21.6	28.8	36	72	144	,,
Saturn	8.55	17.1	25.65	34.2	42.75	85.5	171	,,
Mercury	7.65	15.3	22.95	30.6	38.25	76.5	153	,,

Strictly speaking, 1 minute or more of arc of the various planets yields the above number of days.

But from the practical point, if the fraction of the day is more than half, a full day is taken and if the fraction of the day is less than half, it is omitted.

Another point to emphasise is that in calculating the *Mahadasha,* a year consisting of 365 days and odd hours is taken as constituting 1 year, and a month as 30 solar days (slightly longer than the civil day).

For example, if we have to reckon one year from 1st January 1970, for purposes of the *Mahadasha,* it will be over on 1st January 1971.

Example: Let us calculate the *Mahadashas* of a child born at 5-30 A.M. Indian Standard Time at Delhi on 1st January 1970.

On referring to the Ephemeris we find that the longitude of the Moon was 17° 15′ in Virgo, Now referring to Table I, we find that for 17° 20′ in Virgo the balance of the Moon is given as 4 years 6 months. We have to find what will be the period for 5′ for the Moon *Mahadasha*. It is 22.5 days. In order to avoid fractions we may take it as 23 days. Adding these 23 days to 4 years 6 months, we get the Moon's balance *Mahadasha* as 4 years 6 months 23 days and prepare the *Mahadasha* table as follows:

TABLE III

MAHADASHAS

Planet	Duration Y. D. M.			Till the Age of Y. D. M.		
Balance of Moon's Mahadasha at birth	4	6	23	4	6	23
Mahadasha of Mars	7	0	0	11	6	23
„ „ Rahu	18	0	0	29	6	23
„ „ Jupiter	16	0	0	45	6	23
„ „ Saturn	19	0	0	64	6	23
„ „ Mercury	17	0	0	81	6	23
„ „ Ketu	7	0	0	88	6	23
„ „ Venus	20	0	0	108	6	23
„ „ Sun	6	0	0	114	6	23
„ „ Moon	5	5	7	120	0	0

Normally astrologers do not complete the cycle of 120 years. They leave it at about 80 or 90 years which is generally the longest span of life. But one may calculate beyond that age.

ANTARDASHAS

The *Mahadasha* is at times referred to as *Dasha* (an abbreviated form of *Mahadasha*) and the *Antardasha* is also referred to as *Antar* only (an abbreviated form of *Antardasha*). In South India generally *Antardasha* is referred to as *Bhukti.*

There are nine planets, so there are nine *Mahadashas.* There are nine planets, so there are nine *Antardashas* also. Each *Mahadasha* has nine *Antardashas.* The first *Antardasha* in each *Mahadasha* is of the *Mahadasha* lord and the subsequent *Antardashas* are of other planets in the order of *Mahadashas,* e.g., in the Sun's *Mahadasha* there will be nine *Antardashas* of the Sun, Moon, Mars, Rahu, Jupiter, Saturn, Mercury, Ketu, Venus. In the Moon's *Mahadasha* there will be nine *Antardashas* of the Moon, Mars, Rahu, Jupiter, Saturn, Mercury, Ketu, Venus and Sun.

The period of an *Antardasha* in a *Mahadasha* is in proportion to the durations of the *Mahadasha* lords.

Example:

What will be the duration of the Suns' *Antardasha* in the Moon's *Mahadasha.*

The duration of the Sun's *Mahadasha* is 6 years and that of the Moon 10 years.

In 120 years Sun gets 6 years

In 1 year Sun gets $\frac{6}{120}$ Years

In 10 years Sun gets $\frac{6 \times 10}{120}$ years

$= 6$ months.

The Tables giving *Antardasha* periods for each *Mahadasha* follow:

TABLE IV

1. Ketu (17 years)				2. Venus (20 years)				3. Sun (6 years)			
Ketu	0	4	27	Venus	3	4	0	Sun	0	3	18
Venus	1	2	0	Sun	1	0	0	Moon	0	6	0
Sun	0	4	6	Moon	1	8	0	Mars	0	4	6
Moon	0	7	0	Mars	1	2	0	Rahu	0	10	24

Mars	0	4	27	Rahu	3	0	0	Jupiter	0	9	18
Rahu	1	0	18	Jupiter	2	8	0	Saturn	0	11	12
Jupiter	0	11	6	Saturn	3	2	0	Mercury	0	10	6
Saturn	1	1	9	Mercury	2	10	0	Ketu	0	4	6
Venus	0	11	27	Ketu	1	2	0	Venus	1	0	0

4. Moon (10 years)				5. Mars (7 years)				6. Rahu (18 years)			
Moon	0	10	0	Mars	0	4	27	Rahu	2	8	12
Mars	0	7	0	Rahu	1	0	18	Jupiter	2	4	24
Rahu	1	6	0	Jupiter	0	11	6	Saturn	2	10	6
Jupiter	1	4	0	Saturn	1	1	9	Mercury	2	6	18
Saturn	1	7	0	Mercury	0	11	27	Ketu	1	0	18
Mercury	1	5	0	Ketu	0	4	27	Venus	3	0	0
Ketu	0	7	0	Venus	1	2	0	Sun	0	10	24
Venus	1	8	0	Sun	0	4	6	Moon	1	6	0
Sun	0	6	0	Moon	0	7	0	Mars	1	0	18

7. Jupiter (16 years)				8. Saturn (19 years)				9. Mercury (17)			
Jupiter	2	1	18	Saturn	3	0	3	Mercury	2	4	27
Saturn	2	6	12	Mercury	2	8	9	Ketu	0	11	27
Mercury	2	3	6	Ketu	1	1	9	Venus	2	10	0
Ketu	0	11	6	Venus	3	2	0	Sun	0	10	6
Venus	2	8	0	Sun	0	11	12	Moon	1	5	0
Sun	0	9	18	Moon	1	7	0	Mars	0	11	27
Moon	1	4	0	Mars	1	1	9	Rahu	2	6	18
Mars	0	11	6	Rahu	2	10	6	Jupiter	2	3	6
Rahu	2	4	24	Jupiter	2	6	12	Saturn	2	8	9

Antardasha at Birth:

Having specified the period of each *Antardasha* in each of the *Mahadashas* what remains to be explained is how to calculate the *Antardasha* at birth. This we shall explain by taking a concrete example.

Example:

We have found above that the Moon's Mahadasha at birth was 4 years 6 months 23 days. Had the native a full quota of 10 years of the Moon's *Mahadasha*, there would have been no need to explain. As the first *Antardasha* is always of the *Mahadasha* lord, the first ten months would have been the Moon's *Antardasha* in his own *Mahadasha*, the next seven months of Mars' *Antardasha* in the Moon's *Mahadasha* and so on (see Table IV). But the fact that there is a balance of only 4 years 6 months 23 days of the Moon's *Mahadasha* shows that out of the full quota of 10 years of the Moon's *Mahadasha,* 5 years 5 months 7 days were over before birth. This period already undergone prior to birth shows that the following *Antardashas* had already lapsed before birth:

	Y.	M.	D.
Moon in Moon	0	10	0
Mars ,,	0	7	0
Rahu ,,	1	6	0
Jupiter ,,	1	4	0
Saturn ,,	1	2	7
	5	5	7

And the balance *Antardasha* of Saturn was (1 year 7 months minus 1 year 2 months 7 days) 4 months 23 days. So we write as follows:

TABLE OF ANTARDASHAS IN THE MAHADASHA OF MOON

	Duration			Till the Age of		
	Y.	M.	D.	Y.	M.	D.
Balance of Saturns' Antardasha in the Mahadasha of Moon at birth:	0	4	23	0	4	23
Mercury in Moon	1	5	0	1	9	23
Ketu ,,	0	7	0	2	4	23
Venus ,,	1	8	0	4	0	23
Sun ,,	0	6	0	4	6	23

TABLE OF ANTARDASHAS IN THE MAHADASHA OF MARS

	Duration			Till the age of		
	Y.	M.	D.	Y.	M.	D.
Mars in Mars	0	4	27	4	11	20
Rahu ,,	1	0	18	6	0	8
Jupiter ,,	0	11	6	6	11	14
Saturn ,,	1	1	9	8	0	23
Mercury ,,	0	11	27	9	0	20
Ketu ,,	0	4	27	9	5	17
Venus ,,	1	2	0	10	7	17
Sun ,,	0	4	6	10	11	23
Moon ,,	0	7	0	11	6	23

And in a similar manner we calculate the *Antardashas* in the subsequent *Mahadashas.*

CHAPTER 14

MAHADASHAS—MAJOR PERIODS OF PLANETS AND JUDGMENT

THIS IS the most important chapter dealing with the timing of events. Each step has to be carefully followed and the various points of view carefully understood and synthesised. If readers go by one point of view alone, the judgment is likely to be misleading. In the first instance, the various factors determining the effects of *Mahadashas* may appear too many or at times contradictory, for example, if a planet is strong by sign and placed in a good house, it should naturally show good effects; but if he is the lord of an evil house or aspected by *Papas*, he should show evil effects. But we shall explain how to reconcile these opposite views and declare the resultant effects he will show during his *Mahadasha*.

The simple solution is that he will show both the good as well as the evil effects. For example, if Taurus is the rising sign and Saturn is in the fifth house as lord of the ninth and tenth houses he will prove good for the affairs of these two houses, but due to his fifth house tenancy, he may impair the affairs of the fifth house — cause stomach troubles, formation of gases, damage the digestive tract or cause ill-health to children.

Or take another example. Suppose the sign Cancer is rising and Jupiter, the lord of the sixth and ninth, occupies the tenth house. Now as lord of the ninth in the tenth, he will give fillip to official status and position and increase the respect commanded by the native. Jupiter in the tenth will fully aspect the second house; thus there may be increase in wealth also. Jupiter will fully aspect the fourth house, so additions to landed properties may also be expected. Jupiter is *Karaka* for sons, piety, religion, etc., and during Jupiter's *Mahadasha,* sons may prosper; or if the native is young there may be birth of a son, the native may go on a pilgrimage, he may perform special religious services connected with devotional worship. But since Jupiter in the above example is the lord of the sixth house also, his *Mahadasha* may give rise to increased enmity and opposition.

Thus the planet shows the effect (1) of the house he owns, (2) the house he occupies, (3) the sign he is in, (4) the houses he aspects, (5) he also kindles into action the effects of the planet or planets he aspects or conjoins with, (6) he himself is modified in yielding effects according to the planet or planets that conjoin or aspect him.

In Chapter 8 have been given the effects of planets in the different signs and in Chapter 9 the effects of the planets in houses. What each house stands for has been fully discussed in Chapter 7. Readers will thus be able to arrive at fairly good judgment in regard to the quality and effects of each *Mahadasha* if they refer to the effects delineated in Chapters 7, 8 and 9 and then draw conclusions from them. We have come across a large number of text-books on Hindu astrology in which we find paragraphs describing the effects of *Mahadashas.* But since no two horoscopes are alike how can this ready-made prediction like ready-made suits fit every one? The result is that the predictions go wrong. It is to guard against such pitfalls that we invite reference to previous chapters. If a planet has been according to the canons of astrology, described as yielding certain effects, he will during his *Mahadasha* yield those results. If the natal effect has been described as good, he will during his *Mahadasha* yield good results as described for the planet. If his effect given in the previous chapters is evil, he will yield evil results in regard to those matters which have been stated earlier. If on some counts he is good radically and evil on others, he will show mixed trends. But in judging the quality sometimes there is a set-off also. For example, a planet is lord of good houses and occupies a good house, but occupies his sign of debilitation or is aspected by a *Papa.* Under such circumstances his intensity of showing good effects will be set-off, due to occupation of a weak sign or receiving a *Papa* aspect. Conversely, a planet may be lord of an evil house and occupy evil house, but if he tenants his exaltation sign or own sign and is conjoined with a benefic, he may not yield such evil results as his lordship and tenancy of houses warrant.

Different streams of evaluation in regard to *Mahadashas* and *Antardashas* flow in one channel and state principles for judging the *Mahadasha* effects. We give four of these below:

(A) Judge each planet as giving effect, during his *Mahadasha,* in respect of matters for which he is a *Karaka* or which is signified by him. If he is well placed by sign and house, conjoined with or receiving the aspect of benefics, he will show good effects in respect of all matters he is significator for. If on the other hand, he occupies an evil sign, an evil house, and is conjoined with or aspected by *Papas* he will show evil effects in regard to matters for which he is a significator or a *Karaka.* We shall explain this. Suppose Jupiter is good and strong and beneficially conjoined and aspected. Jupiter is *Karaka* for wealth, sons, education, religion, respect, etc. So, during his *Mahadasha,* all these matters would augment and show good effects. Now take the reverse example. Suppose Jupiter is afflicted in a weak sign, and evil house and conjoined with a malefic, or aspected by a *Papa.* Then under such circumstances all matters, such as, wealth, sons, religious undertakings, respect, etc., would suffer. In short, if the planet is strong the matters for which he is a *Karaka* prosper; if he is weak and afflicted, these suffer.

(B) Another point of view in judgment is the ownership of houses. Various matters have been assigned to each house. Matters governed by each house have been given in detail, but one need not take into consideration each one of them. One has to pick and choose. For example, cattle are judged from the fourth and the sixth also. People living in large cities and towns have no facilities for keeping cows or buffaloes. So it would be idle to take cattle into consideration — whether they would increase or decrease during the *Mahadasha* of the lord of the fourth or the sixth house. But when we are examining the birth chart of an agriculturist, it may be a relevant point worth considering. But such matters as health, wealth, happiness are common to all. We need not add that common sense would prelude consideration of marriage or birth of a son if the native is only a child. Strong *Marakas* (death inflicting planets) do not kill the native if he is young, if his health is good and he is ordained to live a long life. But if the same *Mahadasha* were current in old age, it would kill the native. This is just to show how we have to discriminate in fixing the role of the *Mahadasha* according to the stage in life and probabilities. Here again we have to examine each lord of the house whose *Mahadasha* is current. If the lord of the house is strong and well placed he would produce good effects pertaining to the matters of the house he is lord of, tenants and aspects. If the lord of the first house is well placed and strong, whether malefic or benefic, he does not damage the house he tenants or aspects; but if the planet is a malefic and not the lord of the first but of other houses, then during his *Mahadasha* he may bestow good effects in matters governed by the house or houses he owns, but being a natural malefic he would spoil the house he occupies or aspects. Here also all benefics are not always wholly benefic nor all malefics wholly malefic.

(i) A natural benefic, if he owns a good house such as a trine becomes fully benefic.

(ii) A natural benefic if he owns an evil house acts in a beneficent as well as a malignant manner. For example, if the sign Taurus is rising, Venus would be the lord of the first and the sixth house, and if he occupies the seventh house, then due to ownership of the sixth house, he has a streak of malignancy also and his placement in the seventh would give pleasures of sex, partnership, etc., but would damage the health of the wife as well.

(iii) A malefic, if he is the lord of an evil house, would be fully malignant.

(iv) A malefic, if he is the lord of good houses, will not be so malignant and would not greatly damage the house tenanted. For example, if Cancer or Leo is rising, Mars would be the lord of an angle and a trine and his occupation of a house would not damage it very much. To revert to the main point, if the planet is strong and well placed, he would show good effects pertaining to matters governed by the house or houses he is lord of. The third point usually followed by astrologers is as given below.

(C) The third point of view is in a way an offshoot of (B) above. Certain planets have been declared as yielding good results during their *Mahadashas* according to the sign rising; others have been declared to yield unfavourable results. Here the main criteria are the ownership of houses and their *Sambandha* with lords of other houses. In subsequent pages we shall take up each of the ascendants and state which planets would yield good results for a particular ascendant and which would create evil effects.

(D) In the fourth place we shall group all miscellaneous considerations which assist in ascertaining the quality of the *Mahadasha.*

A. MAHADASHA EFFECTS ON THE BASIS OF KARAKAS

Each planet is *Karaka* for certain matters and affairs. According to the delineation of effects of planets in signs and houses, readers have to exercise their judgment and find out whether a particular planet is strong or weak, good oı bad. If he is good he will promote the matters and affairs for which he is a *Karaka.* In Chapter 6 on planets, have been given some of the matters for which a particular planet is *Karaka.* Here we are giving a consolidated list, so that readers may at a glance know whether (if the Karaka is strong) benefits would accrue from or pertaining to the matters governed by him or he will come to harm or suffer in respect of the matters (if the Karaka is weak and afflicted).

Sun. The soul, self-realisation, worship of lord Shiva, body, health, belly, eye, bile, diseases of the head, power, splendour, strife, harshness, courage, valour, strenuous effort, royal favour kingdom, government, position, activity in public, high status, long standing anger, hostility, capture of the enemy, enmity, intense severity, good strength, father, fortress, fire, heat, taste, bitter articles, thorny trees, grass, timber, forest cattle, old people, land, square or circular shaped things, bones, medicines, position, roaming over mountains, travelling, rubies, pearls, orange or red coloured articles, coarse or rough cloth, the eastern direction, etc.

Now we shall explain how to interpret these. If the Sun is strong, during the Sun's *Mahadasha,* the soul will feel strong, the native may make efforts for self-realisation, live splendidly, may travel far and wide, may be engaged in strife or hostility which may yield him good dividends. His father may have a rise or he himself may benefit from his father; he may have rise of position and status, exhibit physical strength and courage, gain by dealing in timber, thorny trees, forest contracts, circular or square shaped articles, coarse cloth, medicines, medicinal herbs, poisons, red or orange coloured articles, and so on. On the other hand, if the Sun is weak and afflicted, he may feel inner weakness, his physical and mental prowess may decline, there may be health troubles, diseases of the stomach, eyes, teeth or mental ailments. He may suffer at the hands of his father, or his father may suffer in health or die. There may be demotion in rank and status, displeasure of the government, loss by dealing in timber, forest contracts, medicines, coarse cloth, round or circular shaped things, etc.

Each item for which the Sun is *Karaka* or any planet is *Karaka* cannot in the very nature of things apply to all individuals. In this world there are millions of things. They fall in the portfolio of some planet or the other. Thus, a planet is a *Karaka* for thousands of matters and things. Every native, according to his environment, is connected with a few of them only, and the astrologer has to discriminate which items are likely to affect him. If a person is in government service the favour of the government or a rise in position are likely effects, if the Sun is strong; but if the Sun is weak, he may miss the chance of promotion or may be reprimanded or demoted or suffer a dismissal if the planet is severely afflicted. The art of interpretation is a delicate one and requires commonsense as well as practice and experience. We have merely given the guidelines for interpretation and the readers have to exercise their own judgment and discrimination.

Moon. Intelligence, mind, heart, disposition, happiness, pleasure, splendour, fame, eating good food, blood and vital energy, favours, face, beauty, facial lustre, impartiality, diseases arising out of wind (*Vata*) and phlegm, sleep, lethargy, epilepsy, belly, enlargement of spleen, consumption, fluid formations in the body, fevers due to cold, typhoid fever, mother, good perfume, flowers, women comforts of the bed, wells, tanks, pearls, the nine gems, middle aged people, nourishment, saline taste, white articles, shining things, silver, bell metal, royalty, wealth, getting a job, north-western direction, fish and other aqueous animals, fine cloth, silk, sugarcane, good fruit, Brahmans, worship of goddess Gauri, etc.

Thus if the Moon is well placed by sign and house and beneficially aspected, the native may during the Moon's *Mahadasha* have a cheerful heart, a happy and vigorous mind, his facial lustre may increase; he may have at his disposal flowers and perfumes, and comforts of the bed. He may obtain a good job or there may be rise in status or there may be gain of money from women or the favours or patronage of women or from a queen; he may gain by dealing in silver, pearls, gems, sugar-cane, aqueous products, white articles and from the north western direction, he may pay homage to Brahmans and worship goddess Durga, etc. But if the Moon is afflicted, his health may suffer, he may have ailments arising out of imbalance of *Vata* (such as, blood pressure) or *Kapha* (phlegm) or from enlargement of the spleen, typhoid fever, etc., he may lose a job or there may be demotion in rank or status, there may be loss from or quarrel with women, displeasure of the queen, enmity with women and loss thereby. The native may not feel sufficiently energetic and may be lethargic, indolent, sleepy. There may be loss by dealing in sugar-cane, silver, silk, etc. His mother may suffer ill-health or die, etc.

We have to pick and choose some items which may be applicable to the native, his environment and probabilities.

Mars. Prowess, stamina and strength, hostility, virility, generosity, anger, cleverness, firmness, quarrels, enemy's strength, kingship, arms, wearing arms (for battle), battle, service, ministership, wickedness, fickleness of mind, hatred, independence, sound of a trumpet, seeing, eating meat, bile, blood, heat, wounds, urinary diseases, hot and inflammatory diseases, marrow, breaking of a limb, axe, forester, quadrupeds, brothers and sisters, land, earthen things, burnt things, jewels, gold, goldsmith, copper, beautiful cloth, red articles, square shaped things, southern direction, wild animals, an authority inflicting punishment, serpent, god Subrahmanya, Kshatriya caste, people of young age, pungent taste, etc.

Now, if Mars is strong and well placed during his *Mahadasha*, there may be gain from brothers, favour from persons wielding authority, entry into or promotion in military, quasi-military or police service where one has to bear arms, or if already in service promotion therein, acquisition of land and property, gold, copper and jewels, benefit from the southern direction or the native may travel in that direction. The native's health would be good, he would be optimistic and have a feeling of strength and stamina, he would be dashing and courageous and achieve much with his daring and persistence, etc. But if Mars is weak and afflicted, the native may have a fall, break his limbs or have wounds, suffer from urinary complaints or deterioration of the blood, may suffer at the hands of a magistrate, always be in a quarrelsome mood, exchange hot words, there may be enmities, litigation and hatred and loss thereby. He may be put to loss by a person of the *Kshatriya* caste; there may be loss of wealth, gold, copper, etc. The art of interpretation varies from circumstance to circumstance and with the subjective appreciation of the astrologer. The background of the native must be known — one in military service may lose a limb in the thickness of battles, a factory worker may do so while operating a machine, a civilian may have an accident. All items cannot apply to all people alike.

Mercury. Speech, neck, navel, softwords, modesty, the nervous system, jocular disposition, education, wisdom, writing, impartiality, mathematics, astrology, proficiency in languages, logic, dealing with others in commercial or political spheres, trading, doctors, maternal uncle, relations, friends, tranquillity, activity, movement, flourishing of the family, dust, garden, horses, treasury, infantry, new garments, palatial buildings, green colour, sculpture, pilgrimage, worship of lord Vishnu, devotion, people of the trading class, the northern direction, wet things, alloys, gold, mercury and all products in which this metal is used, emerald, jewellery, the art of testing precious stones, mixture of things, etc.

Now if Mercury is strong and well placed by sign and house, the native would be during his *Mahadasha* inclined to devote his time and energy to studies, writing, reading, lecturing or in dealing profitably with others; he may act as a middle man, or secure the agency or distribution of some product or may be engaged in publishing and publicity. There may be gain from friends and relations; he may travel to the north or there may be financial benefit from that direction; he may be associated with young people and may pass a happy time with them or they may be a source of monetary gain, etc.

But if Mercury is weak and afflicted, the native may have to suffer from nervous diseases, a bad liver, loss due to bad friends and relations; suffer a loss in sculptures, publishing, jewellery, or may be the victim of fraud or cheating, or he may be brought to book due to his own dishonest acts like cheating, forgery, antedating of documents, or for defamation and the like. Consider those items which may suit the circumstances of the individual.

Jupiter. Knowledge, wisdom, philosophy, Vedic texts, sacred incantations, religion, devotional worship, morals, piety, inclination to oblige others, doing good, physical health, stamina, happiness, gentleness, misery, devices, softness, brilliance, beautiful house, comfortable living, paraphernalia, savings, wealth, treasury, topaz, jewels, ornaments, money, eldest brother, grand-father, holy water, pilgrimages, Brahmans, cows, chariots, horses, elephants, palanquins, sons, grand-sons, disciples, yellow coloured things, elliptical articles, sweet taste, sweet juice, long things, worship of Lord Shiva, north-east direction, diseases arising out of imbalance of *Kapha* (phlegm) and fat in the body due to corpulence and good living, etc.

When Jupiter is strong and well placed or forms good *Yogas*, the native is during his *Mahadasha* inclined to learning and increase of knowledge. It is one of the best *Mahadashas* during school and college career. If the *Mahadasha* comes in middle age a good Jupiter confers wealth and bestows sons; the native may have a good and comfortable life, go on a pilgrimage and have auspicious celebrations, such as, investiture of the sacred thread ceremony; he may gain from yellow articles, gold, juicy and sweet products. In old age, the *Mahadasha* may bestow grandsons, better income, finances. There may be gain from Brahmans and religious people, etc.

However, if Jupiter is afflicted by sign, house and aspect, his *Mahadasha* would thwart education, bring poverty and cause misery. The native would commit irreligious or evil acts, his efforts in the north-eastern direction may end in frustration and failure, he may lose cows, horses, etc., if he possessed any. His sons and grand-sons may suffer or be hostile to him. In other words, instead of there being gain and happiness, there will be loss and misery and the negative aspect would predominate.

Venus. Art, artistic things, beauty and aesthetics, women, love, love affairs, sexual enjoyment, semen, eyes, sexual parts, marriage, company of women, gentleness, kindness, co-operation, amiability, harmony, flowers, scents, perfumes, happiness, all kinds of pleasures, passions, desires, dancing, dancing girls, drama, theatres, cinemas, singing, music, musical instruments, poetry, esteem, respect, good luck, courtesans, short things, sour taste, scratching, black hair, taste, happiness from wife, lustre, attendants, gems, pearls, silver, silk, white and soft materials, liquids, buying and selling, horses, elephants, articles of variegated colour, swimming, people of the Vaishya caste, people of middle-age, beautiful girls, handsome boys, a minister, supporting women, decoration, south-east direction, etc.

Now, according to the rules of interpretation indicated earlier, if Venus is well placed, the native will during his *Mahadasha* acquire things of art and pleasure, he will co-operate with others in a harmonious manner and will receive their reciprocal cooperation. He may gain from or through the agency of any of the things enumerated above. Love between husband and wife may increase or the native may have love affairs. If unmarried, the native may be married, daughters may be born or there may be other festivities in the house. The native may rise due to the patronage or favour of some lady, and so on.

On the other hand, if Venus is afflicted the native may suffer from imbalance of wind (*vata*) and *phlegm* (*kapha*), he may have urinary or venereal diseases, his sexual powers may be at a low ebb, he may get entangled with some woman and earn a bad name and also suffer monetary loss. Favours may be lacking; there may be want of cooperation and disharmony at home and outside. The circumstances differ from case to case and the above is not an exhaustive list of the good and bad effects possible, but only illustrative of them.

Saturn. This planet presides over sorrows, deaths, disabilities, diseases arising out of imbalance of *Vata* (wind), an extreme example of which is paralysis, gout, rheumatism, ketabolic activity in the human body, old age, decay, annihilation, destruction, meanness, stinginess, cheating, treachery, distress, pain, melancholia, misunderstanding, downfall, accusations, liability to be prosecuted, agnates, misdirected strength, indigestion, wandering, servants, dependants, old persons, low caste people, labour, labourers, ugly hair, goats, sheep, buffaloes, theft, cruel deeds, woods, secluded places, regions where oils and minerals are found, dirty places, iron, tin, lead, wool, woollen goods, oil, oilseeds, coarse grain, black grain, ashes, articles of black colour, servility, unrighteous acts, sins, falsehood, western direction, agriculture, machinery, etc.

If Saturn is well placed and occupies a good position in the birth chart, the native may during his *Mahadasha* rise in service by his own strenuous efforts and hard work; he may derive benefit from agriculture, cattle, oil, factory, iron, goats, sheep and other matters connected with Saturn. He may receive a legacy. But if Saturn is afflicted, he may suffer from diseases due to malnutrition, poverty, litigation, etc. There may be quarrels and disputes with old people, deaths in the family or among those near and dear to the native. He may have to lead a miserable life due to distress all around. There may be impediments and obstacles in his path of progress.

This delineation is based mainly on the *Karakatwa* (attributes of the *Karaka*), but there are other governing and modifying features which we shall deal with later.

Rahu and Ketu should not be considered unimportant for Rahu's *Mahadasha* extends over 18 years and Ketu's to 7 years. Thus these nodes together cover 25 years out of 120, a fairly long span of time. As we shall have occasion to discuss later, these nodes produce effects according to the sign and house they occupy and reflect during their *Mahadashas* the attributes of the planets they are conjoined with but they have significance of their own also. It is therefore necessary to specify matters and affairs they are significators for.

Rahu. Kingdom, power, accumulation, gathering, harsh speech, falsehood. low caste people, wicked females, cohabitation with quadrupeds, impurity, wickedness, breathing, catarrh, acute pain, grandfather, movements, travelling, moving in the opposite direction, change of place, sorrows, servants, reptiles, south-west direction, mountains, old age, an irreligious person, liaisons with females or wicked people, bone, enlargement of the spleen, cutaneous diseases such as ringworm, eczema, diseases arising from imbalance of *Vata* (wind) and *Kapha* (phlegm), a bad swelling, tumour, serpent bite, creeping and crawling creatures, royal insignia of umbrella and *Chamar**, vehicles, cheating, gambling, speculation.

All the above are governed by Rahu. If Rahu is well placed and strong, the native may rise in governmental favour by resorting to falsehoods, tricks and cunning; he may resort to all kinds of unscrupulous methods and gain thereby, such as, black marketing, thefts, evasion of taxes. He may have liaisons with females and get enjoyment as well as riches out of them. It is, however, observed that there is during this *Mahadasha* change of place of residence or activity. *Rahu* is a planet presiding over gambling and speculation and a strong Rahu may bring in much money.

* Bushy tail of *Bos grunniens* used as a fly-whisk or fan and reckoned as one of the insignia of royalty.

But if Rahu is afflicted there may be loss due to matters signified by him. The native may suffer from aberration of mind, schizophrenia, hallucinations and illusions. He may suffer from asthma, eczema and other cutaneous diseases. In places where serpents abound, there are chances of snake-bite also. It is one of the worst *Mahadashas* for education and if it occurs when the native is at school or college his educational career may be broken or disrupted. During Rahu *Mahadasha,* if the planet is evil there may be loss of money and loss of reputation through liaison with females of loose morals, particulary widows, and complications might arise through them.

Ketu. Worship of God Shiva, Chandi, Ganesh, etc., philosophy, divine knowledge, salvation from earthly bondage, all kinds of wealth, great penance, religious austerities, friendship, conferring of prosperity, luck, all kinds of luxuries, doctor, freedom from disease, causing of trouble to enemies, maternal grandfather, belly, consumption, pain, hunger, stupidity, thorn, witchcraft, eye diseases, wounds, fever, an outcaste, dog, deer, vulture, cock, horned animals, and company of servants.

If Ketu is well placed in the chart the native would during his *Mahadasha* devote time and energy to the perusal of works of philosophy and engage in worship, derive much income by practice of medicine, and have domestic comforts and luxuries. He will be devoted to gods and Brahmans and pay homage to them. He will have good luck and freedom from disease.

But if Ketu is ill-placed in the chart, he may suffer intense pain of body and anguish of mind, may have wounds and fever. He may be the victim of an accident, have low company and suffer bad consequences through them.

We have succinctly given in the above paragraphs the matters and affairs in the portfolio of each planet and tried to provide guide-lines how these are to be interpreted in the individual chart. Examples for each of the items could not possibly be provided in a book of this kind and it is left to the reader to follow the guide-lines and come to conclusions relevant to the age, status and environment of the native, whose chart is under study.

Now we shall take up the next point of view—the second stream in the channel of interpretation of the effects of the *Mahadashas,* according to the ownership of the house. Before we do so, we shall deal with two more features in respect of the effects of

Karakas' during his *Mahadasha*.

(i) If a *Karaka* is adversely placed from the house he is a *Karaka* for he does not produce very good results in respect of the house for which he is a *Karaka*. A *Karaka's* location has therefore to be judged not only from the ascendant, but also from the house for which he is a *Karaka*.

(ii) If the *Karaka* aspects the lord of the house for which he is a *Karaka*, then during his *Mahadasha* the affairs of the house will progress well.

B. MAHADASHA EFFECTS ACCORDING TO THE OWNERSHIP OF HOUSES IN THE BIRTH CHART

A large number of rules have been given in the previous chapters to indicate whether a planet should be deemed to be good and if so to what extent, or evil and if so in what measure. All planets act as good if they are well placed by sign and house and are conjoined with benefics or aspected by them, or evil if they are ill-placed by sign and house and conjoined with malefics or aspected by them. Having provided these guidelines, we shall deal with the *Mahadasha* of each lord according to whether he is good or evil in the particular chart. Here the expression 'good or evil' should not be confused with 'natural benefic or malefic,' because in a particular chart, say, for Taurus ascending, Saturn in the ninth in Capricorn may be called a natural malefic; but may be positively good conversely for Capricorn ascendant, the Moon being a natural benefic, the lord of the seventh conjoined with the Sun in the eighth in Leo may be evil. So in going through the *Mahadashas* of various planets, according to the house they own as given below, we should appraise each house lord on his merits or demerits in the birth chart.

1. (a) If the ascendant lord is strong, the native would during the *Mahadasha* of the lord of the ascendant rise to an eminent position, will be happy and maintain good health. His prosperity will gradually increase.

(b) However, if the lord of the ascendant is ill-placed, the native's health will suffer, he may be held up or become accussed in a case. He will be under apprehension and suffer mental anxiety. He will not be able to make any distinctive progress during the *Mahadasha;* rather his attempts will result in failure and frustration.

2. (a) If the lord of the second is well placed and strong, then during his *Mahadasha* there will be additions to the family, acquisition of wealth, good letters will be written and received, the native will be able to achieve success due to his speech and he will have good food and have a happy time.

(b) But if the second lord is weak and ill-placed, there will be heavy expenditure, the bank balance will be depleted, the native will write impolitic letters and also receive unpleasant ones; there will be eye troubles, the meals will not be savoury; the native will not be able to deliver learned discourses, rather his powers of expression and eloquence will be at the lowest ebb. There will be fear from the government.

As indicated in Chapter 12, the birth chart must be examined to determine whether the native is destined to have a short, medium or long life and if the *Mahadasha* runs at the appropriate time, the lord of second has the propensity to kill the native, particularly if he occupies the second, seventh, eighth or the twelfth house and has *Sambandha* with the lord of the seventh.

3. (a) If the lord of the third house is strong during his *Mahadasha*, there will be a spirit of love, help and cooperation between the brothers, good news will be received; the native's power and prowess would yield good dividends. The native will rise in his career and his work would be commended by others.

(b) However, if the lord of the third is weak and ill-placed, then during his *Mahadasha*, there will be quarrels and misunderstandings with brothers and neighbours, the health of a brother or sister may suffer or there be demise of one of them, if there is such an indication in the radix. Bad news will be received. The trips undertaken will not be successful. There will be mental uneasiness and the native will suffer humiliation.

4. (a) If the lord of the fourth house is strong and well placed, then during his *Mahadasha* there will be help from and given to relations, there will be happiness in respect of the mother, lands, agriculture, cattle and conveyances. There may be acquisitions of immovable property and vehicles, happiness from wife, friendship with people, promotion in career, contented and peaceful period.

(b) But if the lord of the fourth house is weak and afflicted during his *Mahadasha*, there will be distress to the native's mother, quarrels with friends and relations or sickness may afflict them; loss of cattle or immovable property or litigation in connection with it, discomfort in respect of conveyance, danger from water, general unhappiness and no tranquillity of mind.

5. (a) If the lord of the fifth is strong and well placed, then during his *Mahadasha*, there will be increase in education and learning, birth of sons, or their affairs may progress well, increased devotion to God, promotion in career. If the native is in the run for a ministership, he may get it. The native has good food and drink. His actions will be good and he will earn praise for his conduct. He will gain money; there may even be sudden gains, if the radix so indicates.

(b) But if the lord of the fifth is weak and afflicted, then during his *Mahadasha*, there will be illness to children or loss of child or children, if the radix so indicates; inharmonious relations with sons, failure in examination, decline in worship of God. The native may have mental troubles, aberration or confusion of mind; there will be likelihood of his being the victim of fraud or deceptions, and wearisome wanderings. The intellectual powers will be at a low ebb and there is likely to be failure of the efforts made.

6. (a) If the lord of the sixth is strong (but not stronger than the lord of the ascendant) the native would during his *Mahadasha* vanquish his enemies, the native's courage would enhance, he would be triumphant over his rivals, compete successfully and would have the satisfaction of surpassing others. His health would be good, he would earn well, be generous and will not be cowed down by others. He will do well in service.

(b) However, if the lord of the sixth is afflicted, the native will during the *Mahadasha*, perform evil acts and will have to pay the penalty for them; he will suffer reverses in fortune and be constantly troubled by enemies. His health will suffer and there may be some disease as indicated by the sign on the cusp of the sixth house or the sixth lord. He will have mental anguish and will have to subordinate his wishes to others and suffer humiliation; he will have trouble from servants, loss of cattle or pets, etc. He may lose a job.

7. (a) If the lord of the seventh is strong and well placed, the native will during his *Mahadasha* purchase additional items of luxury, will be happy and enjoy pleasure in the company of

his wife or other women. There will be auspicious festivities in the family connected with marriages, etc. If the native is not married, he will get married. He may enter into a business partnership or travel successfully. There will be harmony and co-operation from all parties the native associates with.

(b) But if the lord of the seventh is weak and afflicted, there will be distress to the native's son-in-law, separation from his wife and difficulties and calamities arising out of partnership or connected with his wife. He will have liaisons with women and suffer from venereal diseases. He may fall ill and if as determined by other factors, such as, those shortening the life, or making it medium or long, the *Mahadasha* synchronises with the *Maraka* period, death may occur and particularly so if the lord of the seventh is in the second, seventh, eighth or twelfth and has *Sambandha* with the lord of the second, eighth or the twelfth.

8. (a) If the lord of the eighth is strong but not stronger than the first lord and aspected by benefics then during his *Mahadasha*, if the native is under debt, he will discharge his debts. There will be a cessation of quarrels; acquisition of cattle, addition of servants. The native's affairs will advance favourably and he will have elevation in rank. He may gain a legacy, if there is a probability of one. He may gain from the import-export business, if he is in that line.

(b) But if the lord of the eighth is weak and has *Sambandha* with *Papas*, during the *Mahadasha*, the native will suffer in health, he will undergo distress and sorrow, there will be rivalry, jealousy and enmity and the native will suffer. There will be loss of wealth and reputation. He will be insulted, his endeavours will fail and he will wander fruitlessly without achieving his objectives. The lord of the eighth is a potential killer also, but for this look to the span of life as ascertained by other factors. The *Maraka* qualities of the lord of the eighth are increased if he occupies the second or the seventh house.

9. (a) If the lord of the ninth is strong and well placed, then during his *Mahadasha* the native will have a prosperous time in the company of his wife and children and grand-children if there be any. He will gain in wealth and rank. He will perform acts of religious merit and will be much respected.

(b) But if the lord of the ninth is weak and afflicted, then during his *Mahadasha* the prosperity of the native will be on the wane due to the wrath of some deity, because of his own actions in this birth or previous ones. He will suffer in the domestic sphere and in respect of children and grand-children (fifth from fifth). His actions will not be good and his financial position will be weak.

(10) (a) If the lord of the tenth is strong and well placed, the native will during the *Mahadasha* of the planet be successful in his undertakings, will have elevation of rank and status, his prosperity will enhance and he will earn name and fame for himself.

(b) But if the lord of the tenth is weak, afflicted and occupies an evil house, there will be a fall from his station in life; he will meet with much disrespect, his efforts will be unsuccessful; his trips or travelling will only be a source of discomfort and loss. His actions during the *Mahadasha* will not be good and there will be a general setback in his career.

11. (a) If the lord of the eleventh is strong and well-placed then during his *Mahadasha,* there will be a continuous influx of money and there will be happiness in association with family members, relations and friends. There may be gain of money from associations of people, such as, societies, companies, the government, etc. The native's hopes and desires will be fulfilled. There will be an addition to the number of servants and employees. Good news will be received.

(b) But if the lord of the eleventh is weak and afflicted, then during his *Mahadasha,* the native will hear bad news, there will be trouble to brothers and sons, poverty and humiliation, ear trouble. The native may be cheated by others.

12. (a) If the lord of the twelfth is strong and well aspected, and does not occupy the second or the twelfth house, then during his *Mahadasha* the native will spend money on good causes; he will have pleasures and luxuries. He will gain in respect. His actions will be good. If the lord of the twelfth is a benefic and in his own house in the twelfth or if he occupies the eighth house, there will be accumulation of money also.

(b) If the lord of the twelfth is weak and afflicted, then during his *Mahadasha* the native's vitality will be lowered and he will suffer in health; he may go abroad or there may be hospitalisation. If the lord is very much afflicted and a malefic is in the twelfth and if the lord of the sixth is stronger than the first lord, there may be imprisonment. The native's wealth will be dissipated and he will incur debts.

GUIDE-LINES FOR DEDUCTIONS

We have succinctly stated the *Mahadasha* effects of a planet according as to whether he is the lord of a particular house and (i) strong and well placed, or (ii) weak and afflicted. We will leave it to the ingenuity of readers to derive corollaries from the main propositions. Those who have gone through a number of birth charts and compared events actually occurring during a particular *Mahadasha*, will with the prognostications in the radix, have enough experience not to need any guide-lines; but for the benefit of those who are new to the subject, we are furnishing below a few guide-lines on how to derive corollaries from the main proposition.

(i) If the lord of the third is weak and afflicted, the third being sixth from the tenth (father) he may cause illness to father. Conversely, if the lord of the first is well placed and strong, the first house being lord of the fourth from the tenth (father), the native's father may during the *Mahadasha* of the strong lord of the first, acquire property or conveyances.

(ii) This principle should be applied to the *Karaka* also. Suppose the lord of the seventh, as counted from the native's radical Venus is strong and well placed, the native may marry or if already married may have an enjoyable time. Conversely, if the lord of the seventh from Venus is weak or afflicted, there may be illness of the wife or even loss of the wife if the radix so indicates.

(iii) Another type of corollary derived from the delineations, is as follows: suppose the lord of the sixth is weak and afflicted and tenants the fifth house (because a contact has been established between the fifth and the sixth houses, due to sixth lord's location in fifth), the son of the native may be antagonistic to the father or the son may fall ill. Let us take the converse example: if the lord of the sixth is strong and well placed by sign in the ninth and well aspected, there may be increase in the general good luck and fortune (ninth house) due to an enemy (sixth). He may win in litigation. In olden times Indians used to capture their enemies' properties. A man may have to visit another place due to sickness (sixth house) and contacts there may lead to a lucrative business, and so on. Circumstances differ from native to native and from case to case.

(iv) Barring the Sun and the Moon, the other five planets have two houses each. Rahu and Ketu's domain is generally confined to one house each, the house tenanted by him. But when Rahu or Ketu conjoins a planet he bestows the effects not only of the house he tenants but of the planet he is conjoined with and if such a planet owns a house or two houses a contact is established between Rahu (or Ketu) and the houses owned by the conjoining planet. For example, say, in a nativity with Leo as ascendant, Rahu and Saturn are in Aries in the ninth. Now apart from Rahu showing the effect of being in Aries, he has become linked with the ninth house (due to his location in the ninth) and the sixth and the seventh houses (due to conjunction with Saturn, lord of sixth and seventh houses). What we intend to convey is that excepting the Sun and the Moon, each of the five planets owns two houses. And when there is *Mahadasha* of a planet owning two houses, during the *Mahadasha*, there may be a connection or correlation between the effects pertaining to the two houses. For example, if Gemini is rising, Mercury will be the lord of the first and the fourth and the native may acquire immovable property (fourth) due to his personal efforts (first). Or to take another example, suppose Gemini is rising and Venus, lord of the fifth, is afflicted, he causes financial loss or heavy expenditure during his *Mahadasha*. Then the loss of money or expenditure (twelfth house) may have a connection with education, sons, pleasures, speculation—any one or more items governed by the fifth house.

In this way, intelligent readers can draw inference. We cannot be so exhaustive in this book as we would like to be, and no doubt some readers would like us to be; but the above examples will help to develop the power of reasoning on the lines indicated.

C. FAVOURABLE AND UNFAVOURABLE MAHADASHAS FOR THE VARIOUS ASCENDANTS

The point of view we are dealing below is based on a Sanskrit work called *Udu-daya Pradeep* ('a lamp to shed light on the propensities of *Mahadashas*'). This work is also known as *Laghu Parashari* (abridged to *Parashari* method). Sage Parashar flourished thousands of years ago and wrote a monumental work on predictive astrology. Several texts of this large work have been published, but there are doubts if the texts available are correct versions of the original written by the great sage, who is in a way treated as the father of Hindu astrology.

As regards the abridged work *Laghu Parashari* or *Udu-daya Pradeep*, it is doubtful when it was abridged or compiled and by whom; but during the last several centuries, it is being followed by astrologers all over India and has acquired a pre-eminent place for delineating *Mahadasha* and *Antardasha* effects. In this system the criteria of good and bad, auspicious and inauspicious, are different from those described earlier in the book and the rules propounded hereunder should not be mixed or confused with those given earlier. What is common to this system and others will also be explained.

1. The signs, lordship of signs, the signs of exaltation and debilitation of planets, their aspects, the houses—their order or what each of them signifies, the method of calculation of the balance of *Mahadasha* at birth, the duration of each *Mahadasha* and the order in which they follow each other, the durations of *Antardasha* in each *Mahadasha* and the order in which each *Antardasha* follows the other—all these are common to this system and others.

2. But the definition of *Shubhas* (auspicious) and *Papas* (sinful) as given here is different from that given according to general precepts in other systems. According to general precepts, Jupiter and Venus are auspicious; the Moon (strong in *Pakshabala*) and Mercury not associated with *Papas* are also auspicious; the Sun, Mars and Saturn are malefics in increasing order; Rahu and Ketu are also *Papas;* the Moon (weak in *Pakshabala*) and Mercury associated with malefics are also *Papas*. But according to this system, the natural benefics are not treated as benefics nor are natural malefics treated as malefics, because the criteria are different. The division of planets into the two groups, (i) benefic and (ii) malefic is not according to their natural qualities or attributes, but founded on the basis of ownership of houses. A natural benefic may become a benefic if he owns certain houses or may become a malefic if he owns certain others. Similarly, a natural malefic may become a benefic in a particular chart, but he may become a malefic if he owns certain other houses in another chart.

Thus, according to ownership, a natural benefic may become a *Papa* or a natural malefic may be treated as *Shubha*. Ownership of which houses makes a planet *Shubha* and ownership of which others makes any planet inauspicious are dealt with below.

(A) All lords of trines bestow auspicious results. Any of the seven planets if he owns a trine, is auspicious. Because Rahu and Ketu do not own any sign, they are not included here. Even a natural malefic, such as the Sun, Mars or Saturn, if he owns a trine, becomes auspicious. If natural benefics own a trine they become even more auspicious. Of the two lords, those of the fifth and the ninth, the latter is stronger in his auspicious attributes than the former.

(B) The lord of the third or the sixth or the eleventh is a *Papa*. Whether a natural benefic or malefic, if a planet owns any of these three houses, he will be deemed a malefic. Naturally, a malefic lord of the third would be a greater *Papa* than a benefic lord of the third. The lord of the sixth is more malefic than the lord of the third, and the lord of the eleventh a greater malefic than the lord of the sixth. For Aries rising, Mercury will be the lord of the third and the sixth. Similarly, for Libra ascendant, Jupiter will be the lord of the third and the sixth houses. Thus, when one and the same planet becomes the lord of the third and the sixth houses, he becomes a still greater *Papa*. For Gemini ascendant, Mars would be lord of the sixth and the eleventh: similarly for Sagittarius rising Venus would be the lord of the sixth and the eleventh. In these two cases, the same planet being lord of the sixth and the eleventh houses, he would become a more malefic *Papa*.

A question and a very relevant one now arises as to what happens when a planet owns two houses and one of these houses happens to be a trine and the other the third, sixth or eleventh. For example, when Cancer is the ascendant, Sagittarius will be the sixth sign as counted from Cancer and therefore the sixth house and Pisces will be the ninth sign as counted from the ascendant and therefore the ninth house. Let us reiterate the basic principle of Hindu astrology that the signs and houses are synonymous and houses are counted from sign to sign. Western astrologers are requested to forget about Placidian or other house division methods. Astrologers of India are also requested not to bring in Shripati's method or Keshava's method of house division by trisecting the distance between the meridian and the rising degree and marking the domain of each house. Here in this book has been stated the oldest and the most authoritative method of counting houses signwise.

Let us revert to the point under discussion. For Cancer ascendant, Jupiter becomes lord of the sixth and the ninth; for Virgo rising, Saturn becomes the lord of the fifth and the sixth; for Capricorn ascendant, Mercury becomes the lord of the sixth and the ninth. Under these circumstance, when in the portfolio of these three planets, one house is the sixth and the other a trine (fifth or ninth), what will be the resultant position — whether in the above cases cited are Jupiter, Saturn and Mercury to be declared *Shubha* (due to ownership of a trine) or evil (due to ownership of the sixth)? The reply to the above enquiry will be that for Cancer ascendant, Jupiter and for Capricorn ascendant, Mercury has been declared a *Shubha* (auspicious). For Virgo ascendant, his good ownership of the fifth is set off against the evil ownership of the sixth house and so Saturn has neither been declared as auspicious nor as inauspicious.

(C) Ordinarily, the lord of an angle if a benefic, is auspicious, and if a malefic he is not auspicious. On the other hand, if a malefic is the lord of an angle and also the lord of a trine, he confers good results. If a benefic is the lord of an angle and also the lord of the third, sixth or the eleventh house, he does not during his *Mahadasha* confer auspicious results. But if a *Papa* is the lord of an angle and also a lord of the third, sixth or the eleventh, he confers during his *Mahadasha, Papa* results.

(D) The lords of the second and the twelfth houses by themselves, if isolated from other influences, have neither been declared as *Shubha* (auspicious) nor as *Papas*.

If the lord of the second or the twelfth has *Sambandha*,

(i) with the lord of a trine, he confers auspicious results;

(ii) with the lord of third, sixth or the eleventh, he confers *Papa* results;

(iii) with the lord of an angle who is a *Shubha*, he is *Shubha;*

(iv) with the lord of an angle who is a *Papa*, he confers *Papa* results;

(v) with the lord of the eighth, then too he is a *Papa*.

Excepting the Sun and the Moon, the other five planets own two houses each. So if the other house owned by the lord of the second or the twelfth is,

(i) a trine, he is a *Shubha;*

(ii) third, sixth, or eleventh, then he is a *Papa;*

(iii) an angle and the planet is a natural benefic, then he confers results as a *Shubha;*

(iv) an angle and the planet is a natural malefic, then he is a *Papa.*

Lords of the first, fourth, seventh and the tenth are strong in increasing order, i.e., the lord of the fourth is stronger than the lord of the first.

(E) We have dealt with the criteria for judging the lords of the fifth, ninth, third, sixth, eleventh, fourth, seventh, tenth, second and twelfth. The ascendant is considered both an angle and a trine and the lord of the first is always auspicious. Thus the lords of all the twelve houses, except the eighth, have been discussed. As regards the lord of the eighth, because he is the lord of the twelfth (expenditure) as counted from the ninth house (good luck, fortune and general prosperity), he is not auspicious. Two provisos have, however, been added to this dictum.

(i) If one and the same planet is the lord of the first and the eighth, he is auspicious. This can apply only to Aries and Libra ascendants because when Aries is rising, Mars becomes the lord of the first and the eighth, and when Libra is rising, Venus is the lord of the first and the eighth houses.

(ii) When the Sun or the Moon is the lord of the eighth house, no *Dosha* or stigma is attached to the luminary on account of ownership of the eighth house. One view is that slight *Dosha* is attached, but being negligible it is ignored. However if the Sun is in Leo in the eighth, or the Moon in Cancer in the eighth, they have no *Dosha.*

One of the corollaries arising from the above is that the lord of the twelfth as counted from each of the houses will be detrimental (because it represents expenditure, exhaustion, emaciation) to the house from which it is the twelfth lord. Thus a lord of the twelfth from the seventh, i.e., the sixth lord, will during his *Mahadasha,* damage the seventh house, the lord of the twelfth from the fifth, i.e., the fourth lord, would damage the fifth house affairs, and so on.

(iii) If the Sun or the Moon be the lord of the eighth and posited in the eighth, he is *Shubha.*

(iv) If the lord of the eighth owns the first, fifth or the ninth also (for Aries and Libra ascendants, he will own the first as well; for Leo and Aquarius he will own the fifth as well; for Gemini, he will own the ninth also) and is posited in the eighth, he confers good results during his *Mahadasha*.

(F) Having discussed the lordship of the twelve houses and the general circumstances under which he becomes a *Shubha* or a *Papa*, certain additional rules are provided.

A natural malefic, if he owns an angle, does not become a *Shubha* only by virtue of lordship of an angle. He becomes a *Shubha* only when he owns a trine also. For example, let us consider three charts where Mars is the lord of an angle.

(i) When Cancer is the rising sign, Mars is the lord of the fifth and the tenth.

(ii) When Leo rises, Mars becomes the lord of the fourth and the ninth.

(iii) When Aquarius is the ascendant, Mars rules the third and the tenth houses.

Here in (i) and (ii) above Mars owns an angle as well as a trine. He is, therefore, a *Shubha* for Cancer and Leo ascendants. But in (iii) above, while Mars owns an angle (the tenth house), he does not own a trine, so he does not become a *Shubha* but remains a *Papa*.

(G) The eighth is the house of longevity; when we look at the positive side of this house, it is called longevity; when we look to the negative side, it is called death. From the eighth from the eighth, i.e., the third house also, we judge longevity and as stated earlier, the twelfth from each of these two houses (the eighth and the third), i.e., the seventh and the second houses, stand for expenditure, exhaustion or annihilation of longevity, i.e., end of life. The second and the seventh therefore are called *Maraka* (killing) houses and the lord of the second and seventh are *Markesha* (killer). Of the seventh and the second lords, the latter is a stronger *Maraka* than the former. And if the *Mahadasha* of any of these two is running, when according to the general examination of the radix—the birth chart—and determination of longevity as discussed in Chapter 12, the death of the native may appear probable, then the *Mahadasha* of the lord of the second or the seventh may prove fatal.

Further if the Moon, Mercury, Venus or Jupiter owns the seventh house his Maraka, — the death inflicting — powers are enhanced, and particularly so if the planet tenants a *Maraka* house, i.e., the seventh or the second.

Under the above circumstances, the four planets Moon, Mercury, Venus and Jupiter are stronger for the worse in increasing order. Mercury is more fatal than the Moon, Venus more fatal than Mercury and Jupiter most fatal of them all.

The Parashari system enumerates on the basis of the above dictum certain planets as good and the others evil on the basis of the sign rising or the ascendant in a particular chart.

(H) If the sign rising is:

(i) *Aries*: Saturn, Mercury and Venus are *Papas*, Jupiter and Sun are *Shubhas*. Mere *Sambandha* between Jupiter and Saturn does not confer *Raja Yoga* here, because Jupiter is the lord of the twelfth also, and Saturn the lord of the eleventh also, they yield evil results in addition to conferring good results. Venus is a full killer (extremely fatal) and a *Maraka*. Saturn and other *Papas* have also the power to kill.

(ii) *Taurus*: Jupiter, Venus and the Moon are *Papas*. Saturn and the Sun are *Shubhas*. Saturn alone is *Raja Yoga Karaka*. *Papa* planets — Jupiter, Venus, the Moon and Mercury — have attributes of *Maraka* (death inflicting propensities).

(iii) *Gemini*: Mars, Jupiter and the Sun are *Papas;* Venus alone is *Shubha*. Mere *Sambandha* between Jupiter and Saturn does not confer a *Raja Yoga*, here Jupiter is the lord of the seventh house also and Saturn the lord of the eighth also. A combination of Mercury and Venus confers *Raja Yoga*. If the Moon is not conjoined with *Papa*, he does not prove fatal during his *Mahadasha*.

(iv) *Cancer*: Venus and Mercury are *Papas*. Mars and Jupiter are *Shubhas*. Only Mars is *Raja Yoga Karaka*. Saturn alone is the killer. Other planets have *Maraka* propensities only.

(v) *Leo*: Mercury and Venus are *Papas;* only Mars is *Shubha*. No *Raja Yoga* is conferred by *Sambandha* of Venus and Jupiter only. Mercury, etc., having *Maraka* propensities kill the native.

(vi) *Virgo*: Mars, Jupiter and Moon are *Papas*. Venus alone is *Shubha*. *Sambandha* between Mercury and Venus causes good *Raja Yoga*. Venus is a killer; others, Mars etc., are *Marakas*.

(vii) *Libra*: Jupiter, the Sun and Mars are *Papas*. Saturn and Mercury are *Shubhas*. A *Sambandha* between the Moon and Mercury causes *Raja Yoga*. Mars kills; Jupiter, etc., have *Maraka* propensities and are also killers.

(viii) *Scorpio*: Mercury, Mars and Venus are *Papas*. Jupiter and Moon are *Shubhas*. A *Sambandha* between the Sun and the Moon causes *Raja Yoga*. Jupiter is the killer; Mercury, etc., have also *Maraka* propensities and are killers.

(ix) *Sagittarius*: Venus alone is a *Papa*. Mercury and the Sun are *Shubhas*. *Sambandha* between Mercury and Sun gives rise to *Raja Yoga*. Saturn is the killer. *Papas* like Venus, etc., have *Maraka* propensities and are killers also.

(x) *Capricorn*: Mars, Jupiter and the Moon are *Papas*. Venus and Mercury are *Shubhas*. Mars, etc., may prove fatal during their *Mahadasha* or *Antardasha* because they have *Maraka* propensities. Venus alone causes good *Yoga*.

(xi) *Aquarius*: Jupiter, the Moon and Mars are *Papas*. Venus alone is *Shubha*. *Sambandha* between Mars and Venus gives rise to *Raja Yoga*. Jupiter is the killer. Also Mars, etc., have *Maraka* propensities.

(xii) *Pisces*: Saturn, Venus and the Sun are *Papas*. Mars and the Moon are *Shubhas*. *Sambandha* between Jupiter and Mars confers *Raja Yoga*. Mercury and Saturn yield *Maraka* results during their *Mahadashas* and *Antardashas*.

A brief outline has been furnished above of the way of looking at lords of houses. But the ancient text does not specify the lord of each house for each ascendant. We, have, however, discussed at length earlier the criteria for determining whether the lord of a particular house should be deemed a *Shubha* or a *Papa*.

In giving above a faithful translation of the Sanskrit text, we have not added that a *Shubha* planet confers good and benefic results during his *Mahadasha* or *Antardasha* and a *Papa* yields evil results during his periods, because that is understood; we are dealing in this chapter with the effects of *Mahadashas* and naturally any topic dealt herein pertains to *Mahadashas*.

Certain further explanations are, however, necessary at this stage.

For Scorpio ascendant, the text states that Jupiter is a *Shubha* and further on we find stated that Jupiter is a killer. A doubt may naturally arise. Are these two statements mutually contradictory? No, because the author intends to convey that Jupiter being lord of the second and the fifth will show good results during his *Mahadasha* and *Antardasha*, but if the Jupiter's *Mahadasha* commences or continues, when according to the rules determining longevity, the native's life term is about to be over, then Jupiter inflicts death. So, a planet may play a dual role, because he is the lord of two houses, one of which, i. e., the fifth, is absolutely good on account of being a trine, but the other, the second, is a giver of wealth as well as a killer. Thus, where a planet has two traits of character, one good and one evil, both of these have been stated and there is no contradiction. Similarly, under Virgo, we find Venus stated as a *Shubha* due to the lordship of the ninth and also a killer due to lordship of the second, and so on. If the time of death is not ripe, such a planet will give good results in regard to wealth and prosperity.

Planets which have been described as *Papas* may cause illness, but if placed in their own house (except lord of the second in the second, lord of the seventh in the seventh), they will confer good results pertaining to the house they own and occupy. For example, the lord of the eleventh is a *Papi*, but if he is in the eleventh, he will in regard to income and finances bestow very good results during his *Mahadasha*.

(I) So far we have discussed the lords of the various houses which cover the seven planets. Now we shall provide some rules in regard to judging the *Mahadashas* of Rahu and Ketu.

(i) Rahu and Ketu produce effects as determined by the house they tenant. For example, if Rahu tenants a trine or an angle or the eleventh, he will give good results, though in the seventh, he will have *Maraka* propensities as well. Rahu in the second or the twelfth, if afflicted, may cause loss of wealth during his *Mahadasha;* so also Rahu in the eighth. Rahu in the third and the sixth would increase valour and activities of the native. So with Ketu. Look to the effects described for planets in the different signs and houses as given in Chapters 8 and 9.

(ii) Rahu and Ketu also reflect during their *Mahadashas* the effects of the planets they are conjoined with. Suppose for a Cancer ascendant Mars is in the third and Rahu in Virgo conjoined with Mars; Rahu will reflect the effects of Mars also. In other words, Rahu will produce all such effects as can be bestowed by Mars. Suppose for the Leo ascendant Saturn and Rahu are conjoined in the ninth in Aries; then Rahu will produce effects of the ninth house and of Saturn as well.

(iii) One of the schools of Hindu astrology interprets the Sanskrit text as meaning that Rahu or Ketu also bestow the effects of the dispositor*. For example, if Rahu is in Aries, he will reflect during his *Mahadasha* the effects of Mars as well; suppose Rahu is in Taurus, then he will reflect the effects of Venus as well, and so on. We, however, do not accept this view, but confine ourselves only to (i) and (ii) above.

(iv) If Rahu or Ketu is in an angle and conjoined with the lord of a trine, it is an excellent *Raja Yoga* and Rahu or Ketu so conjoined will cause *Raja Yoga* results during his *Mahadasha* or *Antardasha.*

(v) Similarly, if Rahu or Ketu occupies a trine and is conjoined with the lord of an angle, such Rahu or Ketu so conjoined will give rise to *Raja Yoga* results during his *Mahadasha* or *Antardasha.*

(J) We shall now discuss the excellence or otherwise of the *Mahadashas* of the various planets.

(i) The lord of an angle having a *Sambandha* with the lord of a trine, bestows very good results. Thus it follows that the lord of a trine if conjoined with the lord of an angle will also confer excellent results.

(ii) The above *Sambandha* of the lords of an angle or trine bestows very good results if not diluted by *Sambandha* with the lord of an evil house. For example, if the lord of an angle and a trine form simultaneously a *Sambandha* with the lord of the third, the sixth, the eighth or the eleventh, the efficacy in regard to good results is marred in some measure.

(iii) If the lords of a trine or an angle themselves have some *Dosha,* notwithstanding such *Dosha* they become stronger for the good and confer good results during their *Mahadashas.* Of course, the *Dosha* will be a pulling down weigh and the result cannot be so good as it would have been if there had been no *Dosha.*

(iv) (a) As stated earlier if the lord of an angle has *Sambandha* with the lord of a trine, he would confer good results during his *Mahadasha.* If the lord of the angle has *Sambandha* with both the trine lords, his *Mahadasha* will be still better.

(b) Similarly, if the lord of a trine has *Sambandha* with the lord of one angle, it is good; if with lords of two angles, it is

* The word dispositor means the planet, who owns the sign in which another planet is. For example, if the Sun is in Scorpio—then Mars lord of Scorpio is the dispositor of the Sun. This is a technical term used in astrology.

better; if with the lords of three angles, it would be still better, and if with the lords of all the four angles, it would be the best placement for conferring excellent results.

(c) While evaluating (a) and (b) above, it should be kept in mind that the ninth lord is more powerful than the fifth lord and among the lords of the first, fourth, seventh and the tenth, the latter is stronger than the former.

(d) It follows that the ninth lord in the tenth and the tenth lord in the ninth or both together in the ninth or the tenth or even the lord of the ninth in the ninth and the lord of the tenth in the tenth would confer excellent results during their *Mahadashas.*

To appraise how far the *Sambandha* between the lord of an angle and trine will be devalued due to *Sambandha* with lords of undesirable houses, readers are referred to *Kendra — Trikona Yogas* in Chapter 11.

(K) It is now necessary to deal with the question as to which *Mahadasha* is capable of causing death. We would state in this context that the determination of the time of death is a very complicated issue which bristles with difficulties and we would advise beginners not to predict death. It requires a life-time of experience and a study of more detailed rules to determine death than can possibly be given in a simple book on astrology such as this, which merely provides an outline of the subject. The prediction regarding death creates a fear and horror in the mind of the native; besides it creates a very unfavourable chain of adverse psychological repercussions.

Moreover, a *Maraka* planet at times does not actually kill; it may make the native seriously ill or he may be disgraced or thrown out of his job, or involved in a civil or criminal case with evil consequences, or his finances may be appreciably depleted and so on.

The general rule is that the lords of the second and the seventh houses are *Marakas,* but as we had occasion to examine earlier, Jupiter is *Shubha* as well as *Maraka* for Scorpio ascendants, Venus is *Shubha* as well as *Maraka* for Virgo ascendants, and so on. Now if the native is destined to live long and the *Mahadasha* of Jupiter or Venus runs during youth or middle age they will only prove *Shubha* and not *Maraka.* The crucial point to decide is whether a particular native has a short, medium or long life and which *Mahadasha* synchronises with the probable period of death. If the *Mahadasha* so synchronising has been described as *Maraka*, it will kill the native. To sum up, the following *Mahadashas* are capable of proving fatal:

(i) Lord of the second
(ii) Lord of the seventh
(iii) Planets in the second or the seventh
(iv) *Papis* conjoined with the lord of the second or the seventh
(v) Lord of the twelfth
(vi) Lord of the eighth
(vii) If no *Mahadasha* of any of the above synchronises with the expected period of death, then in the *Mahadasha* of a *Papa*
(viii) Saturn having *Sambandha* with *Marakas*. Generally Saturn in the above circumstances has priority over other planets in causing death.

Having discussed the Parashari system, we shall now pass on to the fourth stream. We have stated earlier that in the matter of judgment of a *Mahadasha*, four parallel streams flow side by side in the same channel and a judicious conclusion has to be arrived at after taking into consideration the various points discussed under each head. We shall now deal with the fourth stream which does not enunciate a new code or school, but under this we have grouped the various general principles for evaluation of the *Mahadasha*, as stated in various ancient texts.

D. OTHER FACTORS FOR EVALUATING THE EFFECTS OF A MAHADASHA

(i) If a planet is exalted, his *Mahadasha* will be very good provided he occupies a good house. It may be stated that of the two positions, (i) weak by sign but placement in a good house, such as the eleventh, and (ii) good by sign position but placement in an evil house, such as the eighth, the former is better if we have to choose between the two evils.

(ii) A planet in his own house is always expected to yield good results in his *Mahadasha*. If the house occupied is also a good one, the results would be still better.

(iii) A planet in great friend's house shows during his *Mahadasha* benefit from friends or through the agency or patronage of friends.

(iv) A planet in a friend's sign will show good results and benefit due to the assistance of friends, but not in the same measure as in (iii) above.

(v) A planet occupying a neutral's house, maintains the status quo neither augmenting his fortunes nor scaling them down.

(vi) A planet occupying his enemy's house causes various kinds of opposition and impediments during his *Mahadasha.*

(vii) A planet occupying his great enemy's sign causes during his *Mahadasha* all the ill effects stated in (vi) above, but with greater intensity and rigour.

(viii) A planet debilitated in sign unless occupying special degrees as mentioned for each planet in Chapter 8, causes during his *Mahadasha.* intense distress. If the planet is retrograde also, he is not so evil.

(ix) A combust planet, if otherwise good, is incapable of bringing about during his *Mahadasha,* fully good effects. A combust planet, if a malefic and prone to cause ill effects, causes during his *Mahadasha* much distress.

(x) Planets which have crossed their deepest debilitation points and are proceeding towards their highest exaltation points show good results; while those which have crossed their highest exaltation points and are proceeding towards their deepest debilitation points show adverse results during their respective *Mahadashas.*

(xi) A retrograde planet if benefic becomes stronger to do good and his *Mahadasha* is good. The reverse is the cause with malefics in retrogression.

(xii) When a malefic and a benefic together conjoin, the malefic would yield better results than if he were not so conjoined. But the benefic is sullied due to conjunction with a malefic and does not yield during his *Mahadasha,* such results as he would have done otherwise.

(xiii) Similar to (xii) above is the case when a planet in exaltation is in conjunction with a planet in debilitation. For example, if, Mars and Jupiter both occupy Cancer, under such circumstances, the effects of Mars *Mahadasha* are improved, but those of Jupiter are devalued.

(xiv) A planet in a sign rising with its hind parts first* becomes more malefic than he is otherwise; while a planet in a sign with the front portion* rising becomes more benefic than he would have been. Thus they yield effects during their *Mahadashas* accordingly.

(xv) Planets if in movable signs cause much movement and travelling during their *Dashas*, while planets in fixed signs curtail movement and travelling in some measure. In common signs, this special effect is not so marked.

(xvi) Signs correspond to houses. Aries would correspond to the first house. Taurus to the second, and so on. A planet in a sign would confer during his *Mahadasha* the effects as modified by this factor. For example, a benefic in Taurus may during his *Mahadasha* cause acquisition of money; a malefic therein may give rise to complaints of the throat or eyes.

(xvii) Planets in signs with the hind parts rising may show their full effect during the latter part of the *Mahadasha;* a planet in Pisces in the middle one-third of the *Mahadasha;* and a planet in a sign rising with the front part first, in the initial period of the *Mahadasha.*

(xviii) Another rule for judging when the effect of a planet, good or evil, will be felt in an intense manner is to examine whether the planet is in (a) the first ten degrees, (b) the middle ten degrees, or (c) the last ten degrees of the sign. If in (a), the intense effects would be felt during the initial period of the *Mahadasha;* if in (b), during the middle period: if in (c), during the last one-third part of the *Mahadasha.*

(xix) It is frequently observed that a *Mahadasha* proves good for certain matters but evil for others. For example, a person may during the course of *Mahadasha* rise in his career, but suffer the loss of a son. Therefore, while assessing a *Mahadasha* for general effects, its effect for each house should also be appraised. For this the following guide lines will prove useful.

(a) A weak planet, particularly if he is a malefic, will during his *Mahadasha* annihilate (i) the house from which he is placed in the twelfth, and also, (ii) the house as counted from which he is the twelfth lord. For example, if a weak malefic is in the fourth, then because he is in the twelfth from the fifth, he wil'

*See Chapter 5 on signs.

be detrimental for fifth house matters and a. .rs. This is an illustration of (i) above. Now let us take another example to illustrate (ii) above. Suppose a weak lord of the ninth is located anywhere in the chart. Then because the ninth is the twelfth from the tenth, the tenth house affairs will suffer.

What has been stated in regard to a planet tenanting the twelfth from a house, or being the lord of the twelfth from a house, should also be applied if he is in the sixth or eighth from a house or lord of the sixth or the eighth from a particular house.

(b) A strong and well-placed planet will during his *Mahadasha* augment the affairs of (i) the house from which he is in the eleventh, and (ii) the house as counted from which he is the lord of the eleventh. Let us illustrate; a strong and good planet in the second will promote the fourth house affairs because the second house is the eleventh from the fourth. This is an illustration of (i) above. Now let us illustrate (ii) above. The lord of the second if strong and well placed anywhere will promote the affairs of the fourth house because he is the lord of the eleventh from the fourth.

(xx) The *Mahadasha* stretches over a long span of years — Jupiter extends to 16 years, Saturn to 19 years, and so on. When a *Mahadasha* is current find out which natal house in the birth chart he is transiting. If he is strong radically, when during the *Mahadasha* he transits a good sign, exalted, own or great friend's and a good house in the natal chart, he will confer good results. For example, suppose a native with Scorpio ascendant has Jupiter's *Mahadasha,* and Jupiter is placed in Pisces in the fifth house, i.e., well placed by sign, and in the fifth house in the radix; now when during Jupiter's *Mahadasha,* Jupiter transits Cancer, his sign of exaltation and also the ninth house in the radix during that one year, he will confer excellent results. Now take the reverse case. Suppose in a birth chart with Cancer ascendant, Saturn is in the twelfth and Saturn's *Mahadasha* is current. When by transit he is in Aries in the tenth, he will spoil the tenth house affairs because he will be transiting his sign of debilitation.

(xxi) When the *Mahadasha* of a planet is current and he is combust, he shows evil effects during his period of combustion. Similarly, when the *Mahadasha* lord gets conjoined with a malefic or is aspected by a malefic during the course of his *Mahadasha,* he shows evil results. But when his *Mahadasha* is current and he becomes conjoined with a benefic or is aspected by a benefic, he produces good results.

(xxii) Apply all the general principles stated in Chapter 10 and also those discussed in Chapter 12 and apply them to *Mahadashas*. For example, a malefic in the third may during his *Mahadasha* increase the personal courage or valour of the native, but may be evil for his brother's health (third house governing brothers) and also for the mother (twelfth from fourth; expenditure for the vitality of mother—fourth). Or take another example. A planet in the eleventh may be good for the native's own income, but may prove detrimental to the native's father (second from tenth: *Maraka* for father).

What has been stated in respect of location in the eleventh from a house or being lord of the eleventh from a house, should also be applied where a planet is lord of the second, fourth, ninth, or the tenth as counted from any house or located in the second, fourth, ninth or the tenth from a particular house.

(xxiii) In judging a *Mahadasha*, if most of the planets are in the sixth or the eighth from the *Mahadasha* lord, the *Dasha* will not be good; but if the benefics are in the first, fourth, fifth, seventh, ninth, or the tenth and benefics or malefics in the 11th from him, the *Mahadasha* will be good.

(xxiv) The *Mahadasha* of a planet is unfavourable for those houses whose lords are the *Mahadasha* lord's enemies, and particularly so, if the two lords are in quincunx.* To illustrate this, suppose Leo is the sign rising. The sign is owned by the Sun. Now Saturn is an ememy of the Sun, so Saturn's *Mahadasha* would be detrimental for the matters and affairs governed by the first house. This will be particularly so if the Sun and Saturn are in quincunx.

Space does not permit stating all the subtleties and niceties which should be applied to determine whether a planet's *Mahadasha* would be good and if good in what respects; or evil and if evil in which particulars; but the above discussions will help to develop a sense of discrimination and that is ultimately the most important factor which helps in determining the good and evil effects of a planet exercised and felt during his *Mahadasha*.

* Quincunx: Sixth and eighth from each other.

CHAPTER 15

ANTARDASHAS (Minor Periods)

THE PRINCIPLES and rules laid down for determining the qualities, the goodness or badness of *Mahadashas* should also be applied to *Antardashas.* We have in Chapter 14 referred to four parallel streams running in one channel and all the four streams apply to *Antardashas* also. It is therefore unnecessary to repeat the same principles in relation to *Antardashas* as we have stated earlier in regard to the evaluation of *Mahadashas.*

1. The first principle, therefore, is that if the *Mahadasha* of a particular planet due to his strength, placement in sign and house, ownership of house or houses or due to conjunction with benefics, lords of good houses or due to receiving aspect from them is good, his *Antardasha* will also be good. Conversely if on the various counts enumerated above, the *Mahadasha* is evil, then his *Antardasha* will also be evil.

2. (a) If the *Mahadasha* is good and the *Antardasha* also appears to be good, very good effects will be felt; (b) if the *Mahadasha* is evil, even a good *Antardasha* will not be able to affect affairs so favourably; but there will be a slight improvement in the status and partial good effects will be felt, (c) if the *Mahadasha* is evil and the *Antardasha* also evil, then extremely evil effects will be felt; (d) if the *Mahadasha* is good and the *Antardasha* evil, the general trend of goodness will be arrested, just like the Sun who is eclipsed for the time being and during

the currency of evil *Antardasha*, there will be impediments and difficulties, opposition and setbacks, but the basic structure of progress will not suffer any serious damage.

In this connection readers are requested, not to overlook the radix or the birth chart. When the foundation is strong, a tempest may shake the branches of a tree but will not uproot it. Similarly, when the *Mahadasha* is strong, an *Antardasha* may affect the blossoming of the tree or drying up of the leaves of the tree, according as it is good or bad, but does not uproot the tree.

3. The location of the *Antardasha* lord, as counted from the *Mahadasha* lord is also an important factor. If the *Antardasha* lord is in the sixth, eighth or the twelfth from the *Mahadasha* lord, it is evil, but if the *Antardasha* lord is in trine or an angle or in the eleventh or in the second or the third or conjoined with the *Mahadasha* lord, it is good. The conjunction of the *Mahadasha* and the *Antardasha* lords would intensify the effects and if both are evil, as judged by the principles elaborated in Chapter 14 their conjunction would intensify the evil effects.

4. The mutual relationship between the *Mahadasha* lord and the *Antardasha* lord is another important factor. If they are enemies, despite both being good independently, the *Antardasha* will not be so good. If they are friends the *Antardasha* will be better. But if as adjudged separately both are evil and happen to be enemies also, the *Antardasha* will prove very evil.

5. The *Antardasha* of a benefic in the *Mahadasha* of a benefic is generally good, but the *Antardasha* of a *Papa* in the *Mahadasha* of a *Papa* is very evil. For example, Rahu in Mars or Mars in Rahu, Saturn in Rahu or Rahu in Saturn, Mars in Saturn or Saturn in Mars, produce evil results.

Antardashas in Evil Mahadashas

6. On a similar principle, the *Antardasha* of the lord of an evil house in the *Mahadasha* of the lord of an evil house is considered evil. On this principle, if the *Mahadasha* and the *Antardasha* lords are both afflicted the following *Antardashas* prove very evil for health and may even cause death, if occurring at the appropriate time:

(i) In the *Mahadasha* of the lord of the eighth *Antardashas* of (a) lord of the sixth, (b) of a *Papa* tenanting the sixth house,

(c) a planet conjoined with the lord of the sixth, (d) a planet aspected by the lord of the eighth.

(ii) In the *Mahadasha* of a *Papi* (natural malefic) posited in the eighth house, the *Antardashas* of (a) lord of the sixth, (b) a *Papa* tenanting the sixth house.

(iii) In the *Mahadasha* of the lord of the sixth, the *Antardashas* of (a) lord of the eighth, (b) a planet occupying the eighth house.

(iv) In the *Mahadasha* of a *Papa* in the sixth, the *Antardashas* of (a) the lord of the eighth, even if the lord of the eighth is in the eighth.

(v) In the *Mahadasha* of the lord of the twelfth, the *Antardashas* of (a) the lord of the second, (b) a planet conjoined with the lord of the second, (c) a planet fully aspected by the lord of the second, (d) a *Papa* tenanting the twelfth house, (e) a *Papa* conjoined with the lord of the twelfth in the second.

(vi) In the *Mahadasha* of a *Papa* tenanting the twelfth house, the *Antardasha* of (a) *Papa* having *Sambandha* with the lord of the second.

(vii) In the *Mahadasha* of the lord of second, the *Antardasha* of (a) lord of twelfth (b) a planet in twelfth and aspected by the lord of the twelfth.

Shubhas and Papas According to Parashari

7. Another school of Hindu astrologers states that in the *Mahadasha* of one of the following, the *Antardasha* of another may prove fatal if occurring at the appropriate stage of life, as determined by the rules given in Chapter 12.

(a) Lord of the second house, (b) *Papa* tenanting the second house, (c) lord of the seventh house, (d) a *Papa* tenanting the seventh house, (e) a *Papa* conjoined with the lord of the second house, (f) a *Papa* conjoined with the lord of the seventh house, (g) lord of the eighth, (h) lord of third or the eighth if conjoined with the lord of the second or the seventh, (i) Saturn conjoined with a *Maraka*, (j) lord of the sixth, (k) the weakest planet in the birth chart.

8. A planet who is a *Maraka* and whose *Mahadasha* is current does not kill during the *Antardasha* of a *Shubha* (lord of the fifth or the ninth) although such a *Shubha* may have *Sambandha* with the *Mahadasha* lord, who is a *Maraka*.

9. A planet who is a *Maraka* and whose *Mahadasha* is current

kills in the *Antardasha* of a *Papa*, according to ownership, even though such a *Papa* may have no *Sambandha* with the *Mahadasha* lord, who is a *Maraka*.

10. A *Maraka* planet during his *Mahadasha* does not confer wealth and in a good *Antardasha* even, there is no gain of money, but only increase in respect.

11. If there is *Mahadasha* of a *Papa* that is lord of the third, sixth, eleventh or the eighth, then the *Antardasha* of *Shubha* which does not have *Sambandha* with the *Mahadasha* lord, gives *Papa* results; the *Antardashas* of *Shubhas*, who have *Sambandha* with the *Mahadasha* bestow mixed results and the *Antardasha* of a *Yoga Karaka Shubha* who does not have *Sambandha* with the *Mahadasha* lord gives extremely *Papa* results.

Antardashas of Lords of Trine and Angles

12. The lord of a trine, if he has *Sambandha* with the lord of the angle, will show good results in his *Antardasha* in the *Mahadasha* of the lord of an angle. Thus (a) *Antardasha* of the lord of the fifth in the *Mahadashas* of (i) lord of first, (ii) lord of fourth, (iii) lord of seventh, and (iv) lord of the tenth, will show good results. And (b) the *Antardasha* of the lord of the ninth will show good results in the *Mahadasha* of (i) lord of the first, (ii) lord of the fourth, (iii) lord of the seventh, (iv) lord of the tenth.

13. The lord of an angle will, if he has *Sambandha* with the lord of the trine, show good results in his *Antardasha* in the *Mahadasha* of the lord of the trine. Thus the *Antardasha* of (a) lord of the first in the *Mahadasha* of (i) lord of fifth, (ii) or lord of the ninth, and (b) lord of the fourth in the *Mahadasha* of (i) lord of fifth (ii) lord of the ninth, also (c) lord of seventh in the *Mahadasha* of (i) lord of the fifth, (ii) lord of the ninth, and (d) lord of the tenth in the *Mahadasha* of (i) lord of the fifth, and (ii) lord of the ninth will be good.

14. In (12) and (13) above, it is necessary that there be *Sambandha* between the *Mahadasha* lord and the *Antardasha* lord. If there is no *Sambandha*, the result will not be good; that is, the *Antardasha* of a trine lord in the *Mahadasha* of the lord of an angle or the *Antardasha* of the lord of an angle in the *Mahadasha* of the lord of the trine will not be good and particularly so, if the lord owns an evil house in addition to the lordship of trine or an angle.

15. The ascendant is both an angle as well as a trine. Therefore, if the lord of the ascendant has *Sambandha* with the lord of the fifth or the ninth house, this should be treated as *Sambandha* between the lords of an angle (ascendant) and trine (fifth or ninth). Similarly, if the lord of the ascendant has *Sambandha* with the lord of an angle (fourth, seventh or tenth), it should be treated as *Sambandha* between the lord of a trine (ascendant) with the lord of an angle (fourth, seventh or tenth).

Thus during the *Mahadasha* of the lord of the ascendant, if he has *Sambandha* with the lords of any of the following, he will bestow good effects during the *Antardasha* of the planet with whom he has *Sambandha*:

Lord of (i) fourth, (ii) fifth, (iii) seventh, (iv) ninth, or (v) tenth. Similarly, during the *Mahadasha* of the lord of (i) fourth, (ii) fifth, (iii) seventh, (iv) ninth, or (v) tenth, if the lord of the ascendant has *Sambandha* with the lord of the *Mahadasha* of above, then during the *Antardasha* of the ascendant lord, there will be rise and prosperity.

16. The effect of *Shubhas'* (lord of the fifth or the ninth) *Antardasha* is good, if the *Antardasha* lord has *Sambandha* with the *Mahadasha* lord.

17. In the *Mahadasha* of a strong lord of the tenth or the ninth, even *Shubha* planets, having no *Saṁbandha* with the *Mahadasha* lord, bestow good results.

Antardasha in Own Mahadasha

18. A *Mahadasha* lord does not show his full good or evil effects in his own *Antardasha*. Readers are reminded that a *Mahadasha* has nine *Antardashas*, the first *Antardasha* being his own. Now as soon as the *Mahadasha* commences, the general trend and tenor of the native's life and career will change in keeping with the traits and effects of the planet whose *Mahadasha* commences. But the full effect will not be felt in his own. *Antardasha*. It will only become full in the *Antardashas* of *Sadharmi* and *Sambandhi* planets.

(i) *Sadharmi* means planets having a similar disposition: (a) lords of angles are *Sadharmi* of one another; (b) lords of trine are *Sadharmis* one in respect of the other; (c) the lords of the third, sixth and the eleventh form a group by themselves and are mutually *Sadharmi*; (d) lord of the eighth stands by himself.

This is one way to classify planets into four groups, each member of one group being *Sadharmi* of the other members of the same group. Here we have enumerated lords of ten houses and grouped them, but the lords of second and the twelfth have been left out. The Sun and the Moon own one house each. If the luminary is lord of the second or the twelfth and is conjoined with a planet, the luminary will be classed with the conjoined planet, according to the ownership of such planet. For example, if the luminary is conjoined with the lord of an angle, he will go to group (a); if conjoined with the lord of a trine, he will go to group (b); if conjoined with the lord of the third, sixth or the eleventh, he will be classed in group (c); and if conjoined with the lord of the eighth, he will be placed in group (d).

But if the luminary — the Sun or the Moon, is lord of the second or the twelfth and is not conjoined with any other planet, he would be grouped under (a), (b), (c) or (d), according as he occupies an angle, trine, etc.

Planets other than the Sun and the Moon own two houses each. And a planet lord of the second or the twelfth will fall in group (a), (b), (c) or (d), according to the ownership of the other house.

This is one definition of *Sadharmi,* meaning having similar disposition. Another way of demarcating planets into *Sadharmi* groups is as follows: members of the following one group are *Sadharmi* of each other:

(i) The lords of the first and the seventh
(ii) The lords of the second and the twelfth
(iii) The lords of the third and the eleventh
(iv) The lords of the fourth and the tenth
(v) The lords of the fifth and the ninth
(vi) The lords of the sixth and the eighth

We have explained at length what the Sanskrit word *Sadharmi* means. *Sambandhi,* means, planets having *Sambandha.* We have explained already in Chapter 10 what a *Sambandha* is between two planets, so we shall not repeat ourselves here. One of the general principles is that a *Mahadasha* lord shows the impact of his influence in the *Antardasha* of a *Sadharmi* or *Sambandhi* planet. If the *Antardasha* lord is neither a *Sadharmi* nor a *Sambandhi* of the *Mahadasha* lord, his trend would not be the same or similar but of a contrary nature. Under such circumstance, the reader has to exercise his individual judgment as to which would prevail over the other. When the *Mahadasha* lord and the *Antardasha* lord have contrary trends and they are neither *Sambandhis* nor *Sadharmis*, if the *Mahadasha* lord is overwhelmingly strong his effects would prevail; but if the *Antardasha* lord is extra powerful, his influence would predominate. Each planet has to be determined on his own merit and no hard and fast rule can be laid down as to which of the two contrary influences would prevail.

Sometimes it happens that the influence of the *Mahadasha* lord and the *Antardasha* lord, both of contrary nature, show their effects in different spheres. For example, the native may have a strong *Mahadasha* for political career, high office and position. Due to the general strength of the birth chart and potency of the *Mahadasha* lord, the native continues to be at the helm of affairs even during adverse *Antardashas*. But during an adverse *Antardasha*, health may suffer or one of the family members may die or even his political image be blurred, but not completely broken. Nehru continued to be the Prime Minister of India from 1947 to 1964. But during this period he suffered from paralytic stroke, he lost his only son-in-law and in 1962 when China invaded India and routed the Indian army, his prestige as a political leader suffered a serious set-back. Thus we come across long periods of time in the lives of an individual when he appears to be at the zenith of his life, but suffers during intermittent periods from domestic or health troubles. What is intended to convey is that the *Mahadasha* lord and *Antardasha* lord at times may show contrary effects but in different spheres or on different planes.

19. Saturn and Venus have a special feature, whether there be *Sambandha* between these two planets or not: (i) Saturn in his *Mahadasha* shows his effect during the *Antardasha* of Venus, and (ii) Venus in his *Mahadasha* shows his effect during the *Antardasha* of Saturn.

Antardashas in Yoga Karaka's Mahadasha:

20. The *Yoga Karaka* planet is considered extremely good and powerful. A lord of a trine and a lord of an angle get additional power due to *Sambandha* with each other. Without such *Sambandha*, by their individual selves alone, they will not be capable

of producing a third independent force. This third entity, quality, power or force can be produced by their *Sambandha* alone. In Hindu astrology, the angle has been treated as a male and a trine as a female. When a male house lord has *Sambandha* with a female house lord, a third entity a child — may be produced; but if the male and the female are isolated from each other, there cannot be a progeny. But a *Yoga Karaka* planet being lord of a trine and an angle combines in himself the attributes of a male and a female and therefore he does not need *Sambandha* with an outsider like the lord of a trine or angle. So the *Yoga Karaka* planet is in a distinctive class by himself.

21. In the *Mahadasha* of *Yoga Karaka,* the *Antardashas* of Rahu or Ketu if the node tenants an angle or trine, gives good effects.

22. In the *Mahadasha* of *Yoga Karaka,* (i) when there is *Antardasha* of a *Shubha* due to ownership, having *Sambandha* with *Mahadasha* lord, extremely good results are experienced; (ii) but in the above *Mahadasha,* if the lord is a *Shubha* (lord of good houses), and has no *Sambandha,* then instead of extremely good results, fairly good effects only are felt.

23. Even *Papas* having *Sambandha* with the *Yoga Karaka* will due to their *Sambandha,* give good effects during their *Antardashas.*

The inherent power of the *Yoga Karaka* has been domonstrated here. There would be three grades of influences; (i) a *Shubha-Antardasha* having *Sambandha* with *Yoga Karaka* is extremely good; (ii) a *Shubha* having no *Sambandha* with *Mahadasha* lord is fairly good; (iii) a *Papa* having *Sambandha* with *Yoga Karaka* is ordinarily good.

Antardashas of Yoga Karaka:

24. The effects of the *Antardasha* of a *Yoga Karaka* planet are good even if he has no *Sambandha* with the *Shubha Mahadasha* lord. If the *Yoga Karaka* (*Antardasha* lord) has *Sambandha* with the *Shubha* by ownership whose *Mahadasha* is current, the *Yoga Karaka* sometimes bestows very good results due to his being the *Yoga Karaka.* It is necessary to explain the term *Yoga Karaka.* When one and the same planet is the lord of a trine and angle, he is called *Yoga Karaka.* For example, for Cancer ascendant Mars owns the fifth (trine) and tenth (an angle) and is a *Yoga*

Karaka; for *Leo* also he is a *Yoga Karaka* because he owns the fourth (an angle) and ninth (a trine); for Taurus, Saturn owns the ninth (a trine) and the tenth (angle) and is hence a *Yoga Karaka.* For similar reasons, Saturn is *Yoga Karaka* for Libra ascendant and Venus for Capricorn and Aquarius ascendants. The term *Yoga Karaka* has been defined earlier, but is being re-explained here for immediate reference.

Two New Points of View:

We are in this judgment of the *Antardashas* introducing two new elements, which too have to be taken into account.

25. Consider that house as the ascendant, which is occupied by the *Mahadasha* lord and from this position count the houses which are first, second, third, and so on, and see which house or houses are owned by the *Antardasha* lord. He will bestow the effect of these houses during his *Antardasha.*

Illustration: Suppose Leo is the ascendant and Mars is in Scorpio in the fourth. The *Mahadasha* of Mars is current. Now suppose we have to judge the effect of Saturn's *Antardasha.* Then because Saturn is the lord of Capricorn and Aquarius and as Capricorn will be the third and Aquarius the fourth from Scorpio where Mars is natally posited, Saturn therefore would during his *Antardasha* in Mars give the effect of lordship of the third and the fourth also; this is because he is the ruler of the third and the fourth as counted from the *Mahadasha* lord. This does not mean that Saturn will not produce the effect of lordship of the sixth and the seventh from the natal ascendant Leo. It only means that in addition to the lordship of houses as counted from the natal ascendant the lordship as counted from the *Mahadasha* lord should also be considered as an additional factor.

26. The next point is that just as we have recommended taking into consideration of the lordship of the *Antardasha* lord as counted from the house tenanted by the *Mahadasha* lord, so also we have to take into consideration the tenancy of the *Antardasha* lord as counted from the *Mahadasha* lord.

Illustration: For example, in the above illustration, if Leo is the ascendant and Mars in Scorpio in the fourth, and his *Mahadasha* is current, we have to judge the effect of Saturn's *Antardasha* therein. Then if Saturn is radically in Virgo, being in eleventh from the *Mahadasha* lord Mars (in Scorpio), he will confer gain of money, and if he is radically in Libra, twelfth from the Mahadasha lord, he will cause heavy expenditure. This influence will show itself during Saturn's *Antardasha* in the *Mahadasha* of Mars and will be an additional factor to be taken into consideration over and above the general effects of Saturn's tenancy radically in Virgo or Libra, as the case may be.

While discussing these two new points, all references to the positions of the *Mahadasha* lord and the *Antardasha* lord should be considered as in the birth chart and not by transit.

This chapter dealing with *Antardasha* effects appears to be comparatively short, but in fact, it contains many points for judging an *Antardasha,* because all the principles that have been stated in connection with the judgment of a *Mahadasha* should be applied *mutatis mutandis* to *Antardashas* also.

27. *Pratyantardashas*: Just as a *Mahadasha* period is divided into *Antardashas,* so also an *Antardasha* period is divided into *Pratyantardashas.*

In Chapter 13 have been given periods of *Antardashas.* Reference to them would show that the Venus *Antardasha* period in Venus *Mahadasha* is 3 years 4 months. Now how do we calculate the *Pratyantar** periods in Venus *Antardasha* and what will be the order of planets in the *Pratyantars*? Let us take the point of order first.

The first *Pratyantar* is of the planet in whose *Antardasha* we are calculating the *Pratyantar.* Thus in the Venus *Antardasha,* the nine *Pratyantars,* will be Venus, Sun, Moon, Mars, Rahu, Jupiter, Saturn, Marcury and Ketu. What will be the order of *Pratyantars* in Saturn's *Antar*? The order will be Saturn, Mercury, Ketu, Venus, Sun, Moon, Mars, Rahu and Jupiter. Thus, the cycle remains the same, but the first *Pratyantar* commences with the planet whose *Antar* we are dividing into *Pratyantars.* Now what will be the duration of each *Pratyantar*? The Venus *Antar* in Venus *Dasha* is for 3 years 4 months.

When the total duration is 120 years Venus gets 20 years

When the total duration is 1 year Venus gets $\frac{20}{120}$ years

When the total duration is 3 years 4 months his *Pratyantar* is

* For brevity, *Mahadasha* is referred to as *Dasha, Antardasha* as *Antar* and *Pratyantardasha* as *Pratyantar.*

$$\frac{20 \times 3Y4M}{120}$$

$$= \frac{20 \times 10 \text{ years.}}{120 \times 3}$$

$$= 6 \text{ months } 20 \text{ days.}$$

Tables for *Pratyantars*, in each *Antar*, are available in the market and these are therefore not given in this book.

Some *Antars* are of a very short duration and *Pratyantars* in them will be of still shorter durations. For example, the *Antar* of Sun in the Sun's *Dasha* is of 3 months 18 days. It will not be worthwhile to split it into *Pratyantars*.

But when the *Antar* period covers two or three years, it becomes worthwhile to sub-divide it into *Pratyantars*. Then we judge the *Pratyantar* in the *Antar*, as we judge the *Antar* in the *Mahadasha* and we need not repeat what we have stated in regard to judgment of *Antars*.

Sometimes it happens that the *Dasha* is good and the *Antar* is also favourable, but the target is not hit. Suppose Libra is the ascendant and Saturn's *Dasha* is current and Saturn is a *Yoga Karaka*, and Mercury's *Antar* is going, and he as lord of the ninth and the twelfth is harmoniously configurated with Saturn. Now Mercury *Antar* in Saturn *Dasha* extends to 2 years 8 months 9 days. This is a long period so we sub-divide the period of *Antar* into nine *Pratyantars* and fix the time of fruition during the *Pratyantar* of Venus (because he is the lord of the ascendant) if he is strong, well placed, and harmoniously configurated with the lords of *Dasha* and *Antar*, or in the *Pratyantara* of the Moon (because he is the lord of the tenth) if he is strong in the radix and well configurated with the *Dasha* and *Antar* lords.

As sometimes the *Antars* and at times even *Pratyantars* extend over long periods, we are providing below some hints which will help in fixing the time of fruition of the result.

(1) The Sun shows his effects more prominently on Sundays, when the Sun, the Moon or Jupiter transits Leo or *Krittika, Uttaraphalguni* or *Uttarashadha Nakshatras*.

(2) The Moon shows his effects more prominently on Mondays when the Moon, the Sun or Jupiter transits Cancer or *Rohini, Hasta* or *Shravan Nakshatras*.

(3) Mars shows his effects more prominently on Tuesdays, when the Moon, the Sun, Mars or Jupiter transits Aries or Scorpio or *Mrigashira, Chitra* or *Dhanishtha Nakshatra.*

(4) Mercury shows his effects more prominently on Wednesdays, when Mercury, the Moon, the Sun or Jupiter transits Gemini or Virgo or *Ashlesha, Jyestha* or *Revati Nakshatras.*

(5) Jupiter shows more prominently his effect on Thursdays, when the Sun, the Moon or Jupiter transits Sagittarius or Pisces or *Punarvasu, Vishakha* or *Poorvabhadra Nakshatras.*

(6) Venus shows his effects more prominently on Fridays, when the Sun, the Moon, Jupiter and Venus transit Taurus or Libra or *Bharani, Poorvaphalguni* or *Poorvashadha Nakshatras.*

(7) Saturn shows his effects more prominently on Saturdays, when the Sun, the Moon, Jupiter or Saturn transits Capricorn or Aquarius, *Pushya, Anuradha* or *Uttarabhadra Nakshatras.*

These are for judging the fruition of good effects. When we have to judge the timings of evil effects, substitute Saturn instead of Jupiter in paras 1, 2 3, 4 and 6 above. In para 5 add Saturn along with, the Sun, the Moon, and Jupiter. In para 7 omit Jupiter.

If the readers do not want to work out the entry of planets into and transits through *Nakshatras,* the following rule may be followed.

More prominent effects of planets are shown during the following months:

(i) Sun — 16th August to 16th September
(ii) Moon — 15th July to 15th August
(iii) Mars — 13th April to 13th May and 15th November to 16th December
(iv) Mercury — 15th June to 15th July and 16th September to 16th October
(v) Jupiter — 16th December to 14th January and 12th March to 12th April
(vi) Venus — 14th May to 14th June and 16th October to 14th November
(vii) Saturn — 14th January to 12th March

When the *Antardasha* of a planet is current there is greater likelihood of the fruition of effects during the above periods according to the *Antar* of the planet.

CHAPTER 16

TRANSITS

WHAT IS a transit? Transit means the passage of a heavenly body —a planet—through the zodiac. We prepare the birth chart on the basis of time, that is, the date and year of birth. To judge the transits, we need an Ephemeris for the year for which the good or bad effects by transits are to be judged.

Suppose you desire to judge the effects for a person born earlier, for the year 1969. Then we require two data: (i) the birth chart, rising sign and longitudes of planets at birth, (ii) an Ephemeris giving the daily longitudes of planets for the year 1969.

The transit system consists of appraising the positions of the nine planets at a particular time for which the good or bad effects are to be ascertained together with the planetary positions and the rising sign in the birth chart. Suppose, at the moment the Sun is in Libra, then for a correct and detailed appraisal we must judge how the Sun in Libra agrees with the rising sign and the nine planets in the birth chart. If he is favourable from the majority, the Sun in Libra should be declared as yielding good effects; but if he is unfavourable from the majority of the natal positions of the planets, he should be declared unfavourable. This kind of appraisal would no doubt be more detailed and scientific, but it involves too much time and labour. This detailed examination of the influences exerted by a planet through his passage in the zodiac has been discussed at length in Hindu texts, but the detailed calculations involved do not make it a very popular practice.

One of the basic theories of Hindu astrology is that all influences of planets fructify through the Moon, i.e., the Moon being the heavenly body nearest to the earth, the influences filter through the Moon. Besides, all happiness and unhappiness is experienced by the mind or the heart.

In Hindu astrology, the reasoning faculty is ascribed to the mind, presided over by Mercury and all emotional feelings to the heart, presided over by the Moon. The Moon has been figuratively described as the 'heart' of God and in every nativity the Moon signifies the 'heart' of the native.

In Western astrology transits of planets are judged *vis-a-vis* the radical longitudes of the planets and the ascending degree; but in Hindu astrology the popular and the most widely practised method is to judge the transits from the natal Moon. The sign in which the Moon is at birth is popularly called the *Rashi* of the native. *Rashi* literally means a cluster or a heap. But since the signs in Hindu astrology are identified with constellations (which contain a heap or cluster of stars, forming a particular geometric pattern); the word *Rashi* has, by extended meaning, come to mean a sign and when only the *Rashi* of a particular native is referred to it means the Moon-sign.

From times immemorial the Moon-sign has acquired the pride of place and just as in western astrology, popular predictions are made and even published in magazines on the basis of Sun-signs, so also in Hindu *Panchangas* (Ephemerides) and astrological magazines and journals, and sometimes even in newspapers, predictions are published on the basis of the Moon-sign, i.e., the sign in which the Moon was at the time of birth. This Moon-sign is succinctly referred to as *Janma-Rashi* — the sign occupied by the Moon at birth. We shall also, hereafter, refer to the Moon-sign at birth as *Janma-Rashi*.

For purposes of judging the transit influences so much importance is given to the *Janma-Rashi*, that if the date or time of birth of the native is not known and his birth chart cannot be erected and the position of the Moon cannot be ascertained, it is fixed according to the initial syllable of the name of the individual. It is an accepted principle of Hindu astrology that the first syllable of a person's name vibrates with certain influences and these correspond to certain positions of the Moon in particular signs. We give below a table showing the correspondence between the initial syllable of the name and the particular Moon-sign.

Aries: chu, choo, che (e as in they) cho (as in chosen) la, a (as in woman or father) li, le, lu, loo, la (a as in late) lo.

Taurus: I, e, u (as in put), a (as in aid), va, wa, vi, wi, ve, we (as in we), wu (u as in put), woo, ve or wé as in (weight), vo, or wo (as in woe).

Gemini: ka, ki, ke, ku, koo, ka (a as in kate) ko — also all syllables beginning with c having the sound of k as in Catherine, Carol, gh, chha, ha (a as in harm).

Cancer: hi, he (as in he) hu, hoo, hé (e as in Henry) ho, da, di, de, du doo, dé (e as in devil) do (o as in so). (The sound of d in this para is as in deed, door etc.).

Leo: ma, mi, me (as in me), mu, moo, mé (e as in menthol) ma (as in Mary), mo (o as in so), ta, ti, te, tu, too, ta (as in tail). (The sound of t in this para is as in tea or total).

Virgo: to (to as in token) pa, pi, pe (as in Peter) pu, poo, tha (hard sound as in Thomas) pa (as in pain), po (o as in so).

Libra: ra, ri, re, ru, roo, ra (a as in rain), ro (o as in rover) ta, ti, tee, tu, too, té (as in Telangana). (the sound of "t" is soft as in French).

Scorpio: to (t soft as in French, o as in so), na, ni, nee, nu, noo, ya, yi, ye, yu, yoo.

Sagittarius: yé (as in yes) ya (as in yale) yo, bha, bhi, bhe bhu, bhoo, dha (dh soft as in French) dhe (e as in they), pha or f, phe or fe, phe or fi, any word begining with ph or f, bhe.

Capricorn: bho, ja, ji, je, kha, khi, khe, khu, khoo, khe (e as in they), kho (o as in so), ga (sound of g as in gun), gi, ge.

Aquarius: gu, goo (as in goose), gé (as in get), ga, go (as in go) sa, si, see, sé (as in sentry), sa (as in said), so, da (sound of d soft as in French).

Pisces: di, dee, due, doo, dé (sound of de as in they or that), do (o as in so), (sound of d in this para is soft as in French), cha (as in chunk or chart), chi, chee.

These letters or syllables have been transliterated from the Sanskrit alphabet. They therefore appear to have no system. But they do have a system in Sanskrit. But why a particular letter or syllable should have particular sign allotted to it is a moot point

A discussion of the entire proposition — correlation between sound vibrations and signs of the zodiac — is too intricate and wide a subject to be discussed at length in a text book intended for beginners. Besides, such a discussion would be more academic than practical.

If an individual's birth date and time are known and he wants to know his Moon-sign, the best and the quickest way is to get an Ephemeris for the year and look up the position of the Moon on that particular date, at that particular time (time of birth). Readers are reminded that the Ephemeris must be one which gives the position of the Moon in the sidereal zodiac. If the reader does not possess an Ephemeris giving the sidereal positions, after ascertaining the Moon's longitude in the tropical zodiac, the precession of equinoxes and nutation on the date of birth has to be deducted from the tropical zodiac to arrive at the sidereal longitude of the Moon.

But when the date and time of birth are unknown, one has to go by the above Table. The letters not found in the above list should be determined as follows:

(i) For b look up v or w
(ii) For g as in go look up g; for g as in German, look up j
(iii) For q look up k
(iv) For sh look up s
(v) For x as in xaivier, look up j

If the Moon sign at birth is not known, the guide to the Moon-sign by the initial letter or syllable of the name is the next best data. In Western numerological methods, each letter is assigned a value and the values of all the letters constituting the name are added up and the same is taken as the basis for ascertaining the harmonious or inharmonious numbers. In Hindu astrology, however, what is important is the first syllable of the name which determines the name *Rashi* (Moon-sign by name) and that is taken as the basis for further prognostication.

Having dealt with the *Janma-Rashi* (Moon-sign at birth) and with name *Rashi* (Moon-sign according to the name), we shall deal with the transits of the planets in particular signs as counted from the Moon-sign.

Transits of the Sun:

The Sun transiting the third, sixth, tenth, or the eleventh house as counted from the *Janma-Rashi* (Moon) is auspicious. For example, if the Moon sign is Scorpio, the Sun's transit through Capricorn, Aries, Leo and Virgo is good. In the rest of the signs it will not be good.

The effect of the Sun's transit through each of the houses as counted from the Moon-sign at birth is as follows: (1) loss of house or position, travelling; (2) loss, fear; (3) gain of money, happiness; (4) fear of ailments, loss of respect; (5) humility, poverty, loss of money, expenditure; (6) happiness, annihilation of enemies; (7) travelling, loss of money; (8) sickness, fear; (9) loss of lustre, inclination to indulge in evil acts; (10) success in undertakings, happiness; (11) gain of money, happiness; (12) loss of money, apprehension of sickness or trouble.

Transits of the Moon:

The Moon completes one cycle of the zodiac in about 27 days. He is in one sign, for about two days and a quarter. Suppose the Moon at birth is in Scorpio; then the Moon by transit in Scorpio will be in the first house; the Moon by transit in Sagittarius in the second house, and so on. The effects of the transiting Moon as counted from the *Janma-Rashi* (sign occupied by Moon at birth) will be as follows:

(1) Good health, increase, gain; (2) ordinary gain of money; (3) good income, happiness; (4) sickness, loss of money, loss of respect; (5) happiness but lack of success; (6) gain of money; (7) happiness, good income; (8) fear of trouble, an evil time; (9) respect, fear from the government; (10) aupicious time, happiness; (11) gain from various sources; (12) sickness, loss of money, heavy expenditure.

Thus it will be observed that the transiting Moon is auspicious in the first, third, sixth, seventh, tenth and the eleventh houses as counted from the radical Moon.

Transits of Mars:

Mars bestows good effects when he transits the third, sixth or the eleventh house as counted from the *Janma-Rashi*. The effects of Mars, by transit through various houses as counted from the radical Moon, are as follows:

(1) Fear, trouble — physical or mental; (2) eye troubles; loss of money; (3) happiness, gain of wealth; (4) trouble, fear from

enemies; (5) apprehension of sickness, loss of money; (6) happiness, gain of wealth; (7) poor health, heavy expenditure or loss of money; (8) fear, inclination to indulge in sinful acts; (9) apprehension of ill-health; (10) happiness, also distress; (11) gain of money and happiness; (12) sickness, distress.

Transits of Mercury:

The effects of Mercury during transits, as counted from the radical Moon are as follows:

(1)Fear of being confined; (2) gain of money; (3) fear from opponents or enemies; (4) gain of money and happiness; (5) sickness, distress; (6) no gain, status quo; (7) apprehension of trouble, quarrels; (8) gain of money and commodities; (9) apprehension of ill-health, loss of money; (10) happiness, good enjoyment; (11) good time, gain of money; (12) sorrow, loss of money, heavy expenditure.

Transits of Jupiter:

Jupiter stays in one sign for about a year. Jupiter is a heavy planet and while the transits of Mercury, Venus or the Sun, being about a month in each sign, are fleeting Jupiter's stays for a long period in each sign and this entitles him to greater importance and weightage. When Jupiter during his transit aspects any planet, he excites the good influences of that planet which he aspects from his transiting position. For example suppose the native's ascendant is Scorpio and the Sun is the lord of the tenth house in Pisces. Then when Jupiter transits Cancer or Scorpio, he will be fully aspecting the radical Sun; or when Jupiter actually transits Pisces he will pass over the radical Sun and excite the solar influences and the native would benefit in respect of all matters governed by the Sun, i.e., the tenth house affairs, because the Sun in our example is the lord of the tenth house and all matters for which the Sun is a *Karaka*. So judge Jupiter's transit in relation to other planets also.

The effects of Jupiter's transit through the various houses as counted from the *Janma-Rashi* will be as follows:

(1) Fear of unfavourable circumstances. In Western astrology Jupiter by transit over the radical Moon is considered good. Not so in Hindu astrology; (2) gain of money and commodities; (3) fear, sickness; (4) loss of money, fear; (5) gain, happiness; (6)

sickness, distress; (7) respect, happiness; (8) adversity, troubles, both physical and mental; (9) happiness, enhanced prestige, respect from others; (10) humility, i.e., loss of respect; (11) happiness, gain of money; (12) sickness, fear.

Transits of Venus:

When Venus by transit occupies various houses as counted from the Moon-sign of birth, the effects are as follows:

(1) Happiness, annihilation of enemies; (2) gain of money; (3) happiness, gain of wealth; (4) gain of money and comforts: (5) gain, happiness in respect of child or children; (6) trouble, increase in the number of enemies or adverse effects caused by opponents; (7) distress, great apprehension, adversity, loss of money; (8) gain of money; (9) happiness, gain; (10) loss of religious merit — the native may indulge in irreligious acts, want of happiness; (11) mental distress but gain of money; (12) increase in wealth.

Transits of Saturn:

The transit of Saturn is generally unfavourable in respect of the house (from the radical ascendant) he transits unless he be transiting his own house or unless he be the lord of the ascendant. (i.e., unless Capricorn or Aquarius is the rising sign), when he does not damage the affairs of the house he transits. For example, if Scorpio is the ascendant and Saturn by transit is in the first house, he will be inclined to cause ill-health. When he transits Sagittarius he will have a tendency to adversely affect finances. In Capricorn, he will not during his transit damage the third house because Capricorn is his own sign. When he transits the fourth house Aquarius then also he will not damage the fourth house affairs because Aquarius is his own sign. When he transits Pisces, the fifth house, he will spoil the fifth house affairs of the native. The native may have stomach troubles due to sluggish digestion or formation of gases (traits of Saturnine diseases), or the native's children may suffer in health or career, and so on.

Saturn also has a depressing influence on the radical planet whom during the course of his transit he aspects. For example, suppose Scorpio is the ascendant and the Sun, the lord of the tenth, is in Pisces. Now when Saturn during his transit, stays in Gemini, he will be fully aspecting the radical Sun (the Sun occupying Pisces in the birth chart), with the result that affairs pertaining to the Sun may suffer or have a setback. The Sun is the lord of the tenth house, so the native's career may have a setback or advancement may be thwarted. Saturn is the planet of death and delay and so he spoils matters by prolonging issues or keeping them pending and by procrastination. He also causes harm from low people, aged persons, labour, servants, enemies and opponents. In the above example, the Sun is the lord of the tenth and we have explained how his transit would adversely effect the native's career. But the Sun is also *Karaka* for health, vigour, personal push, respect, father, government, persons in authority, and so Saturn during his transit through Gemini will also spoil or damage one or more affairs over which the Sun presides. In this way Saturn by transit spoils the affairs pertaining to the planet he aspects. But if he be the lord of the ascendant, he will not do so, or if he does any harm it will not be in such great measure.

Now we shall revert to our original line of delineating the effects of planets: The effects, of Saturn in the twelve houses as counted from the Moon-sign are:

(1) Great distress and destruction; (2) sorrow, loss of wealth; (3) happiness, gain of money; (4) apprehension of trouble, physical and mental ailments, fear; (5) loss of wealth, distress to sons or children; (6) happiness, gain of money; (7) infirmities, physical sickness or mental ailments; (8) increase of enemies or added onslaught by enemies, illness or distress; (9) indulgence in sinful actions, loss of wealth, retarded income; (10) increase of enmity; (11) gain of money, happiness, (12) trouble all round, upsetting of status quo — a very unfavourable time.

Saturn stays for two and a half years in one sign; so his transits are very important. When Saturn transits the twelfth, the first and the second house as counted from the radical Moon the period comes to seven and a half years (two and a half years in each of the three signs) and the combined period of seven and half years is generally referred to in India as the *Sadhe Sati* (the phrase literally means seven and a half years). This is generally considered a period during which the native does not have peace of mind, one thing after another crops up to keep the native worried. Few indeed are lucky who do not have a death in the family during these seven and a half years.

Here again persons in whose nativity the Moon is in Taurus (because Saturn would be the lord of the ninth and the tenth, both good houses from the Moon sign) or Libra (because Saturn would be the lord of the fourth and the fifth, both good houses as counted from the radical Moon) or Capricorn or Aquarius (because Saturn would be the lord of the Moon sign radically) do not fare so badly as natives in whose nativities Saturn is the lord of an evil house as counted from the natal Moon.

Transits of Rahu:

The effect of Rahu's transit through the twelve houses as counted from the *Janma-Rashi* is as follows:

(1) Loss, trouble both physical or mental; (2) loss of wealth, heavy expenditure; (3) good health, gain of money; (4) enmity, sorrow; (5) loss, sorrow; (6) happiness, gain of wealth; (7) loss, quarrels; (8) illness, fear; (9) inclination to indulge in sinful acts; (10) enmity, happiness; (11) happiness, gain of money; (12) loss, illness.

Transits of Ketu:

The effect of Ketu's transit through the twelve houses as counted from the radical Moon are as follows:

(1) Loss, ill-health or disease; (2) loss of money; (3) happiness, gain, increase, (4) fear, trouble both physical or mental; (5) sorrow, loss of money; (6) happiness, gain of money; (7) evil state of affairs, illness; (8) loss, threatened trouble; (9) sinful actions, humility; (10) fear, sorrow; (11) good name and fame, gain of money; (12) physical ill-health or mental distress, enmity.

Having stated succinctly the effects of transits of the nine planets through the twelve houses as counted from the radical position of the Moon, we shall explain a new feature. This is called *Vedha.*

What is Vedha?

Vedha in Sanskrit means penetrating, piercing, perforating, also a measure of time. When a particular position of a transiting planet say A, is obstructed by another transiting planet B, the latter B is said be obstructing the planet A's influence. Suppose light is coming from a particular source. If we put an obstruction between the source of light and the spot illuminated, the light will be obstructed and would cease to illuminate the spot where it was formerly falling. Similarly, suppose the Sun is transiting the third sign as counted from the radical Moon. Now if a planet other than Saturn is in the ninth, the influence emitted by the Sun, being third from the Moon, will be obstructed and the influence due to his transit through the house from the natal Moon will not be felt. When describing *Vedha* for the Sun, we have said that any planet other than Saturn will do so. This is because the Sun is the father of Saturn, and the Moon the father of Mercury. There is no *Vedha* by the son to the father or by the father to the son. The Sun therefore does not cause *Vedha* for Saturn nor does Saturn do so for the Sun. The Moon does not cause *Vedha* to Mercury, nor does Mercury cause *Vedha* to the Moon.

We give below the corresponding *Vedha* positions:

Sun: Auspicious places	3 6 10 11
Vedha places	9 12 4 5
	(except by Saturn)
Moon: Auspicious places	1 3 6 7 10 11
Vedha places	5 9 12 2 4 8
	(except by Mercury)
Mars: Auspicious places	3 6 11
Vedha places	12 9 5
Mercury: Auspicious places	2 4 6 8 10 11
Vedha places	5 3 9 1 8 12
	(except by Moon)
Jupiter: Auspicious places	2 5 7 9 11
Vedha places	12 4 3 10 8
Venus: Auspicious places	1 2 3 4 5 8 9 11 12
Vedha places	8 7 1 10 9 5 11 6 3
Saturn: Auspicious places	3 6 11
Vedha places	12 9 5
	(except by Sun)
Rahu: Auspicious places	3 6 11
Vedha places	12 9 5
Ketu: Auspicious places	3 6 11
Vedha places	12 9 5

Here the auspicious place and the corresponding *Vedha* place are both counted from the radical Moon. Suppose the Moon at birth is posited in Cancer and the Sun is transiting Virgo—third from the Moon. He would bestow a good effect by transit through the third house from the Moon. Now the corresponding *Vedha* place for the third from the Sun is the ninth house. If therefore any planet other than Saturn is transiting Pisces, which is the ninth sign from the radical Moon, there will be no good effects of the Sun's transit through the third sign from the radical Moon. The Sun's influence would be checked, held up or obstructed.

Reference is invited to the auspicious places of the Sun's transit as counted from the radical Moon. They are 3, 6, 10 and 11. The corresponding *Vedhu* places are 9, 12, 4 and 5. Thus if the Sun is in the third from the radical Moon, a planet other than Saturn in the ninth from the radical Moon, would obstruct; if the Sun is in the sixth, the *Vedha* place is the twelfth; if the Sun is in the tenth the corresponding *Vedha* place is the fourth, and if the Sun is in the eleventh the corresponding *Vedha* place will be fifth.

The figure under each auspicious place is the corresponding *Vedha* place in relation to it.

Converse Vedha

(i) We have discussed the auspicious places of planets as counted from the radical place of the Moon and corresponding places—also counted from the Moon—which obstruct or check the influence emanating from the transiting planet.

(ii) We now give below the inauspicious places of the transiting planets, as counted from the radical Moon and the corresponding *Vedha* places, which hold up or check the unfavourable influence; but here while the inauspicious places are counted from the radical Moon, the corresponding *Vedha* places are *not* counted from the radical Moon but from the transiting planet. For example, the Sun transiting the fourth from the radical place is inauspicious. Suppose the Moon is in Cancer; now fourth from Cancer will be Libra. So if the Sun transits Libra, his influence would be unfavourable to the native. Now if a planet other than Saturn, because the Sun and Saturn do not mutually *Vedha* each other, is in the third from the Sun (not from the Moon), i.e. in Sagittarius, he will obstruct the evil influence of the Sun. By this converse *Vedha* not only is the adverse influence nullified, but even the evil transit becomes good.

Below are given the inauspicious places of transit as counted from the radical Moon, and under each such place is also given the corresponding *Vedha* position as counted from the transiting planet:

Sun: Inauspicious places	4	5	9	12	
Vedha places	3	6	10	11	
Moon: Inauspicious places	4	5	8	9	12
Vedha places	3	6	7	10	11
Mars: Inauspicious places	5	9	12		
Vedha places	3	6	9		
Mercury: Inauspicious places	3	6	7	9	12
Vedha places	2	5	8	10	11
Jupiter: Inauspicious places	3	4	10	12	
Vedha places	2	5	9	11	
Venus: Inauspicious places	6	7	10		
Vedha places	2	5	9		
Saturn: Inauspicious places	5	9	12		
Vedha places	3	6	11		
Rahu: Inauspicious places	5	9	12		
Vedha places	3	6	11		
Ketu: Inauspicious places	5	9	12		
Vedha places	3	6	11		

It is further reiterated that the Sun does not cause *Vedha* to Saturn nor Saturn to the Sun, similarly the Moon does not cause *Vedha* to Mercury nor Mercury to the Moon.

Some Factors which Modify Transit Influences

Of all the factors which modify the transit influences, the most important is the *Vedha*. But there are some other factors also which modify the influences. These are as follow:

(i) If the planet is strong in the radix, he shows very good results, when he is good by transit and even when transiting an adverse house, he does not show such evil result and particularly so if he tenants the third, sixth, tenth or the eleventh house from the ascendant in the birth chart. By strong, we mean in his sign of exaltation, in his own sign or great friend's or friend's sign and conjoined with a benefic and well aspected.

(ii) If the planet is weak and afflicted in the radix, he does not even when transiting a good house show very good results; and when he transits an evil house, he shows very evil results. By weak and afflicted we mean in his sign of debilitation, in great enemy's or enemy's sign, conjoined with or aspected by malefics.

(iii) A planet expected to yield good results does not do so if he is aspected by a malefic during the transit.

(iv) A planet expected to yield unfavourable results does not do so if during his transit he is aspected by a benefic.

(v) If during the course of transit, a planet becomes combust or conjoined with a malefic or transits his sign of debilitation or great enemy's or enemy's sign, his power to do good is curtailed and his power to do evil is enhanced.

(vi) If during the course of his transit, a planet is in his sign of exaltation, own sign or great friend's or friend's sign and conjoined with a benefic, his power to do good is enhanced and his power to do evil is curtailed.

(vii) A benefic, when during the course of his transit becomes retrograde, becomes more benefic. Conversely, when a malefic during the course of his transit becomes retrograde, his power to do evil is enhanced.

(viii) While judging the effect of the transit primarily from the radical Moon, the house transited by the planet should also be adjudged from the ascendant. For example, if Virgo is the ascendant in a nativity and Moon is in Cancer, Saturn's transit through Leo, being second from the radical Moon, will be evil. Now, Leo is twelfth from the ascendant and the house of expenditure and losses as counted from the ascendant. So Saturn's transit through Leo will be doubly evil. Let us take another example. Suppose Pisces is the rising sign or the ascendant and the radical Moon is in Leo in the sixth. When Jupiter transits Sagitarius, fifth from the Moon, he will be auspicious. But as counted from the ascendant, Jupiter lord of the tenth will be transiting tenth. So Jupiter will be doubly good.

(ix) When the Sun, Mars, Jupiter and Saturn are simultaneously transiting the first, eighth or the twelfth from the radical Moon, it is a very evil time for the native. It may cause loss of position, loss of wealth, serious illness, any one or all of these.

(x) The Sun in the fifth, Moon in the eighth, Mars in the seventh, Mercury in the sixth, Jupiter in the third, Venus in the sixth, Saturn in the first and Rahu in the ninth, bring about loss of honour and wealth and even danger to life, if all the above transits occur simultaneously.

(xi) The Sun and Mars have a tendency to show their effect

when they enter a sign and their influence is more prominent in the initial ten degrees of the sign; Jupiter and Venus bestow their full effect by transit when they transit the middle of the sign, from the eleventh to the twentieth degrees, and the Moon, and Saturn in the last one-third of the sign that is, from the twenty-first to the thirtieth degrees. Mercury and Rahu show uniformly good or evil effect throughout their passage through the sign from zero to thirty degrees.

(xii) The good effects of a house as counted from the ascendant, are felt when the lord of the ascendant or the lord of the house or *Karaka* for the house transits the house concerned. For example, suppose we have to determine the birth of a son. This is judged from the fifth house. When the lord of the first house, lord of the fifth house or the *Karaka* for son, i.e., Jupiter, when one or more of these planets transit the fifth, there is likelihood of the birth of a son or if sons are already adults, their affairs may prosper.

(xiii) When the house is transited by the lord of the eighth as counted from the house concerned, the affairs pertaining to the house transited suffer.

(xiv) To judge when good effects pertaining to a house will prosper add the longitudes (signs, degrees, minutes and seconds) of the lord of the house, lord of the ascendant and the *Karaka* of the house when Jupiter transits this point, it will be good.

(xv) Whatever effect has been delineated due to a planet's location in the birth chart, it comes to pass when that planet transits the ascendant.

(xvi) The good or evil effects pertaining to a planet are stirred into action when the lord of the ascendant passes during transit over the radical position of the planet.

(xvii) When several planets are simultaneously transiting good places and the *Mahadasha* and *Antardasha* current are also good, very good effects are felt.

(xviii) When several planets are simultaneously transiting evil places and the *Mahadasha* and *Antardasha* current are also evil, very adverse results are experienced.

(xix) A conjunction of two or more *Papas* near about the ascending degree or the longitude occupied by the radical Sun, Moon or any planet is evil.

(xx) An eclipse over the ascending degree, Sun or Moon is evil.

What has been said above is quite sufficient for delineating the effects of transits. A large number of astrologers base their predictions on transits alone and do not take the trouble of erecting a complete birth chart or calculating the *Mahadasha* or *Antar-dasha.* It is hoped readers will take advantage of this book and learn astrology correctly and those who have already read a few books on the subject. will also find here many things both new and stimulating.

APPENDIX

PRECESSION OF EQUINOX AND NUTATION FROM 1880 TO 1972 ON THE 1ST JANUARY OF EACH YEAR

Year			*Deg.*	*Min.*	*Sec.*
1880	...	...	22	11	20
1881	...	...	22	12	12
1882	...	...	22	13	0
1883	...	...	22	13	47
1884	...	...	22	14	33
1885	...	...	22	15	18
1886	...	...	22	16	13
1887	...	...	22	16	47
1888	...	...	22	17	32
1889	...	...	22	18	20
1890	...	...	22	19	9
1891	...	...	22	20	00
1892	...	...	22	20	52
1893	...	...	22	21	47
1894	...	...	22	22	42
1895	...	...	22	23	38
1896	...	...	22	24	34
1897	...	...	22	25	29
1898	...	...	22	26	23
1899	...	...	22	27	15

1900	...	...	22	28	5
1901	...	...	22	28	52
1902	...	...	22	29	39
1903	...	...	22	30	24
1904	...	...	22	31	8
1905	...	...	22	31	53
1906	...	...	22	32	38
1907	...	...	22	33	24
1908	...	...	22	34	12
1909	...	...	22	35	2
1910	...	...	22	35	54
1911	...	...	22	36	47
1912	...	...	22	37	42
1913	...	...	22	38	38
1914	...	...	22	39	34
1915	...	...	22	40	29
1916	...	...	22	41	24
1917	...	...	22	42	17
1918	...	...	22	43	8
1919	...	...	22	43	57
1920	...	...	22	44	45
1921	...	...	22	45	31
1922	...	...	22	46	16
1923	...	...	22	47	0
1924	...	...	22	47	44
1925	...	...	22	48	30
1926	...	...	22	49	17
1927	...	...	22	50	6
1928	...	...	22	50	56
1929	...	...	22	51	49
1930	...	...	22	52	43
1931	...	...	22	53	38
1932	...	...	22	54	33
1933	...	...	22	55	30
1934	...	...	22	56	25
1935	...	...	22	57	19
1936	...	...	22	58	11
1937	...	...	22	59	2
1938	...	...	22	59	50
1939	...	...	23	0	37

1940	...	...	23	1	23
1941	...	...	23	2	9
1942	...	...	23	2	54
1943	...	...	23	3	37
1944	...	...	23	4	23
1945	...	...	23	5	10
1946	...	...	23	6	0
1947	...	...	23	6	51
1948	...	...	23	7	44
1949	...	...	23	8	39
1950	...	...	23	9	35
1951	...	...	23	10	31
1952	...	...	23	11	25
1953	...	...	23	12	20
1954	...	...	23	13	15
1955	...	...	23	14	7
1956	...	...	23	14	56
1957	...	...	23	15	45
1958	...	...	23	16	31
1959	...	...	23	17	16
1960	...	...	23	17	55
1961	...	...	23	18	38
1962	...	...	23	19	24
1963	...	...	23	20	11
1964	...	...	23	20	59
1965	...	...	23	21	49
1966	...	...	23	22	41
1967	...	...	23	23	35
1968	...	...	23	24	30
1969	...	...	23	25	25
1970	...	...	23	26	21
1971	...	...	23	27	17
1972	...	...	23	28	11

GLOSSARY OF ASTROLOGICAL TERMS

Afflicted. When a planet is unfavourably placed by sign and house and is conjoined with or aspected by a malefic or malefics.

Angles. The first, fourth, seventh and tenth houses.

Aquarius. The eleventh sign of the zodiac.

Aries. The first sign of the zodiac.

Ascendant. The sign which is rising at the eastern horizon at birth.

Aspect. See Chapter 6.

Benefics. Moon in the bright fortnight, Mercury not associated with malefics, Venus and Jupiter are benefics in increasing order.

Cadent. The third, sixth, ninth and twelfth houses or the planets there in a horoscope.

Cancer. The fourth sign of the zodiac.

Capricorn. The tenth sign of the zodiac.

Caput Draconis. The northern node of Moon called Rahu.

Cauda Draconis. The sourthern node of the Moon called Ketu.

Combust. When a planet is not visible due to nearness to the Sun. See Chapter 10.

Common signs. Gemini, Virgo, Sagittarius and Pisces.

Configurated. The relative position of planets in a horoscope.

Conjunction. Location of two planets in the same sign.

Constellation. Group of fixed stars called *Nakshatras.*

Daily motion. The average motion of a planet in twenty-four hours.

Debilitation. Certain planets in certain signs are considered weak. See Chapter 6.

Degree. One-thirtieth part of a sign and 1/360th of a circle.

Degree rising. The exact degree on the cusp of the first house, i.e., rising at the eastern horizon at birth.

Direct motion. When a planet is moving forward this is direct motion. The Sun and Moon have direct motion. Other planets have retrograde motion also. Rahu and Ketu have always retrograde motion.

Directional Strength. See Chapter 6.

Dispositor. The lord of the sign in which a planet is. Suppose the Moon is in Taurus, then Venus is the dispositor of the Moon.

Ecliptic. The imaginary belt which the Sun appears to move in. In fact, it is the path traversed by the earth in going round the Sun in one year. This path is not circular but elliptic.

Exaltation. Certain planets are strong in certain signs and then they are called exalted. See Chapter 6.

Fixed signs. Taurus, Leo, Scorpio, Aquarius.

Gemini. The third sign of the zodiac.

House. The division of the zodiac into twelve parts, each part being called a house. See Chapter 7.

Ill-placed. Unfavourable location by sign and house and conjoined with or having the aspect of a malefic or malefics.

Jupiter. One of the nine planets (presiding over Thursday).

Latitude. On the earth, as given in geographical maps the distance in degrees north or south of the equator. In the heavens, distance in degrees north or south of the ecliptic line.

Leo. The fifth sign of the zodiac.

Libra. The seventh sign of the zodiac.

Local Mean Time. See Chapter 4.

Longitude. On earth as given in geographical maps, the distance east or west from Greenwich meridian. In the heavens, it is the distance from 0 or beginning of Aries.

Lords. Certain planets are lords or rulers of certain signs. See Chapter 5.

Malefics. The Moon in the dark half, Mercury associated with a malefic, Sun, Ketu, Mars, Rahu and Saturn are malefics in increasing order.

Mars. One of the seven planets presiding over Tuesday.

Mercury. One of the planets presiding over Wednesday.

Meridian. On earth, longitude of Greenwich. In the heavens, the degree passing over the cusp of the tenth house.

Mid-heaven. The cusp of the tenth house, the meridian above the earth.

Moon. One of the seven planets (presiding over Monday).

Movable Signs. Aries, Cancer, Libra and Capricorn.

Natal. As at the time of birth.

Native. The person whose birth chart is being made or is under discussion.

Nativity. The birth chart or the horoscope.

Node. Nodes of the Moon called Rahu and Ketu in Hindu astrology.

Own house. Certain planets are deemed to be lords or rulers of particular signs. When the sign falls in a particular house, the planet is said to own the house or be lord or ruler of the house in which his sign falls.

Pisces. The twelfth sign of the zodiac.

Planets. Sun, Moon, Mars, Mercury, Jupiter, Venus, Saturn, Rahu and Ketu.

Precession of the Equinoxes. See Chapter 1.

Quincunx. In sixth and eighth from each other.

Radical. As in the birth chart.

Radically. As in the birth chart.

Retrograde. The backward motion which the planets appear to have at times on account of the position and motion of the earth. Rahu and Ketu are always retrograde. The Sun and Moon are never retrograde. The other planets are at time retrograde.

Rising sign. The sign rising at the eastern horizon at the birth place at the time of birth.

Ruler. See Lord and own house.

Sagittarius. The ninth sign of the zodiac.

Saturn. One of the seven planets presiding over Saturday.

Scorpio. The eighth sign of the zodiac.

Sidereal Time. Angular distance of the first point of Aries in the tropical zodiac. If we convert the hours, minutes and seconds on the basis of fifteen degrees for each hour, it would give the right ascension of the meridian cusp in time.

Signs. The ecliptic or the zodiac is divided into twelve parts each comprising 30°. The twelve signs in order are Aries, Taurus,

Gemini, Cancer, Leo, Virgo, Libra, Scorpio, Sagittarius, Capricorn, Aquarius and Pisces.

Standard Time. Time by the watch prevalent in a particular country. The Indian Standard Time is 5 hours 30 minutes ahead of Greenwich Mean Time. This is since 1906. Before that Madras Time was the Indian Standard Time.

Stationary. When a planet due to the earth's motion appears to be stationary. This is either when a planet changes from direct motion to retrograde motion or vice versa.

Succedent house. The second, fifth, eighth and eleventh houses.

Sun. One of the seven planets (presiding over Sunday.)

Taurus. The second sign of the zodiac.

Transit. The passage of any planet through the zodiac.

Trine. The fifth and the ninth houses. The first house is a trine as well as an angle.

Venus. One of the seven planets (presiding over Friday).

Virgo. The sixth sign of the zodiac.

Well-placed. Location is a good sign and house and conjoined with or aspected by a benefic or benefics.

Zodiac. The imaginary belt comprising 8 degrees on either side of the ecliptic. See Chapter 1.

INDEX TO SANSKRIT TERMS

Below are being given Sanskrit words, used in this book and the references to pages where they have been explained. This will also serve the purpose of the glossary referred to on page 187.

Abhijit, 5
Adhi, 109
Adhika masa, 23
Adhiyoga, 194
Amala, 205
Amavasya, 23
Ambara, 84
Anala, 20
Ananda, 20
Anapha, 197
Angira, 20
Antara, 257
Antardasha, 257
Anuradha, 5
Apachaya, 185
Apoklima, 62
Ardra, 4
Aroha, 69
Ashadha, 21
Ashlesha, 4
Ashtami, 23
Ashubhamala, 206
Ashwina, 21
Ashwini, 4
Asta, 185
Astra yoga, 210
Asura yoga, 211
Asus, 34
Atiganda, 26
Ativasuman, 194
Avanti, 84
Avaroha, 69
Avayoga, 212
Ayanansha, 34
Ayushmana, 26

Bahudhanya, 20
Balava, 24
Bandhus, 153
Basti, 53
Bava, 24
Beeja Sanskara, 28
Bengali San, 19
Bhadra, 21
Bhadra, 31
Bhadra yoga, 202
Bhagya yoga, 211
Bhagya, 97
Bharani, 4
Bhava, 20
Bhava, 107
Bheda, 83
Bhukti, 257
Brahma, 26
Brahma, 81
Brahmanas, 58
Buddha, 19

Chaitra, 21
Chamara, 270
Chamara yoga, 210
Chara, 59
Chaturdashi, 23
Chaturthi, 23
Chatushpada, 24
Chera, 57
Chhatra yoga, 210
Chitra, 4
Chitrabhanu, 20
Chola, 57

Dainya yoga, 209
Dama yoga, 206
Dana, 83
Danda, 83
Daridra yoga, 214
Dasha, 251
Dashami, 23
Dhanishtha, 5
Dhanu, 8
Dharma, 110
Dharmashala, 112
Dharmasthana, 119
Dhata, 20
Dhatu, 62
Dhenu yoga, 210
Dhriti, 26
Dhruva, 26
Dhundiraja, 108
Dosha, 185
Dreshkana, 100
Durga, 81
Dundubhi, 20
Durmati, 20
Durmukha, 20
Durudhara, 197
Duryoga, 213
Dushkriti yoga, 213
Dusthana, 187
Dwadashi, 23
Dwapara, 19
Dwiswabhava, 59
Dwiteeya, 23

Ekadashi, 23
Ekavaliyoga, 207

Gaja Kesari Yoga, 198
Ganda, 26
Gandanta, 66
Gara, 24
Gauri yoga, 199
Gautamika,[1] 84
Ghatis, 27
Grahas, 3
Gola yoga, 205
Gunas, 78
Gurus, 85

Hansa yoga, 202
Hanuman, 81
Harsha yoga, 213
Harshana, 26
Hasta, 4
Hemalamba, 20
Hora lagna, 236

Indra, 26
Indra, 81
Ishtam, 35
Ishwara, 20

Jaimini,[2] 92
Jaladhi yoga, 210
Janma-Rashi, 307
Jatakabharana,[3] 108
Jataka Parijat,[4] 87
Jatakaratna,[5] 111
Jaya, 20
Jeeva, 62
Jyeshtha, 21
Jyeshtha, 5

Kahala yoga, 204
Kala purusha, 52
Kalayukta, 20
Kalinga, 84
Kaliyuga, 19
Kalyan Varma,[6] 159
Kama yoga, 211
Kanya, 8
Kapha, 78
Karaka, 84, 87, 187

Karakatwa, 270
Karana, 24
Karka, 8
Karnata, 57
Kartika, 21
Kaulava, 24
Kedar yoga, 205
Keelaka, 20
Keeta, 61
Kemadruma yoga, 197
Kendra, 61
Kendra-Trikona yoga, 216
Kerala, 57
Keshava,[7] 280
Ketu, 3
Khala yoga, 209
Khanda, 66
Khandanta, 66
Khara, 20
Khyati yoga, 211
Kinstughna, 24
Kleeva yoga, 208
Kollam era, 19
Kollasa, 57
Koshala, 57
Krishna, 23
Krishna Paksha, 23
Krittika, 4
Krodhan, 20
Krodhi, 20
Krura, 89
Kshatriya, 58
Kshaya, 20
Ksheena Chandra, 83
Kuhoo yoga, 212
Kumbha, 8

Laghu Parashari, 278
Lagnam, 14
Lagna Rashi, 52
Lakshmi yoga, 203

Madhya yoga, 208
Maghadha,[8] 84
Magha, 4
Magha, 21
Mahabhagya yoga, 200
Mahadasha, 251
Mahapurusha yoga, 202
Mahayoga, 208
Malavya yoga, 203
Malaya,[9] 57
Malika yoga, 207
Makara, 8
Manchaka, 6
Mandapa, 104
Mangal yoga, 208
Mangalika, 234
Manmatha, 20
Mantras, 159
Mantreshwar,[10] 92
Maraka, 187
Maraka Sthana, 186
Mardala, 6
Margashirsha, 21
Mathas, 98
Meena, 8
Mesha, 8
Mithuna, 8
Mlechchhas, 81
Moola, 5
Moola, 62
Moola Trikona, 70
Mridanga, 6
Mrigashira, 4
Mritiyoga, 212
Musala yoga, 211

Naga, 24
Nakshatra, 201
Nandan, 20
Navami, 23
Navansha, 86
Neechabhilashi, 70
Nirayan, 42
Nirbhagya yoga, 213
Niswa yoga, 212

Paddhati, 93
Pakshabala, 121
Pala, 27
Palabha, 34
Pamar yoga, 213
Pan, 240
Panaphar, 62
Panchala,[11] 57

Panchami, 23
Panchanga, 24
Pandya, 57
Papa, 82
Papa Kartari, 194
Papi, 90
Parabhava, 20
Parashara,[12] 87
Paridhavi, 20
Parigha, 26
Parthiva, 20
Parvata, 84
Pasha yoga, 206
Patala, 57
Pausha, 21
Phaladeepika,[13] 87
Phalguna, 21
Pingala, 20
Pitta, 78
Plava, 20
Plavanga, 20
Poorvabhadra, 5
Poorvaphalguni, 4
Poorvashadha, 5
Poornima, 23
Prabhava, 20
Prajapati, 20
Pramathi, 20
Pramoda, 20
Prashna marga,[14] 100
Pratipat, 23
Pratyantardasha, 303
Prishthoday, 63
Prithvi, 81
Priti, 26
Punarvasu, 4
Punya, 106
Pushkala yoga, 200
Pushya, 4

Rahu, 3
Rajasika, 78
Raja yoga, 189
Rakshasa, 20
Raktaksha, 20
Rashi, 51
Rashi, 309
Raudra, 20
Revati, 5
Rohini, 4
Ruchaka yoga, 207
Rudhirodgari, 20
Rudra, 81
Rudra, 98

Sadharana, 20
Sadharmi, 298
Sadhya, 26
Saindhava,[15] 57
Sama, 83
Sambandha, 189
Sambandhi, 299
Samvata, 20
Sandhi, 60
Sanhara Khand, 66
Sanketnidhi,[16] 100
Saptami, 23
Sarala yoga, 213
Saraswati yoga, 205
Saravali,[17] 159
Sarini, 34
Sarvajit, 20
Sarvadhari, 20
Sarvartha Chintamani,[18] 87
Satayuga, 19
Satwika, 78
Saubhagya, 26
Saumya, 89
Saumya, 20
Shachi, 81
Shakata yoga, 199
Shaka, 20
Shakuna, 24
Shankha yoga, 214
Shanti, 31
Sharvari, 20
Shasha yoga, 203
Shashthi, 23
Shastras, 97
Shatabhisha, 5
Shesha, 81
Shirshodaya, 63
Shiva, 26
Shiva, 195
Shobhana, 26
Shobhana, 20

Shoola, 26
Shoola yoga, 205
Shorya yoga, 210
Shravana, 5
Shravana, 21
Shri Kantha, 195
Shrimukha, 20
Shrinatha yoga, 214
Shripati,[19] 280
Shubha, 82, 83, 89, 90
Shubha, 26
Shubha Kartari, 193
Shubhamala, 206
Shubhakrit, 20
Shudras, 58
Shukla, 20
Shukla, 21
Shukla, 26
Shukla Paksha, 21
Siddhartha, 20
Siddha, 26
Siddhi, 26
Sinha, 8
Srishti Khanda, 66
Sthira, 59
Sthiti Khanda, 66
Subhanu, 20
Subrahmanya, 81
Sudarshan Chakra, 52
Sukarma, 26
Sunapha yoga, 197
Suparijata yoga, 211
Surya-Siddhanta,[20] 27
Sushubha, 194
Swati, 4

Taitil, 24
Tamasika, 78
Tarana, 20
Tithi, 21
Torana, 6
Trayodashi, 23
Tretayuga, 19
Trika, 192
Trikona, 216
Triteeya, 23
Tula, 8

Ubhayachari, 197
Uchchabhilashi, 69
Ududaya Pradeepa, 278
Upachaya, 192
Uttarabhadra, 5
Uttarakalamtrita, 100
Uttara Phalguni, 4
Uttarashadha, 5

Vaidhriti, 26
Vaidyanatha,[21] 100
Vaishakha, 21
Vaishya, 58
Vajra, 26
Vali, 6
Vallaki yoga, 206
Vanija, 24
Varaha Mihir,[22] 129
Variyan, 26
Vashi, 197
Vasuman, 198
Vata, 78
Vedas, 104
Vedha, 314
Veena, 55
Veena yoga, 206
Veshi, 197
Vibhava, 20
Vidya, 97
Vijaya, 20
Vikari, 20
Vikram, 20
Vikram Samvata, 20
Vikrit, 20
Vilamba, 20
Vimala yoga, 214
Vipala, 27
Viranchi, 196
Virodhi, 20
Virodha Krit, 20
Vishakha, 5
Vishkumbha, 26
Vishnu, 81
Vishti, 24
Vishwavasu, 20
Vriddhi, 26
Vrischika, 8
Vrisha, 20

Vrishabha, 8
Vyadhi, 109
Vyaghata, 26
Vyatipata, 26
Vyaya, 20

Yajnas, 206
Yamaganda, 31
Yantras, 105
Yavana, 57
Yavana, 84
Yoga, 25, 26
Yoga, 192
Yogakaraka, 192
Yogas, 192
Yogi (ascetic), 189
Yoni, 6
Yudhisthira, 19
Yuga yoga, 205
Yuva, 20
Yogakaraka, 192

Foot Note—

It is difficult to identify ancient names for some geographical regions with the names of the modern regions, so they have been given as stated in the old texts. 1 The present Godavari river. 2, 6, 7, 10, 12, 19, 21 and 22-Ancient masters of Hindu Astrology. 3, 4, 5, 13, 14, 16, 17, 18, 20 Classical Sanskrit texts on Hindu Astrology. 8, part of modern Bihar. 9 part of modern Kerala. 11 the modern Punjaba. 15 the modern Sindha. 23 Yamaganda: Divide the duration of day (sunrise to sunset) by 15 and multiply by 9, 7, 5, 3, 1, 13 and 11 to arrive at the time of yamaganda on the seven week days (beginning from Sunday) respectively.

INDEX

Actions, 99, 104-106, 112, 120, 124, 127, 131, 136, 139, 140, 142, 144, 154, 157, 158, 160, 161, 163-167, 171, 172, 174. Also see *yogas*.

Adverse, ascendant degrees 32, 49, 66 — Constellations 31 — degrees of Moon 31-32, 65-66 —*karanas* 31 — lunar dates 30-31 — *yogas* 41.

Angles, Planets in 178, 179, 207.

Antara, balance of first 258-259 — calculation of 257 — duration of 257 — general principles to judge 260 — 303 — special rules to judge 302 — table of 257-258.

Antar and *Dasha* Lords, both malefic 294-295 — both benefic 294-295 — mutual disposition 295 — of contrary nature 294, 300 — relationship 295, 299, 300

Antardasha, See *Antar*

Antara in, evil *dasha* 294, 295 296 — good *dasha* 294, 297 — own *dasha* 298 — *yogakarak's dasha* 300, 301.

Antar Lord, location of 295 — lordship of 295, 296 — transit of 304, 305.

Antara of Ketu, in *yogakarak's dasha* 301.

Antar of, lords of angles 297 — lord of eighth 296, 298 — lord of eleventh 298 — lord of second 296 — lord of sixth 295, 296, 298 — lord of third 298 — lord of trine 297 — lord of twelfth 296 — *papa* 296, 297, 301 — *sadharmi* 298, 299 — *Sambandhi* 296-300 — Saturn 296 — *shubha* 296-298, 301 — *yogakaraka* 297, 300, 301.

Antara of Rahu, in *yogakarak's dasha* 301.

Antara of Saturn, in Venus *dasha* 300.

Antara of Venus, in Saturn *dasha* 300.

Appearance, 46-49, 76, 77, 96, 100, 107, 117-119, 123-125, 127, 128, 130, 134-137, 139-141, 150, 152-155, 161, 163-167, 171, 172, 174.

Aquarius, as ascendant 49 — attributes of 55-63 — benefics for 285 — Jupiter in 137 — Ketu in 145 — malefics for 285 — Mars in 130 — Mercury in 133, — Moon in 49, 125 — parts of the body 53 — Rahu in 145 — Saturn in 145 — Sun in 120, 121 — Venus in 141. Also see Signs.

Aries, as ascendant 46 — attributes of 55-63, benefics for 284 — Jupiter in 134 — Ketu in 145 — malefics for 284 — Mars in 126 — Mercury in 130 — Moon in 46, 122, 123 — parts of body 53 — Rahu in 145 — Saturn in

141, 142 — Sun in 116, 117 — Venus in 138. Also see Signs.
Ascendant, 13-16, 33, 43-50 — calculation of 38-42. Also see Aries, Taurus etc. and House I.
Ascending Degrees, 15, 49, 50.
Ascending Sign, see Ascendant.
Aspects, benefic 73-75, 177, 184, 220, 222, 227 — malefic 75, 176-178, 184, 187, 220, 227 — of planets 73-75, 181, 184 — strength of 74, 182, 183, 220.
Astrological Terminology, 324-327.
Backward Motion, 3, 11, 66, 178
Birth chart 13, 38-45 — data 13, 38 — date of 13, 38 — place of 13, 38 — time of 13, 38
Birth Chart, Calculation of 38-45 — patterns of 43-45.
Blind Signs, 60
Body, humours of 78 — ingredients of 76 — parts of — see body and its parts
Body and its Parts, 46-49, 76, 78, 99, 100-113, 116, 119, 122-130, 134, 140, 142, 145, 154, 155, 161, 168
Bright Fortnight, 21, 22, 23
Cadent Houses, planets in 179, 207
Calendar, different 19, 20 — years 19, 20, 256
Cancer, as ascendant 32, 47 — attributes of 55-63 — benefics for 284 — Jupiter in 135 — Ketu in 145 — malefics for 284 — Mars in 127 — Mercury in 131 — parts of body 53 — Rahu in 145 — Saturn in 142 — Sun in 117, 118 — Venus in 139 — tropic of 10, 11, 12. Also see Signs
Capricorn, as ascendant 48 — attributes of 55-63, — benefics for 285 — Jupiter in 137 — Ketu in 145 — malefics for 285 — Mars in 129, 130 — Mercury in 133 — Moon in 48, 125 — parts of body 53 — Rahu in 145 — Saturn in 144 — Sun in 120 — Venus in 140, 141 — tropic of 10, 11, 12. Also see Signs
Caput Draconis, 3, 66, see Rahu
Castes of, planets 81, signs 58
Cauda Draconis, 3, 66, see Ketu
Characteristics of planets — see planets — signs, see Signs
Colour of, planets 78 — signs 57
Combust Planets, see Planets
Comforts, 46-49, 104, 112, 113, 114, 123, 128, 135, 139, 153, 155, 158, 160, 163-165, 169, 174
Commencement of year, 20, 21
Common Signs, planets in, 180
Conjunction of Planets, 168, 181, 182, 221, 222, 243
Constellations, 4, 5, 31 — and *dashas* 251, 252 — and signs 7, 9 — eunuch 201 — female 201 — jurisdiction of 7, 9 — longitudes of 6-8 — male 201 — names of 4-6 — number of stars 6 — shape of 6.
Crawling signs, 61
Cusps of Houses, 12, 94
Cycle of Sixty Years, 20
Dark Fortnight, 21, 22, 23
Dasha, balance of first 252-256 — calculation of 251-257 — computation of years 256 — duration of 251 — first 251-256 — judgment of 260-293 — due to ascendant 260, 261, 263, 264, 278-286 — due to *karaka* 261, 263-272 — due to other considerations 261, 282-293 — due to ownership of houses 260-263, 272-289 — order of 251, 252 — table to ascertain -- 253-255
Dasha and, Constellations 251, 252 — *karaka*, effect of 264-272 — *karaka's* location 272 — ownership 272-289 — *sam-*

bandha 264, 273, 281, 284, 285, 287-289.

Dasha and Ascendants, Aquarius 285 — Aries 284 — Cancer 284 — Capricorn 285 — Gemini 284 — Leo 284 — Libra 284 — Pisces 285 — Sagittarius 285 — Scorpio 284, 285 — Taurus 284 — Virgo 284.

Dasha Lord, *arohi* 290 — *avarohi* 290 — benefic 263 — combust 290-292 — enemy of any house lord 293 — in conjunction with 290, 292 — in 2nd, 4th, 9th, 10th or 11th from any house 292 — in 6th, 8th or 12th from any house 291 — location of 293 — malefic 263 — retrograde 290 — transits of 292.

Dasha Lord in Sign, common 291, correlation with house 291 — fixed 291 — in particular degrees 291 — movable 291 — Pisces 291 — *Prishthodaya* 291 — *Shirshodaya* 291.

Dasha Lord in Sign of, debilitation 290 — enemy 290 — exaltation 289, 290. — friend 290 — great enemy 290 — great friend 290 — neutral 290 — own house 289, 290.

Dasha of. Jupiter 267, 268, 284, 285 — Ketu 271, 272, 286, 287 — Mars 266, 267, 284, 285 — Mercury 267, 268, 284, 285 — Moon 265, 266, 284, 285 — Rahu 270, 271, 286, 287 — Saturn 269, 270, 284 — Sun 264, 265, 284, 285 — Venus 268, 269, 284, 285.

Dasha of Lord of, angles 281-283, 287 — eight 275, 281, 282, 287 — eleventh 276, 280, 281, 287 — fifth 274, 282, 288 — first 272, 273, 282, 288 — fourth 273, 274, 282, 288 — ninth 275, 276, /282, 288 — second 273, 281, 288, 289 — seventh 274, 275, 282, 288, 289 — sixth 274, 280, 281, 287 — tenth 276, 282, 288 — third 273, 280, 281, 287 — trine 280, 283, 287 — twelfth 276, 281, 282.

Dasha of *Maraka*, 283-286, 288, 289.

Day births, 178.

Deaf signs, 60.

Death, 288, 289. Also see *Dasha* of *Maraka*.

Declination, 10, 11.

Debilitation of Planets, 68

Degree Rising, see Ascending degree.

Diseases, 47, 48, 84, 85, 95, 101, 106, 107, 110, 114, 117, 119, 121, 122, 126-130, 136, 139-142, 144, 149-151, 153, 155-159, 162, 164-172, 174, 175, 208, 222.

Dispositer of, Ketu 169 — Rahu 169.

Duration of, *karanas* 24, 25, 30 — lunar dates 21-23, 30 — sign rising 18, 33-34 — *yoga* 25, 26.

Earth, 1, 3, 11, 16-19 — axis of 34 — path of 2, 14, 34 — revolution of 1.

Ecliptic, 1-4, 11, 13, 17 — path on 34, 52 — plane of 14.

Effect of Planets, 116-176.

Eight House, See House viii

Electional Astrology, 5

Eleventh House, See House xi

Emotions, 46-49, 84, 85, 102, 114, 118, 119, 123, 125, 126, 128, 135, 149, 170. Also see Tastes and Temperament.

Enemies, 48, 49, 84, 85, 100, 101, 106, 108, 110, 112, 114, 118, 121, 125, 128-130, 133, 141, 151-153, 160-162, 164-167, 169, 171, 175

Enmity of Planets, 71, 72

Ephemeris, 2, 3, 12, 23, 25, 27-29, 36, 38, 40-43

Equator, 10, 14

Equinoctical Degrees, 11

Equinoxes, See Precession of Equinoxes
Exaltation, degree 68, 69 — planets in 68.
Even Signs, 58
Eunuch, constellations 201 — planets 80, 81
Female, constellations 201 — planets 80-81 — signs 58
Fifth House, see House V
First House, see House I
Fixed signs, 59—planets in — 179, 180
Fixed stars, 1,- 10. Also see Constellations
Fixed Zodiac, see Sidereal
Flavour, 78
Fortnight, 21-23
Fourth House, see House IV
Friends, 47, 102-104, 108, 114, 120, 121, 126, 127, 132, 135, 136, 145, 150, 152, 158, 161, 164-166, 170
Friendship among Planets, 71-73
Gain, 121, 127, 128, 136, 138, 140, 141, 149, 150, 165, 167, 170, 172, 174. Also see Houses I, II, IV, VII, VIII, IX, X and XI and lords thereof
Gemini, as ascendant 46 — attributes of 55-63 — benefics for 284 — Jupiter in 135 — Ketu in 145 — malefics for 284 — Mars in 127 — Mercury in 131 — Moon in 46, 123 — parts of body 53 — Rahu in 145 — Saturn in 142 — Sun in 117 — Venus in 138 — Also See Signs
General Principles of Judgment, 177-185
Geocentric Longitudes, 13, 28, 29
Great, enmity among planets 72, 73 — friendship among planets 72, 73 — years of planets 241
Happiness, 47, 84, 85, 98, 101, 104, 114, 120, 137, 139, 143, 149, 152, 153, 158, 160, 161, 167, 170, 172, 173, 175. Also see *Yogas*
Health, 95, 101, 106, 109, 114, 116, 127, 129, 150, 151, 153, 156, 166, 170, 172. Also see Diseases and *Yogas.*
Houses I and VI and lords thereof
Herschel, 2
Horizon, 13, 15, 33
House, aspects on 177, 178 — cusp of 94 — definition of 16, 91, 221 — division of 15, 91-94, 280 — domain of 93 position of 15
Houses and, judgment 177-187, 220-249. Also see *Yogas* — *karakas* 87, 88 — lords — see Lords — matters judged from 95-115 — order and position 15-17 — parts of body 54, 110-114 — planets in 149-176, 178 — signs, correlation with 15-18, 91, 116, 145 — *Yogas* based on —see *Yogas*
House I, judgment of 177-185, 221-224 — Jupiter in 161, 222 — *karaka* for 87, 88 — Ketu in 172 — Mars in 155, 222 — matters judged from 95-96, 100, 101, 114, 230 — Mercury in 158, 222. Moon in 151, 222 — parts of body 54, 100, 101, 114 — planets in 178 — Rahu in 169 — Saturn in 165, 222 — Sun in 149 — Venus in 163, 222. Also see *Yogas*
House II, judgment of 177-185, 220, 224-226 — Jupiter in 161, 224, 225 — *karaka* for 87, 88 — Ketu in 172, 173, 224 — Mars in 155, 224 — matters judged from 97, 98, 101, 102, 114, 220, 224 — Mercury in 158, 224 — Moon in 152, 224 — parts of body 54, 101, 102, 114 — planets in 178 -- Rahu in 169, 170, 224, 225 — Saturn

in 166, 224, 229 — Sun in 149, 224 — Venus in 163, 224, 225. Also see *Yogas*

House III, judgment of 177, 185, 226, 227 — Jupiter in 161, 227 — *karaka* for 87, 88 — Ketu in 173 — Mars in 155, 226 — matters judged from 102, 103, 114 — Mercury in 158, 226 — Moon in 152, 226 — parts of body 54, 102, 103, 114 — planets in 178 — Rahu in 170, 226 — Saturn in 166, 226 — Sun in 150, 226 — Venus in 164, 227. Also see *Yogas*

House IV, judgment of 177-185, 220, 227, 228 — Jupiter in 161 — *karaka* for 87, 88 — Ketu in 173 — Mars in 155, 156, 228 — matters judged from 97, 98, 103-105, 114, 220 — Mercury in 158, 159 — Moon in 153 — parts of body 54, 104, 114 — planets in 178 — Rahu in 170 — Saturn in 166, 227, 242 — Sun in 150, 228 — Venus in 164. Also see *Yogas*

House V, judgment of 177-185, 228-230 — Jupiter in 162 — *karaka* for 87, 88 — Ketu in 173, 230 — Mars in 156, 230 — matters judged from 105, 106, 114 — Mercury in 159 — Moon in 153, 232 — parts of body 114 — planets in 178 — Rahu in 170, 230 — Saturn in 167, 230 — Sun in 150, 230 — Venus in 164. Also see *Yogas*

House VI, judgment of 177-185, 230-232 — Jupiter in 162, 226, 228 — *karaka* for 87, 88 — Ketu in 173, 231 — Mars in 156, 226, 232 — matters judged from 106, 107, 114, 231 — Mercury in 160, 240 — Moon in 153 — parts of body 54, 105, 54, 106, 114 — planets in 178, 179 — Rahu in 170, 231 — Saturn in 167, 232 — Sun in 150, 232 — Venus in 164, 228. Also see *Yogas*

House VII, judgment of 177-185, 232-236 — Jupiter in 162 — *karaka* for 87, 88 — Ketu in 173, 174 — Mars in 156 — matters judged from 107-109, 114 — Mercury in 159, 160 — Moon in 153 — parts of body 54, 107-109, 114 — planets in 178 — Rahu in 170, 171 — Saturn in 167, 227 — Sun in 150, 233 — Venus in 164, 165. Also see *Yogas*

House VIII, judgment of 177-185, 220, 236-240 — Jupiter in 162, 226, 228 — *karaka* for 87-88 — Ketu in 174-231 — Mars in 156, 157, 224, 226 — Matters judged from 98, 109, 110, 114, 220 — Mercury in 160, 228 — Moon in 153, 178, 224 — parts of body 54, 109, 110, 114 — planets in 178, 179 — Rahu in 171, 231 — Saturn in 167 — Sun in 150, 224 — Venus in 165, 224, 228. Also see *Yogas*

House IX, judgment of 177-185, 220, 240-242 — Jupiter in 162, 163, 240 — *karaka* for 87, 88 — Ketu in 174, 240 — Mars in 157, 240 — matters judged from 99-111, 114, 220, 242 — Mercury in 159, 228 — Moon in 153, 240 — parts of body 54, 110, 114 — planets in 178 — Saturn in 167, 240, 241 — — Rahu in 171, 227, 240, 241 Sun in 150, 151, 226, 240 — Venus in 165, 240. Also see *Yogas*

House X, judgment of 177-285, 242-244 — Jupiter in 163 — *karaka* for 87, 88 — Ketu in 174 — Mars in 157, 242 — matters judged from 99, 111, 112, 114, 242 — Mercury in

160 — Moon in 153, 154 — parts of body 54, 111, 112, 114 — planets in 178 — Rahu in 171 — Saturn in 167, 168, 244 — Sun in 151, 242 — Venus in 165. Also see *Yogas*

House XI, judgment of 177-185, 220, 245-247 — Jupiter in 163 — *karaka* for 87, 88 — Ketu in 174, 175 — Mars in 157-227 — matters judged from 112-114, 220 — Mercury in 160 — Moon in 154 — parts of body 54, 112-114 — planets in 178 — Rahu in 171, 172 — Saturn in 168 — Sun in 151 — Venus in 165. Also see *Yogas*

House XII, judgment of 177-185, 247, 249 — Jupiter in 163, 226, 228, 247, 248 — *karaka* for 87, 88 — Ketu in 175 — Mars in 157, 226 — matters judged from 113, 114 — Mercury in 160, 161, 228 — Moon in 155 parts of body 54, 113, 114 — planets in 178 — Rahu in 172 — Saturn in 168 — Sun in 151 — Venus in 165, 228, 247. Also see *Yogas*

Houses-Lords of, antardasha of — see Antar — judgment of — see Planets in signs and houses — location of — see yogas — mahadashas of — see Dasha — see also Lords of Houses

Human signs, 61

Humours of Body, 78

Inauspicious Degrees of Moon, 65, 67

Incest, 86, 87

Indian Standard Time, see Time

Ingredients of Body, 76. Also see Body and its parts

Ingresses of the Sun, 23

Intercalary Month, 23

Jewels and Planets, 80

Judgment of, achievements 242 — actions 222, 242 — activity 222 — agricultural land 228 — bodily vigour 223, 231 — brothers and sisters 226, 245 — business 242 — children 229, 230, also see sons and daughters — company 223 — complexion 224 — conveyances 227 — courage 227 — daring 223 — diseases 224-226, 228, 229, 231, 232, 248 — digestive power 229 — education 228 — eloquence 229 — enemy 231 — energy 223 — environment — family 224 — father 243, 245 — food 225 — fortune and prosperity 240, 241 — friends 227 — gain 245 — happiness 228 — health 222, 231, 232 — honour 227 — hurt (bodily) 222, 226, 227 — income 245 — intelligence 222, 228 — learning 228 — living in places 223, 232 — logical faculty 228 — longevity 236, 240 — low acts 228 — matrimonial affairs 232 — matrimonial happiness 233-235 also see wife — memory 228 — mother 227 — parts of body 223 — personal efforts 242 — philanthropy 247 — political power 242, 243 — position 242 — poverty 243, 246, 247, — property 227 — religiousness 240, 247 — respect 242, 243 — sedentary habits 223 — shyness 229 — sons and daughters 225, 231 — speech 224, 225, 228, 229, 247 — spending 247, 248 — success 242 — victory 231 — wealth 224, 225 — wife/husband — appearance and temperament of 232 — harmony with 233 — longevity of 233-235 — separation from 233 — set off of malefic influences 234 — wisdom 222. For all kinds of judgment also see

planets in signs and houses and *Yogas*.
Judgment of *Antardasha*, see *Antara*.
Judgment of *Dasha*, see *Dasha*
Judgment of Houses, general principles 177-185 — House I 221-224 — II 220, 224-226 — III 226-227 — IV 220, 227, 228 — V 228-230 — VI 230-232 — VII 220, 232-236 — VIII 236-240 — IX 220, 240, 242 — X 242-244 — XI 220, 245-247 — XII 247-249. For judgment please also see Planets in signs and houses and *Yogas*.
Jupiter in, houses 161-163 — signs 134-138 — *yogas* 194-205, 208, 210, 212, 215
Jupiter's, *antardasha* — see *Antar* — attributes of 75-89 — debilitation 68 — enemies 71-73 — exaltation 68 — friends 71-73 — *mahadasha* — see *Dasha* — *Moola Trikona* 71 — neutrals 71-73 — signs 64. Also see Planets.
Jupiter significator for, 84-89, 224, 232, 244.
Karaka, 84-88, 95, 164, 180-184, 187, 188, 220, 221
Karana, 24, 25, 30, 31
Ketu, conjoined with a planet 145, 168, 172, 286 — what is 3.
Ketu in, angle 168, 172 — any house 168, 172 — houses 172-173 — signs — see Aries, Taurus etc. trine 168
Ketu's, *antardasha* — see *Antar* — characteristics — see Planets — *mahadasha* — see *Dasha*.
Ketu significator for, 85
Latitude, 2, 6, 7, 13, 18, 34, 67
Lagnam, see Ascendant
Lame signs, 60
Leo, as ascendant 47 — attributes of 55-63 — benefics for 284 — Jupiter in 135 — Ketu in 145 — malefics for 284 — Mars in 128 — Mercury in 131, 132 — Moon in 47, 124 — parts of body 53 — Rahu in 145 — Saturn in 143 — Sun in 118, 226 — Venus in 134. Also see Signs.
Libra, as ascendant 48 — attributes of 55-63, benefics for 284 — Jupiter in 136 — Ketu in 145 — malefics for 284 — Mars in 128 — Mercury in 132 — Moon in 24, 48 — parts of body 53 — Rahu in 145 — Saturn in 143, 144 — Sun in 119 — Venus in 139, 140. Also see Signs.
Local Time, 36
Local Mean Time, 38-42
Long signs, 62
Longevity, 84, 85, 98, 101, 105, 106, 109, 110, 114, 151-156, 158, 160, 161, 163, 167, 171, 173, 174, 236-240
Longitudes of Planets, 42, 43
Lord of the House 181, 183, 184, 221-224 — I 180, 183, 185, 188, 225-227, 230, 231, 241, 242, 245, 246, 248 — II 185, 188, 224, 225, 229, 245, 246 — III 185, 188, 226, 246, — IV 185, 188, 227, 228, 241, 245, 246 — V 185, 188, 227-229, 243, 245, 246 — VI 179, 185, 188, 230, 231, 246 — VII 188, 232, 233, 246 — VIII 179, 185, 189, 229, 231, 246 — IX 185, 188, 227, 241-243, 245, 246 — X 185, 188, 226, 245, 246 — XI 185, 188, 226, 245, 246 — XII 179, 185, 189, 224, 246-248
Lordship of Signs, 64
Loss, see House XII and lord thereof
Lunar Ascendant, 184
Lunar Dates, 20-23
Lunar Months, 21
Lunar signs, 63

Mahadasha, see *Dasha*
Male, costellations 201 — planets 80, 81 — signs 58
Maraka 187, 188, 189 — See Houses II, VI, VII, VIII and XII also lords thereof.
Married Happiness, 84, 85, 107, 108, 119, 131, 139, 143, 149 — 151, 156, 158, 171, 232-235. Also see wife/husband
Mars in, houses 155-157 — signs 126-130 — *yogas* 190, 195, 197, 199, 201 — 204, 207-210.
Mars' *antardasha* — see *Antar* — attributes of 75-89 — debilitation 68 — enemies 68 — exaltation 68 — friends 71-73 — *Mahadasha* — See *Dasha* — *Mool Trikona* 70, neutrals 71-73 — signs 64. Also see Planets.
Mars significator for, 84-89
Matters Judged from Houses, 95-115, 220-249
Measures in Space, 2
Mental Qualities, 46-49, 84, 85, 97, 101, 102, 104-106, 111, 114, 117-120, 123, 124, 126, 131, 133-136, 138, 139, 142, 144, 149, 150, 153, 155, 158, 159, 161, 163, 167, 169-171, 173, 174.
Mercury in, houses 158-161 — signs 130-134 — *yogas* 194-195, 197-199, 201-205, 214, 215
Mercury's *antardasha* — see *Antar*—attributes of 75-89, debilitation 68 — enemies 71-73 — exaltation 68 — friends 71-73 — *mahadasha* — see *Dasha* — *Moola Trikona* 70 — neutrals 71-73 — signs 64. Also see Planets
Mercury significator for, 84-89, 224, 244
Meridian cusp, 37
Metals and Planets, 79
Mid-Heaven, 13, 15
Mineral signs, 62
Month, intercalary 23 — names of 21
Mool Trikona, 70
Moon in, houses 151-155 — signs 122-126 — *yogas* 194-200, 203, 205, 208, 210, 215
Moon's, adverse position 31, 32, 65, 66, 178 — *antardasha* — see *Antar* — association 122, 222, 231, 232 — attributes of 75-89 — auspicious degrees 65 — constellation position 7, 8, 233 — debilitation 68 — enemies 71-73 — friends 71-73 — inauspicious degrees 65 — latitude 3 — *mahadasha* — see *Dasha* — *Moola Trikona* 70 — motion 21 — neutrals 71-73 — nodes 3, 47, 53 — *pakshabala* 225 — path 3 — strength 121, 122, 179 — sign 49-51, 64, 184. Also see Planets
Moon Significator for, 84-89
Movable signs, 59 — planets in 179, 180
Motion Backwards, 3, 11
Nakshatra, see Constellations
Name first syllable of and Moon-sign, 308
Neptune, 2
Night Births, 178
Ninth House, See House IX
Northern Declination, 10, 11
Northern Latitude, 2, 3, 66
Northern Node of Moon, 3, see Rahu
Nutation, 11 — also see Precession of Equinoxes
Papa, see *Papi*
Papi Planets, 82, 83, 89, 90, 186-188, 222, 231
Parallax, 28, 29
Path of, earth 2, 14, 34 — planets 2, 3
Patterns of Chart, 43-45
Pisces, as ascendant 49 — attributes of 55-63, benefics for 285 — Jupiter in 137 — Ketu in 145 — malefics for 285 — Mars in

130 — Mercury in 134 — Moon in 49, 126 — parts of body — 53 Rahu in 145 — Saturn in 145 — Sun in 121 — Venus in 141. Also see Signs

Planets, age of 79 — *antardashas* of — see *Antar* — *arohi* 69, 187 — aspects of 73-75, 182 — *avarohi* 69, 187 — benefic 75, 82-83, 89, 90, 177-179 — biped 82 — birds 82 — caste of 81 — characteristics of 75-90 — colour of 78 — combinations of — see *yogas* — combust 181, 185, 187, 205, 210, 215, 224, 228 — complexion of 76 — conjunction of 176, 181-183, 187, 195, 196, 221 — crawling 82 — debilitation 68, 71, 176, 179, 184, 185, 216 — *dhatu* 82 — enemies interse 71-73 — exalted 68-69, 71, 176, 178 — effects of — see Planets in Signs and Houses — friends interse 71-73, 179 — glance of 77 — great enemies interse 71-73 — great friends interse 71-73 — great years of 241 — how to put in houses 94 — in angles 178, 179, 182, 183 — in cadent houses 177 — in common signs 179, 180 — in enemy's house 176 — in fixed signs 179, 180 — in friend's house 176 — ingredients of body 76 — in houses 149-175 — in movable signs 179, 180 — in own house 176, 178 — in signs 116-148 — in succedent houses 179 — *Jeeva* 82 — *karakas* for 84, 88 — longitudes of 42, 43 — *mahadasha* of — see *Dasha* — malefics 75, 82, 83, 89, 90, 177, 179, 233, 234 — *Moola* 82 — *Mool Trikona* 70 — *neechabhilashi* 69 — neutrals interse 69 — owning two houses 183, 185 — *papa* 82, 89, 224 — Also see *Papi* — path of 2 — quadruped 82 — retrograde 178, 179, 215 — rising both ways 82 — rising with back 82 — rising with front part 82 — sex of — 80, 81, 227, 230, 247 — *shubha* 82 — significators for 75-89 — tenanting own house 178 — transits of — see transits — *uchchabhilashi* 69

Planets and, cloth 82 — constellations 251, 252 — deities 81 — directions 81 — directional strength 82 — elements 81 — flavour 78 — *gunas* 78 — humours of body 78 — jewels 80 — manner of winning over 83 — metals 79 — order of *mahadashas* 250-253 — own house 64 — parts of body 76, 231 — periods — see *Dasha* and *Antar* physical characteristics of 77 — places 80 — regions 84 — relationship interse 71-73, 179 — relations governed 81 — seasons 80 — signs, correlation with 53, 54, 116 — temperament 77 — *yogas* — see *Yogas*

Planets, latitude 2, 3 — longitudes 42, 43 — path of 3

Pluto, 2

Pratyantar Dasha, 303-305

Precession of Equinoxes, 11, 12, 25, 28, 29, 34, 35, 37, 42, 43, 221

Principles of Judgment, general 177-185 — for each house 220-249

Property, 46, 47, 84, 85, 97, 98, 101, 104, 105, 110, 114, 136, 140, 150, 152, 153, 155, 156, 158, — 160, 166, 168, 173

Prosperity, 46-49, 84, 85, 97, 98 101-105, 107, 108, 110, 113, 114, 117-120, 122, 124, 127-134, 137, 140-142, 144, 145, 149, 151, 153-156, 158, 160, 161, 163-

167, 169, 170, 172-174, 240, 241. Also see *Yogas*
Quadruped, planets 82 — signs 61
Rahu, in houses 168-172 — in signs 71 — in *yogas* 195 — What is 3
Rahu's position, in angle 168, 172 — in trine 168, 172 — in association 145, 168, 172, 286.
Rahu's, *antardasha* — see *Antar-Mahadasha* — see *Dasha.*
Rahu significator for, 84, 86
RAMC, 41
Rank and Position, 48, 84, 85, 100, 101, 104-106, 110, 111, 114, 118, 119, 123, 126, 128-130, 132-136, 138, 140-145, 150, 152, 154, 156, 157, 159-162, 163, 165-168, 171, 172, 174, 175. Also see *Yogas*
Regions and, planets 84 — signs 51
Relations signified by Planets, 84, 85
Relations, brother 46, 81, 84, 102, 103, 111, 112, 121, 123, 132, 140, 150, 152, 157, 158, 161, 166-168, 170, 173 — children 95, 123, 132, 134, 145, 152, 156, 160, 162, 167 — daughter 46-48, 50, 84, 85, 114, 123, 152, 154 — family 101, 102, — father 48, 70, 81, 84, 95, 99, 100, 102, 104, 105, 111-114, 117, 145, 150, 156-158, 162, 166, 168, 170, 171, 174, 179 — husband see wife — mother 47, 81, 84, 95, 102-104, 114, 123, 151, 155, 161, 166, 168, 170, 173 — relations 46, 48, 95, 100, 101, 103, 104, 106, 111-113, 117, 120, 125, 129, 133, 138, 141-143, 156-159, 164, 168, 170-173, 175 — sister 46, 81, 84, 102, 103, 111, 112, 150, 152, 158, 166 170 — son 46, 47, 49, 50, 105, 114, 120, 121, 124, 128, 129-132, 134-136, 141-145, 149-150, 152-154, 156,157, 160, 161, 164-168, 171, 174, 175 — wife/husband 47-49, 81, 85, 88, 99, 100, 104, 105, 107, 108, 113, 114, 121, 122, 123, 128, 131-134, 141, 150, 156, 157-159, 161, 164, 165, 167-170
Relationship among Planets, natural 71-73 — temporal 71-73
Religiousness, 48, 103-106, 110-112, 114, 118, 125, 126, 130-132, 134-139, 144, 145, 150, 153, 156, 159, 161-163, 169, 171, 174
Religious Propitiation, 31, 32
Reptile signs, 61
Retrograde Planets, 66, 178, 179, 216
Revolution, 1, 14, 18
Right Ascension of the Meridian cusp, 37, 41
Rising Sign, see Ascendant
Rising Parts of, planets 82 — signs 63
Sagittarius, as ascendant 32, 48 — attributes of 55-63 — benefics for 285 — Jupiter in 136-137 — Ketu in 145 — malefics for 285 — Mars in 129 — Mercury in 133 — Moon in 32, 48, 125 — parts of body 53 — Rahu in 145 — Saturn in 144 — Sun in 119, 120 — Venus in 140. Also see Signs
Saturn in houses 165-168 signs 141-145 — in *yogas* 194, 197, 201-204
Saturn's *antardasha* — see *Antar* — debilitation 68 — enemies 71-73 — exaltation 68 — — friends 71-73 — *mahadasha* — see *Dasha* — *Moola Trikona* 70 — neutrals 71-73 — signs 64. Also see Planets.
Saturn significator for, 84, 85, 244
Scorpio, as ascendant 48 — attributes of 55-63 — benefics for 284, 285 — Jupiter in 136 — Ketu in 145 — Malefics for

284 — Mars in 128, 129 — Mercury in 132, 133 — Moon in 48, 124, 125 — parts of the body 53 — Rahu in 145 — Saturn in 144 — Sun in 119 — Venus in 140. Also see Signs
Second House, see House II
Seventh House, see House VII
Sidereal, 1, 10 — longitudes 12, 25, 28, 29, 35, 42, 43, 221 — signs 10, 42, 224 — time 38, 40 — zodiac 4, 10, 12, 28
Signs, abode of 55, 56 — animal 62 — appearance of 55 — ascending, see ascendant — attributes of 53-63 — biped 61 — blind 60 — castes of 58 — colours of 57 — commencing degrees 66 — common 59, 223 — crawling 61 — deaf 60 — debilitation 64, 184, 185 — direction of 15, 16, 60 — diurnal 160 — duration of 14, 15. 18, 33, 34 — even 58 — exaltation in 68 — fag end of 66 — female 58 — fixed 59, 223 — human 61 — in opposition 18 — interpretation of planets in 146-148 — lame 60 — long 62 — lordship of 63, 64 — lunar 63 — male 58 — measure of 8 — mineral 62 — movable 59, 223 — names of 8 — nocturnal 60 — odd 58 — peculiarities of 55, 56 — planets in 116-145 — properties of 55, 56 — quadruped 61 — reptile 61 — rising, calculation of 38-41 — rising, effects for — see Ascendant — rising bothways 63 — rising with back 63 — rising with read 63 — sectors of 66 — sex of 58 — short 62 — sign rising, what is 15 — solar 63 — tenanting Moon 51, 52, 184 — vegetable 62 — waterless 59 — watery 59, 61 — *yogas* involving signs — see *yogas*.
Signs and, constellations 8, 9 — degrees 9, 10, 66 — houses, interrelation with 15-18, 53, 54, 91 — parts of body 53 — parts of country 57
Sixth House, see House VI
Southern Declination, 10, 11
Southern Latitude, 2, 66
Southern Node of Moon, 3 — see Ketu
Space, measurement in 2
Standard Time, see Time
Stellar Zodiac, see Sidereal Zodiac
Succedent Houses, planets in 178
Sun in, houses 149-151 — signs 116-121 — in *yogas* 194-198, 200, 203, 204, 207, 208, 215.
Sunrise, 10, 13, 20, 35, 36
Sun's, *antardasha*, See *Antar* — debilitation 68 — enemies 71-73 — exaltation 68 — friends 71-73 — *mahadasha* — see *Dasha* — *Moola Trikona* 70 — motion 21 — neutrals 70-73 — path 1, 10 — sign 64. Also see *Planets*.
Sun's Ingress, 23
Sun Significator for, 84-89, 221, 244
Table of, *antardashas* 257, 258 — houses 37, 41, 42 — *mahadashas* 251, 253-255 — precession of equinoxes 321-323
Tastes and Temperament 46-49, 101-105, 95-114, 117-119, 124, 126-128, 130, 132, 135, 136, 138, 139, 141, 142, 149, 152, 159, 160, 164, 166, 169
Taurus, as ascendant 46 — attributes of 55-63 — benefics for 284 — Jupiter in 134 — Ketu in 145 — malefics for 284 — Mars in 126, 127 — Mercury in 131 — Moon in 46, 123 — parts of body 53 — Rahu in 145 — Saturn in 142 — Venus in 138 — Also see Signs.

Tenth House, see House X
Third House, See House III
Tide, high and low 122
Time, cycle of 19 — Greenwich Mean 29, 38, 39 — Indian Standard 39, 40 — local 36 — local mean 38, 40, 41 — of rising of signs 33, 34 — sidereal 38, 40 — standard 38, 39, 40 — units of 27
Transits, general principles 306-309
Transit of, Jupiter 311, 312, 315, 317 — Ketu 314, 315, 317 — mars 310, 311, 315, 317 — Mercury 311, 315, 317 — Moon 310, 315, 317 — Rahu 314, 315, 317 — Saturn 312-315, 317 — Sun 309, 310, 315, 317 — Venus 312, 315, 317
Transit of Planets, Judgment by name of the native 308, 309 — modification of influence 317-320 — special rules to judge 317-320
Trine, planets in 178 — quality of 178
Tropical, longitudes 28, 221 — signs 10, 42, 221 — zodiac 4, 11, 12, 33, 35, 42, 43
Tropic of Cancer 10, 11, 12 — Capricorn 10, 11, 12, 28
Twelfth House, see House XII
Vegetable signs, 62
Venus in, houses 163-165 — signs 138, 141 — *yogas* 194-200, 202-205, 210, 214, 215
Venus, *antardasha* — see Antar debilitation 68 — enemies 71-73 — exaltation 68 — friends 71-73 — *mahadasha* — see *Dasha* — *Moola Trikona* 70 — neutrals 71-73 — signs 64. Also see Planets
Venus Significator for 84-85, 232
Virgo, as ascendant 47, 48, 229 — attributes of 55-63 — benefics for 284 — Jupiter in 135, 136 — Ketu in 145 — malefics for 284 — Mars in 128 — Mercury in 134 — Moon in 47, 48, 124, 229 — parts of body 53 — Rahu in 145 — Saturn in 143 — Sun in 118, 229 — Venus in 139. Also see Signs.
Wealth, see Prosperity
Years, commencement of 21, 23 — cycle of 20 — different kinds of 19, 20 — lunar 20, 23 — names of 20 — solar 20
Yogas, (soli-lunar distances) 25, 26
Yogas involving aspects 194-196, 198-201, 208-210, 211, 212 — constellations 201 — day births 200, 201 — night births 200, 201 — Saturday 208 — Tuesday 208
Yogas involving Houses, I 193-195, 197-199, 203-205, 207-209, 210, 212, 214, 215 — II 193-198, 208-210, 212, 214, 215 — III 194, 195, 198, 207, 210, 212, 214 — IV 195, 197-199, 203, 207, 208, 210, 212 — V 198, 199, 203, 204, 207, 208, 210, 213 — VI 194, 195, 198, 207, 208, 210, 211, 213, 215 — VII 194, 197-199, 203, 204, 211, 213 — VIII 194, 195, 198, 199, 207, 208, 211, 213, 215 — IX 195, 198, 199, 203, 205, 207-209, 211, 213, 214 — X 194, 195, 197-199, 203-205, 207, 208, 211, 213, 214 — XI 194, 195, 198, 207, 208, 211, 214 — XII 193, 195, 197-199, 207, 208, 211, 214, 215 — angles 195, 196, 198, 199, 202-204, 207, 208, 211, 214, 215 — house positions 205, 206, 210-211 — trines 195, 196, 203, 204, 208, 211, 214, 215
Yogas involving Lords of Houses of, I 195, 196, 200, 203, 208-210,

212, 215, 217-219 — II 196, 199, 208, 209, 210, 212, 214 — III 209, 210, 212, 217 — IV 195, 208 — 210, 212, 215, 217-219 — V 196, 199, 208-210, 213, 217-219 — VI 209, 210, 211, 213, 215, 218 — VII 208, 209, 211, 213, 217-219 — VIII 209, 211, 213, 215, 218 — IX 195, 196, 199, 203, 209-211, 213, 214, 215, 217-219 — X 204, 208, 209, 211, 213, 214, 215, 217-219 — XI 199, 208, 209, 211, 214, 218 — XII 209, 211, 214, 215

Yogas involving Planets, benefics 193-195, 197, 201, 205, 207, 210 — combust 210, 211, 215, 216 — conjunction of 195, 196, 214 — directional strength 215 — Jupiter 194-205, 208, 210, 212, 215 — Mars 194, 195, 197, 199, 201-204, 207-209, 210 — malefic 193, 197, 201, 211, 212, 215 — Mercury 194, 195, 197-199, 201-205, 214, 215 — Moon 194-200, 203-205, 208, 210, 215 — *papas* 199, 215 — Rahu 195 — retrograde 215, 216 — Saturn 194-197, 201-204 — strength of 195, 196, 208 — Sun 194-198, 200, 203, 204, 207, 208, 215 — Venus 194-200, 202-205, 207, 210, 214, 215

Yogas involving Signs, Aquarius 194, 197, 201-203 — Aries 194, 195, 197, 200-204 — Cancer 194, 197, 201-204, 209 — Capricorn 194, 195, 197, 201, 202, 204 — debilitation 195, 209, 215, 216 — degrees in signs 194-198, 200, 202 — enemy's sign 196, 215 — exaltation 195-197, 199, 202-205, 208, 210, 211, 214, 215, 216 — friend's sign 195, 202 — Gemini 194, 197, 201-209 — Leo 194-197, 201, 204, 210 — Libra 194, 196, 197, 201-204, 207, 210 — own sign 195, 197, 199, 201-204, 210, 212, 214 — Pisces 194, 195, 197, 200-204 — Sagittarius 194, 195, 197, 201, 202, 204 — Scorpio 194, 197, 201, 202, 209, 210 — Taurus 194, 197, 199, 201-204 — Virgo 194, 196-198, 201-204. For Sanskrit names of *yogas* please refer to pages 329-334

Zodiac, 1, 2, 3, 4, 7, 10, 17, 28, 33, 42, 51, 52

Zodiac, fixed 10, 12 — sidereal — see Sidereal, tropical — see Tropical

Zodiacal Belt, 1

Zodiac-Division of, in constellations 7, 8, 9 — in signs 9, 10